Stolen Childhoods

Stolen Childhoods

*The Untold Story of the Children
Interned by the Japanese in the
Second World War*

NICOLA TYRER

Weidenfeld & Nicolson
LONDON

First published in Great Britain in 2011
by Weidenfeld & Nicolson

1 3 5 7 9 10 8 6 4 2

© Nicola Tyrer 2011

A CIP catalogue record for this book
is available from the British Library.

ISBN: 978 0 297 85878 2

Typeset by Input Data Services Ltd, Bridgwater, Somerset

Printed in Great Britain by CPI Mackays, Chatham, Kent

The Orion Publishing Group's policy is to use papers that
are natural, renewable and recyclable and
made from wood grown in sustainable forests. The logging
and manufacturing processes are expected to conform to
environmental regulations of the country of origin.

Weidenfeld & Nicolson

Orion Publishing Group Ltd
Orion House
5 Upper Saint Martin's Lane
London, WC2H 9EA

An Hachette UK Company

www.orionbooks.co.uk

For Keith, Alice and Edmund

Contents

PART THREE: Dark Days

PART FOUR: Freedom At Last

Acknowledgements

The most surprising aspect of writing this book has been the size of the response from former internees. Eager, no doubt, to contribute to a story which has never been told in its entirety, they responded by the score to my initial letter of introduction; it is a source of regret that I have not been able to include in my book the testimony of everyone who offered to participate. I would like to take this opportunity to thank all those who offered their time and reassure them that, even though they may not all be mentioned by name, their experiences have played a vital role in helping recreate the feel of those far-off scenes of captivity where so many important childhood years were played out. Many of them have lent me out-of-print books, and entrusted me with their unique photos, precious documents and mementoes of camp life, and I am grateful for that trust.

There are some people whose helpfulness and enthusiasm for this project makes them deserving of special mention. Head of the list is Ron Bridge. Interned at the age of nine, for ten years Ron was chairman of the Association of British Civilian Internees Far East Region (ABCIFER), the organisation whose dogged pressure finally resulted in the last government granting £10,000 in compensation to the vast majority of former civilian prisoners. There is no answer to any question about the lore of civilian internment that is not to be found on Ron's personal database; his patience and good humour when faced with my lack of expertise made dealing with him a pleasure.

I would also like to thank Rod Suddaby of the Imperial War

Museum for all his support for the project and his readiness to introduce me to the rich archive of unpublished testimonies by so many people whose childhoods were blighted by a Japanese prison camp.

Internment affected tens of thousands of people from multiple nationalities in scores of camps; no one setting out to write about it could hope to master the subject without recourse to what is universally referred to as the internees' Bible – Greg Leck's authoritative and compulsively readable account of internment in China, *Captives of Empire: The Japanese Internment of Allied Civilians in China, 1941–1945*. I owe him thanks for permission to quote excerpts from the book, reprint photographs and for his many helpful and encouraging communications.

I would also like to thank the three children of the late William Sewell – Ruth Baker, Daphne Erasmus and Roger Sewell – for permission to include extracts from *Strange Harmony*, his vivid account of life in Stanley camp in Hong Kong. No other writer has written so tellingly of internment from a parent's point of view. My thanks are due, too, to the heirs of men and women whose unpublished accounts of imprisonment are lodged with the Imperial War Museum and who generously gave their permission for me to quote from these accounts.

I am chiefly indebted, however, to the internees whose own stories have provided the framework for this book: people such as Barbara Glanville, Sylvia Williams, Iris Krass, Barbara Tilbury, David Nicoll, Colin Palmer, Maureen Collins and Dick Germain; Keith Martin, who was one of the first to tell me his story, and who, sadly, died before my book was completed; Jose Chamberlain, who agreed to be interviewed, despite poor health; Joyce Storey, who spent days copying out sections of her 'liberation' diary for me; Bill Macauley, whose remarkable involvement in the battle for Hong Kong as a fifteen-year-old led to multiple interviews and who has been generous with his time and his library; Richard Dobson, who had never before spoken about his experiences in the camps on Java and had to be persuaded to give an interview. No less vital have been my long-distance contacts, people with whom, although living far away, I have been in regular touch. These include Cyril Mack, who is able to call up events of seventy years ago in scintillating detail and make them seem as if they took place last week; Neil Begley and Margaret Blair, both authors of fine books, and Ralph Armstrong, who has recorded his experiences in the terrible Sumatran camps where his mother and both his sisters died. I have made every effort to trace copyright holders for photographs and quotations, but this has not always been successful. If any have been overlooked I would be happy to acknowledge them in future editions.

I would also like to add my thanks to my husband Keith who uncomplainingly took over the reins of the household while I was absorbed in this book and who encouraged and goaded as appropriate. Lastly my appreciation is due to my editor Bea Hemming, whose enthusiasm and calm made light work of the final stages.

From the time I was interned and whilst growing to adulthood, I had no one to turn to for advice and comfort. I had to stand on my own feet. It was a very difficult and lonely time. My father would not discuss Shanghai or internment and I learned not to ask questions … My own memories are still very few, and even things I would expect to have remembered remain blank. I put this down to the trauma suffered as a child during internment and the ensuing years.

The Japanese and their internment of civilians deprived me in my childhood of a normal family life and the security a child should have while growing up. I feel that in many ways, since I was interned at nine years I have brought myself up with some assistance from various people, none of whom were very close or seemed to care what happened to me …

Jose Chamberlain, who was interned in a Japanese civilian prison camp in Shanghai at the age of nine, reflects on her internment fifty-five years after being freed

Introduction

The children in this story experienced things no child is meant to experience – shipwreck, hunger, death of loved ones and even of playmates, prolonged separation from parents, violence, fear. Today we would readily acknowledge that many received psychological wounds in the process. But these boys and girls returned from their Japanese internment camps with little advice on how to cope in their new lives beyond 'don't talk about it', the catch-all motto of that stiff upper lip era. As a result many of the people who appear in this book have never spoken about how they felt while they were interned. The literature of internment has not focused on the unique problems encountered by the children who spent their formative years as prisoners.

Childhood memories are supposed to be happy – 'the happiest years of your life', as adults were fond of saying in those days. A great many memories described in this book are not happy ones. Yet, happy or sad, the memories of childhood possess a unique intensity, rarely matched by things we remember from later on. I have been struck by how often, describing incidents that happened more than sixty years ago, the teller's eyes – men as well as women – filled with tears. These are people now in their seventies and eighties. 'The past is always with me,' as one put it.[1] Several broke down when they recalled the loyalty and devotion of servants, many of whom trekked for miles to find them in newly liberated camps. Their emotion is undoubtedly bound up with the increasingly negative way colonialism has been depicted in the post-war era. Its image today is a blend of exploitation and heartlessness, which fails to acknowledge the mutual loyalty and affection that existed between many servants and their masters; many who lived through that era find this a hurtful misrepresentation. 'We can't have been that brutal if these people were prepared to run such risks to find us and help us,' was how one former prisoner expressed it.[2] Many of the memories remain intensely painful. One man wrote to me from Australia describing how, as a twelve-year-old in a camp in China, he was so hungry after he had eaten his meagre ration that he cried, instantly prompting his father to give him his portion. He added, 'After so many years, typing this has brought tears to my eyes.' Others still feel grief at yet another wound inflicted by internment – losing a parent at a young age. The adults – particularly the fathers – emerged from camp with an assortment of health problems and found adapting to the post-war world hard. Many buckled under the strain. Of male prisoners between the ages of forty and fifty who returned from the Far East, 70 per cent were dead by sixty.

If for some recollections of camp are as fresh as if they happened yesterday, for others it is the opposite. Where their contemporaries have incidents branded into their minds, they have a blank. Memory is highly sensitive to shock and, consciously or unconsciously, these memories have been excised. One man who was in a camp in the Netherlands East Indies suppressed all memories because he felt that if he had dwelt on what he had gone through he would never have found the energy to start on his professional life.

For others the process was less conscious. One survivor, who as a fourteen-year-old girl watched mesmerised when Japanese soldiers administered a protracted beating to a woman caught smuggling, has no memory of the event today. She only knows she saw it from witnesses. A woman who found herself an orphan at nine when her mother died in camp remembers keenly the misery of being unwanted, but few details about her mother, or day-to-day life in camp.

What unites all the child victims of internment is the conviction that the dropping of the two atomic bombs on the Japanese cities of Hiroshima and Nagasaki was horrific but necessary. The prevailing view today, especially among people born after the war, is that this was an unjustified atrocity because of the bomb's terrible power to maim and abort the most innocent of victims, the future generations.

The people in this story, who were prisoners of the Japanese, were aware that the Japanese army had instructions to kill all Allied prisoners the moment there was a landing on the Japanese homeland. For them, the situation looks different. One girl was celebrating her twelfth birthday on 9 August 1945 in a camp on Java, where women and children were sick and dying for lack of decent food and medical drugs. Though the prisoners were unaware of it, it was the day the second bomb was dropped, this time on Nagasaki. She speaks for the overwhelming majority of ex-internees when she says that without the dropping of those bombs she would have been unlikely to have seen another birthday and nor would hundreds of thousands of other soldiers and civilians.[3]

Many of these former prisoners have derived a measure of closure through a dogged campaign for compensation fought by the Association of British Civilian Internees Far East Region (ABCIFER). After six years of lobbying, about 3,000 civilian ex-internees, all that was left of the 20,000 originally interned, received an ex-gratia one-off payment of £10,000. This was paid out by the Labour Government headed by Tony Blair. Regrettably, about forty ex-internees are still waiting for their promised ex-gratia claims to be honoured. Many, while feeling that the payment did at last acknowledge their sufferings, were sad that it came too late to help their parents.

The miracle is that so many of these former internees have managed to put the past behind them. The majority have led useful and fulfilling lives and have raised families – with children and grandchildren who tease them uncomprehendingly about their strange, thrifty, hoarding habits. Surprisingly, perhaps, the internees are not resentful of what they endured. They are glad merely to have survived when so many did not. As one woman put it, 'I had an extraordinary childhood. I give thanks that my children had an ordinary one.'

PART ONE

———

A Colonial Childhood

I

Caught in a Net

The world is familiar with the shocking Japanese treatment of adult prisoners during the last war (nearly a third of the 57,000 British troops held in the Far East died). What is largely unknown, however, is that thousands of children spent the war incarcerated in Japanese prison camps too.

Among them were British children – nearly 4,000 under the age of eighteen. These youngsters were the sons and daughters of an educated and energetic colonial elite, many of whose families had settled out east generations earlier – as teachers and missionaries, army officers, merchant seamen, civil servants, policemen, rubber or tea planters, bankers, businessmen and engineers. Before the Japanese entry into the war their children had enjoyed an idyllic life, waited on by devoted servants and distanced from the chaotic ways of oriental society by the time-hallowed colonial habit of importing the traditions of home – British food (kippers, roast beef and potatoes, not rice), British architecture and British education. Their destiny was to take over the reins of Empire from their parents: the boys as customs officers, architects, engineers, accountants, the girls as leisured wives and mothers playing tennis, bridge or mah-jong and attending tea dances.

But Japan had other plans. They saw the war in Europe and the success of Hitler's armies as a golden opportunity to add to their substantial territorial victories against the Chinese in the east. The British and Dutch empires with their rich resources were now vulnerable. America was reluctant to enter the conflict, and the way to a vastly enlarged Japanese empire lay open. On 8 December 1941 they attacked with unprecedented force. The simultaneous lightning strikes against their key targets – Pearl Harbor, where they destroyed much of the American Pacific Fleet, Hong Kong and Malaya – were a prelude to the overrunning of much of the Pacific.

The conflict wiped out the future for many thousands of colonial families who found themselves suddenly transformed from the masters to enemy aliens. The children were caught up in this turmoil. Overnight their world fell apart. They were pitchforked into the adult world of the prison camp where they were no longer protected from anything. They may have been civilians, but much of what the military POWs endured, they endured too. They were hungry. They were fed filthy food not fit for dogs – rotting vegetables and rice thick with grubs and cockroach excreta. The hunger reduced teenage boys to tears, forcing them to root through bins for discarded scraps. By the end many were too weak even to play games. Nearly all of them suffered ill health, and not just the ailments that characterise any childhood: they suffered repeated attacks of malaria and dysentery – conditions easily treatable in peacetime but not in a prison camp, where the Japanese withheld drugs. Lack of essential vitamins and minerals caused skin and eye problems; many were covered with boils when they were liberated. These pampered children of the West now found themselves in a world of terrifying casual violence from which their parents could no longer shield them. They saw their mothers repeatedly slapped round the face by bullying Japanese guards who used whatever it took – their hands, wooden sticks, rifle butts – to enforce respect from the hated white races; they were made to watch savage punishments for breaches of discipline. In one camp all the children were made to watch a father being beaten because his hungry daughters had stolen vegetables. Every time they cried out they beat him again. In another, mothers were ordered to brand their young sons with red-hot pokers because they had broken a glass door pane. They became precociously familiar with death as people around them – sometimes friends their own age – died from preventable diseases. One man, sadly recalling the death from beriberi of an older woman who had been kind to him, pointed out that a jar of Marmite, with its vitamin B, could have saved her.

One of the cruellest aspects of internment was its randomness. When the Japanese launched their blitzkrieg in the first week of

December 1941 it was as if a gigantic hunting-net had dropped from the sky, trapping people where they stood, and preventing those parted from loved ones from reaching them. Where they were when the net fell was due to chance, but its effects would, in many cases, be felt for the rest of their lives. So many of the children in this story, who have been scarred by what happened in camp, could have avoided the whole experience – had Fate been on their side. One fifteen-year-old girl fled Shanghai and the impending war in December 1941 together with her mother and younger brother and sister. They left their father behind and headed for the safety of Australia. Their ship put in at Manila on the very morning the Japanese attacked. When the Japanese overran the city they were taken to an internment camp where they remained for four years, separated into three units. The girl went to the women's section, her brother to the men's and her mother and sister to a different location. They were not reunited with their father until 1950. If they had left Shanghai a day earlier they would have remained free.

A fifteen-year-old boy who lived with his parents in Canton returned to his boarding school in Hong Kong for the autumn term of 1941 looking forward to the cricket season. On 8 December the Japanese attacked the airport, a few miles from his school. After finding himself caught up in the bloody battle for Hong Kong, dodging bombs and shells and running messages for the British services, he was sent to a prison camp, alone, the following month. A year later, when food rations had been cut and conditions were very harsh, he heard that his parents had been safely repatriated back to Britain. He did not see his relatives again until the autumn of 1945. If he had delayed his return to school, he would have spent the war in Britain with his family.

A university professor working as a missionary in West China made the long journey to Hong Kong to meet his wife and three young children who were returning from a trip visiting relatives in Canada. Their pleasure at being reunited was short-lived. Within a matter of hours Japanese planes began bombing the colony. Caught up in the battle they spent weeks living rough in bombed-out houses, foraging for food, before they too were interned. He had to watch helplessly as his children got thinner and weaker, until his once sparky and mischievous elder daughter lay listlessly on her bed all day. If that ship had docked two days earlier the whole family would have avoided the war altogether as West China was outside the war zone.

The situation was worst for missionary families who had sent their young children to what was regarded as the best school east of Suez in Chefoo, in the far north of China. It was the tradition to send children to this school from the age of seven. Because of the huge distances involved – one little girl travelled 3,000 miles – the parents only visited once a year, leaving the children to board year-long.

When the Japanese marched into the school on the morning of 8 December, in a display of violence which terrified the children, barging into classrooms, taking away the head of the school and punching elderly female teachers, the parents were thousands of miles away. These children were eventually interned, with their teachers, in Weihsien camp. There, like children in other camps, they endured hunger, cold, inadequate clothing and, for the girls, the embarrassment of having to sew – and wash – their sanitary towels. The teachers did their best. But spinster teachers in the formal 1940s were no substitute for parents. Unlike other interned children, they had to endure it all without the protective hugs, reassurance and encouragement that children take for granted when they are part of a family. For many in this group it would be five years before they were reunited with their families again.

In one of the saddest cases a girl of nine found herself orphaned in camp. She had already suffered a major shock when the kempeitai, the Japanese version of the Gestapo, burst into her family home in the small hours and took away her father. Her mother later died in camp, leaving her to fend for herself for the rest of the war.

The camps ran into hundreds – there were nineteen in Shanghai alone – and were scattered over a huge area ranging from Weihsien in the north of China down to Java and Sumatra in the former Netherlands East Indies, now Indonesia, and including Burma, Thailand (then Siam), Malaya, Borneo, the Philippines and Japan itself. In many camps as many as a third of the prisoners were children. The women's section of Changi jail in Singapore held 1,000 women and 330 children, Stanley camp in Hong Kong held 2,500 adults and 300 children. Santo Tomas camp in the Philippines 3,200 adults and 400 children and Lunghwa camp in Shanghai 1,700 adults and 300 children. On islands such as Java and Sumatra there were more than 40,000 prisoners of which 1,500 were British.

The Japanese, whose military strategy was so ruthlessly pre-planned, had no plan for accommodating prisoners. Their own martial code forbade surrender and the sheer numbers of Allied prisoners took them by surprise. There was no organisation with overall responsibility for their care and the administration of the camps varied according to geography. Many were run by Japanese civilians – this was the case with all the camps in China. The commandants were often diplomats and were, on the whole, decent men who did their best for the prisoners. Camps in the Netherlands East Indies were run by the military. Other camps, such as those in Manila, Singapore and Hong Kong, oscillated between civilian and military regimes. Takeover by the military invariably led to a decrease in rations and an increase in punishments and beatings.

Prisoners on the islands that had formed the Netherlands East Indies (NEI) endured far worse conditions and treatment than any other group, and children shared their suffering. This applied to military and civilian prisoners alike. One fifteen-year-old girl was locked up in a prison cell on Java with her mother and thirty-three other people, nine of whom were children. One group consisted of five children: the eldest was a little boy of eight. As his mother was ill in hospital (she later died), the eight-year-old had to look after his three younger brothers and his two-year-old sister. The lavatory was a stinking fly-infested hole in the corner, the cell's earth floor was running with water and their diet was one spoonful of boiled rice three times a day. After three and a half months, sixteen of the original thirty-three were dead and one woman had gone mad.[1]

Everything that happened in other camps was magnified in the Netherlands East Indies. The appalling way civilian internees were treated mirrored that of military POWs interned on these islands, where men died in their hundreds. Many things were different in these camps. Families were separated and not allowed any written contact. The men were held in different camps from the women, and as soon as they reached the age of twelve, and sometimes sooner, the boys were classed as men, torn from the arms of their weeping mothers and sent to men's camps to work. Whereas in almost all the camps elsewhere in the east the adults were allowed to set up some form of education for the children, in most of the NEI camps it was banned. This was an essential, and in some camps explicitly stated, first step in the zealous crusade to destroy European colonial culture. Books, paper, writing materials, money and photographs were also banned. People found in possession of any of these items were beaten. Food rations were so inadequate that the children ate snakes, snails and roots. One of the most haunting images of internment in this region is of little girls so lacking in energy that they sit pretend-playing with their hands because they haven't the energy to run about. Whereas in many of the camps in China doctors had been free to take a basic supply of drugs into the camps with them, there were few medical supplies in the Netherlands East Indies. This led to the dreadful phenomenon of life-saving operations being performed without anaesthetic.

Some of the effects on children of experiencing and witnessing so much suffering are predictable and visible. A great many former internees took a long time to return to full physical health after the war. Adjusting to normal eating and returning to healthy body weights was straightforward enough. Many, however, after being repatriated to Britain, were endlessly ill with coughs and chills, a syndrome the Victorians would have understood as 'failure to thrive' and we would probably attribute to a damaged immune system. Those who contracted malaria went on suffering attacks for as long as ten years after their release. The lack of calcium in the camps wreaked its effect on teeth, bones and growth. Many former child internees lost all their teeth young and those diagnosed with osteoporosis later in life attribute it to lack of calcium in the vital growing years. A particularly cruel effect of malnutrition in childhood is the impact it has on future fertility. A high number of girls who were interned shortly before they reached puberty have not had children.

The experience of internment also had other more insidious effects that, in some cases, continued to make themselves felt for years after the war was over. The harsh regime in camp, which for some had included torture, the difficulty of coming to terms with having lost everything, the struggle to start afresh in a demoralised inward-looking society all took their toll. For many, internment quite simply destroyed family life, which was never the same again. One of the saddest things was the premature death of so many of the fathers.

These deaths not only left sons and daughters mourning a parent, but also bequeathed them the burden of the dependent widow. One girl who wanted to get married was required by her mother to remain living at home for three years after her father's death 'to keep her company'. In many cases the children undertook a lifelong financial commitment to their widowed mothers.

The most poignant victims are the boys and girls who were separated from their parents. In those vital, vulnerable years, when children are groping their way towards the kind of person they want to become and have such need of loving role models, they were on their own. Many have struggled all their lives to overcome the effects of this, suffering from depression and breakdowns. There have even been suicides. As for family life, the longed-for return home after such a long separation was often stormy. Mothers could be savagely critical of these children they hardly recognised – their anger perhaps a mask for their own guilt at not having been there. And many children were angry, too, feeling that their parents had abandoned them.

But it wasn't anybody's fault. You were where you were when the net fell. More than anything the story of the children who lost their childhood is that of a group of people who found themselves in the wrong place at the wrong time.

2

Paradise Lost

It was an enchanted life that the young sons and daughters of Empire led before the war in the Far East. Childhood is usually carefree but these children were uniquely privileged, certainly compared to the children of Oriental races who surrounded them, but also to their cousins back in Britain. Children of middle class parents – civil servants, architects, missionaries, engineers, oil men, police officers – led the kind of life that in Europe only the super rich could afford. Chauffeured about in rickshaws, they lived in lands where the sun always seemed to be shining. They had spacious modern homes with multiple bathrooms and played in gardens with emerald lawns and trees which dripped luscious tropical fruit; they splashed in pools at state-of-the-art Lidos their English cousins had only seen in films; they shopped in luxurious department stores with moving staircases and were taken to see their fathers' racehorses. While most British children of that era were expected to lend a hand with household chores like cleaning the bath or laying the table, these children didn't even sharpen their own pencils. A fleet of submissive and devoted servants was perpetually on hand – to take them on picnics, cook them their favourite snack, do their washing or tidy their room.

Barbara Bruce (later Glanville) was the only daughter of five children whose father managed a tin mine in Kuala Lumpur. Because education was better in Singapore than Malaya in 1941 the children lived in her grandmother's well-appointed house set in two acres of gardens, immaculately maintained by two gardeners, in Paya Leber, a semi-rural residential district. The garden contained a huge variety of tropical fruit trees, all flourishing in the warm, moist climate, and providing a juicy sticky treat for children – coconuts, pineapple bushes, guava, durian, rambutans, star fruit and custard apple, known as chikoo, which were so delicious that if you left them to ripen on the tree the birds would eat them, so they were picked unripe and buried in dry rice to ripen.

Barbara's French grandfather had been a university professor of mathematics at the Sorbonne. Her mother came from a well-to-do Dutch family who had settled in Malaya and bred racehorses which ran at the Singapore racetrack. The family enjoyed a typically leisured colonial lifestyle with a car and a chauffeur, known as 'syce' from the old Raj term for groom, a cook and an amah to look after the children and the cleaning. 'It was a very lazy life. We didn't have to lift a finger. We'd come home from school, take off our school uniform and throw it on the floor. The servants would pick it up, wash and iron it and put it back in the wardrobe for next time. All we did was play.' They played old-fashioned open-air games: find the ball, a variant of hide-and-seek, hopscotch, five stones. Barbara was a great tree climber and there were no shortage of huge trees in her grand-parents' garden.

From the age of seven she attended the Convent of the Holy Infant Jesus as a boarder, where the school day ran from 8 a.m. to 1 p.m. to accommodate the heat. Her grandmother was strict and trips into the centre of Singapore were limited to visits to the ultra-modern Lido swimming pool complex and the Botanical Gardens. Sometimes the children would be driven to Saturday morning pic-tures at the Cathay cinema, where amah would chaperone them for the 11 a.m. matinee. After the show syce would be waiting to take them home, or on rare occasions, on to meet their parents for tiffin at Raffles Hotel. Barbara's grandmother took her to see *The Wizard of Oz* at the air-conditioned Cathay cinema.

Singapore in the 1930s was a dynamic and glamorous city with a worldwide reputation for exciting nightlife. Run as a British colony since its foundation in the early nineteenth century by Sir Thomas Stamford Raffles, its status as a free port meant prices were low and the good life came cheap. Crammed onto the small island were a multitude of nationalities – Indians, Malays, Chinese, English, Dutch, Germans. These races, each with their own quarter, contributed to the island's reputation for gaiety and diversity. The hub of Singapore's shopping area was the opulent tree-lined Orchard Road with its boutiques displaying samples of their expensive goods – handbags, gloves, perfumes – in glass cabinets along the pavements.

A great treat for children was to be taken to one of the island's three amusement parks, The Great World, The Happy World and the New World, lit at night with hundreds of Chinese lanterns and frequented by huge groups of laughing and chattering extended Chinese families. These were palaces of fun conceived on a giant scale, combining the standard funfair offerings of rides, shooting galleries and stalls with dance halls, and banqueting rooms where one could entertain as many as forty friends to fifteen-course feasts, puppet shows and Chinese and Malay operas.

Ralph Armstrong was another member of Singapore's gilded youth. Ralph's father worked in various parts of the British admin-istration, including Highways and the Harbour Master's Office. He had been manager of Robinson's, the island's leading department store, whose reputation was founded on the boast that you could buy a house and furnish it all in the one store. Ralph, who was thirteen when war broke out, was the youngest in the family. His two older sisters, Dixie and Grace, were zestful and attractive, with the glossy hair, tanned legs and cheeky hats that we associate with the film stars of the 1930s. Ralph spent his free time watching films at the Pavilion Cinema in Orchard Road or going for a spin in the latest open-topped cars, sitting in the back while a boyfriend of his sister's drove them to the seaside, to have lunch, or see a film.

As far as the British were concerned, protected by the island's avowedly impregnable fortress with its massive guns, this wonderful life would go on forever. A matter of months before the fall of Singapore itself the supposedly invincible forces of the British Empire continued, peacock-style, to flaunt their pageantry to anyone who cared to be impressed by it. Barbara Bruce's older brother Mel attended a parade which took place on the Singapore esplanade not far from Raffles Hotel and included all the regiments stationed in Singapore. Though no one realised, it was almost certainly the last of its kind. 'The march past included units from the Royal Navy, various Army units, also units from the Royal Air Force base at Tengah and Seletar, and also units from the Argylls, the Ghurkas and followed by units from the Police, and detachments of the Nursing and medical staff and from the Military and Civilian hospitals, and last but not least, the Boys Brigade and Boy Scouts, and Girl Guides. The salute was taken by the then Governor Sir Shenton Thomas. It was ... a marvellous sight ... There was also a fly past of aircraft from both the RAF bases at Tengah and Seletar.'[1]

It wasn't just in Singapore that British children had found their place in the sun. Seven-year-old Sylvia Williams's family were living in Manila in the Philippines when the Japanese attacked Pearl Harbor. Her father worked for Shell. 'We lived in a beautiful house, painted white and covered in purple bougainvillea. It had huge polished hardwood floors scattered with rich oriental rugs on which I liked skating. I had a lovely little dachshund called Frisky.' They had servants: a gardener, a chauffeur, an amah for Sylvia, a cook, a houseboy and a lavandera who was in charge of the laundry. Sylvia attended the American school. 'Like many only children I spent a lot of time with my parents. They liked going to the Polo Club or the Social club, where they drank whiskey and sodas or gin and tonic. I swam in the pool or played ball.'

Sylvia's father, unusually, was critical of the sybaritic life led by Europeans in the Far East, where stints of work were punctuated by trips home aboard luxury liners which took eight weeks to reach England. With more insight than shown by most of his compatriots, he referred to it scathingly as a 'fool's Paradise'. Sylvia, however, was serenely happy. 'I loved the warm, humid climate, where I was never cold and could play outside all the time and I loved the vividness of everything in the tropics.'

Sensing that war with Japan was now a certainty, Sylvia's father booked a passage to Australia for his wife and daughter. But when it came to the moment, like many other wives of ex-pats, her mother refused to leave her husband.

European children growing up in the big cities of China were not colonials in the strict sense – but they might as well have been. Historic trade agreements between Imperial China and Western traders in the mid-nineteenth century had led to the foundation of treaty ports. Foreign communities had quickly grown up in these towns and the desire to protect these citizens – diplomats, missionaries, travellers and merchants – from the lawless ways of the pre-war Orient had led to the creation of foreign concessions. Within their designated boundaries these territories operated as autonomous mini-states, with their own legal system, local government administration, police force, foreign schools and hospitals. Businessmen could thus conduct their affairs unaffected by Chinese law or taxation. The terms of the lease stated explicitly that Chinese and nationals of other countries could be excluded. Of these Shanghai was the largest, followed by Peking. By the outbreak of war with Japan, Tientsin, another city with a high European population, had nine foreign concessions. Because of the high incidence of theft and looting in China, Western families living outside the concessions invariably made their homes in walled compounds manned by guards.

Life in northern China lacked the languid glamour of the tropics, but the extremes of the climate brought their own variety of exuberant childhood pastimes – all supervised and facilitated by the faithful band of servants. Nine-year-old Neil Begley spent his early years in Peking, which, as well as being the exotic and mysterious Imperial city, contained the second largest British population in China after Shanghai. His father was a missionary with the Salvation Army. Missionaries formed the largest Western professional group in China: when war broke out there were over 8,500 missionaries living in China.[2] Even missionaries, whose pay in no way compared to some of the top civil servants or businessmen, had their complement of servants. 'We had a cook, an amah, and a rickshaw coolie who doubled as yardman. Each Monday my father had a meeting with the cook to establish the week's menu, after which the cook would arrange everything from the purchasing of the foodstuffs to the preparation and serving of the meals. Apart from looking after us, the amah was responsible for the general housework, the washing, the ironing and the mending. Each morning she'd come to my bedroom and lay out my clothes, then help me dress. After I'd gone down to breakfast she'd make my bed and tidy up my room.'[3]

In the cold winters of the north skating was popular with Europeans. 'In the yard we youngsters made a small skating-rink by dividing off a portion of the garden with an earth wall about four or five inches high and then hosing the enclosure each day. After a few days there was a layer of ice strong enough to support our weight as we learned how to skate on ice skates we'd bought from a second-hand stall. When we'd become more proficient we were allowed to go to Pei Hai Park where a section of the frozen lake had been fenced off ... to form a public rink.' Later on, as the weather warmed up, there would be visits to the Summer Palace 'with its picturesque gardens and lakes with humpbacked and zigzag bridges built to foil the progress of evil spirits' and its extraordinary Marie Antoinette-style toy, the Marble Boat. This was a gigantic fantasy boat built of marble and arising from a lake.

Summers in northern China were stiflingly hot and characterised by red dust storms that blew in from the Gobi Desert, reducing visibility to a few feet. To escape the heat, missionary families often spent the summer holidays at the Western Hills in a large rambling rest house set in extensive park-like gardens. A favourite trip was to hire donkeys and mules and ride through the hills in search of a secluded picnic spot. A highlight of the picnic was the cool home-made ice cream made on the spot by the servants.

To today's readers the imperious attitude of Europeans towards Orientals might seem offensive, but this was an era when a racial hierarchy, with the white man enthroned at the top, was unquestioned in Western circles. This applied as much in religious communities as in more worldly society. 'As foreigners we kept ourselves quite apart. We were surrounded and far outnumbered by Chinese but we had little to do with them and, apart from our servants, dealt with them only as tradesmen or shopkeepers. We took it for granted that coolie labour was used for everything ... and that the average life expectancy of a rickshaw boy was twenty-eight years. What did it really matter that there were 450,000,000 of them and most of them were starving?' The only thing Neil was expected to do for himself was clean his shoes – an activity that was considered character-building.

Hong Kong offered the familiar bubbling cosmopolitan cocktail of other Chinese cities, but here it was laced by a heavy dose of British-ness, characterised by an entrenched belief that things work best when ordered along hierarchical lines of class and race. Westerners in Shanghai, where the existence of the International Settlement made for a more relaxed atmosphere, regarded colonial Hong Kong as a 'stuffy backwater'.[4] This stuffiness and Britishness was the result of Hong Kong's having been a British colony since 1842 when, with the signing of the treaty of Nanking, China ceded it to the British Crown in perpetuity. Bill Macauley had started as a boarder at the Diocesan Boys' School in Kowloon in 1938 at the age of twelve with his older brother Jim. Bill was one of five siblings but he had a special bond with Jim. Although the elder by only four years Jim took his role as older brother seriously, combining physical protectiveness with an awareness, in the absence of their father, of the need to be a moral mentor. 'In 1937 when the Japanese launched their war against the Chinese we were on a train which was bombed. The blast blew out all the windows in the carriage. We had to get out and hide in a field. We lay down in the mud and stones and Jim lay across me to protect me. That was typical.'

The boys' father had been out east since before the First World War and was a chief appraiser in the Chinese Maritime Customs. In the years leading up to war the family was based in Canton and Bill and his brother went home for the holidays. Jim left school in July 1941 and that autumn Bill returned to school on his own as head prefect. 'I had finally made it into the First Eleven and was looking forward to the cricket season. There was a lot of cricket played in Hong Kong but admission to the various clubs was strictly according to social position and race.'

During the years they had attended the school together Bill and Jim had made plenty of friends in Hong Kong and made sure they went out at weekends. 'Weekday evenings were taken up with prep as later that term I was due to take School Cert. That was the stepping stone to Matric, which influenced your choice of career. If I wasn't studying I was practising in the nets for cricket.' At weekends Bill and Jim used to take the Star Ferry over to the island to go the cinemas. In those days all the cinemas produced printed programmes giving a synopsis of what they were showing. The school expected pupils to go to something educational, but Bill and Jim liked cowboy films. 'We would go into one of the cinemas showing a cultural film and pick up their programme so that if we were questioned back at school we'd have a cast-iron alibi.' A favourite haunt was the Dairy Farm, a combined food store and café which, in those pre built-up days, actually had cows and fields.

Bill's brother Jim had decided he wanted to follow their elder brother who was already in England at radio school prior to joining the Royal Air Force as a radio transmitter. His ship was due to leave Hong Kong on 17 November 1941 and Bill went down to the docks to see him off on SS *Neleus*, a thirty-year-old passenger ship of the Blue Funnel Line, which plied between the Far East and Liverpool. It was almost certainly the last Blue Funnel ship to sail from Hong Kong before the attack on Pearl Harbor.

'Before he got into the sampan which would take him out to the ship, which was anchored in the middle of the harbour, Jim hugged me close. His parting words were "always to try to play with a straight bat". I was crying my eyes out. I really looked up to him and I didn't know when I would see him again.' Bill took a taxi back to school. Noticing his distress the head took him to task. 'He reminded me that I was a prefect and that I was British. The British, he said, don't cry.'

Teenagers are endlessly hungry and on Bill's trips into the city with Jim food had played a central role. In the interval between his brother's departure and the outbreak of war he pursued his gastronomic interests blithely unaware of the sword of Damocles poised above his head. 'I would go anywhere where there was the chance of a free meal. Two weeks before Pearl Harbor I went to an American Evangelist meeting. The preacher was said to provide wonderful teas to the faithful. I went back to school with a nice little box of cakes and sandwiches.'

There were Japanese populations in all Chinese cities. Many Europeans had Japanese friends and went to Japan for holidays. On the first weekend in December Bill went to see a Japanese family he had got to know with Jim. 'They owned a shoe shop on Nathan Road. They had children about the same age as us and we used to play together. They were very nice people and always made us welcome. The added attraction was that there, too, there was always a slap-up tea of buns and cake.'

How could those people from different cultures, innocently sipping tea together that afternoon, suspect that events were in preparation which were about to change their lives forever?

Singapore and Hong Kong offered a pleasant, easy life to foreigners, but European children growing up in Shanghai believed that,

compared to them, everywhere else was stuck in the dark ages. It was a supremely modern city, boasting the latest lifestyle technology. Hollywood films and the hottest American dance records came to Shanghai long before they reached London. From its relatively recent beginnings the port had risen to be among the six largest in the world importing and exporting on a prodigious scale – half of all goods coming into China passed through Shanghai and more than a third of the country's exports left through the city's harbour. Moreover, Shanghai was a seething hive of industry and manufacture in its own right with paper and cotton mills, shipyards and engineering plants. Everything that was needed to make the wheels of life turn was made in the city by thousands of highly skilled workers: iron and steel, machinery, textiles, soap, drugs, cigarettes, candles, matches, dyes and electrical supplies.[5]

Shanghai was a genuinely international city with the accompanying feelings of energy and can-do spirit. In December 1941 the city's population numbered 8,000 British, 2,500 French, who lived in their own concession, 2,500 Portuguese, 2,000 Americans, 40,000 White Russians who had poured over the border fleeing the Bolsheviks in 1917, four million Chinese and up to 25,000 Japanese civilians. The heart of the city was the International Settlement, an area of 9 square miles, which had been formed in the middle of the previous century by the amalgamation of the old British and American Concessions and was independent of Chinese law. At the outbreak of war a million and a half Chinese were living in the International Settlement.

The International Settlement was effectively run by the British. They dominated the Shanghai Municipal Council, the settlement's governing body, and ran the police force, the fire service, the waterworks and the gasworks. The SMC maintained its own defence force, the Shanghai Volunteer Corps, and encouraged its staff to join. The top posts in the Chinese Maritime Customs, a huge organisation responsible for collecting duty from imports and exports, and which had staff in all the treaty ports throughout China, were held by British men. The city swarmed with taipans, highly paid Western businessmen who ran the big multinational companies, known as hongs, who had offices in China: Jardine Matheson, Butterfield & Swire, Patons and Baldwins the knitting wool manufacturers, British

American tobacco, Ford, Singer, ICI, The National City Bank of New York. It was also the headquarters of the Hong Kong and Shanghai Banking Corporation, now known as the HSBC and based in London.[6] Most people arrived in Shanghai by ship, sailing up the Whangpoo River and arriving eventually at the famous Bund. This was a wide road facing the river, and was home to many of the city's most important buildings, the majority built in emphatically Western neoclassical or Director's Roman style.

Compared to London or Paris, Shanghai was a dazzlingly modern city. It had wide streets crowded with the latest models of cars, plumbing that worked, electric lighting and an efficient public transport system boasting trams, electrically operated trolleybuses and single and double decker buses. One of the city's four giant department stores, the Sun Company, even had escalators, much to the delight of children who begged to be taken to the store to be allowed to ride them. But shadowing the sleek plutocracy of the Westernised city was a different Shanghai: a desperate place characterised by hunger, violence and crime. The crime rate put Shanghai at the very top of the world league, right behind Chicago. The 1937 Japanese invasion of China had laid waste hundreds of towns and villages forcing destitute families into the city in search of work and handouts. Most of the Chinese in the city were desperately poor. Jostling for space with the motorised traffic in the street were thousands of hand-pulled rickshaws, pedicabs, barrows and handcarts owned by Chinese scraping a living at subsistence level. Many had no income at all and were reduced to begging. Shanghai was notorious for its beggars. In 1938 over 100,000 'exposed corpses' were picked up off the street. Many froze to death. In a really cold winter 400 bodies a day might be picked up.[7]

It was estimated that before 1941 about 10 per cent of all the sausages sold in Shanghai were made of human meat. The more unscrupulous Chinese sausage manufacturers, who ran the sausage factories in the back streets, would drag the dead beggars off the street before the garbage cart could collect them, and turn them into sausages. Prior to 1941 this was not illegal. A law was then passed by the Shanghai Municipal Council to make it illegal and punishable by a fine of Chinese $100 (US $10 or £5) to make sausages out of human meat.[8]

Newcomers to the city found conditions shocking. For Hope Lee, a British woman whose husband was a social worker for the Society of Friends, the squalor was nauseating. 'If there was an odd space anywhere it was covered with vile litter and used as a lavatory. The spitting in the streets and buses made me sick .... There was one terrible beggar without arms or legs who rolled on the ground in front of you, screaming.'[9]

In front of this chaotic and often cruel oriental backdrop, British children, chaperoned by the ever-faithful amah, continued to lead extraordinarily British lives. These lives were characterised by pride in Empire, English cooking, English education and visits to English-style public parks.

Cyril Mack's father, who came originally from Norfolk, had been in Shanghai since the late 1920s. Ten years later he was an inspector in the Distribution and Inspection Department of the Shanghai Waterworks, responsible for the purity of Shanghai's drinking water. Cyril and his older brother Roy lived with their parents and servants in the western end of the International Settlement, on the other side of Shanghai's racetrack. Unwilling to let standards slip just because he was out east Cyril's father insisted on kippers for breakfast every Saturday. He was a member of the Shanghai Municipal Police Specials – the Waterworks had their own division, known as the Water Lilies – and kept a .45 handgun at home.

Cyril and his brother's lives mirrored those of thousands of other foreigners in the city. At times they even had a private rickshaw. While the amahs looked after the children their mother spent her days having her nails done, listening to the latest popular music, meeting friends for coffee and knitting and doing needlework. Tailors visited at home to measure the men for suits and shirts, the women for dresses, copied from the latest edition of *Vogue* or similar Western fashion magazines. Even shoes were custom-made. Again, only a photograph was needed.

Like many city children Cyril and Roy's favourite outings centred on Shanghai's open spaces. The racecourse, in the heart of the city, was a focal meeting place for Westerners, its huge wide, flat, treeless central area the setting in summer for all kinds of sports – football, cricket, hockey, rugby, a small golf course and polo. The boys loved the military tattoos, which featured mainly British troops. The biggest draw for children, however, was the huge sandpit in the racecourse's public recreation ground. Wearing sunhats or topees and carrying buckets and spades the children would hurry to the tram stop, followed by amah laden with picnic 'tiffin'. Another destination popular with the brothers was the Public Gardens on the Bund overlooking the point where the Soochow Creek joined the vast Whangpoo River. They liked watching the huge variety of craft – junks, sampans, barges, tugs, ferries, steamboats and cargo boats – and listening to the cacophony of honks, toots, whistles and blaring horns that accompanied them.[10]

Jose Chamberlain's father Harry had first gone out to China in 1911. Starting work as a Post Office messenger boy in Birmingham he had risen through the ranks of the Shanghai police force and by the late 1930s was superintendent in charge of the Riot Squad. Harry was a tough, unsentimental man and Jose has photographs of him executing Chinese civilians. He spoke Mandarin and had fought in the First World War. He returned to China with his Birmingham-born wife in the mid-1920s.

The family's attitude to Chinese culture was typical of other Westerners. 'We didn't eat Chinese food. The cook boy's speciality was sirloin of beef and cold ox tongue. I liked water chestnuts but I was not allowed to eat them "as you didn't know what the water they grew in was like".'

Before the war they were living in a three-storey semi-detached house attached to the headquarters of the riot police. At that time there was a lot of civil disturbance among the Chinese caused mainly by the opium trade. 'Dad had a lot of men under him – Sikhs, Chinese, Russians and British. They used to tour the streets in red marias, which had a gun turret at the back on which a machine gun was mounted. Dad was in charge of the machine gun.'

Jose was an only child and spent a lot of time reading and playing with her toys or keeping her mother company. She liked comics like *Tiny Tots*, and cardboard cut-out dolls which could be dressed in different outfits which you clipped on. She loved dolls and had a dolls' pram and dolls' house, which had been made for her by prisoners in the jail. As is often the case with only children, mother and daughter were very close and in the late afternoon Jose often accompanied her mother to tea dances, which were held regularly in elegant Art Deco hotels like the Cathay. At other times they went to the Da Lo swimming pool, an ultra-modern Lido, where there was a 30-foot-high diving board and a snack bar selling ice cream and popcorn. In the summer she and her mother would go for walks in one of the many large landscaped cemeteries in the city where the plane trees provided shade from the heat.

At five Jose began as a pupil at the Shanghai Cathedral School for Girls, an establishment run along ultra-British lines, with English teachers, a smart uniform and a curriculum and exam system prescribed by Cambridge University. Jose travelled to school every day with a friend in a rickshaw pulled by a coolie.

Ferried around by rickshaw and waited on like lordlings, the quality of life of these children of the colonies was vastly superior to that led by children of similar backgrounds in Britain. Physically cosseted they obviously were, but in some ways they were less insulated and more streetwise than their British cousins. The east was a violent place with very different ideas about the sanctity of life or the finality of death from those prevailing in the West. Many of these children had witnessed sights no youngster in Britain would expect to see – dead bodies, vicious ethnic bullying, gruesome accidents. The toughness they had developed through these experiences would be severely tested in the immediate future.

Western children were brought up not to show compassion to beggars. Ron Huckstep was a bright fifteen-year-old whose father was the Director of Education in Shanghai. He was told by his parents never to move the body of a beggar if they died outside one's property. This was because under Chinese law at that time, one was liable not only for burying the body but also for caring for the relatives of the beggar for the rest of their lives.

'I remember ... a dead beggar lying outside our garage door for three days. We were unable to move the body or open the garage door for the car while the relatives waited expectantly on the opposite side of the road.

'Many a time, as a young child walking to school particularly on a hot summer's day, I would pass a beggar crying for water. I was told never to approach too closely, as there was then no really effective way of treating either cholera or typhoid in those days, and there was a risk of contracting the disease oneself. On the way back from school the beggar was sometimes dead.'[11]

As a result of their victory in the Sino-Japanese War the Japanese occupied China for about 100 miles inland and surrounded Shanghai. In the city, checkpoints were set up on all the routes leading from occupied China into the International Settlement. These were manned by Japanese soldiers who searched all the Chinese peasants entering the city in case they were smuggling rice or other foodstuffs into the Settlement. The checkpoints were often the scene of repellent cruelty as the Japanese tormented – and on occasion even murdered – defenceless Chinese citizens, uninhibited by the crowds of observers. As a youngster Ron Huckstep found himself drawn to them: 'I used to watch the searching, and sometimes punishment meted out to those caught smuggling at the checkpoint at the end of our road on the main Shanghai–Nanking railway. The penalty for smuggling rice was to make the culprit eat large quantities of raw rice and then drink great quantities of water. This would cause the rice to swell up in the stomach and intestines and often cause the victim to die slowly in agony.'

Occasionally women would pretend to be pregnant and carry the rice in the bulge in front of the abdomen. The Japanese got into the habit of ripping up the front of the dress of such women with a bayonet. 'Unfortunately sometimes the woman would actually be pregnant, and the bayonet would rip up her belly. The foetus and guts would then fall out on to the road together with the agonised woman, much to the horror of the onlookers.'[12]

The fighting between the Chinese and the Japanese during the war led to many children witnessing disturbing sights. Devastation was caused one summer afternoon in Shanghai at the height of the war when a Chinese bomber targeting a Japanese warship accidentally dropped two bombs in the crowded downtown commercial district of the city, killing 700 and injuring hundreds more. Cyril Mack, who was then four years old, was ill at the time and was taken to the family doctor. He and his mother had to step over scores of gravely wounded Chinese soldiers to get to the consulting room, a sight that horrified him. 'Some with limbs amputated, others obviously with not long to live, bandages stiff with congealed blood, many lying in their own body waste. Flies swarmed over their unwashed bodies dripping with sweat, the heat was suffocating and the stench was retching.'

Parents doubtless did their best to protect children from the more unpleasant sights but they weren't always there. Neil Begley and his brother were returning to their school at Tientsin in north China from a holiday trip when they heard a commotion in a first class carriage. Neil was about eight at the time. 'At the end of the corridor a Japanese man dressed in a plain white kimono was kneeling on a white mat ... In front of him were ... a small pottery bowl and an ornate looking dagger ... he seemed to be in some sort of trance. As he knelt with his hands resting on his thighs he spoke in a dull monotone. We watched, not knowing quite what to expect. After a short while the talking stopped. He reached forward deliberately, grasped the dagger with both hands and held it pointing towards his lower abdomen. He paused for a moment. Then drawing the dagger towards him, he plunged it deep into his stomach, moved it around, up and across, then with a forward flick of his wrist disembowelled himself. For what seemed like an eternity he knelt there, glazed eyes staring into a nothingness in front of him, then slowly leaned forward and collapsed in the mess of blood and intestines on the mat.'

Extreme as it was, such a sight formed an integral part of the unique blend of suffering and luxury that made up a colonial childhood in the Far East. But, even as these privileged children continued to play the carefree games of childhood, Paradise was being lost. The coming years would bring the kind of suffering that they had previously accepted as the lot of others. This time they and their families would be the victims.

3

Melted Like Butter

O n Monday, 8 December 1941 just after eight o'clock in the
morning fifteen-year-old Bill Macauley was starting his prefect's duty of dormitory inspection at the Diocesan Boys' School in
Hong Kong. The school was built on a hill on the mainland in
Kowloon, overlooking the narrow strait to Hong Kong island. Dormitory duty involved checking that the two dozen middle boys' beds
were properly made and lockers tidy. Suddenly he heard a series of
deafening thumps.

'I looked out of the window and saw wave after wave of low-
flying aircraft coming in from the north-east and bombing the
airport, which was no more than two miles from the school. We
were on the third floor and though we couldn't see the runways
we could see clouds of dust and debris billowing up from the
wrecked planes.'

The boys' instinct was to stay and watch, but the headmaster had
given them strict instructions as to what to do in case of attack. 'We
were expected to file down in a disciplined fashion to makeshift air
raid shelters, which were just covered storerooms,' Bill explained. 'By
now it was really noisy with anti-aircraft guns popping away all round
us and the Japs switching their attention to other targets, like the
dockyards.'

The headmaster had been called up over the weekend and had
enlisted in the Hong Kong Volunteer Defence Corps. Before leaving
he had sent the 300 day boys home to their families, leaving a young
American teacher and a middle-aged English matron in charge of
the eight boarders, of whom Bill was one.

'The authorities must have known an attack was imminent because the HKVDF were all in position by Sunday, 7 December. The last I saw of the headmaster was a week earlier.' His wife was about to give birth and he came back to school to collect her and take her over on the ferry to St Mary's Hospital on Hong Kong island. Bill, whose family were in Canton, was put in charge of the remaining boys. Still under attack from the air the boys spent the day emptying the upper floors of the school, throwing the mattresses off the upper walkways and stacking them up in their air raid shelter, which became their dormitory. This included Matron and her Scottie dog Missie. With commendable presence of mind Bill made every boy pack a small suitcase containing a change of clothes to be kept at the foot of the bed – 'I thought if we had to get out fast it would be a good idea.'

A thousand miles away in Tientsin, in north China, on the same morning Neil Begley was hurrying to school from the hostel where the children slept. Nine-year-old Neil, the son of Salvation Army missionary parents, had failed Matron's hand inspection on this cold bright morning and was worried he was late. As he neared the school he realised something was wrong.

'Two soldiers in padded khaki Japanese uniforms with little cloth peaked caps on their heads stood guard outside the gates, weapons at the ready. They wore those funny rubberised canvas ankle-length boots that Japanese soldiers wore which separated the big toe from the rest of the foot, and carried Mausers – large curious-looking pistols that could fold out to become rifles.' Neil tried to edge past the soldiers but one of them lashed out at him with the butt of his rifle, catching him just above the right eye. Sobbing and terrified, he fled back to the hostel, a mixture of tears and blood streaming down his face onto his school blazer.

By now Japanese soldiers were everywhere. Some marched down the middle of the road in the characteristic half-walk, half-jog that would become so familiar before long. Others moved along the footpaths wielding bamboo sticks, lashing out at screaming passers-by. The terrified boy tried to get back into the hostel but the gates had been sealed by the Japanese and the gatekeeper refused to let him in. Tearing a piece off his shirt to try to staunch the bleeding from the gash above his eye he made for the school playing fields and hid there, finally getting back into the hostel by climbing a drainpipe.

Inside the school there was an air of calm. The older girls were ordered into their dormitories and told not to look out of the windows. The headmaster summoned the entire school and called for dignity and self-control, telling them: 'You are British and must deport yourselves with pride and dignity. God is on our side, God is for the right and the right will win. God save the King.' He then led them in the singing of the school song and 'There'll Always be an England'.

Throughout the morning Japanese soldiers burst into classrooms unannounced, shouting unintelligible orders and cuffing people out of the way. The terrified children were screaming and sobbing. Brigadier McKenzie, a strict elderly spinster who was matron of the hostel, known as 'Auntie Kenzie', tried to stand up to the Japanese only to become their first victim under the horrified gaze of the children. 'One officer was particularly belligerent and when Auntie Kenzie tried to stop him he felled her with a vicious blow. We watched terrified as his retinue stood guard at the door. When the officer emerged he aimed a kick at the inert body of Auntie Kenzie, then marched down the stairs and out of the hostel.'[1]

While Neil Begley's sheltered life in north China was being shattered by the ugly intrusion of war, in the Philippines, a fifteen-year-old girl, also British, gazed up happily at the cloudless sky. Iris Krass was on her way to Australia with her mother and her younger brother and sister, her father having decided that Pacific war seemed imminent and Shanghai was no longer safe for women and children. The *Anhui*, the Chinese steamer which was carrying them, had just entered Manila Bay on that brilliant December morning. 'It was a really beautiful day, warm and tropical after wintry Shanghai. The sky was deep blue and so was the sea. We were basking in the warmth.'

At about noon they heard the roar of engines overhead. They looked up to see the sky filled with scores of Japanese planes. The noise became deafening as the planes began a devastating bombing attack on the shipping in the bay. 'It was absolute pandemonium. My mother was in another part of the ship with my sister who had got herself locked in the lavatory. A member of the crew told us all to put on our lifejackets, get below and lie under a table. There were other children there and they were screaming and crying, but I froze. I didn't cry. I just went stiff. I suppose it was shock. It was absolutely terrifying – the noise of the planes' engines, the bombs exploding, people's screams ... Two or three times our ship was shaken by massive convulsions and we thought we had been hit. One man jumped overboard because he thought we would sink. When the bombs fell right by us they exploded under the sea sending up great towers of water making the ship rock and plunge as if she had been damaged.'

The raid went on for hours but eventually the noise stopped and the terrified passengers realised that the planes had left. 'It was dark when we felt brave enough to venture back up on deck. It was a terrible sight. The whole bay was lit up by burning ships.'

The next morning the captain told the passengers that Japan had declared war on the Allies the day before and that it would be too dangerous for him to proceed with them to Australia. He would therefore be landing them in Manila. 'As we landed we were met by the Red Cross who managed to find billets for us all in different parts of the city.' Iris and her family were taken to a golf club.

The group of mothers and children, some of whom were only babies, remained in the golf club for several weeks, sleeping on mattresses on the floor, while the Japanese continued their assault on strategic targets in Manila. During this time Iris contracted typhoid. 'I collapsed very suddenly and developed a very high fever. I was pretty ill and just lay on my mattress semi-conscious for weeks.'

Soon after Christmas their worst fears were realised when word went around that the Japanese were on their way. 'The women were in a panic as the golf club, naturally, was full of whisky and gin. My mother, who was a teacher in Shanghai, took charge. She ordered all the women to get rid of the spirits for fear that the Japanese would find them. There was no knowing what the Japanese would do if they were drunk. All night they smashed bottles and poured the stuff away. Some drank it and got quite drunk, including a girl we called

Fatso, who was only a few years older than me; some buried bottles in the grounds – 'for later' – as no one had any idea how long the war would last. Some of it went to Filipinos. Word had somehow got around and they turned up with empty tins and went away with them brimming with gin and whisky.'

The following day the Japanese started to drift in, a small contingent of between twenty and thirty, looking travel-stained and dishevelled. 'My mother went out to meet them. Their officer was a captain and appeared to be an educated man. In fact my mother told me later that she had a sore hand because the officer had stubbed his cigarette out on it. He told her that his men were dirty and needed to use the showers. His advice to her was that the women stay out of sight.'

The frightened women did as he suggested. Iris's mother went back to her daughter's bedside. Suddenly they were joined by a Japanese soldier. 'I was lying on the bed with my eyes closed. I was feeling very ill but I was still terrified. Unlike my poor mother, I didn't know anything about rape, but I was fearful he might harm me. He flung back the bedclothes to get a look at me. I was wearing pyjamas. I kept my eyes tight shut as I felt that would be best but I could feel him looking. My mother was appealing desperately to him, saying that I was ill, very ill, that I was highly infectious. She was saying, "She has typhoid." We had no idea if he could understand or not but eventually he left. We didn't see any of the soldiers after that.'

Just as Iris had felt exhilarated by the blue sky over Manila Bay, so Keith Martin, aged thirteen, was feeling on top of the world. He was staying with his aunt and uncle in Shanghai and he had gone to bed the night before worrying about his School Certificate exams, which he was in the middle of sitting.

At 3 a.m. on 8 December, however, he woke up. 'In the pitch-black we heard the sound of distant explosions. We learned later that it was the Japanese sinking of the gunboat HMS *Peterel*. A Japanese launch had gone out from the mainland, boarded the ship and told the captain that as a state of war existed between Japan and Great Britain he would have to surrender the ship. The captain's reply was: "Get off my bloody ship." The launch then withdrew and launched a red rocket. This was a signal to the Japanese on the mainland to attack the ship.*

'In no time everyone in the house was up. My aunt didn't know exactly what was happening but she said something like: "the balloon's gone up" and I guessed what she meant. Torn between fear and relief, I was thinking two things simultaneously: one – we're trapped; the other – no more exams tomorrow.'

For seven-year-old Barbara Bruce, who was living with her family in Singapore, 8 December was also a day she would never forget. 'It was Dad's birthday and we were really worried because he was miles away on the mainland of Malaya. He had joined the military reserve in Malaya (the SSVF – Strait Settlements Volunteer Force) and had been ordered not to leave. His instructions were to stay behind and blow up the tin mines so the Japs couldn't use them. My mother had refused to be evacuated so we were trapped on the island. My father just managed to get back to us before the Japs blew up the causeway joining Singapore island to the mainland.'

Barbara remembers the first air attacks on the island. 'They bombed the massive fuel storage tanks, which lit up the night sky with red and orange lights. The fires burned for eight days. British troops were putting up guns all along the front. There was an air of rising panic, especially amongst the servants who were really scared of the Japanese.'

What the world woke up to on 8 December was the almost unbelievable news that the Japanese air force, in a succession of lightning raids, had all but destroyed the US Pacific Fleet at Pearl Harbor. The timing seemed right. In North Africa British forces had been driven back by Rommel towards Egypt and in Russia, Japan's Nazi

---

* The Americans had an identical ship moored nearby and were also requested to surrender. They complied. When the survivors of the crew of HMS *Peterel* were taken to the detention centre where the US crew had already been taken, they were soaking wet and cold. When they asked for fresh clothes the Japanese pointed to the US sea chest and told them to help themselves. The Americans protested. 'That's ours,' they exclaimed. 'You didn't fight. They fought,' was the Japanese reply. The acting CO of the *Peterel*, Lt Stephen Polkington, was later awarded the Distinguished Service Cross for his actions.

ally was sweeping towards Moscow and apparently unstoppable. Britain's Atlantic supply line was in peril from German U-boats. America, though aiding the British war effort, was still reluctant to come into the conflict.

Pearl Harbor turned out to be merely the starting gun. With synchronised precision the Japanese war machine powered into lethal action as its armed forces launched multiple attacks on key Western strongholds or occupied foreign concessions. While the raid on Pearl Harbor was taking place they launched their first bombing raid on Singapore; simultaneously hundreds of Japanese troops landed at Kota Bharu in northern Malaya. On the morning of 8 December the Japanese air force destroyed Hong Kong's airfield and crippled its docks. The next night the Japanese 23rd Army landed on the mainland of Kowloon from where they bombarded the island of Hong Kong, knocking out the water supply and forcing the British to surrender three weeks later. As a triumphalist editorial in the *Hong Kong News* expressed it in the days following the surrender: 'the vaunted supermen of the white race have melted . . . like butter'.

In the north of China the takeover was less bloody, but no less organised. Japanese troops marched into the foreign concessions in Tientsin and Peking taking over and shutting down key institutions. Even those working in remote mission stations and outposts received visits from members of the Japanese army that day. A Japanese officer heading a squad of men marched into the compound and brusquely informed the occupants that Japan and the United States and Britain were at war.[2]

In Shanghai, after sinking the *Peterel*, the Japanese marched across the Garden Bridge from Hongkew, the Japanese sector of the city, and seized building after building. At 6.40 a.m. low-lying planes roared over the St John's University campus.[3] By 10 a.m. sentries were posted at the American, British and Dutch consulates, newspaper offices, the Country Club, the racecourse and cable offices. Columns of Japanese soldiers marched through the city. All over China long-distance phone calls were interrupted or disconnected. In Hankow enemy nationals were summoned to the Hankow club where Consul General Tanaka informed them that from now on passes would be required to leave their houses; meetings and trips were banned, transfer of property was not allowed and telegrams and radios were prohibited.[4] Two days later the two most powerful vessels of the Royal Navy's eastern fleet, sent by Churchill to defend Malaya and Singapore against invasion, the state of the art battleship HMS *Prince of Wales* and the battle cruiser HMS *Repulse* were both sunk by Japanese bombers with the loss of 840 lives.

Back in Hong Kong, as the colony fought for its life against over-whelming odds, Bill Macauley became embroiled in the sort of adventure teenage boys usually only read about. Overnight he was transformed from ink-stained schoolboy to special agent complete with gun. The colony was composed of two parts: Hong Kong island, and Kowloon and the New Territories. These were on the other side of a narrow strait and formed part of China, which leased them to Britain in the nineteenth century. Kowloon held out for less than four days and the Allies withdrew to the island of Hong Kong on 11 December. By lunchtime that day, as news spread that the Allies were evacuating the mainland, British authority began to crumble. As the military and the police scrambled into whatever boats they could find, crowds of Chinese headed for the port area of Kowloon, where guards attempting to protect the godowns (warehouses) filled with lucrative cargo were overwhelmed. Looting and panic were widespread. While Bill and another boy were patrolling the grounds of the school they found a Chinese with an axe down among the pine trees. The man said he was just collecting firewood. 'But Jimmy Hulse, the master in charge of us, said we should stop him so we rugby tackled him and took him to the local police station.'

The next day, with air raids still going on intermittently overhead, a naval officer turned up at the school. 'He asked the six older ones among us if we would like to become dispatch corps messengers with ARP. [Air Raid Precaution, a volunteer service set up to protect civilians from the danger of air raids.] If so we were to report for duty the next day wearing our khaki Scout uniforms. The next morning two cars drew up at the school containing a turbaned Indian soldier and a driver and an officer. We were to deliver messages, in the form of printed cards, to all the families of service personnel telling them to be ready to assemble on the waterfront the following day.'

Being treated almost like officers thoroughly appealed to the boys.

'We had a great time rushing round in our cars. Our officer stayed with us until tiffin when we set off for the Peninsula Hotel. This was very smart, the best hotel in Kowloon – my father had never been able to afford to stay there. Suddenly the car was surrounded by angry threatening Chinese bent on robbing us. I knew how to use a gun and I had to use the officer's pistol to frighten them off. He seemed to freeze in the face of danger so I grabbed the pistol out of his holster and brandished it to clear a way so that the car could make it to the hotel.' But in the highly volatile situation they had hardly finished their lunch when the order came through to evacuate the mainland. 'We were told to get back up to the school, collect the two younger boys and Mr Hulse, the master, and Matron and get back down to the waterfront asap. There was a mob of Chinese carrying baseball bats and axes approaching the school. If we'd been there they'd have beaten and robbed us.'

When they headed back down to the waterfront to try to get a boat to the mainland the roads were almost impassable. The streets were filled with a heaving mob of shouting, looting Chinese, who jumped onto the running board of the car as it drove along trying to wrench anything they could seize from the fleeing whites. 'As we drove down Nathan Road, which in normal times was a lovely, elegant shopping street, it was Bedlam. It was an open car and I was sitting on the folded down hood hanging out, with Nicholas, who was a hefty lad, holding my legs to stop me falling out, and wielding a lathi (a bamboo stick) to beat back the crowds. There were no police and no military so the Chinese were looting everything in sight. At the top of Nathan Road I saw a woman with a small boy having her coat and suitcase literally torn off her.'

By now it was dark. They managed to push their way through to the dock and found a boat, an unwieldy water lighter owned by two Americans. 'They were shouting "We can take more people but we're going to have to shove off soon." We managed to get everyone on board, including Matron and Missie. It was pretty grim. There were air raids going on against military targets as we boarded the boats and during the crossing we were under shellfire from the Japanese guns on Kowloon. Boats in the harbour ahead of us were being shelled.'

One of their fellow passengers was the woman who had had her coat stolen. She was still in shock at what had happened and Bill remembers saying a prayer with her to try and comfort her. He also gave her his Burberry raincoat as it was winter and she was only wearing a summer dress. 'I was left in just my Scouts uniform and sweater and had cause to regret that when we ended up in camp. The other boys had brought the suitcases I had told them to have ready, but when we rescued them from school we were in such a hurry I didn't have time to get my suitcase. I had only the clothes I stood up in.' As they neared the dock on Hong Kong island a boat moored less than 20 feet away was hit by a shell and began sinking. 'It was terrible. The boat was lower than the wharf so it took time to get people off. People were rushing off the boats screaming and panicking.'

Once they had landed, Bill went to see his 'charges'. 'Jimmy Hulse, the American master, was meant to be in charge, but he didn't seem able to take control of things. They were all pretty frightened. Jimmy Hulse said: "Thank you. I think you saved our lives."' Army trucks took the terrified civilians away from the docks and left them to find shelter where they could. The first night Bill and his charges slept in an office block, with Bill taking special trouble to make Matron comfortable. 'I was very fond of her. Her name was Muriel Hassard and she was a widow. In 1941 she would have been in her early fifties. I felt a special bond with her as I had fallen ill at school in 1939. The school doctor had diagnosed merely a bad throat but Matron suspected it was diphtheria, and kept insisting the school got a second opinion. She turned out to be right and I got the serum I needed just in time. She nursed me through it and probably saved my life.'

From 13 to 21 December, still in their Scout uniforms, but now equipped with tin hats and gas masks, Bill and his three fellow pupils continued to run messages for the ARP. They worked six-hour shifts running messages within HQ – and outside.

The last external message Bill ran was in conditions of extreme danger four days after the Japanese had landed on the island and only four days before the surrender. 'The four of us were called in and told there was a very important message that had to get through to the ARP HQ in Happy Valley, home of the famous racecourse in the northern part of the island. We were told both pairs would be delivering the same message, in case one of us failed to get through – so we realised that this was serious stuff.

'We got onto the tram but before we reached Causeway Bay district, which was only part of the way, the tram was shelled. The terrified driver got out and ran off and I don't blame him. We scarpered inland and as we knew the island well, managed by using back roads to get to the ARP in Happy Valley. Both groups got through and arrived at more or less the same time.'

The journey back was even more hazardous as they realised that they were effectively in no man's land and had become moving targets. 'There were deep typhoon ditches alongside the road and we threw ourselves into them to avoid the shells. For the rest of the time we decided to try Scout's pace. You run ninety paces and walk ten. You covered a lot of ground fast but you kept your stamina up.'

All four boys got back to HQ in one piece, which was more than could be said for a Bren gun carrier they had met on the way. 'We passed it not far from where we had originally seen it. It was lying on its side beside the road, burnt out. The bodies of the four soldiers who had hailed us were scattered round on the ground.'

On 23 December, with the situation looking very grim, Bill and one of the other boys (Nicholas Masters) decided to enlist. 'We went to the recruiting office and a chap asked me if I knew how to use a firearm. I said I did so he handed me a rifle and asked me to load it. I did as he asked and cocked the trigger. We were on the point of getting uniforms and guns when the phone rang. It was Wing Commander Puckle, my boss from ARP.

'"Have you got two of my lads down there?" he demanded. "If you have, send them back up here double quick. They're under age."'

On Christmas Eve, Bill and Nicholas came off night duty at six o'clock in the morning. As they walked round to the north side of the cathedral they saw two servicemen trying to bury a dead soldier. 'I asked them if they knew him, or knew his name and they said "No, but we're going to bury him anyway." We offered to help and the four of us gave the poor lad a temporary burial.' Like many incidents during those last desperate days the lonely resting pace of the anonymous trooper, a young man little older than himself, remained vivid in Bill's memory. As we will discover, half a century later their paths would cross once more in moving circumstances.

The cathedral had been damaged by a shell in the fighting, but the Dean was determined that Christmas Day services would be celebrated whatever the enemy had in mind. 'We boys set to and worked like dogs to get the cathedral cleaned up so that it was ready first for Communion and then Matins. A lot of people came to the services.' Despite the fact that they were virtually surrounded, with the Japanese in control of all the strategic high ground on the island, the atmosphere among the British that morning was one of defiance. 'The Governor had turned down one Japanese request to surrender, saying we would fight to the last. I thought I would end up fighting alongside the Indian soldiers.' Christmas dinner was a spartan affair. 'We had a slice of corned beef and a tomato each, but we did have a slice of Christmas pudding – with Carnation milk.'

Then, after a burst of artillery fire, everything went silent. Surprisingly, the telephones on Hong Kong continued to function perfectly throughout the battle and at three o'clock the phone rang. Bill answered. 'It was a friend of Matron's. She said "We've surrendered, Bill." And it was true. We looked out and saw white flags everywhere.'

An agonising wait began. When would the Japanese come? How would they behave? The Chinese, with the memory of the terrible massacre of Nanking fresh in their minds, were terrified. After the capture of the city in 1937 hundreds and thousands of civilians and disarmed troops had been slaughtered and tens of thousands of women raped. 'The sexton of the cathedral was Chinese and he had a beautiful Chinese wife. I remember her coming in looking unrecognisable. She had smeared ash in her hair and across her face to make her look like an old woman. They both knew the risk she faced from victorious Japanese troops.'

It was not long before Bill made his own unpleasant discovery. 'A few days after the surrender I decided to go and check up on a female cousin of mine who lived higher up in the hills. On the way I was stopped by six Japanese soldiers. They started in on me straight away, punching with fists and kicking me with their boots. The Far East was a tough place and my father had always impressed upon me the need to stay upright if I were set upon. I was sporty and pretty fit and did judo and I managed to remain on my feet. It probably saved me. At any rate they got tired of knocking a useless kid around and wandered off.'

The next encounter provided Bill with brutal evidence of what victorious troops can do to their victims in the absence of authority. 'I met a Japanese NCO leading a young Chinese woman along by a rope, which was tied round her neck. She was sobbing, "Save me. Save me", and he was dragging her along. A Chinese man, whom I suppose was her husband, was also pleading with the Japanese to release her. I shouted at the Jap something like, "I say old chap, don't you think you should let that woman go?" His response was to shove his pistol in my face. It was pretty frightening. I had no choice but to back down. When I came back down I found the body of the man lying in the road, shot. The Japanese had vanished with the woman.'

You would think that after close encounters like these Bill would have had enough of risk-taking. But that was not the case. In the uncharted atmosphere that followed the surrender, when even the Japanese didn't always know the rules, the cheekiest gestures sometimes paid off. Sometime before the surrender a young artilleryman who had lost the rest of his unit had joined them at the hall. He was in uniform, carried a pistol and had a car at his disposal. He had a shrapnel wound in his hand which needed attention. 'It wasn't getting any better so one day, after the surrender, he said he thought he would get it seen to. We set off in his car for Bowen Road Hospital, which was the British military hospital in Hong Kong. Off we went with me helping him change gear. We had to get past two Japanese guards to get in – the chap merely waved his injured hand at them. The guards let us through, the guy got his hand seen to, we drove out again and they let us through again without a murmur.'

While Bill was still waiting to learn what the Japanese had planned for him, nine-year-old Neil Begley in Tientsin was already discovering what was in store. His school and hostel were swiftly commandeered as a Japanese barracks and the children were told to go home. Those unable to join their parents, including Neil, whose parents were in Hong Kong, were to be cared for by missionaries in Peking. They were put in cattle wagons on a freight train.

'Although there had been a heavy frost in the night, the sun was now shining and it was pleasantly warm as it streamed through the bars of the freight truck. That was until the train started moving, and the icy wind bit into us, freezing our ears, fingertips and faces

.... We huddled closely together, shivering as chilblains formed on our fingers, toes and ears ... finally, around four in the afternoon ... [the train] ground to a halt outside a small village. Our trucks were shunted onto a siding and the train went on without us. It was getting dark. We were frightened, frozen and terribly hungry. We'd had nothing to eat or drink since breakfast and the freight truck was becoming putrid from lack of toilet facilities.'

After dark some Chinese visited them, bringing boiled rice and hot tea. They were then coupled to another train and arrived in Peking in the late afternoon where they were let out by Japanese soldiers, escorted to the main exit and told to wait. Neil had wet his pants in the night and hurried off to the lavatory. When he returned, to his horror, the rest of the children had disappeared – including his brother. A sympathetic Chinese woman, noticing the little European boy all alone, asked him what had happened. Neil replied that he had nowhere to go. Ignoring the potential risk of harbouring an enemy alien, the woman took pity on Neil and, leaving the station, told him to go with her. She led him through a network of back alleys to her family and then returned to catch her train. For several extraordinary days Neil lived with this Chinese family, who generously shared their meagre rations with him. He slept with them, and played and joshed with Di Urr, one of their children, who was the same age as him, as if he had known him for ever. (The boys in a Chinese family were often not given names. Instead they were numbered. Di Urr is second son in Mandarin.) Di Urr's knowledge of English stopped short at 'sonofabitch', an insult that was traded to their mutual mirth. The womenfolk cared for Neil with kindness and gentleness.

The extraordinary culture-crossing interlude came to an end all too soon. The Chinese family had contacted the Swiss Red Cross and a representative called to see Neil a few days later. He was in touch with the missionaries who were looking after Neil's brother and sister. 'Tearfully I took leave of the Chow family, told Di Urr that he was my sonofabitch and set off in a rickshaw with the Red Cross man, for the other side of Peking.'

In Peking things once again returned more or less to normal, although Japanese soldiers now patrolled the streets. Neil noticed that people who attracted their displeasure were cuffed and then made to stand to attention inside a chalk circle. Any straying outside the circle resulted in fresh cuffing and a prolonging of the standing. No dispensation was granted for visits to a toilet, with the attendant humiliation.

In China and Hong Kong the Japanese allowed some families separated by hostilities to become reunited. The Begleys were among the lucky ones. Major Begley and his wife were released from internment in Hong Kong and allowed to return to Shanghai on 24 December 1942. A few months later Neil and his brother were allowed to travel down by train to Shanghai from Peking, escorted by a major in the Salvation Army who was a Swiss national, and therefore neutral.

Shanghai was now very changed from the flourishing cosmopolitan melting pot the Begleys had known before the war. All enemy nationals over the age of thirteen were issued with numbers and had to wear red armbands with their nationality and individual number printed on the armband in black. In Shanghai British armbands featured the letter B in a circle. A curfew was imposed. Roadblocks divided the subdued city. Propaganda posters appeared extolling Japan's Greater East Asia Co-Prosperity Sphere. Giant maps hung from buildings showing Japan's expanding empire and increasing control over South East Asia.[5] Roving checkpoints made of rolls of barbed wire appeared without notice, trapping people and cutting them off from worried families for hours at a stretch. Enemy aliens caught within the barricades would be expected to produce their identity papers and proof that their cholera and typhoid inoculations were up to date.[6] Food was running short and prices spiralling.

The Japanese had set about systematically seizing property and foreign concerns, taking over everything that Shanghai produced – from machinery to medicines, electrical equipment to flour and silk. Within three months they controlled the telephone, electric, water, gas, tramway and bus companies. On 12 February a joint announcement by the Japanese army and navy justified these takeovers as part of the plan 'to wipe out the influence of the United States of America, Britain and other enemy countries who made the Shanghai Area the centre of their exploitation of East Asia for over a century.' By early April private cars were requisitioned, forcing Westerners to take to bicycles. The staff of the Shanghai Municipal Council were all sacked and money became a real problem as the Japanese froze all bank accounts. The decision to let enemy nationals draw a meagre monthly allowance was soon swallowed up by galloping inflation. From 1942 to August 1945 Shanghai prices would increase by 26 per cent a month![7]

As Neil Begley was enjoying being reunited with his family, however, other children had already suffered bereavement as a result of the war. Keith Martin had barely recovered from the delight of not having to take his School Certificate exam when he discovered that his uncle had been killed in one of the first battles of the war.

Keith and his family had been living in Hong Kong where he had been born. In June 1940 the authorities in Hong Kong decreed that dependants should leave the colony because they feared a Japanese attack was imminent. Keith's mother was not able to leave as she was in a reserved occupation and decided to send Keith and his younger sister to Shanghai to stay with her sister. Keith was now a pupil at the Cathedral School for Boys in Shanghai, run by P. C. Matthews, an ordained Anglican priest in his fifties.

One morning in December 1941 Keith was called out of class and told that his uncle wished to see him. 'He had received an order to sail to Hong Kong and said he would be seeing my mother. He knew she would like to know he had seen me recently. My uncle sailed to Hong Kong as the Japanese launched their attack. He was ordered to scuttle his ship, which he did, and then he joined the dockyard Defence Corps. He was commanding a tug in Hong Kong harbour when it was attacked from the air. He lost both legs and died the next day.' It would be five years before Keith and his sister saw their mother again.

For many Western children trapped in occupied Shanghai life seemed, at least on the surface, almost to resume its old lazy current. For several months schools continued to function, with some pupils actually sitting important public exams. And even where the cataclysm had triggered a dramatic drop in living standards, for the young it was all an adventure.

David Nicoll's father worked for the Chinese Maritime Customs and was evicted from the family's elegant flat in the Custom House within weeks. They were offered temporary accommodation in the Church Hall adjoining Shanghai's Anglican Cathedral. This was an imposing edifice in red stone, built in Victorian Gothic style and even boasting a cloister. They moved in on 23 December. It is a night David, who was ten at the time, will never forget. 'What a miserable night that was,' he recalled, 'the four of us in that large cubicle in that dark, high-ceilinged hall, our furniture and belongings strewn around us ... and all lit by the one light ... Our beds were piled high with blankets as there was no heating.'

Things began to look up on Christmas Eve when more families moved in and a coal stove was installed. Christmas Day, however, passed with no celebration and no Christmas dinner. The gloom of the preoccupied adults was further deepened by the news that Hong Kong had surrendered. Now the community comprised 21 people – 11 adults, 3 teenage girls and 7 children under 12. For sleeping they separated themselves into family units. Each family had a large cubicle partitioned by black material to a height of 6 feet, inside which they arranged whatever furniture they had brought with them – wardrobes, dressing tables, beds and dining tables. The centre of the hall became the communal sitting room comprising all the families' settees and armchairs arranged round their carpets. At first meals were taken communally round a long refectory table, but after a few weeks each family took to eating in its own cubicle.[8]

There was a problem with the WCs, which had been installed for the children who used the hall. David saw that the adults tried hard to keep up old standards but these lapsed with time: 'In the lavatory a blanket was rigged up to screen off part of the urinal but this was not very practical and everyone soon accepted our altered mode of living and the blanket was removed. Another attempt at clinging to past customs was the making of a wooden box of normal WC height to be placed over one of the small WCs but this too was dispensed with in time.'

For the adults, used to servants to wait on them, this first taste of cramped communal living was exceedingly taxing, but to the children having so many friends around to play with and so much space was paradise. 'The compound had a large yard to play in safely, away from strangers and wheeled traffic, and beyond the cloisters was the front of the cathedral with its vast lawn; by the lawn was a clump of trees, also a bamboo thicket, and all this open space was virtually a park for our private use … the cloisters … were a great place to play on rainy days.' After a while the gang were joined by a Mrs Rees and her son Sonny, which meant that each family living in the Church Hall had a son. Sonny, who was twelve, was an instant hit. 'Because Sonny was the oldest and also good-natured we three other boys all looked up to him; he attended the Cathedral School but during the week lived with friends … we used to look forward to his return every weekend.'

While their parents chafed at the humiliation of having to wear armbands, the boys regarded it as a badge of honour, conferring manly status. 'It became a matter of pride to display a red armband and whether in a shop or out in a street we could not help pointing out the presence of another armband-wearer … George Noel and I were envious of Sonny for 5th November would soon come around and as that day was his 13th birthday he would have to wear an armband from that day.'[9]

David's family were Catholic. The normality of these first months was such that, not only did he go to school (although now it was mornings only), he also prepared for his first Communion. His mother selected a convent in Frenchtown and sent him there for catechism classes. Beyond the confines of the cathedral the once vibrant city appeared transformed.

In September 1942 the Japanese ordered all schools for enemy nationals to shut down. But some families in Shanghai were determined that, however their lives were affected, their children were still going to receive an education. Cyril Mack's father was one of these. Having had a deprived childhood in rural East Anglia he had gone out to China, worked his way up to the rank of inspector in the Shanghai Waterworks and completed his education as a mature student. He was determined his two sons would have the benefits he had had to struggle for. When all the Allied-run schools shut down he refused to give up.

'To Dad the solution was obvious – join the enemy. First he enrolled us in the German school – that lasted a couple of days, there was no way that we could get around the language problem. Then he tried the Italian school where we had a little more success because the teachers gave us separate, specific tasks to do, but the problem once again was in the language.' Still unbeaten Cyril's father had one more card up his sleeve – the Shanghai Jewish School. 'The teachers were very friendly but ... we were really not on the same wavelength ... Dad decided to call it quits and Roy and I finally joined the happy band of British children on enforced holiday.'[10]

Another British family who took education seriously, war or no war, were the Hucksteps. Ron and his younger brother John were the sons of Shanghai's Director of Education. Ron, like Keith Martin, was in the middle of taking his School Certificate when the Japanese bombed Pearl Harbor. Unlike Keith, however, he was not let off the second part. About half the children due to take the second and final week of the exam decided to abandon it, believing the chance of the papers surviving the war to be slim. But Ron's father, knowing his son was very bright (he was more than two years younger than most of the other boys in his class), insisted. The venue was a school several miles away from the family's home and Ron had to cycle to reach it. 'I ... managed to get past the Japanese roadblocks for the next five days, and to complete the exam. I feel that my youth helped me past the Japanese soldiers.'

Astonishingly, Ron's paper did reach England. This was due to a blend of foresight on the part of his father, faithfulness on the part of a Chinese colleague and the wonders of the diplomatic bag. Fearing that war was imminent Ron's father provided him with carbon paper and told him to write in pencil. The copy was hidden by a Chinese friend for the duration of the war and sent to Britain in 1945. The original reached England in the diplomatic bag about two months after it had been written through the goods offices of the neutral Swiss. The results, when they came through years later, made all the efforts worthwhile. 'I did not hear until 1946, four and a half years later, that I had by some "fluke" gained a Matriculation after only one and a half years of secondary schooling.'

The realisation that life had changed definitively for Ron Huckstep came early, and it concerned his family's prize possession. 'In January 1942 ... our beautiful Ford V8 we had bought in Detroit in 1937, taken across to Britain on the *Queen Mary*, and then back to Shanghai by ship through the Suez Canal, had to be delivered to the Japanese metal yard about 5 miles away.' It was part of the Japanese method, repeated all over their conquered territory, to show the Chinese (their partners in the Greater East Asia Co-Prosperity Sphere) how they had triumphed over the white races. By way of extra humiliation they were not allowed to drive the car to its destination, despite the fact that it had plenty of petrol in its tank. 'We ... had to push the heavy car all the way through the streets of Shanghai ... It was then crunched flat and loaded onto a small Japanese freighter bound for Japan. The freighter with its load of hundreds of crushed cars then steamed down the Whangpoo River to the mouth of the Yangtze, and out into the Yellow Sea.' The only consolation for Ron was that the family pride and joy was never destined to help the Japanese war effort. In the Yellow Sea the vessel transporting it was torpedoed by an American submarine. 'Now the beautiful streamline green Ford V8, licence number 3539, lies at the bottom of the China Sea.'

For most of 1942 children of British families in Shanghai continued to lead lives that were constricted, but still reasonably secure. Food was increasingly scarce, roadblocks divided the city, fathers worried about money, but at least families were together. This was not the case in Malaya. Here within days of the surrender, Japanese troops had stormed into British homes dragging the men off to prison camps and helping themselves to anything that took their fancy.

Singapore, the supposedly impregnable fortress that stood proud guard over all Britain's territories in the Far East, had surrendered on 15 February 1942.

Barbara Glanville's older brother Mel, who was twelve at the time, will never forget the day that war came to him: 'We awoke the next morning to a stillness that was almost unreal, and venturing to the front louvre windows to gaze out, I saw three Japanese soldiers calmly sitting on our front porch enjoying a cigarette and talking between themselves. I rushed back into Mum's bedroom, to tell them what I'd seen, and dad had only sufficient time to get back into bed, with Mum throwing the covers over him, before we heard the front door burst open and these soldiers walked into our house as bold as brass.'

One of the soldiers then chased after 'Sai Mui', their Chinese servant, who had rushed screaming in terror through to the servants' quarters at the back. 'The other two soldiers came into the bedroom, where dad was lying in bed with Mum and us kids cowering round her, all absolutely terrified. One soldier pointed his rifle at Mum and us indicating that we should back away from Dad in the bed. Somehow she seemed to manage to explain that Dad had an injured leg ...'

A soldier then noticed the father's treasured gold half hunter pocket watch on the dresser and picked it up for a closer look. 'He looked at Mum and Dad as if to say I want this and ... placed it in his pocket. His companion spied dad's silver cigarette case and combined lighter, and took this for himself, then they both continued to search the house right through, indicating that we were all to stay where we were. All during this time every one of us was terrified at what they would do next.'

Eventually all three soldiers left, though the horrified family were too frightened to venture out of the room for some time. Sai Mui was sobbing hysterically and the children's mother tried in vain to comfort her. 'We later learnt that poor Sai Mui had been raped in her quarters at the back of the house ... but of course we children had no idea of what had been done to [her].'

Days later the Japanese returned, this time in more formal mode. 'A Japanese army officer arrived with an interpreter to inform us that my dad was being taken away and interned in a prison camp. He would be allowed only a few personal belongings and toiletries together with some changes of clothing. Then he was told to be ready to be picked up in a truck in about an hour together with other European civilians. The truck arrived already half full of other internees, some of which we were acquainted with, Dad was showed out to the truck limping because of his injured leg amid tearful goodbyes from all of us – we had no idea where he was being taken ... [or if] ... we would ever see each other again.'[11]

While British families in Malaya and Hong Kong were being torn apart by internment, throughout most of 1942 families in Shanghai were still free and leading lives that by comparison were almost normal. 'There were no new movies so the cinemas regurgitated the old ones but the Japs insisted upon including short propaganda films and we would wait with impatient anticipation until they appeared when everyone would laugh, jeer and whistle. It was more entertaining than the old movie we had come to see, so the Japs closed all the cinemas.'[12]

Having seen how people who annoyed the Japanese got slapped and cuffed Western children developed a safety-first technique for dealing with roadblocks. Cyril Mack, who was used to travelling about Shanghai on his own, knew it was crucial not to provoke the Japanese. 'It was always a one on one situation. I would fix my eyes steadily at my own level, never dropped them, never stepped back, but avoided eye contact. We never smiled – Dad's orders.'

Despite the Japanese occupation some young people were worried about a career and keen to get qualified. Fifteen-year-old Ron Huckstep, who had doggedly braved roadblocks to sit part two of his School Certificate, decided to try to train as a civil engineer and enrolled in a Chinese engineering institute in Shanghai called the Lester Institute, which trained students up to the standard of an external BSc. in Engineering from London University. Still aged only fifteen Ron passed the first year of Engineering, the inter BSc., in June 1942. He was three months into his second year when the Japanese clamped down on the movements of Westerners and he was no longer able to cycle to the Lester Institute.

The only university close to the family home was a French university run by Jesuits. It didn't have a faculty of engineering, but it did have a medical school so Ron decided to switch subjects and study for an external medical degree from the University of Paris. The only problem was that he would be taught in French. He had the distinction of being the only student in the university who wore an armband denoting that he was an enemy alien, the French being classed as allies of the Japanese thanks to the Vichy Government. Being, equally, the only Anglican, he never mastered the all-important grades of precedence in the various religious ranks, but found an ingenious way of masking his ignorance by addressing all priests by the respectful title 'mon père'.

Conditions in Shanghai continued to deteriorate throughout 1942. In September all schools for 'enemy nationals' had to shut down and all schooling ceased.[13] More and more Westerners became homeless, turned out to make way for Japanese or forced to seek more modest accommodation because of diminishing funds. For those 'enemy nationals' who still had jobs the Japanese had pegged wages at

Chinese $2,000 (before the war Chinese $2,000 had been £125, but by 1942 it was nearer £50). Fresh milk disappeared and was replaced by dried soya milk, described by one unappreciative child as 'a steaming, thick, dirty yellow beverage with a slightly gritty texture'.[14] Rationing was introduced for bread and flour. By the end of 1942 the daily ration had been cut from 10 to 8 ounces per person. Ten-year-old Cyril Mack and his family had been living in a suite in a comfortable hotel, but had to leave to make way for a pro-Japanese Chinese family. They eventually found refuge in a squalid one-room ground-floor flat 'infested with rather large rats that ran amok during the night' with neither a kitchen nor bathroom.

They had lost the use of the large radio aerial on their building's roof. Squalid conditions were not going to deter an inventive engineer of the calibre of Cyril's father, however. He devised an ingenious human aerial instead. 'Dad would put his finger on the terminal on the back of the radio – we all joined hands forming a chain across the living room and in this way managed to pick up a passable reception from the BBC Overseas Service.'

Early in the year the Japanese had ordered that household goods belonging to Westerners had to be labelled with stickers describing them as the property of the Emperor. Any item, once labelled, was not to be removed from the premises. The justification for this piece of bureaucracy, which was accompanied by an itemised list given to each householder, was that it would protect them from becoming the booty of war. Perhaps predictably most families found on their return from imprisonment that their homes had been entirely stripped of their possessions.

The drop in living standards suffered by Westerners surprised some of the Japanese as they arrived to carry out the stickering procedure. This was clearly the case when the Japanese visited the primitive flat the Mack family had moved into. They explained that in addition to items of furniture, telephone and 'cooking stove' they had to put a sticker on the 'bathtub'.

'We had difficulty in persuading them ... that we used the landlord's bathtub on the second floor and the tiny public toilet with wash basin under the ground floor staircase. They had a sticker that they had nowhere to stick and so there was disbelief ... before their bureaucratic minds accepted that the bathtub did indeed belong to the landlord and what we had told them was true.'[15]

As the months drew on, however, the defiant optimism with which Westerners had originally contemplated the notion of long-term domination by the Japanese began to give way to apprehension. It was as if a noose were tightening. Children like David Nicoll rushed home from school to check that their fathers were still safe. There was talk of the much-feared kempeitai, the Japanese secret police whose speciality was torture, and their henchmen, the Pao Chia, an auxiliary Chinese force who travelled on bicycles.

Cyril Mack's school was located in an area with a high crime rate. He and his friend would do anything not to get trapped in the lightning drag net. 'If the whistles blew while we were at school it was not a problem – we stayed put. However, several times, the whistles started just after George Houlston and I had left school for home. We could tell from the tone and pitch of the whistle that it was a Pao Chia whistle .... We knew we were in for a race so we started running like hell for home, all the while glancing over our shoulders to keep an eye on the man on the bike and to check on the ropes going across the road behind us. He was faster than us but we knew that he would have to stop at each intersection to give instructions, so, in theory, we had the edge on him.'[16]

The terror began on 5 November 1942. Several hundred British, American and Dutch men, many of whom were prominent members of the Shanghai Municipal Council, journalists and broadcasters, policemen or representatives of international companies were arrested without warning and taken to a former US Marine barracks in Haiphong Road. Throughout the 1930s Haiphong Road was just a neutral name, like the name of any road. The sadistic torture and relentless interrogations that took place there, however, which not infrequently ended in death, meant that by the end of the war, the name Haiphong Road meant a place of pain and suffering.

The day is etched on the memory of Jose Chamberlain, the little girl who used to go to tea dances with her mother. Things had been steadily deteriorating for the Chamberlain family. Nine-year-old Jose's father had had his job as a superintendent in the Shanghai police force terminated at the end of July. Jose's school, the Shanghai Cathedral Girls' School, had been ordered to close its doors. The family had been forced out of their police accommodation, but not before a team of Japanese assessors had come round and placed the required stickers on all its contents. As they left a seal was placed across the door and they were ordered not to return. Little did Jose know, as she went to bed the night before in their new, more modest house, that what was about to happen would set in motion a chain of events destined to cast a shadow over the rest of her life.

'It was very early in the morning. It was cold and still dark. Suddenly there was a very loud thumping at the door. Japanese soldiers burst in shouting and told us they were taking dad away. They told him to get enough things for an overnight stay and then they took him away on an open truck. It was horrible. I cried so much I made myself sick.'

The reality of war had come to Jose and her distraught mother, but for other children, freed from the burden of lessons, their families still intact, life was fun. David Nicoll, whose family were now celebrating a year of communal living in the Church Hall, remembers Christmas 1942 as almost lavish compared to the previous year. 'For us living in the hall Christmas was a very good time: we were ... warm and reasonably comfortable, and we had all adapted to living together ... We had a marvellous communal lunch on Christmas Day with a wide array of food, even a side of ham dotted with cloves ... we played party games and careered among the library books.'

In those straitened times presents were not extravagant, but David received three: a pencil-sharpener, a diary and – the cherry on the cake – a bicycle coat. 'It was pale fawn waterproof, thickly padded and lined with flannel and the sleeves had an inner lining with elastic at the wrists ...'[17] Little did he know what a godsend that ultra-warm garment would prove in the years to come.

4

Goodbye to All That

The multiple attacks of 8 December had shown the martial Japanese at their deadliest and most organised best. When it came to the internment of the thousands of alien civilians whose lives their perfectly planned victories had disrupted, they were less well prepared. Indeed the problem of what to do with all these civilians seemed to take them by surprise. There was no organisation with overall responsibility for internment; there was no overall policy on how the prisoners would be held, whether in family groups or segregated by gender; there was a lack of suitable accommodation, and the Japanese authorities seem to have given little thought to how much food the thousands of prisoners would need. It is, of course, probable that, with their overwhelmingly militaristic code of ethics, they didn't care. As Japanese historian Utsumi Aiko has put it, 'Japan went to war with virtually no policy for the treatment of prisoners, especially enemy civilian internees. It could further be said that this problem was not even one of great concern for the Japanese Government.' Whereas the audacious attacks that reduced the stunned Allies to submission took only weeks to achieve their aim, internment took years. How much time you spent in camp was the result of what we today would call a post-code lottery, with families in Manila and Hong Kong being interned in January 1942 and people who lived in Shanghai remaining free for another eighteen months. The last few hundred Allied nationals in Shanghai were only interned at the end of June 1944.

For children the discrepancies in timetable were echoed by the differences in the way their experiences of internment began. Some, whose parents were given plenty of time to prepare, saw it as an adventure and couldn't wait to go. They enjoyed watching the adults commissioning tailor-made luggage and stockpiling food, as if they were going for a jolly, extended picnic. For others, wrenched away from deeply loved relatives, weeping amahs, adored family pets – in many cases never to see them again – the moment remains, more than half a century later, seared on the memory as an experience of still-raw pain.

In Manila in the Philippines Sylvia Williams got up on 9 January 1942 in a cheerful mood. It was not going to be a normal day, but she little knew how unlike a normal day it would prove to be. It was exactly a month after the raid on Pearl Harbor. 'It was my eighth birthday and I was standing in the kitchen watching the cook ice my birthday cake. Friends of my parents, whom I called Auntie Fran and Uncle Stan, were staying with us. Suddenly a truck driven by a Japanese soldier drew up and stopped outside our house. My mother told me I could bring my beloved doll. We were told to leave the house and found an open lorry waiting outside. We all climbed up, me, my mother and father and Stanley and Frances Lloyd, and were driven to the university campus in Manila.'

The whole thing came as a complete shock to Sylvia. Her parents had said nothing to her. 'The Japanese visit was not a surprise to my parents. A few days earlier another truck had come and some Japanese had told them that we were going into a camp and that we could each take a small suitcase and some tinned food with us.' She was not worried or frightened. 'They told me we were going to Santo Tomas, the university campus in Manila. I knew the building. Its massive concrete buildings were a landmark and dominated the skyline. Besides, I was with my mother and my Auntie Fran.'

In Santo Tomas families were broken up, with the men and women sleeping in separate rooms and meeting only during the day. The first night in camp was very uncomfortable.

'It was hot anyway because of the climate, but it was unbearably stuffy because we were so crowded. There were forty to fifty women in a room. There were no beds. We had to lie down on the bare concrete floor. There were a few mats and my mother let me have one, lying on the bare concrete herself.'

*

In another location in Manila fifteen-year-old Iris Krass, who had contracted typhoid after her ship was attacked in Manila Bay on 8 December was still very ill when the lorries came to take her and the rest of the refugees to camp. Now another shock lay in store: the family would be separated.

'The boys went on a different transport from the women so my brother Peter, who was a year younger than me, went off on his own. My mother and my younger sister were sent off to a different camp, which housed mothers with small children. Because I was infectious I was taken to a Filipino hospital in Manila where I remained for several weeks.'

Towards the end of January, when she was deemed to have recovered, an open truck, which already had several adult passengers, drew up outside the hospital. 'We were taken to what we learned was Santo Tomas university campus. We went through the main gates and saw two large buildings, quite far apart from each other. My impression was of several layers of fences. I didn't see my brother. He was in the men's part of the camp and, sadly, for the next three years our paths hardly crossed.' Iris was directed to a large room on the first floor of the main building. 'The building had evidently been destined for refurbishment as all the doors and windows had been removed. The weather was always mild so we didn't feel cold, but it was strange.'

The Krass family's trunks had been left on the ship (they were found after the war, exhaustively looted). All Iris had with her was a small bag containing 'one or two bits of clothing and a towel'. The room contained thirty wooden beds topped with straw mattresses with a space of 3 inches between each bed. Being older than many of the other children in the camp Iris was keenly aware of how dramatically her world had changed. 'I had gone from leading a protected life, one might even say over-protected, to one where I was completely left to fend for myself in the most primitive way.'

Between the surrender on 25 December and the start of internment on 5 January British civilians in Hong Kong were still free to go out and shop. Life was becoming increasingly dangerous, however. Anyone out in the streets had to explain their business to Japanese guards who barred their way as they tried to walk along the pavement.

Separated from his parents and responsible for several younger boys with whom he had fled the Japanese attacks on Kowloon, Bill Macauley was obliged to go out foraging for food. In the highly volatile atmosphere following the Allied defeat, he and Don Devan, a young artilleryman who had joined them in the Church Hall, found it was prudent not to own up to being British. 'You got punched and thumped if you said you were British. That included women. We saw British women being hit for the first time. That was quite a shock. We pretended to be Irish or French.'

With food prices spiralling it was a case of every man for himself. 'We used to go out to where we knew we could get black market stuff. A tin of corned beef, which before the surrender was thirty cents, was now selling for four or five dollars. We used to edge up on the guy selling, take a tin, leave a couple of dollars and run for it.'

On 4 January the Japanese announced that all enemy nationals were to report the next day to the Murray Parade Ground, bringing what they could carry. The parade ground was in front of the Murray barracks, which had been home to the Middlesex regiment. Bill had managed to acquire an empty suitcase in the chaotic flight from Kowloon and had packed it with food. 'I had been to the Dairy Farm, a well-known food store, and bought various types of tinned food – corned beef, a loaf of bread in a tin and a three-pound Cheddar cheese. Several of the girls who worked in the Dairy Farm were Portuguese. They gave me a handful of toothbrushes. I didn't know it then, but they were to prove as valuable as gold ingots where I was headed.'

Monday, 5 January 1942 was bright and sunny, but, unusually for Hong Kong, there was a pronounced nip in the air. Bill was wearing his Scouts uniform of shirt, shorts and pullover, topped by a padded shirt, which had been supplied by the Red Cross for Chinese refugees and which the dean of the cathedral had given to some of the scantily clad boys. To protect his legs from the chill wind he was wearing a pair of silk Ali Baba pantaloons, borrowed from the Church Hall's theatrical costume department.

'It was only about a ten-minute walk from the cathedral to the parade ground. There we were marshalled into groups. We parted company with most of the other boys because they weren't British. Our party now numbered just me, a younger boy called Bobby Parker, who was fourteen, Don Devan, the soldier who had got separated from his unit, and Matron.'

From the parade ground they were marched off in batches of 50 to 100 in the direction of the waterfront. The Chinese turned out in force to watch the humiliating spectacle of their former masters, dishevelled and anxious after weeks of living rough, carrying their own luggage and trudging through the streets on foot. 'Their reactions varied. Some were sympathetic. One man, when one of the prisoners dropped something, rushed forward to pick it up. Others spat and threw stones at us. The Japanese guards laid into all of them indiscriminately with rifle butts.'

Their destination, to the horror of the adults, were three seedy Chinese-run hotels two roads back from the waterfront of the sort sailors hired by the hour to take girls to. The bedrooms, small cubicles whose wooden partitions didn't reach the ceiling, were just large enough to accommodate a double bed and a washbasin. There were two toilets per floor.

'We arrived at about lunchtime and were just told to get on with it. The instruction was three to a room. It was a free-for-all. There was no one in overall command, so people just thought of themselves, pushing and shoving and grabbing what they could. It wasn't at all the way I had been brought up to think of as British behaviour. We were a very mixed crowd. I got friendly with a sea captain in the Merchant Navy. He was sharing a room with three gorgeous young girls. He slept on the floor, under the washbasin, and they shared the double bed. Don and I found a corner room with a bit more space on the third floor and we settled Matron there with her dog.'

No arrangements had been made to feed the prisoners, who were thrown back on whatever they had brought with them. Bill and his friend hatched a cheeky plan and, due to the disorganised nature of that first day, managed to get away with it. 'Don asked me if I had any money and I said I had five dollars. He suggested we try to get a takeaway sent in. I spoke enough Cantonese to be able to order Chow Mein and fried rice, so I went out onto the balcony that ran the length of our floor and shouted down to a Chinese man in the street, "Can you do a takeaway for three for five dollars?" He said he could, and, half to our surprise, when we went down to collect it, the Jap guard let it through.' As the three of them devoured their feast with gusto, and Missie the dog finished off the scraps, they could not have guessed the rigours that lay ahead or how long it would be before they tasted such food again.

After two days the Japanese organised a meagre daily delivery of basic rations of bread, porridge oats and a small quantity of malodorous fish. The only cooking facilities were a primitive wood-fuelled stove and a giant wok located on the flat roof of the hotel and used, in normal circumstances, by the hotel's Chinese owners. Most of the prisoners, who were used to a pampered life where the simplest domestic task was performed for them by servants, as if paralysed by the down-turn in their fortunes, refused to perform any chores and remained in their rooms complaining.

Despite his youth, Bill found himself taking charge. 'We had to get some sort of order into the system. At the beginning, when the bread was delivered, it was dog eat dog, with everyone helping themselves and stealing as much as they could. The people on the third and fourth floors complained that by the time they got down there was nothing left. We decided that each floor would appoint two representatives. They would go down and collect the bread for their floor and then cut it up when they got back.'

Bill and his squaddie friend Don mastered the giant wok, which had been plentifully supplied with firewood. They cooked the porridge in the morning, which gave everyone about half a cup, and then fried the fish, which was eaten with bread at lunchtime. There was no evening meal. 'Each loaf had to be shared among ten people so we each had a one-inch thick-piece of bread a day. A lot of people didn't eat the fish so that gave us some leftovers. We tried to make tea but there wasn't enough fuel so all we had to drink was water from the tap.'

The diet, the water, which was probably less than pure, and the overcrowding, took their toll on the prisoners, who succumbed to various digestive disturbances. Bill used to get up between five and six in the morning to use the lavatory. 'At that time of day they had just been cleaned by the hotel staff. But with fifty people per floor, only two lavatories among them, and many of those people ill, by the end of the day they were in a revolting state – and nobody wanted to clean them.'

The adults became withdrawn, spending most of the day in their rooms, brooding on their fate. Bill spent his time walking up and down the balcony to get a bit of exercise, or up on the flat roof where the air was fresh.

Three weeks later on 26 January they were told to be ready to leave the next morning, taking, as before, what they could carry. 'We knew we were going to Stanley [the internment camp that had been set up on a peninsula on the southern side of the island]. And we realised that our stay in the hotel was an interval while they got the place in some sort of order. It was in a bit of a mess as there had been fighting all through the place before the surrender, with scores of unburied corpses and ruined buildings.'

Once again they marched through the streets, watched by hundreds of Chinese, this time impassive. Every prisoner was body searched before he was allowed onto the ferries that were waiting to take them round the west coast of the island to Stanley peninsula. They were strictly forbidden to take in books or paperwork of any kind. 'They weren't very thorough. Everyone took books in. I managed to smuggle in *Eastern Visas* by the Australian writer Audrey Harris, which I had picked up in the Church Hall. Professor Forster, of Hong Kong University, managed to smuggle in the complete works of Shakespeare.'

Heavily overcrowded, the boats lay low in the water as they embarked on the journey south. Several hours later Bill, Bobby, Don Devan and Matron and Missie were climbing the steep cliff path that led up from the jetty to the camp, with Bobby carrying Matron's camp bed. At the top they were greeted by fellow prisoners, who directed them to their heavily overcrowded quarters. Unbeknown to them, these were to be their home for three and a half long years, a home from which some members of the little group would, sadly, never emerge.

The plight of the prisoners in Stanley, who had been interned with so little notice and had been able to take so little in with them, filtered back to Westerners in Shanghai, who were horrified at the reports they heard of intolerable overcrowding and inadequate food. They resolved that when their turn came, as it undoubtedly would, they would be better prepared. And it was just a matter of time. As members of the Japanese gendarmerie were banging on doors in

Shanghai and dragging fathers off for interrogation in the former barracks in Haiphong Road, the net was closing in the north.

On 27 October 1942 a group of Allied civilians from Tsingtao were interned in a run-down hotel 3 miles outside the city. A month later Chefoo School, a highly regarded establishment run for the children of missionaries, was made to move out of its mission complex. The girls' school, of which twelve-year-old Joyce Kerry (later Storey) was a pupil, was put into a house which they shared with two Trappist monks. 'There were no servants now so the teachers took over the cooking. We slept on mattresses on the floor of the attic, with the older girls at one end. The days were sunny and my memories of that time are happy: scrubbing chopping boards in the sun and leading a healthy, outdoor life.'[2]

After the arrests of 5 November 1942 things took on greater urgency among the Allied population in Shanghai. In December the Swiss consulate warned the British Residents' Association that general internment was imminent and this sterling organisation of 200 volunteers, described by one teenage girl internee as 'very efficient, very kind and very bossy',[3] swung into action. The organisation had been set up in 1939 to support the war in Europe and was run by employees of the Shanghai Municipal Council and their wives. Aware that in occupied Shanghai not every Westerner was thriving, they supplied food, housing, clothing, finance and medical care at reduced prices to the needy. These included destitute pensioners, the families of servicemen on active service overseas, ex-convicts and the mothers of illegitimate children. Conscious of the hardship they were facing, by the end of 1942 the BRA had already sent HK $15 to each person interned in Stanley. As men lost their jobs and the banks closed their doors the BRA played a key role in keeping the British population in Shanghai going by distributing loans of £10 a month repayable after the war.[4]

Aware of how ill-prepared for internment people in Stanley and Santo Tomas had been, the BRA concentrated on laying down vital supplies of food, drugs and soap. It was clear by then that the Japanese had no intention of equipping the camps to an acceptable standard. Drums and kongs for water storage, as well as shovels and mops for cleaning, medical supplies and alum and chlorine for water purification, were all added to the shopping list.[5]

For many children this was a time of intense anxiety. As well as worrying that their fathers might be taken away by the kempeitai, some had to have their beloved pets put down as their parents tried to prepare for an uncertain future. Margaret Blair was six years old. Her father was, like Jose Chamberlain's, a prominent police officer, but had been dismissed from his post as superintendent of the Criminal Investigation Department of the Shanghai Municipal Council's police force in July 1942. The family had been thrown out of their house in the police compound in the International Settlement and made to move to a smaller house across the Soochow Creek in the industrial area of the city. There, for Margaret and her brother Gordon, at least, life continued much as normal. Janey, the family's Cairn terrier, not only survived the tumble down the social ladder but flourished, becoming a mother courtesy of the dachshund next door. They adopted a sickly stray, whom they named Bear, and nursed him triumphantly back to health.

Margaret writes touchingly of the unique bond that develops between dogs and their young charges. When the little dog had puppies and three were found dead, the survivor was treated like a prince and had a special swinging bed made by Gordon using his Meccano set. Unusually, the sire took a husbandly interest in mother and child. 'Then began the amazing last chapter in Janey's life, her life as a mother. She played with and guarded her puppy carefully. Each evening Janey ventured out in the street with it, always accompanied by the dachshund. The two older dogs, with the young one between them, walked along the village road and came back to return him carefully to his home. I shall always remember the poignant sight of the two little dogs with a tiny one between, walking together along the dusty village street.'

Then came the bombshell. With the prospect of internment growing ever more real the parents of the uprooted families took the harrowing joint decision to have all their pets put down. Shanghai vets were so distressed by having to put down scores of healthy animals that it was hard to find one willing to do the deed. Finally a Portuguese vet was found. Margaret's mother explained to the horrified children that as the animals would not be able to go with them, giving them a painless death was the most humane solution.

'Parents dug a grave behind our house, and there was a burial ceremony. Very slowly and reverently the other children of the village walking in single file carried their dead pets, and laid them gently down in the earth, which was lined with sheets. The adults carefully folded the sheets over the dead animals and birds and filled in the open grave. The children sang a hymn, 'All Things Bright and Beautiful', in benediction and farewell. Gardens were blossoming in their last glorious burst before the winter, and to complete the ceremony the children picked whatever they wanted. They came and went until they transformed the muddy grave into a mound of brilliant flowers.'

Margaret was too upset to take part in the funeral ceremony, but watched in tears from the house 'as my brother slowly followed the others in procession and carried the small bodies of our dogs to their grave. I thought of curling up in a chair with Janey, of seeing Janey with her puppy, and playing with Bear. It was hard to grasp that I would never again see them. Our dogs were so alive, and then suddenly not alive. I thought that surely this dreadful thing could be undone and they would come to see us again. I had never felt that sense of loss, never cried like that before.'[6]

Margaret Blair was not the only little girl to associate this period with grief and separation. In Barbara Bruce's home in Singapore, after their horrific experiences in the days following the fall, when Japanese soldiers had burst into their home and raped a servant, things had become calmer. They now had to wear red armbands when they went out and observe a 6 p.m. curfew, but they were still free. Then, one day in late summer, the family were woken by banging at the door. They got up to find a lorry manned by Japanese soldiers waiting to take them away. 'We weren't allowed much time to prepare and were not able to take very much in the way of clothes and possessions. Lack of clothing was a major problem for many in the camps we were in.'

The soldiers asked them who was living in the house. 'My grandmother was Dutch and was quite dark-skinned so they weren't interested in taking her. It was horrible and very frightening. We were all crying. My grandmother didn't want them to take her daughter and tried to hang onto her. The Japanese shouted "you stay" and pushed her away. I was nine and a half, and my two younger brothers, one of whom was only eighteen months old, didn't want to leave Nan and we were wailing and clinging onto her … The soldiers were really rough. "Get in lorry," they said and shoved all five of us in. As we drove by the market area some people recognised my mother and waved to her, but we weren't allowed to speak to anyone. We had picked up that we were going to Changi.* We didn't know much about the prison but we had heard that the Japanese had released all the convicts and murderers to make way for the British.'

When they arrived in front of the high, forbidding walls of the prison they discovered that it was Japanese policy to class all boys over twelve as men, and as such eligible for manual labour. 'We were to be split up and my two older brothers, aged fifteen and fourteen, were going to the men's prison, while me, my five-year-old brother and the baby were going with Mum into the women's prison. My mum was wonderful at comforting us and finding ways to keep us cheerful, but the strain left its mark on her. Not long after we went into camp she had a heart attack. She was allowed to go to the camp hospital – not that there was any medication available – but at least she was allowed to rest. Her hair went white almost overnight.'

As 1942 drew to a close even the children in Shanghai thought of internment in terms not so much of 'if' but 'when'. Margaret Blair's police officer father had been arrested in the same November raid as Jose Chamberlain's. Margaret was sent away to stay with friends and when she returned he had been taken. Neither girl would see their father again for almost three years. The same month all radios thought capable of receiving Allied bulletins were confiscated from Allied nationals.[7] Children whose families were still intact, however, enjoyed an almost normal Christmas. Some Western-run schools even continued to function, only closing their doors for good at the end of February.

At the end of January the Japanese informed the British Residents' Association that internment would begin in weeks, telling

---

* The prison was situated on Changi peninsula on the eastern side of the island and was part of an extensive complex of military barracks that had formed the principal base of the British Army in Singapore. Built to house 700, under Japanese occupation it housed up to 3,400 prisoners.

the Swiss consulate that they expected the process to be completed by 15 March. They were to be interned in four main centres – Pootung, Lunghwa, Chapei and Yangchow, all of which, with the exception of Yangchow, were in or close to Shanghai. Americans were to go to Chapei, the British to Lunghwa; Ash Camp was to be for ex-employees of the Shanghai Municipal Council and Weihsien in north China was to be for all those caught north of the 34th parallel. The BRA decided that as the accommodation at Pootung (the other side of the river from the Custom House) consisted mainly of godowns (warehouses) only unattached men would be sent there. Because Yangchow was a country town 160 miles away they would try not to send the very young and the elderly there as medical facilities might be lacking.[8]

Most of the British community, unable to believe that an untested foe from a society they regarded as inferior could prove victorious against the might of Allied civilisation and skill, went into internment thinking it would last a few months at most. But people in Shanghai had been shocked at the tales of scavenging and fighting and general loss of dignity that had occurred in Stanley and the BRA was determined to be prepared. The association launched a major information campaign, advising future internees what they would need. The BRA began to sell 'many of the items thought necessary for camp life, such as metal framed beds, mosquito nets, enamel mugs and plates, camp-stools, buckets, wooden clogs and bed mats'.[9] The association then wrote to all British subjects asking them to come and collect their 'call-up' papers for internment. The cathedral compound soon filled up with people sitting on benches waiting to be called. In the months leading up to internment they held meetings with British and American doctors to gather information about public health, nutrition, drinking water, heating and the setting up of kitchens, schools and clinics. It was at this point that they decided that each camp should be a self-contained unit with professionals – doctors, nurses, engineers, plumbers and teachers – spread as evenly as possible among them. The BRA, in cooperation with the Japanese authorities, decided which residents went to which camp. Yangchow camps would take married couples and children over five and they would assemble at Church House. Other families were allocated to Lunghwa or Chapei and assembled at the Columbia Country Club.

Shanghai Municipal Council employees and people from Western Shanghai would go to Yu Yuen Road or Ash Camp.

Those with money left were allowed to take it in and could, for a while, buy all the food they wanted.[10] The internees were forbidden to take alcohol or any items from their homes that had been tagged by the Japanese. The list of items they were allowed to take included the following: tableware and non-breakable plates, cups and bowls (usually enamel), a wash basin, chamber pot, writing materials, soap, toilet paper, tooth powder, cigarettes, matches, bed linens, robe, scissors, mirror, can opener, needles, thread and wool, drawing pins, safety pins, hammer and pliers, shoe brush and polish, umbrella, spare spectacles, buttons, shoe laces, sunglasses, candles, hot water bottle, clothes hooks, pegs and hangers, nails, tape measure, tray, passport photos and material.

Internees were instructed to bring with them only what each of them could reasonably carry. Four items only were allowed to be sent ahead: a single bedstead, mattress and bedding, and two trunks, suitcases or kitbags. Each person's name and camp number were supposed to be painted onto the luggage. Doctors brought their medical supplies, teachers their textbooks, musicians their instruments. Unlike the young people who were in Stanley, where books and any form of paper was forbidden, David Nicoll was told by his father he could take in three books. He chose Ballantyne's *The Coral Island*, a Sexton Blake paperback and an American Tom Swift adventure.[11]

The moment, when it came, was deeply unhappy for some. In March 1943 Margaret Blair, who was nearly seven, was less concerned with what she was taking with her than with what she was leaving behind. As her mother, helped by her two faithful Chinese servants, packed up their house, Margaret made her choices. For toys she took a teddy bear, her baby doll and a blue stuffed giraffe. For books *The Tale of Jeremy Fisher* by Beatrix Potter, the first volume of the Children's Encyclopaedia (A-D) and the *Golden Book of Wonder*, a collection of children's poems. 'For one last time, Amah put me to bed. Putting her hands round either side of my head ... she whispered, "Margaret go sleep well". In the morning Amah washed and dressed me, gently brushed my hair and gave me breakfast. I had lost our pets and my father; now I was to lose Ah Ling, my Chinese mother.'

The next morning their heavier luggage, including three camp beds bought for camp by Margaret's mother, were loaded onto a lorry by European prisoners. Margaret, her brother and mother followed in a pedicab, a cross between a tricycle and a rickshaw that allowed the driver to pedal the passengers instead of running between the shafts. Less than an hour later they would no longer be free citizens.

For David Nicoll, on the other hand, the news that they were finally going to camp was the climax of weeks of mounting excitement. For weeks now the curving drive in front of the cathedral had been marked out in squares and people had been directed to their appropriate square for checking according to their camp number. At the end of January David had seen the first group of adult men assemble outside the hall to go to Pootung camp across the Whangpoo River. When the first batch of people destined for Yangchow was to set off David and his friends went up to the forecourt 'and helped by assigning round ginger biscuits, telling people where they could get cups of tea and indicating where the lavatories were'.[12]

Now, finally, it was their turn. 'On 27 February I was descending the cloister steps ... when Sonny, George and Noel came rushing up and told me excitedly that we were all going to Yangchow Camp and that we would be leaving on 11 March. Boy were we thrilled! This was going to be a marvellous adventure and we started to count down the days eagerly.'

After this, each head of the family received two pages of printed instructions from the Japanese Consul General telling them, as the boys had announced, to report at the cathedral Church House on 11 March. The instructions suggested that they bring in not only clothing and provisions but also sports equipment and books and '2 or 3 pairs of shoes and 4 or 5 pairs of slippers'.[13]

The Nicoll family laid in quantities of tinned foods and packets of Chinese dried meat, as well as pounds of bacon, large salami sausages, an Edam cheese, packets and tins of biscuits, six bottles of concentrated cordial, tins of powdered milk and jam. Providently, they also took jars of calcium tablets, cod liver oil and toilet paper.

Other families took similar provisions. Not even the most provident father, however, had any notion of just how long they would be using their kit and provisions – or how inadequate they would prove. Cyril Mack's father, who had been in the army, had splendid kitbags and rucksacks specially made. The red and green kitbags were made of special heavy-duty ship's Chandler canvas and stood 4 feet high when crammed full of provisions. He bought his elder son a new, somewhat cumbersome, folding camp bed, but he didn't buy a mattress. Cyril took his normal bed into camp, 'which was fine except that it was not full size and I grew out of it long before we were released. Towards the end of our internment I had to sleep with my feet dangling over the bottom of the bed. We were all confident that the Japs would soon be defeated by the Allies and that we would all be home by Christmas 1943! – so little things like me growing out of my bed or Roy sleeping on stiff, hard canvas without a mattress for two and a half years were not taken into our planning.'

Nor had they any idea how cold they would be: 'As far as bed linen was concerned we took all the usual – a pillow each, sheets, pillowcases, blankets and a mosquito net each but no quilts because we found that quilts were too bulky to pack.'[14]

As 15 March approached the heavy luggage was sent to the Customs jetty, each piece marked with the person's name, nationality, camp number and name of camp. Having sent their beds off to the docks the Mack family decided to spend their last days of freedom with friends. As they left their flat, there was almost a presentiment that the good life, with Europeans forever on top, was like a spent candle, flickering out, perhaps never to be lit again.

'Before leaving the flat ... we had to make sure that all our household contents were within, in particular those with stickers attached. We had to then lock and seal both the front and back doors with further large stickers. Needless to say that was the last we saw of our chattels.' The family said goodbye to the Jewish owners of the apartment block, who were not being interned. Someone announced that the three rickshaws they had called were waiting. There was the by now customary crowd of silent Chinese onlookers. 'We stepped into the back lane carrying our cases, with haversacks slung and noticed that there was quite a gathering at the gates to the lane so Dad grouped us together, said "chin up, shoulders back, look straight ahead" and we marched the 50 yards to the end of the lane where our rickshaws were waiting.'[15]

For a handful of British children living in Shanghai there would be no excited packing or jubilant countdown. These were the youngsters being cared for by elderly or infirm relatives, who the Japanese had no immediate plans to intern. Ten-year-old Dick Germain was one of these. His father, who worked for the Chinese Maritime Customs, was interned in one camp in the spring of 1943 and in December of that year his mother was interned in Chapei. She managed to persuade the Japanese to allow her youngest son Dick (her older children were at boarding school in England) to stay with his elderly grandfather, who had heart trouble, and an uncle who was also in poor health. Dick's memories of the curious interregnum that occurred after the Japanese takeover of Shanghai and before his own delayed internment (he finally entered camp in June 1944) are days of unmitigated freedom.

'In many ways life continued as normal. I went to school, only this time it was a Jewish school run by German refugees. When I was not at school I roamed Shanghai completely unsupervised.' On one occasion Dick heard that the British Residents' Association had organised a boat to take people across the Whangpoo River to visit relatives interned in Pootung camp. Dick had an uncle there and decided to join the party. 'When I got up to the Bund [the Shanghai waterfront], I found I had missed the boat, but I wasn't going to give up. I found a woman with a sampan and negotiated with her to row me across. When I turned up at the gates of the camp the Japanese guards were quite surprised to see a ten-year-old European boy, but they were quite friendly and let me in. The men made a huge fuss of me and when the visit was over I came back with the BRA boat.'

Being a lone white boy sometimes had its drawbacks, however. The Chinese street children had a favourite game which involved running after lorries laden with bales of cotton and slashing off chunks of cotton with razorblades. 'I was watching them one day and they noticed me. They started by just teasing and then they set about me with the razors. They slashed my coats to ribbons. I took to my heels pursued by them and took refuge in of the warehouses. They were guarded by Sikh policemen who were big fierce-looking men so I knew I would be safe there.'

Yet for those children involved in the big adventure of the spring of 1943, there was everything to look forward to. The mood of David Nicoll and his friends on their last night of freedom was almost jubilant, recalling the children of the Famous Five embarking on a trip into the unknown. 'We were so happy counting down the days and wondering what living in Camp would be like. We did know that we would start ever so much better off than the people of Stanley had been, we were being permitted to take in so much more than they had had; also by this time they had already undergone well over a year of internment and we sensed that conditions for us would not be nearly as bad as their early days had been ... . We thought it would not be easy for the Japanese to be very harsh and we believed that life would be tolerable.'

The day given for their departure was Monday, 15 March and they were to report at the cathedral grounds at 7.30 a.m. It was a cold morning with a weak sun struggling to penetrate the early morning haze as 200-plus British civilians – married couples, elderly folk and excited children – began to muster. All over the normally impeccable sweeping drive and manicured lawns lay mountains of baggage, some spanking new, some improvised. One family had brought their gramophone. Two children were carrying their family's belongings coolie-style on a bamboo pole – shoes suspended by their laces, pots and pans.[16] All the internees by now were wearing their identification labels denoting their name, age, sex and internment number, though some fathers, Cyril Mack's among them, delayed this last act of submission to the last possible moment and did it through gritted teeth. While the adults sought out the British consular officials to report their arrival, the children waited on the drive before being directed to a square on the cathedral lawn according to their camp number. David Nicoll was 10/259, Cyril Mack 14/257.

As the order came to leave, the familiar crowd of silent Chinese came out to observe the peculiar sight of white people carrying their own luggage, and, indeed, this was no time for chivalry and the women were almost as weighed down as the men. As he looked into the crowd Keith Martin, marching with his newly widowed aunt and younger sister, spied his German doctor who had come to wave them off.

The route to the ancient walled city of Yangchow lay by ship down the Whangpoo River and up the Yangtze to Chingkiang, an overnight journey of some 150 miles. Japanese guards accompanied them and took their details. From there a series of barges, dubbed 'chicken boats' by Europeans, pulled by a tug, would take them on the last leg of the journey up the Grand Canal.

As they settled down into the crowded barges and drifted slowly forward there was almost total silence, an unusual experience for residents of one of the noisiest cities on earth. Cyril Mack, having his first protracted glimpse of Chinese rural life, was fascinated. 'To me ... the unusual ... sights and foreign smells – the vast countryside of paddy fields, farmers working with their oxen, small hamlets – the other barges passing on the canal, some with sails up and some being poled, the friendly chat between the bargees as they passed – it was all so different, unexpected and colourful. I was totally absorbed in what was happening around me and for the first time I began to feel a small flutter of excitement.'

The fastidious Cyril had been put out by the dirty state of the bedding on the steamer that had brought them to Chingkiang. The ship had been used as a troopship and the bean-filled sacks that were provided as pillows had impressed him as being 'pungent with the smell of stale sweat and soiled by countless anonymous greasy heads'. But that was as nothing to the dismay of the women and girls when they discovered that there were no latrines on the open barges. They had no alternative to opening a tin of their precious provisions to use as a receptacle. 'A circle formed facing out – with backs to the can and its occupant. Each time the can was used, the waste was emptied into the canal.'[17] It was a sign that they had left the sophisticated West behind them and would henceforth have no choice but to live like the natives.

Cyril Mack detected the deepening anxiety among the adults. 'We children chattered away happily, to us it still seemed as though we were taking part in a big adventure; the adults, however, had been stunned into silence ... Two days previously we had been in the comfort of our own homes in Shanghai and now we were travelling with dozens of strangers on a crowded chicken boat on a canal, surrounded by paddy fields and in the middle of nowhere. We had been deprived of our freedom, were being guarded by armed soldiers, were cut off from the rest of the world and were being transported to an Internment Camp, with the disquieting reality that the uncertain futures of all of us had been placed in the hands of a potentially barbarous and unpredictable enemy.'

Their arrival in Yangchow strengthened their sense that they were truly in an alien land. David Nicoll found the city 'very Chinese-looking ... with no tall buildings, no Europeans visible, apparently no motor traffic ...'. It made Cyril Mack think of the exotic oriental cities in the children's classic Sinbad the Sailor.

It was a dark and brooding city that seemed to have stepped, untouched, straight from the Middle Ages. The place was dominated by its walls built from blocks of dark grey stone that towered 40 feet above the canal. They were so wide at the top that two cars could pass each other with ease. The old fortifications were still intact and the giant wooden gates to the city stood open to greet them. As the internees clambered from their barges, leaving behind Chinese children happily swimming in the canal, they got their first sight of the Japanese guards who from now on would be running their lives. 'There was a large contingent of guards in attendance ... Now most of the guards wore navy blue, almost black uniforms* and carried side arms – Mauser pistols – but none wore the samurai sword, instead they had shorter swords with highly polished scabbards similar to European ceremonial swords.'

After protracted checking and rechecking of numbers the internees were told to move off, escorted by some British prisoners who had arrived at the camp earlier. They walked through the ancient gates and up through narrow streets flanked by high windowless walls. By now, tired after the uncomfortable journey and many struggling with their heavy and cumbersome luggage, few people talked, preoccupied, instead, with what lay ahead.

Their destination turned out to be a former mission compound, whose walled enclosure nestled in the shadow of the city walls. They stopped in front of 'a long grey brick wall about 9 feet in height extending to our left and to our right and set in the wall were solid wooden gates standing, almost invitingly, open'. As they approached the gates and filed through silently the full import of their situation hit them. 'There, before us, in the late afternoon light was our future home – Yangchow Civil Assembly Centre – Camp C.'[18]

---

* These were Consular Police normally used for guarding Japanese embassies and consulates abroad.

PART TWO

Organisation and Optimism

5

Your Safest Refuge

To many children, particularly in China, where there had been months of preparation, internment seemed to promise one long camping holiday, a 'marvellous adventure' as David Nicoll imagined it. They had enjoyed the commissioning of special luggage, the purchase of mountainous reserves of tinned food, camp beds and folding chairs; of thermos flasks and enamel mugs and plates. But as the camp gates closed behind them it was not long before some were facing ordeals which would their make their idyllic childhood seem like a half-remembered dream.

The children who found themselves interned in 1942 and 1943 were used to the best; to eating well-cooked food, and being properly dressed for the extremes of weather offered by the climate of much of the Far East. They were used to washing and undressing in private, to showers, flushing lavatories, safe water ... comfortable beds ... Above all they took for granted a secure family life and had been brought up with a code of behaviour which decreed that men don't use violence against women. All this was to change dramatically in the coming months as the position of the Europeans and the Orientals, seemingly set in stone for a century, was inverted. There are few more ironic symbols of this than the situation in Stanley camp in Hong Kong, where the starving inmates were forced to grow beans up the wires that in happier times had serviced the bells they rang to summon their servants.

In the summer of 1940 the Japanese had launched the concept of the Greater East Asia Co-Prosperity Sphere. Under the slogan 'Asia for the Asians' they painted a picture of the east purged of Western

75

imperialism. In reality, however, their aim was to create a vastly extended Japanese empire, giving them access to wider markets and valuable raw materials. Evidence that the Japanese exploited the idea of all eastern races united against the European interlopers as propaganda to help them in their war aims was revealed in a secret document. 'An Investigation of Global Policy with the Yamato Races as Nucleus', drawn up in 1943, made explicit their belief that the Japanese were superior to other Asian races and that their true aim was domination over Asia. The Japanese lost no opportunity, at the beginning of the war, to show the Chinese how they were humiliating the former colonial masters. From now on the kind of hardship the European families had seen endured by the poorer Chinese – hunger, cold, casual violence – would be visited with a vengeance on the internees.

For the next three years thousands of British children would exchange their airy houses for cramped communal dormitories, alternately fetid and freezing according to the season, where every inch of floor space mattered. There they would sleep alongside strangers, their treasured belongings from a distant and disintegrating world crammed in trunks, suitcases and packing cases, which they shoved under beds, stacked up in corridors or piled on makeshift shelves. Their once leisured colonial timetable was replaced by a day dominated by queuing – queues for endless sittings of wretched, inedible meals, queues for drinking water of dubious quality, queues for ablutions.

For their parents, life was to change even more horrifyingly. It was not just that they were no longer the master race. The men had worked all their lives as executives, administrators, functionaries. They were totally unused to physical labour. Suddenly they were faced with a fight for survival that forced on them an abrupt return to an almost stone age lifestyle on a gigantic communal scale involving exhausting, back-breaking labour, endlessly repeated. In most camps, before any food could be cooked, vast quantities of fuel – coal and firewood – had to be manhandled to the kitchens; before a hot shower could be enjoyed (a luxury not universally available) or filthy clothing washed or tea made, enormous boilers had to be lit and fed remorselessly. When flour supplies ceased internees had to grind rice using huge flat millstones turned by hand – a procedure not seen in the West since the middle of the eighteenth century. All this took its toll, not just on the adults themselves, but on their relationship with their children, who remember them as more irritable than before, or more preoccupied.

As they settled in to what many thought would be an unpleasant experience that would last at best a few months, there was one aspect of internment that everyone detested. The ritual that symbolised internment for everybody, adults and children alike, was roll-call. Whether in Malaya, the Philippines, Hong Kong, China or the Netherlands East Indies, camp life was dominated by this one universally hated event. Invariably it was a long, drawn-out process as the Japanese often got the figures wrong and had to endlessly repeat the exercise. It was usually held outside, which meant that in summer internees were made to stand still for hours in the baking tropical heat, often with no protection from the sun. It was common for people to faint while waiting to be ticked off on the register. In winter prisoners had to dig trenches in the snow to stand in. No talking was allowed during roll-call and internees were forced to stand still with their heads bowed. Sometimes guards would decide that too many internees were on the sick list and insist that the sick join the parade. In some camps, especially if there had been an escape, roll-calls were called in the middle of the night, partly as a punishment, and partly to check there had been no further attempts at escape.

Six-year-old Margaret Blair was interned in Yu Yuen Road camp in Shanghai with her mother and brother Gordon, who was three years older than her. The camp had formerly been the Shanghai Municipal Council's Western District Public School for girls and boys. Four months earlier Margaret had suffered the shock of her father's arrest and imprisonment by the kempeitai, the much-feared secret police. After having to have her beloved dogs put down and say a tearful farewell to her amah only a few weeks before, she soon discovered how much it mattered to be on time for roll-call. Their sleeping quarters were a former classroom, which they shared with another couple and their two children. One night the guards decided to order a roll-call in the night and Margaret's mother didn't hear the summons. Margaret woke suddenly 'to the sound and feel of my mother slammed back across my bed, propelled by blows from a drunken Japanese guard'. His loud enraged staccato created a harsh discord with the frantic cries of their neighbour who begged her husband not to strike the guard. 'In the random flashes from the guard's torch as he waves it about, our bleak room, with its bare walls and worn wood floor, springs haphazardly into focus ... I see the peeling paint of the ceiling with no light bulb, the small metal table where we eat, my yellow teddy bear, blue giraffe, baby doll and well-thumbed books on the floor, the other two beds ... and the curved sword and drawn gun of the guard's companion. I wonder whether he is going to shoot or cut us to pieces.'

The neighbours with whom they shared their room were already standing to attention with their two young sons. Margaret's mother urgently whispered to her children to do the same until they were all in a row, bowing low from the hips. The guard gave another enraged shout at their bowed heads but stopped hitting her. The children waited in silence, fearing the guards would come back, but eventually they heard him stamping upstairs to take roll-call on the floor above. 'Then my mother tells us to go back to sleep and she feels her way along the corridor in the dark to the room with two lavatories and a row of washbasins. There she bathes in cold water to reduce the swelling and bruises that are coming up on the side of her face and body. Our mother washes and washes herself. Over and over the cleaning continues.' The terrified child began wetting the bed as a result of this incident.

The casual bullying violence meted out by the guards to internees came as a profound shock to children, particularly when it applied to their mothers, as it did in many camps. Japanese culture had none of the chivalrous respect for female frailty endemic in Western cultural norms and treated these conquered European females with the lack of consideration they showed their own women, spiced up, in many cases, with racially motivated hatred. Japanese society was rigidly hierarchical and for them prisoners and internees were at the bottom of the social ladder for having surrendered. As Margaret Blair had discovered anything could trigger an attack. All internees were expected to bow when in the presence of one of their captors. Failure to bow was a regular trigger for aggression, as was causing a Japanese to lose face or talking in roll-call. Face-slapping was the preferred method of demonstrating authority, with the punisher slapping both sides of the face with the front and back of the hand, often so violently that the victim would be knocked over.

Barbara Bruce, who was interned in Singapore's grim grey-walled Changi jail at the age of nine with her mother and two younger brothers, hated the violence. 'The guards were rough with the women. There was plenty of pushing and shoving of our mothers, as well as whacks across the head with sticks. This was a terrible shock to us as British men treated women with respect, as did the Chinese, who were very family-orientated and showed particular respect for the elderly. The Japanese were not like that at all.'

For the majority of civilians internment was to prove a bitter experience. This made all the more ironic the sugary, almost evangelical language Japanese officialdom adopted when discussing their victims' loss of liberty. They were sensitive about the word 'camp', preferring instead the term Civil Internment Centre (which the prisoners universally boycotted). In their opinion an internment camp was where families were separated, as they were in the Japanese-occupied Netherlands East Indies.[2] The rules of behaviour sound more like a prescription for life in utopia than a concentration camp: 'The Civil Assembly Centre being the best home for those who live in it, must be loved and cherished by all of them. Each person shall take care of his or her health and live in harmony with each other. There shall be no disputing, quarrelling, disturbing, or any other improper demeanour.'[3]

Internees arriving at Chapei camp, in Shanghai, were welcomed by Commandant Tsurumi, who addressed them in similarly flowery language. 'Unfortunately the prevailing international circumstances have deprived you of your right to free life and necessitated you to enter this place. However, this is your safest refuge, where your rights are best guaranteed and the only abode you are now allowed to live in. You must therefore, cope with the rules and regulations and make possible efforts in the carrying on of this place with a spirit of mutual harmony and with the thought that this is your home, loving it, enjoying it, enjoying your life and duties given to you. Thus, to live in peace and happiness is the wisest and best way for you.'[4]

A month later, when the process was complete, an article in the now Japanese-run *Shanghai Times* congratulated the conquerors on the civilised arrangements they had made their prisoners. The article was in every way a bitter parody of the truth. 'The internment of some 6,000* British, Americans and Dutch which started on Jan 31st is now almost completed. The enemy nationals are living in camps established in Pootung, Chapei, Lunghwa and other suburban districts of Shanghai, and the houses are well built and in good condition .... Much attention has been given to the environment of the internees, and to the construction of their living quarters, with meticulous care being given to their food. In order to maintain their health, walking and sports grounds have been laid out, where the internees are daily playing tennis and volleyball.' This would prove particularly ironic as internees became too weak through hunger to use the sports facilities. As a parting shot the writer declared that the prisoners were grateful for the 'generous and just treatment' they were receiving.[5]

Cyril Mack, the eleven-year-old who had been so excited by his family's custom-made luggage as they prepared for internment, had travelled for nearly two days by steamer and barge to reach the ancient, isolated, inland city of Yangchow. Here, initially, there were to be three internment camps for Allied families from Shanghai. As soon as they arrived in the camp they were summoned to a central point. 'We assembled around the improvised dais and milled about like bewildered passengers waiting for an announcement on an unfamiliar railway station platform. The guards closed in around us and circled slowly with swords clanking softly, threatening, watching.'

The commandant then made a speech of welcome, translated by an interpreter. 'Yamashita laid down a few of his own ground rules which in synopsis amounted to – this is now your home and you have been brought here for your own protection, obey the Camp Regulations, obey and respect the Guards, do as you are told and do not try to escape.'

Some internees from Yangchow C maintain Yamashita warned that any internee who tried to escape would be shot. This was a routine Japanese response and was explicitly mentioned in 'welcome' speeches in other camps. But Cyril remembers the scene differently.

---

* In fact, the total was 7,000.

'When he started to speak a number of people continued to shuffle about and talk between themselves, in particular two foolish teenage girls who continued to laugh and chat loudly. He rounded on them violently and viciously threatened them with dire consequences, letting them know in no uncertain terms what would happen to them, and that included being shot as an example to the rest of us, if they did not shut up and pay attention. The girls were naturally terrified for their safety and after that apoplectic outburst, needless to say, Yamashita also had the full nervous attention of the whole assembly.'

For many children, one of the most traumatic aspects of internment was finding the family broken up. This was what happened to Barbara Bruce who, on arriving with her four brothers at Changi jail found herself, her mother and two younger brothers marched off to one part of the prison while her two older brothers were led off to a different part. Their father had been arrested several months previously and they had no idea where he was. They remained separated for the whole of the war. Sylvia Williams, entering the university building of Santo Tomas in Manila, encountered the same situation, as did Iris Krass, who found herself entirely on her own. Sylvia's father was marched off to the men's section, while she and her mother were directed to a room that housed forty women. In Manila, unlike Malaya, however, married couples were allowed to be together during the day. In other camps, notably those in China, families lived together, usually in rooms containing other family groups, which made a huge difference to the children's happiness.

The treatment of internees in the camps was entirely arbitrary, since, from the time of the attack on Pearl Harbor, the Japanese had had no policy for the taking of prisoners or internees. Japanese military code decreed that soldiers should die fighting and the sheer numbers of Allied troops and civilians who had surrendered took them by surprise. They had not ratified the Geneva Convention, which guaranteed humane treatment of prisoners of war. Their reluctance to do so was largely based on the army's argument that as they didn't expect to be taken prisoner any agreement that acknowledged that foreign troops could be taken prisoner would be one-sided. There was no umbrella policy for how civilian prisoners should be held, whether in family groups or segregated by gender, and no organisation with overall responsibility for them. Internees in China became the responsibility of the Japanese Foreign Ministry, and enjoyed the most humane treatment; in Japan they came under the Ministry of Internal Affairs; in Hong Kong and Singapore they were under army jurisdiction; and in the Netherlands East Indies they were run by the army or navy.

As a result children's experiences varied hugely. Some families, including those living in China, as we have seen, had weeks of notice and were able to take plenty of creature comforts and personal effects into camp. Others, such as those interned in Hong Kong, Singapore and Manila, were rounded up and sent into camp at virtually a day's notice, being instructed to take possessions to last them a few days. This meant that they went in with little more than the clothes they were wearing and no extra food. As a result some found themselves sleeping on bare floors in prison cells, while others had comfortable beds in former schools or university campuses. Food rations differed considerably, too. Some had their meals cooked on modern gas stoves and enjoyed piped water and hot showers, while others, in more isolated surroundings, learned to cook on primitive charcoal stoves and relieve themselves over stinking earth closets. Many ended up forced to adopt the oriental custom of using their own waste on the sickly vegetable gardens they struggled to cultivate in their frantic search for nutrients. There was the same discrepancy in the relationship with their Japanese captors. Some found themselves in camps run by educated commandants who had lived in other countries and were conscious of their duty towards prisoners; others were at the mercy of sadistic thugs.

In August 1942, Barbara Bruce had exchanged a beautiful house in a leafy suburb of Singapore for the small cell in Changi, which she shared with her mother and her two younger brothers, aged five and eighteen months. British families in Singapore had been given virtually no time to prepare for internment and consequently had neither extra food nor clothes for growing children. Without any sheets or blankets, the prisoners slept on the concrete floor of the cell. 'For several weeks Mum had no idea where Dad was, or what had become of her two older children.'

Rations in Malayan camps were meagre from the start. 'There were only two meals a day – breakfast, which was served after roll-call – and lunch. There was no evening meal. Breakfast was rice boiled until it looked like the old-fashioned starch solution, which the Japanese called congee. At 1 p.m. we had to line up to collect our allocation of soup. The men did the cooking in their camp. It was carried over in big wooden vats. Mum queued for our ration, two ladlefuls between the four of us, which she collected in an old tin. We then took it back to our cell to eat it. My youngest brother Errol, who was only eighteen months old, had developed scurvy before we even went into camp because my mother couldn't get milk for him. She was dreadfully upset about it. I remember her crying with worry.'

The children in Changi suffered agonising hunger pains. 'This was particularly true of the babies and toddlers. There was no milk for them. At night it was hard to sleep for their crying because they were so hungry. I was hungry, too. My tummy used to rumble so loudly at night that my mother would tell me to drink water to try to fill myself up. That's what we did. You didn't dare think about food – favourite dishes and that sort of thing – you'd have stayed awake all night. Instead you just thought, tomorrow morning I'll eat again.'

At the start of internment the Red Cross sent in food parcels from South Africa containing tinned milk, sardines and vitamin 'sweets', which helped quell the hunger pangs, but the Japanese did not always distribute them. On one occasion they decided to take some photographs of children in camp for propaganda purposes. Each child was given a Red Cross parcel to hold for the camera. As soon as the photographs had been taken the parcels were removed from the disappointed children.[6]

While Barbara and her mother were trying to adjust to life in their cell her two older brothers were relieved to find themselves reunited with their father. 'Both Sid and I were directed to H block cell no. 2 where we were greeted by our Dad with open arms. He hugged us both, for a while quite overcome with emotion, then asked us how Mum and the rest of the family was, and, on being assured that they were all well and had been taken into the women's wing ... he seemed to heave a sigh of relief, knowing that we were all safe and sound, even though we were still separated.'[7]

The cell, which had been built for eight, now housed eighteen: six boys and twelve adults. One of the other occupants was a Mr Harris who had been chief warder at another well-known prison in Singapore. 'The cell was in two halves, with four suspended cots in each half ... there were two more folding beds in the middle, and the rest of us had to sleep on hessian mats on the concrete floor ... there was a urinal in one corner ... (merely a hole in the floor) which was only to be used during the nights, and turns were taken by us boys to sluice this out each morning after roll-call, using a bucket of water.'[8]

Loss of privacy for washing and primitive sanitary conditions were among the things older children found most difficult. One nine-year-old girl interned in Santo Tomas in Manila saw women showering naked for the first time and was repelled. 'The sight of all those women, many of them fat, with bulging stomachs and huge drooping breasts revolted me. I vowed that I would never let myself get like that.' Some became deeply anxious about defecating and found themselves unable to 'go' if there was any risk of company. This was more difficult as no one wanted to visit the latrines at night, when there was some anonymity, because of the hundreds of giant tropical cockroaches which haunted them.

In the men's wing in Changi an attempt had been made to construct a pastiche of a flush, but Mel Bruce was not impressed. 'There was a large monsoon drain, some 8 to 10 feet deep at the end of the main exercise yard, which normally had a small volume of water constantly running through it. The genius who thought this one up, merely had some twenty or more boxes built over the drain as toilet seats, with a sluice gate at one end to dam up the water supply, which upon reaching a set level, tripped a lever allowing the gate to open and the water would then rush through flushing the drain clean. Imagine being sat on one of these thrones, contemplating one's future when all of a sudden a great torrent of water would rush past your buttocks sweeping all before it, even before you had finished what you were supposed to be doing. During the hottest part of the day, in between flushes, the stench was almost unbearable ... you gauged the time of the next flush and then visited the wall when it was over.'

In the humid tropical climate of Singapore personal hygiene was a priority, but if they wanted to remain clean children and adults had no choice but to strip off in front of each other. And in many camps water only flowed through the pipes at certain times of the day. In 1944 the internees in Changi were moved to another camp which had been an army barracks. Conditions here were even more primitive. Washing was like stepping back in time.

'An area near the huts had been concreted over . . . and had a stand pipe in the centre which fed two troughs. Two lengths of piping led from the stand pipe to each side of the troughs, one simply turned the tap on at the point at which you stood at the trough and stripped and washed or bathed as you desired, absolutely naked, with no privacy at all . . . water at these venues came on at 5.30 am to 9.30 am then again at 4.30 pm to 6.00 pm.'[9]

This time the lavatories were merely boreholes some 10 to 12 feet deep topped by seats made from old tea chests with a hole in the top. There was, of course, no lavatory paper. 'When you used one of these you always made sure you had a tin of water with you to cleanse yourself afterwards (most of us saved a can of water for this purpose when washing each day) or else you used whatever was available to hand, i.e. a turf of grass or Papaya leaf which was akin to using a sheet of leather when dried.'

The urinals were similarly makeshift: 'a long length of corrugated iron folded to form a trough, fixed to two wooden uprights at a downward angle, with a sawn in half palm oil drum at each end to catch the urine. This was then emptied at regular intervals on the various garden plots as manure.'[10]

Most camps had septic tanks, which the men had to clear out. One day in the women's wing, Mel and Barbara's little brother Bryan, curious to see what the men were doing, got too near and fell in. 'Bryan suddenly appeared accompanied by one of the men who had rescued him. Both of them were covered in you know what and Bryan was led away yelling and my Mum clipping his earhole saying, "I told you to keep away". According to Mum, Bryan stank for a week despite bathing several times.'[11]

In Changi the men cooked lunch and delivered it daily to the women's camp. Although there was a no-talking rule messages could be sent and received by this conduit. Some of Barbara's mother's anxiety about the whereabouts of her husband was allayed when 'one day one of the men delivering the midday meal told her that, considering the circumstances, he was fit and well and that my two brothers were in a cell with him'.[12]

Conditions in Changi might have been crowded and basic, but

there was a feeling that everyone pulled together to make the best of things. In Stanley camp in Hong Kong, by contrast, the atmosphere was one of utter chaos, with an unpleasant undercurrent of every-man-for-himself. Fleeing their homes as the battle for Hong Kong raged round them, people had been interned with little more than the clothes they were wearing and lacked the most basic amenities. It was reported that the Americans had sent advance parties who had prepared billets for their countrymen, but that the British advance party had merely secured billets for themselves – close to the kitchen, so that when the bulk of British internees arrived – and there were 2,500 of them – nothing was ready. Three weeks after the battle there were hundreds of bodies lying where they had fallen. Everything was in short supply: beds and bedding, clothing, shoes, toilet materials, brooms and cleaning items, crockery, cutlery, cooking equipment and tools. There were reports that there was nothing to eat or drink and that the children were crying for thirst. With no eating utensils people were reduced to eating with their hands out of disused tins. One young lad's job was to carry rice. Whenever any was spilled other internees were seen scooping up the grains either to eat on the spot or to put in their tins.

This was the situation fifteen-year-old Bill Macauley found himself in as he arrived in Stanley camp in the third week of January 1942. His position differed from the majority of other young people in the camp – there were a little over 200 boys and girls under eighteen – in that that he was on his own.

Bill teamed up with his schoolmate Bobby Parker, who at fourteen was a year younger than him, and was also separated from his parents. The cramped conditions led to intolerant territorial behaviour as people struggled to stake out their own 20 inches of floor space. With more people crammed into one room than had previously occupied whole apartments, generations, genders and races and social classes were stirred up into a potent soup that frequently boiled over. Initially Bill and Bobby shared a cramped room with four women. The room was in a flat in what had been the quarters of the prison officers employed at Stanley. The other occupants included Matron and her Scottie dog, Missie, a middle-aged woman, who would die in camp, and a woman with her elderly mother. 'We had managed to acquire mattresses and Matron still had her camp bed from school and slept by the door. There was no privacy. When the women dressed or undressed we left the room.'

When the Americans were repatriated in June 1942, as part of an exchange of prisoners in which Japanese diplomats held in Britain and the United States were released, more billets became available and Bobby and Bill managed to get a corner of another room, which they shared this time with three other people, a married couple and an elderly male architect. 'I moved around a lot while I was in camp. Sometimes I was with Bobby, sometimes on my own on some veranda.'

The plight of two teenage boys facing internment alone might have been expected to arouse protective feelings in some of the many adults in Stanley. In the event it did not. In contrast to the camps in China, Stanley had been set up in a hurry with minimal planning. In the early days at least, the atmosphere was one of chaos. No family in the camp opened their circle to include Bill or Bobby. 'Insecurity and lack of supplies caused nearly everyone to think first of himself,' as one internee observed. A boy who had been in the year above Bill at school shared a room with his parents and sister in camp. Bill's family and his had been friends since the 1930s and the boy was keen for Bill to join their group, but his parents refused. 'Both families used to go to the same church before the war so they could have given me a hand, but they didn't want to take on the responsibility of an extra child and have another hungry mouth to share their rations with.'

The lack of compassion was further evidenced by the fact that former colleagues of Bill's father in the Chinese Maritime Customs actually pocketed money to which he was entitled. 'After I left school in camp I got a job working in the kitchens. Three chaps who had worked for the Chinese Maritime Customs were already there. Somehow money for people who had worked for the Customs was sent into camp. I didn't see any until one of them came to me one night and gave me thirty dollars, some wong tong, or Chinese brown sugar, and some Chinese bacon. He said, "We haven't been treating you fair." He said I should have been receiving goodies for the previous six months. That thirty dollars kept me going in little extras for six months.'

To be unwelcoming to a lone adolescent like Bill Macauley was bad enough. But in Stanley adults who had already 'bagged' their wretched few inches of floor space did not even show sympathy towards families with babies and toddlers. William Sewell arrived in Stanley camp in February with his wife and three young children. Sewell was a Chemistry Professor at Chengtu University in south-west China. By a grim twist of fate he had gone to Hong Kong to meet his family who were due to return from a visit to Canada on what would turn out to be the day before the attack on Pearl Harbor. Sewell and his wife Hilda were missionaries. Caught up in the battle the family had spent the weeks following the fall of the island living in bombed-out houses and foraging for food in what had once been Hong Kong's most sought-after residential quarter.

On their arrival at the camp with their three children Vee, eight, Joy, six, and Guy, four, the family were directed to the smart modern flats that had been built to house married British prison officers employed at Stanley prison. Instead of a married couple and their children the flat now housed thirty-five people. On the threshold of the room they had been allocated, which he estimated measured about 20 feet by 14 feet, Sewell took in the chaotic scene. 'Our arms were laden with our smaller sacks, while beyond us helpers were bringing some of the larger things. We could not go forward for the room appeared already full. Six camp beds took most of the space, while round the edges of the room were suitcases, bottles, a few pots and pans, two or three chairs, and wedged between the beds, some small round tables. Sitting on chairs and beds were five people eating rice from bowls or plates. They stopped their meal and glared at us. "Well, what do you want?" shouted one of the women. "You cannot come in here." "This room is taken," said another woman with anger in her voice. We saw that there were three women and two men. Obviously we were not wanted. "This is nonsense," the billeting officer shouted over our shoulders, "The room holds ten and there are only five here now. You will have to make room."' Reluctantly, the initial occupiers of the room were forced to admit the newcomers, but, as the tired and anxious family tried to unpack, the unpleasant grumbling continued.

'"It's a shame bringing children in here. We are elderly people and we don't like children," said one of the women in a loud voice. She was a small middle-aged woman, her lips heavily rouged. "Yes," agreed the woman who had first spoken. "It is a shame, pushing people in like this, just as we were settling." It was quite impossible to unpack, though we hunted for our bowl and spoons and the few necessities of our daily life. Our folded blankets and padded Chinese quilts we stacked on the Canadian army mattresses which were to be our seats by day and our beds by night. They took up a very small proportion of the floor.'

Night falls suddenly in the tropics and Sewell and his wife knew fresh hurdles lay ahead as all those inmates without bedsteads competed for floor space. 'Gradually we manoeuvred our mattresses out from the walls; they were each about two feet wide and two and a half feet long. Eventually we got nine of them down flat, winning a space seven feet six inches by six feet, which became ours by right of conquest. True one of the mattress corners was bent up against Em Addy's bed (Miss Addy was an elderly Eurasian spinster) which she defied us to move; but by imperceptible degrees we slid it from us and got our mattress flat, though in future she stepped upon our blankets every time she went to or from her bed.'[13]

William and Hilda lay down on the outside of their mattresses and put the children between them. Neither got much sleep that first night and to add to their woes the two girls were sick.

Lack of privacy was trying for everyone in the camps, as David Nicoll recalled of Chapei camp, where he had been transferred from Yangchow. 'In the silence of the night Mrs White (an internee in Chapei) was occasionally disturbed by the sound of somebody urinating just outside; it turned out to be elderly Mr M who lived upstairs and who could not be bothered to cross the open ground at night to the men's lavatory and just stood at the top of the steps near Mrs White's window.'[14]

Children, on the other hand, found communal living rather fun. Moreover, some camps had a decidedly more positive attitude than others. Cyril Mack's recollection of the way the adults in Yangchow decided to make the best of things, contrasts sharply with what was happening in Stanley. 'Dad went off to find out where we had been billeted ... we gathered up our baggage and quickly made our way over to a house which was numbered on the map as House 4 and our room was to be Room 7, quite a large room with high ceilings. We were the first to arrive and selected a space in the top left hand corner.

Gradually other families started to drift in ... People continued to arrive until there was a final count of nineteen persons of all ages and both sexes, eleven adults and eight children.'

Stunned by the numbers, the next step was to decide where everyone was to sleep. 'Once all the people in our room had retrieved their beds we set about positioning them and spacing them out. It was all completed in an amicable and humorous atmosphere and it was finally calculated that we would be able to have an 18-inch space between the beds – a pretty tight, extremely friendly, shoehorn fit, but no worse than what was occurring in all the other rooms in the camp.'

On the first night Cyril found himself sleeping with his brother on one side and a girl called Evelyn two or three years older than him on the other. But before anyone could get into bed, they had to solve the conundrum of undressing in a room that was 'brightly lit by three light fittings suspended from the ceiling', which could only be turned off in the guard room.

'Somehow, with absolutely no screening and no privacy, we had to work out an acceptable solution. It was an awkward quandary for that first night. We, the children, were prepared for bed by the adults as a sort of sacrificial lamb experiment ... We achieved our objective behind dressing gowns and under the bedclothes under the brilliant glare of the overhead lights.' When the time came for the adults to get undressed, some decided to throw modesty to the winds and simply turn their backs, while the more inhibited 'waited for Lights Out which was controlled by a master switch in the Guard Room and when it came the whole camp was plunged in total darkness'.

That first night Cyril lay awake, acutely aware of the presence of all the other people in the room – 'the whispered private conversations of the adults which you tried not to listen to, the unusual noises, movement and the sounds of many breathing.'

It was Cyril's father who resolved the problem of undressing. 'The next day Dad produced some bamboo canes from somewhere. Having been in the army and experienced barrack room life he had anticipated what communal living with mixed sexes would be like and had come prepared. He tied the canes to the corners of his and Mum's beds and ran string along the top of the canes. Mum unpacked some brown curtains that we had brought with us and attached them to the string thus we at least had privacy around their two beds. This had an immediate effect on our morale. In a very short time nearly all the families had erected some sort of limited screening. The children slept out in the open.'

Lack of privacy was of no great concern to younger children, but their natural energy chafed at the shortage of space. Ann March (later Moxley) was ten when she was interned in Lunghwa camp 8 miles from Shanghai with her father, an architect, her mother and her four-year-old brother. The camp had been a Chinese boarding school which had been badly bombed during the Sino-Japanese War in 1937. The March family were fortunate in having a room, roughly 13 feet by 11 feet, to themselves. 'There was enough room for a trunk under the window which we could sit on for meals, a small table, a camp chair and my bed which left very little play space.' The winter months, when the temperature remained well below freezing for days on end, was the worst time for the children as they couldn't go out to play and their few toys were hard to access because of the cramped conditions. 'The beds were on top of trunks so we had to be very organised about knowing what was in each trunk, as it was such a performance to open them. One bed didn't have a trunk underneath it so that we could play under that, and we could play on top of them if our parents allowed us.'[15]

Mary Hill (later Wedekind) and her family were lucky, also being allocated their own room in what had been one of the old dormitory buildings. It was sited at the corner of the building, which meant it had two windows and provided the children with coveted play space at the end of the corridor when they couldn't go out.

Mary was eight when she was interned with her parents, five-year-old sister and three-and-a-half-year-old brother. She holds fond memories of that corridor.

'The corridor became a post office, or a dolls hospital or whatever was needed at that particular moment.' The Hills considered themselves lucky compared to others: 'People in the classroom blocks had to divide their area off with sheets, and those in the Nissan huts, mostly single, had to live dormitory fashion with no privacy whatsoever.'

Nonetheless for five people, three of them young children, to live, sleep and eat for years in a room measuring 15 feet by 10 feet was not easy. The only storage space they had were two long shelves running the length of one wall. The Hills pushed their trunks out into the corridors and kept everything else under the beds. The untidy, spontaneous way children leading normal lives play with their toys was impossible, but the restraint enforced by their cramped surroundings produced unexpected benefits as the children came to treasure the few toys they did have. 'We could only have the minimum of toys or books out at one time – and it was always very exciting when it was decided to make a change.'[16]

Food played a major role in the health and happiness of internees. By the end almost all prisoners were on starvation rations and many people were ill and dying from malnutrition. In the early stages of internment, however, the amount of food and its nutritional content varied widely. Some recall plenty of variety, while others' memories are dominated by Same Old Stew – known as SOS – or by the cracked wheat that had been sent by America to China as famine relief and had been stored for several years on the floor of filthy warehouses. Frantic parents, worried about the impact of missing calcium on growing bones, forced their children to swallow ground-up eggshells and soya milk made from lumpy, hand-ground beans. Many children are faddy about food at the best of times and these had been pampered children. Accounts of the stinking, ill-kept fodder they were expected to eat – in the light of what they had been used to – are harrowing.

Families interned in Manila, like those in Singapore, endured iron rations almost from day one. This was because the Japanese refused to supply them with food, in flagrant defiance of international law. After several months of negotiation, the Japanese military reluctantly agreed to finance the food of the internees at a cost of thirty-five cents per person. This amounted to roughly eleven pence in today's money.

Sylvia Williams, interned with her father and mother in Santo Tomas in Manila, says that although they were served three meals a day, there was no milk and most days no protein.

'Breakfast was a yellowy corn meal we called mush. For lunch and supper we had rice, eaten with a tropical leaf vegetable known as talinum, which was grown in the camp vegetable gardens, and was a bit like spinach. Sometimes we would get a few shreds of meat, but not every day. I don't remember having any dairy produce for the whole three years we were in camp and this lack of calcium in my vital growing years is without doubt the cause of the osteoporosis I now suffer. The hunger affected us gradually as rations decreased. I was aware from quite early on, that my parents were desperately hungry. My father was well over 6 feet tall and weighed 15 stone when he went in and 9 stone when we came out of camp.'

At the beginning it was permitted for internees to buy extras like eggs, sugar and lard and charcoal to cook on, from outside. 'But to do this people had to borrow huge sums of money from people living outside to pay for them. My family didn't have any contacts as we had only recently arrived in Manila.'

Ann March found the food in Lunghwa deeply unpalatable. When meat did appear she was upset to learn it might be made from the greyhounds from Shanghai's Canidrome, or greyhound racing track. 'We started every day with congee and green tea. Congee is boiled rice, boiled to a kind of mush. It had a purple colour and it was absolutely full of weevils. You couldn't actually eat a spoonful of it without eating the weevils in it too, because there were just too many of them to pick out.

'At lunchtime we had a kind of vegetable soup with sometimes a few bits of very grey scraggy meat, which we were told were greyhounds, and sometimes the odd fish head. In fact the vegetables were mostly market refuse too and were pretty awful. Then in the evening we had congee again, or cracked wheat with weevils and little grey worms or grubs. Sometimes, if we were lucky, we were given a kind of red cattle cake and again, green tea ... Food supplies got less and less ... and we got down eventually to one meal a day for the last six months.'[7]

In Lunghwa children over five were made to drink soya milk made by the adults from roughly ground soya beans. They all detested it. Many parents worried constantly about their children's refusal to eat the unpalatable meals they were served, fearing permanent effects on their development. Some, however, were surprised at their children's reaction. In Stanley camp the Sewells regularly ate what they referred to as 'dustbin stew', which was made of discarded cabbage stalks, carrot tops and turnip tops. Their children coped impressively well with the disgusting diet.

William Sewell remembered: 'Joy and Guy would eat up their rice and stew, though Vee would carefully pick out the cockroach excreta and arrange the little black specks in a ring round the white rim of her bowl. "See no weevil; hear no weevil; eat every weevil is my motto," shouted Guy ... Vee would frequently slip away from our table to see if there were second helpings to be got from the queues ... she once came back flushed with pleasure. "Look what I've got! A great lump of gristle." We divided it and chewed it, until after some minutes Guy asked, "I've chewed it well, now may I swallow?"'[18]

With thousands of people crowded together in these camps water was vital. It was needed to flush the overflowing lavatories, to rinse sweaty bodies, to wash clothes and sheets and floors – and for drinking. In many of the camps, water, with its dangerous potential for importing disease, proved as big a problem as food. Some, like Santo Tomas in the Philippines, had piped water and even got extra pipes laid on to cope with the huge numbers of prisoners. Others, like Stanley, theoretically had piped water, but in such short supply that it only ran at certain times of the day, requiring the prisoners to stand for hours in yet another queue. The camps that were isolated from cities relied on water being brought in carts by Chinese bearers, which had to be boiled and treated before it was safe to drink. In all camps it was in short supply and many prisoners remember thirst as keenly as hunger.

Weihsien, in the north of China, was one of the camps where water dominated the lives of internees. Northern China was known for its extremes of climate. In the unusually cold winter of 1944–45 the thermometer plummeted to -22°C, while on one baking summer day it reached 43°C. In this camp the children were either shivering with cold, or panting with thirst. Weihsien camp, like many of the camps in China, was a former mission compound. At one stage it held more than 2,000 prisoners, but, due to transfers and repatriations, this dropped to 1,600. More than 240 of these were children. Among them were nearly 140 from Chefoo School, which had been interned, teachers and pupils, as a unit. They had arrived in camp in September 1943, having previously been interned in a complex of houses built for foreigners in Chefoo itself.

Estelle Cliff (later Horne) was fourteen when she went into camp. She was one of the many Chefoo pupils who spent their internment separated from their parents. Hers were missionaries based in the interior of China and when she arrived in Weihsien she had already not seen them for three years. 'There was never enough water in camp. The boys had to pump water from the wells all day long in one-hour shifts. And to complicate matters the water had not only to be boiled but distilled as well.' This was because tests carried out by internees when they arrived had found typhoid germs in the water. The result was that on a searingly hot summer day no thirst-quenching drink was available.

'In the summer we queued for hours because the still could not cope with the demand. When we got there the water we collected was piping hot,' remembered Estelle. In the heat some people couldn't resist the temptation of a drink of ice-cold water from the well and died of typhoid fever. It was then that Estelle understood how the Chinese preserved their health, despite primitive living conditions. 'We remembered that the Chinese never drank anything but tea – or boiling water if they couldn't afford tea.'

The lives of the schoolgirls in Weihsien seemed to revolve round water. They were forever washing – their clothes, their bodies … even their sanitary towels, which they made themselves out of a blend of cotton and gauze. 'On Fridays the girls did the school washing. I scrubbed grey sheets on a washboard over a cement trough. The only soap we had was one cake dissolved in hot water and cooled to form a jelly. We dipped our hands in that. I tried to rub off the blood marks from the bedbugs, which were our worst enemy.'

In this world, where they had effectively stepped back hundreds of years into a pre-mechanised past, everything required massive manual effort. The children's dormitories were heated by pot-bellied stoves, which at the beginning had been heated by coal. By 1944, however, the coal had run out. To generate any heat in the freezing dormitories the children had to make coal balls out of a mixture of coal dust and mud, which were then laid out to dry. The morning ablutions were an equally complicated ritual.

'At night we banked up the fire with some wet mix and made a hole through it with the poker. We took turns to wake early to stoke up the fire in the morning, adding new coal balls if it was still glowing, and putting on it the enamel jug of washing water we filled from the big clay kong at the end of the corridor. This the boys kept filled with buckets they carried upstairs for us. We each washed in a little warm water in a basin on the washstand. We had a line on our wrists where we had stopped, until once a week when it was Ladies Day at the showers.'

In the prudish atmosphere of this devoutly Christian school menstruation presented a challenge. 'When everyone had finished washing, those who were menstruating washed their little rags of torn towelling and draped them around to dry ... Our pink slops were collected in a galvanised bucket, emptied for us by the male staff. The boys were not to know about such things.'

There was no running water in Yangchow either. In Yangchow C the three existing wells soon proved insufficient for the 600 or so prisoners who now occupied the compound. The latrines stank and were almost certainly responsible for the many outbreaks of dysentery that occurred in the camp as time went on. The children had to get used to using buckets with a makeshift seat built over them. Showers were out and instead they washed oriental-style by dipping a tin can tied to a bamboo pole into a kong, or giant water vessel, which held cold water, and tipping it over themselves. The water was delivered in carts by coolies and was drawn from the Grand Canal. Talks given by some of the missionary doctors in the camp stressed how unsafe the water was 'as it was used by boats, and people lived on or by it, washing themselves and their clothes in it, and it was their lavatory. All these points were illustrated by quick chalk drawings ... We then looked again at our drinking water and realised that the thick sediment at the bottom might contain rather more than particles of earth and sand."[19] It was, also, always in very short supply. All the water for drinking had to be boiled first in the boiler room in large copper cauldrons, which were then tipped into 5-gallon bamboo buckets and taken to the kitchen. The ration, distributed every morning, was one thermos of boiling water per adult and half per child.[20]

Lunghwa also endured severe water shortages. As in Yangchow it was delivered daily to camp, where it was boiled and handed out to prisoners who carried it, boiling hot, in thermos flasks or teapots, back to their living quarters. Lunghwa internees were allowed a pint per person, available twice a day. Hot water, however, as Estelle Cliff was finding in Weihsien, was little use to thirsty children.

The only water in Lunghwa came either from ponds or from a well; it was brackish and, when used with soap, stubbornly refused to lather. Cold water for washing only ran through the pipes for ten minutes every couple of hours and water dominated eight-year-old Mary Hill's parents' life as they struggled to remain 'decent'.

The prisoners gave areas of camp jokey names that evoked home and better times. Hot water for washing was available from one of the distribution points, which had been given the names Waterloo or Dew Drop Inn – at 6.30 in the morning, having been heated in giant kongs by the stokers, who got up at 4 a.m. to provide this service.

'Dad used to rush to the pond,' said Mary, 'collect two buckets of cold water and place them in the queue outside Dew Drop Inn. After breakfast and roll-call he went back to collect the ONE bucket of water allowed. The reason for the early morning panic was that the buckets of cold water were tipped into the hot water before any hot water was taken out, and if your bucket was at the end, or even the middle of the queue, the probability was that the water you got out was as cold as what you had put in.'

The water, even when it had been boiled, often contained dead tadpoles and pond weed and had to be strained before it could be used. Clothes washing for a family of five with only an enamel basin and one bucket of warm water must have been soul-destroying, but Mary's mother was determined to keep up old standards. 'Mum would do it in the washroom and then wait for ten minutes of running water to rinse it. The wet clothes, sheets, towels etc. had to be carried down to the washing lines in buckets. In winter things froze as she hung them up and they would hang like that for days. Few people bothered to iron at all, but Mum did, using a charcoal iron.'

While many internees remember their skin being caked in dirt as a result of lack of water for washing, Mary's mother was determined her family would remain squeaky clean. 'Dad used to beg half a bucket of warm water from the kitchen in the evening, and this was divided between the four of us in a large enamel basin. Mum washed each of us from top to toe. Bob was the only one who could sit in the basin. Dad used to go off to the washroom with a bucket of cold water and have his wash down. Mum had her wash either when we were asleep, or if there was some left over from washing in the morning and Dad was at work.'

An attempt was made in Lunghwa to upgrade from the hated strip wash and instigate showers for the women but it was not a success. 'They had to take a bucket, soap and a towel. The idea was to soap oneself down, and the women in charge would shout water on and one would try to remove the soap, but invariably the shout water off came before anything like all the soap had been removed. The water was on for about two minutes!'

More successful was the camp's hair-washer who seemed able to lay hands on extra rations, building himself a little shack from which to ply his trade and offering a service in which the wash was hot and the rinse cold. 'We used to go to him because the water was then his problem.'[21]

In Yangchow, Western children found the primitive sanitary arrangements, traditional in central China, hard to get used to. The women who came in once a week to empty the buckets were dubbed with black humour 'glamour girls'. 'The Glamour Girls emptied the thunderboxes into wooden tubs, which swung at each end of the bamboo pole carried on the amah's shoulder. [They] emptied the tubs via a drain running through the wall, behind the laundry. The contents were collected outside the camp, to be spread on the fields as fertiliser by the thrifty Chinese. When there was sufficient water the Glamour Girls gave the buckets a cursory rinse with a bamboo whisk.'[22]

Concerns about hygiene and discomfort at the lack of privacy led some internees to create their own personal lavatory seats in Yangchow. Cyril Mack, missing his family's comfortable Custom House flat in Shanghai, described the peculiarly British embarrassment internees displayed when toting their customised seats. 'Almost overnight these portable devices mushroomed. In rapid time there were people to be seen everywhere, at all hours carrying these wooden frames; casually, embarrassingly, defiantly, shyly, nonchalantly, determinedly, ostentatiously, some standing and chatting, others in groups obviously off to a "conference", a few sliding along quietly trying not to attract too much attention, but all with a single purpose.'[23]

One of the things the children feared was the pitch-black of the camps at night, when any poisonous snake or insect might be lurking, ready to be unwittingly trodden on or grasped. Trips to the lavatory at night were to be avoided, but with so many gastric upsets caused by the doubtful food, the overcrowding and the enforced lack of hygiene, these were frequently necessary. Cyril Mack recalls the feeling of dread triggered by these trips.

'I would call out tentatively into the darkness to ask if there was anyone already enthroned. If there was, out of the blackness would come a reassuring response with knowledge of any "problems" discovered in the cubicle. If there was no answer you were very aware that you were on your own and that you were facing a slightly daunting situation . . . there was no alternative but to progress slowly into the suffocating darkness and grope my way to a cubicle, feel for toilet paper, search for the commode's seat, place my own seat in position on top with every movement preceded by fingertip touch, hoping not to come into contact with anything foul or poisonous (poisonous centipedes were a problem in most camps) and then finally exploring for the lid of the bucket. This last maneuver (sic) always prompted a most fervent prayer from me that the last person to have used the commode had indeed replaced the lid.'[24]

If the Japanese intention in the running of their Civil Internment Centres had been to take the white races down a peg or two they had certainly succeeded. The once-privileged children of empire had slid unceremoniously down the social hierarchy and were now living like the coolies they once commanded. Most of these children were with their families, however, and would bear the rigours cheerfully enough. A minority, however, found themselves coping with these drastic changes in their lives on their own. On these children internment would cast a longer shadow.

6

Writing Exams on Soup Tin Labels

They had almost none of the basics. They lacked paper, pencils, textbooks, dictionaries, maps, qualified staff, even tables and chairs. One thing many of the interned adults did not lack, however, was determination; determination that this setback would not blight the children's future by hampering their education. In camp after camp a small group of highly educated and dedicated men and women used a blend of ingenuity and will, coercion and cooperation to recreate, as closely as the unusual conditions permitted, the orderly classrooms the children had left behind in the pre-war colonial world. There were problems and children in some camps inevitably received a patchy education and found themselves behind after the war. In many cases, however, despite the obstacles, camp education was an outstanding success, with hundreds of children passing their School Certificate, the tough precursors of today's GCSE, just as they might if they had not spent nearly three years in a prison camp.*

They needed the permission of the Japanese authorities to set up schools. People interned in the Netherlands East Indies were explicitly forbidden to provide education facilities for their children, but in most of the camps in China, Hong Kong, Singapore and Manila the Japanese did not oppose the teaching of a basic curriculum. In

---

* The pre-war British education system offered two exams at secondary school age. School Certificate was sat at sixteen and required a pass in five subjects, which had to include English and maths. Matriculation was taken at seventeen-plus and was the gateway to university. Pupils who scored high marks in their School Cert. could be awarded Matriculation Exemption and could apply early to university.

Singapore the authorities were initially reluctant to allow classes but relented when an invitation to the children to learn Japanese met with an overwhelming response.[1] Most commandants imposed a ban on the teaching of history and geography on the grounds that it fostered the European pride in nationhood, which they were pledged to destroy.

The challenges facing the teachers were not limited to a lack of the basic raw materials of education. These men and women were teaching pupils who, as the war wore on, were often suffering the extremes of physical deprivation. Those interned in China were often cold, shivering in unheated huts with broken windows through which poured the snows of a grinding Chinese winter. They were hungry. Fed a tasteless subsistence diet lacking bulk or protein, they began to lack the normal energy of childhood, found it increasingly hard to concentrate and had trouble with their memory. They were ill. Form registers regularly listed children as absent through hospitalisation – brief respites when they were sent to be 'fattened up' or nursed for illnesses brought on by malnutrition, exhaustion and the poor hygiene engendered by overcrowding. In 1944 the school in Santo Tomas camp in Manila closed down and the pupils were told to rest as both teachers and taught were too lacking in energy. And in most camps the older boys were expected to help the men by doing fatigues round the camp on top of their school work.

Of all the various ways adults adapted to the challenges of internment, the way they managed the children's education is the most uplifting. The results – and the work the pupils were expected to put in to achieve them – would win A* in today's world of peace and plenty, but to have achieved such results in the teeth of such a Himalayan array of handicaps seems little short of miraculous. For this was not today's era of multiple choice questions; this was the time when children of nine learned not just French but Latin too and pupils starting secondary school wrote essays of 1,000 words. Many children who had learned their Latin verbs by writing them out with a stick in the dust of a camp parade ground were able to dovetail seamlessly into the British or Canadian or Australian education system after the war; some, who had written their exam answers on lavatory paper or the labels from soup tins, did so well that they went straight from camp to Oxford or Cambridge.

In spite of the fact that they had lost their freedom, there were a number of ways in which the children were fortunate. In many camps they had excellent teachers and small classes. The top class was rarely more than twelve. Before the war in China, Hong Kong and Malaya there were a number of excellent Western schools, the British ones staffed frequently by Oxbridge graduates. Because of this the tradition of sending European children 'home' to boarding schools was less developed than elsewhere in the colonial world. The Cathedral Schools in Shanghai and the corresponding Diocesan Schools in Hong Kong all had an excellent reputation, as did Shanghai's American School. In the north of China, Tientsin Grammar School was highly rated, as were several of the schools run by the Missions, notably that run by the China Inland Mission at Chefoo.

In China and Hong Kong whole communities of civilians had been interned, including many people at the top of their professions. This meant that the children were unusually fortunate in who they had to teach them. In some camps, such as Stanley, in Hong Kong, the entire staffs of high-achieving schools and university campuses had been interned. Bill Macauley, at fifteen, was taught English by the professor of English at Hong Kong University who was a great authority on Shakespeare – 'he would stand with the complete works of Shakespeare in his hand but he never needed to open it. He seemed to know most of the plays by heart.'

Even where this was not the case there were plenty of highly qualified professionals who could be roped in to teach their subject from personal experience without the need for textbooks. Often this made for more lively teaching. There were experts in navigation, surveying, history, trade; there were linguists, doctors, chemists, missionaries with their own academic area of interest. At Lunghwa camp (in Shanghai) there were over a dozen 'teachers', one of whom had been an analytical chemist with the Shanghai Municipal Council and who transformed himself into a physics teacher. A female missionary taught botany and a missionary doctor taught dissection and anatomy to youngsters who were aiming for a career in medicine.[2]

In Yangchow C camp, the boys were taught maths by a man who had been a surveyor: 'To impress on us the value of trigonometry he recounted stories of his surveying days in the wilds of Canada where, if he encountered a frozen lake, he had the choice of breaking the ice and wading or swimming across with a tape measure tied round his waist, or calculating the distance using the help of Pythagoras and trigonometry.'[3] Another teacher was a mountaineer. 'There weren't many places in the world he hadn't been. He'd climbed the mountains he taught us about and crossed most of the rivers.'[4]

In taking on the challenge of educating the children the adults had landed themselves with a mammoth task. Every stage of childhood development was represented in the camps, and each had its corresponding need. It began with the toddlers, who had to be made aware that there was a rich and varied world outside the arid confines of camp life, embraced junior school and ended with those, on the verge of adulthood, who needed to be prepared for university or taught a trade.

Surprisingly perhaps, to those who think that truculent adolescents might be the hardest to discipline, it turned out that it was sometimes the youngest children who presented the biggest headache. Like unbroken colts or pack dogs these children had missed out on the discipline of a normal family-based upbringing and, in a community where many adults had made day-to-day survival their main priority, were running wild.

Hope Lee, a Quaker missionary who was interned in Yu Yuen Road in Shanghai with her husband and small daughter, found parents' growing preoccupation with their own survival made the children very hard to control and intimidated the volunteers. 'Before the winter started ... Mr Southerton, an ex-schoolmaster came ... and asked if I would be willing to help with education for the younger children. It was needed badly enough, most of the children used to run wild like animals, all the parents cared about was to have them out of the way. The difficulties seemed endless ... Many of the helpers became unenthusiastic and had to be coaxed back each week to do their turn ... These were difficult children, or rather they had become difficult children due to circumstances. Many mothers could not see why the children should not be allowed to run wild over the campus all day long, and why it was necessary to organise something for them and exert a certain amount of discipline. Some of us who were [not] keen on our children playing in drains and growing up like savages had to work for all we were worth against the abysmal ignorance and don't care attitude of most of the residents.'[5]

Hope Lee paints an unprepossessing picture of urchins that would do credit to a latter-day Fagin, but the circumstances in which these children were trying to acquire a veneer of education were hardly conducive to civilised behaviour.

William Sewell, another missionary who was interned in Stanley with his wife and three young children, and who was also a university chemistry professor, was concerned at the effect the discomfort and lack of equipment was having on the children's development. 'At first there were no chairs and the children had lessons sitting or lying face down on straw mats on the floor, or kneeling on grass-filled cushions ... The shortage of paper and pencils meant that most of the children suffered from cramped style and lack of power of expression, though many became extraordinarily receptive and developed retentive memories.'

According to Sewell, who taught science at the camp's senior school, the poor diet meant that there was rarely a full class as children went in and out of the camp hospital to be treated for dysentery or to be fattened up. He noted that the school's meagre resources – desks and chairs in particular – had to be guarded from other inmates who would, given half a chance, have stolen them for fuel for private cooking.[6]

Despite these challenges, teachers throughout the camps continued to devise ingenious ways of maintaining a link, if only through imagination, between the youngest children and the world of freedom they had never known.

In Chapei camp (in Shanghai) the children were divided into two halves due to lack of space, with half starting at 9 a.m. and the other half after lunch. Age groups were divided from each other by curtains and discussion of objects not seen in camp became the priority. 'We pooled all our toys and any educational books and magazines ... We made percussion instruments out of old tins, cutting them into different shapes so that they produced a different sort of tinny noise ... we made up songs about motor cars, and various flowers and animals, so that the world outside would not be too strange for these little ones when they were released. In spite of all our educational difficulties, six teenagers sat an Oxford and Cambridge GC examination and they all passed.'[7]

In Changi prison on Singapore the Japanese ended up actively supporting the classes. Barbara Bruce says: 'After the great response to their invitation to us to learn Japanese they allowed us to be taught English and arithmetic. Eventually, due to the high number of school and university teachers in the camp, history and geography were also taught. Everything had to be done from memory as there were no books. Teachers drew maps from memory and the children were given slates and chalks by the Japanese, sitting on little stools, known as *bunkoos*, in a semi-circle in front of the teachers.'

These teachers were able to recite facts and dates, explain formulae, spout Shakespeare and the classics of English literature at length, and draw maps of continents or detailed charts of the rabbit's alimentary canal. And it was lucky for their charges that their elders came from that era of education when learning by heart, scorned by today's educationists as valueless, was deemed a key part of a pupil's development. How else would they have managed?

The teachers coped for the most part with good humour and a liberal dash of British eccentricity. In China during the winter of 1945 when the children were virtually starving, cold was a more bitter enemy than the Japanese. Children in Yu Yuen Road camp (in Shanghai) were taught by a former major in the Shanghai Volunteer Corps. Teaching the children in their coats, the major, who wore jodhpurs and riding boots, regularly interrupted classes to take the children for a 'canter'.[8]

Some took pride in ignoring the Japanese vetoes. Margaret Blair, a six-year-old in Yu Yuen Road was taught by an Anglican clergyman who defied the ban on geography, but taught it in rather an unorthodox style. He had a map of Britain (which the China-born children had never visited), which he pinned up on the wall of his cubicle, and with a long rule pointed out the towns on the railway routes in southern England. After the classes he took down the map and hid it under his bed.[9]

Children interned in Lunghwa were spoilt for choice when it came to teachers. Irene Duguid was sixteen when she went into camp, where the staff of two universities were interned with her. Irene, who was interned with her widowed mother, also a teacher, was taught French by a Belgian count, Latin by Jesuits, physics by an American scientist and other subjects by a mixture of nuns, doctors and missionaries and qualified school teachers. For the first two years the 'school' was a near derelict building outside the main compound and less heavily guarded. After a series of successful escapes this area was closed off and classes had to be in the dining huts. The lack of books and the idiosyncratic nature of camp education allowed teachers to give free rein to their own prejudices.

Irene's dismissive critique, in her English language prose and poetry exercise book, of the talents of many of our most revered writers remains startling:

'1771–1832: Sir Walter Scott wrote his novels at the end of his life to pay off his publishers' debts. Scott wrote poems at the beginning but found that Byron wrote better so he gave up writing poetry for novels which were very popular.'

Byron is described thus: 'Byron was more popular in his own day than any other poet. He was thought of all over the world as a hero of liberty.'

And Shelley: 'Shelley was not a good satirist for he had no sense of humour.'[10]

Her English teacher may have been a person of keenly held opinions, but what sixteen-year-old Irene studied in Lunghwa was a curriculum of impressive breadth, which combined the academic and the vocational. A handwritten copy of her syllabus for the year 1945, headed the 'Lunghwa Academy' and signed by the 'tutor' and the 'principal', shows that she was studying book-keeping, shorthand and elocution, but also English literature and criticism (they had read no less than four Shakespeare plays that year), French (regular dictation, reading, composition, poetry, vocabulary, idiom), ancient history ('Egypt, Sumeria, Babylonia, Greece, Rome to 202 BC based on Breasted's *A Brief History of Ancient Times*), hygiene and – cutting edge material for the time – psychology. The psychology course was described as 'an elementary study of memory, learning, perception, motivation, emotions ... intelligence tests ... industrial psychology'. The camp even boasted a laboratory where Irene learned how to test for malaria and intestinal diseases. Her hygiene course included a study of 'water borne diseases and water supply, airborne diseases and housing. Milk and vitamins. Diseases peculiar to camp. Tropical diseases and infectious diseases. Life history of fly and mosquito.'[11]

Children who graduated to secondary school education during internment, often found that the standards they were expected to reach in camp were substantially higher than the work they had been doing outside. David Nicoll had spent over a year before being interned camping with his parents and siblings in the Church Hall in Shanghai and not being unduly taxed by his studies. His first impression, on arriving in Chapei camp, which was predominantly American and possessed more books than many of the camps, was favourable. The modern, pragmatic style appealed to him. 'We really enjoyed the American books as they presented their subjects in a positive manner which encouraged interest, often including photographs related to the text; this was refreshing after the staidness of British school books . . . the mathematics books explained how to put money in, earn interest . . . in a practical way easy to comprehend.'[12]

After the Easter holidays of 1944, however, David moved up to secondary school and was daunted by the work his classmates were tackling. When you compare this level of study with what is expected of eleven-year-olds today you can see why. 'They were poring over lines from Julius Caesar that they were paraphrasing while I had never read any Shakespeare; French was far beyond my rudimentary vocabulary and I struggled to learn the many new words . . . as for mathematics, I just could not grasp how to calculate the cost of turf while allowing for a circular pond in the middle of a lawn; in Geography I had recently been learning about the Missouri River but the Seventh Grade were studying Japanese economic development during the twentieth century, the power of the five powerful industrial families, and the impact of yerba mate on South American economies.'

In secondary school no allowance was made for the fact that this was an internment camp. Pupils were expected to work in silence and elitism was actively encouraged.

'The headmaster was an American missionary and dedicated teacher, with high expectations of his students and a gift for bringing subjects to life by teaching them in a vividly practical way. He taught the boys astronomy from their superb vantage point out in the tropic night with no light pollution, and took them on field trips round the camp to study botany.

'One task he gave our class was to write a 1,000 word essay on an approved subject, to be completed in about 5 weeks. This seemed a daunting task for a 12-year-old but he started us on our way by writing out an immense list of possible subjects ... once the pupil and he had agreed the subject he would write down all the references to it appearing with his set of encyclopaedias for the pupil to look up. There would follow a further meeting to discuss the proposed layout of the essay and he guided us on how to present the paper to bring out all the points he wanted to make. Topics chosen ... included Volcanoes, Sea Shells, Bridges – mine was The Moon ...'

Chapei school devised its own way of encouraging pupils to win top marks. 'As a spur to grade-loyalty and good behaviour, also to encourage us to do our homework, a system of merits was introduced. Each month the grade in the Upper School with the most merits was awarded the shield for one month. This shield was specially made out of wood and was hung up on one of the notice boards in the Lobby. Any outstanding effort on the part of the Grade could be considered for the award of one or two merits, likewise any pupil's particular performance or behaviour ... At the end of the first month we in the 8th grade were happy to see our Grade's name marked on the shield.'[13]

In Stanley camp, after the Red Cross had supplied tables and chairs, high standards were quickly established thanks to the numbers of qualified teachers who had been interned. Lessons took place in the morning in the hall of St Stephen's College, which, before the war, had been a well-regarded school for Chinese boys. The school by then was within the confines of the camp. Bill Macauley was in the top class with only two other classmates. 'We simply carried on our School Cert. syllabus where we had left off.' The head of Hong Kong's Diocesan Girls' School also taught the older pupils. With no paper available they wrote their exercises out on labels scrounged from the kitchen staff and when supplies of these ran low switched to writing on slates. They could not do practical physics and chemistry due to the lack of any laboratory equipment but they pressed on with their theory. At the end of the school year in 1942 they took exams intended to replicate School Certificate in chemistry, physics, literature, history, geography and maths.

As Bill's academic education ended he moved into professional training. 'I found myself being taught by Charlotte Bird and Mrs Penny, who had been my ARP supervisors during the battle of Hong Kong when I had been a messenger. Before the war they had run a secretarial school in Hong Kong. I was taught typing, Pitman short-hand and book-keeping. We made makeshift keyboards from scrap pieces of wood, all marked out with the QWERTY keyboard. I got up to thirty-six words a minute with my shorthand. At the end of six months we were tested and awarded a certificate. Those skills proved useful. After the war I applied to join the RAF and was put to work in the section where they recruit potential clerks. I ended up marking all their typing papers and the WAAF tester thought I was as good as her. She was stunned when I told her I learned all my skills in a prison camp.'

Stanley was not the only camp to offer professional training but few can have served it up in such an unusual way as the youngsters who underwent their medical training in Lunghwa camp. Ron Huckstep was initially set on an engineering career, but he switched his affections as a result of the highly charismatic missionary doctor who was in charge of the health of the camp. The camp was sited in a Chinese school, which had been badly damaged during the Sino-Japanese War, and was surrounded by miles of paddy fields dotted with dozens of tall Chinese grave mounds dating back centuries.

'When we arrived the camp was in an incredible mess. Ruins, broken drains and unexploded detonators were scattered everywhere, and we all set to clear it up before the hot summer with the risk of typhoid and cholera was upon us. It was while digging and draining that numerous frogs and reptiles were disturbed. Somebody thought of dissecting them, and ... from these small beginnings there gradu-ally grew a medical school.'[14]

There were seven boys in the class. They sat at trestle tables made from spare lumber from around the camp and wrote their notes on brown paper bags. Dr Cater, the Cambridge-trained surgeon in charge of the health of the camp, who was their teacher, had their manual work switched from road-building to public health work 'so that a few practical hours each day in cleaning out cess pools, burying garbage, and laying drains was regarded as part of our Medical Education'. It proved fertile work.

'All sorts of ... animals emerged as we dug under the ruined buildings for pipes and bricks. It used to be quite an art catching a snake without killing it. When full of eggs, or after a meal they were quite slow, and we found they were powerless if grabbed behind the head. The larger ones however tended to wrap themselves round one's arm if their tails were allowed to touch the ground.'

At first the animals had to be kept alive until they could be dissected and this led to scares. 'One chaotic evening ... a six foot snake, two lizards, and a turtle escaped just before roll-call. They were in a cloth bag insecurely fastened at the neck. The snake, of doubtful toxicity, hid itself in a crack between two boxes in a corridor. The Jap on this occasion was a particularly obnoxious guard with beady eyes and he stationed himself in front of the boxes. Little did Snake Eye, as we called him afterwards, know how near the snake's fangs were to one of his Imperial Nipponese calves as he counted us.'

All practical work had to be conducted in secret as the sharp knives used in dissection and the wire-cutting tools used to make apparatus were totally forbidden and their discovery would have led to severe punishment. Things became easier when, while digging under some rubble, the boys discovered the remains of the school's laboratory, bombed six years previously. 'It provided material for practical work ... and also meant that animals could be preserved. It required some experimenting, but a mixture consisting of several unidentified white powders, a few evil smelling liquids, in a basis of crude creosote seemed to do the trick. Toads, snakes, and perhaps a couple of cats were then added to a dilute mixture of this brew in a large tub.' Not for nothing did the motto of the world's most unusual medical school become *Omnia Dissecamus* (We dissect everything).

One of the aspects of the Japanese character which the British found most repellent was their casual cruelty to animals. Hungry wild dogs roamed the countryside round the camp and a favourite pastime for bored guards was to trap the dogs in nooses and then stone them to death as they struggled on the wire. However, it became clear that for greenhorn medical students keen to improve their knowledge of anatomy the unfortunate animals were a godsend. Ron had the honour of retrieving the first victim.

'It was a huge wild brute killed the previous afternoon. After dark I set out to unhook it from the barbed wire. Crawling along a ditch I got within ten yards of it without being spotted. I lifted my head up, the coast was clear; the Japs at least twenty yards away in the guard house. I was just about to crawl the last few yards when I noticed another shadowy figure crouched just the other side of the wire. I said my prayers, and waited for the bullets, but none came. When I looked again the gentleman on the other side turned out to be a Chinaman after the same dog, probably for its skin. He was even more surprised than I was and fled.'

In fact, chronically hungry as they were by now, the boys' first thought as they opened the dog up, was that, instead of dissecting it, they should eat it. 'It was the first real meat that any of us had seen for almost a year, and at the sight of the glistening liver our mouths watered. But, with a few more slashes of the knife our hopes were dashed. The liver turned out to be full of flukes and the heart of long thin worms, so our thoughts turned reluctantly back to dissection.'

As the months wore on Dr Cater became more ambitious. To teach anatomy it was imperative to have a human skeleton. 'We had numerous bones and skulls of lower animals, and also the bones of two Buddhist monks buried several hundred years previously. These were unearthed while draining a swamp and were in large earthen jars. They were however too disintegrated to be of much practical use.'

Operation Skeleton was hatched in the summer of 1944. Half the camp was suffering from malaria, due to the paddy fields being a fertile breeding ground for mosquitoes, and Dr Cater decided something must be done. The Japanese were persuaded to supply the internees with Paris Green, a pesticide, to spray on the paddy fields. 'Two of us would go out every morning with two trigger-happy guards, two sprays, and a bag of Paris Green. We walked the Japs until the evening when they felt tired and their boots pinched. One of us would tell a limping guard that he knew something about medicine and examine the offending foot with a professional air. This he would try to do beside a ten foot grave mound, while the second guard looked on. Meanwhile the other chap would slip behind this mound, and if he could find an eroded pauper's grave would feel through the rotted coffin, and drag out the first bone that came to hand. This was then smuggled into camp in the Paris Green bag.'

It was rarely plain-sailing. 'It was amazing how many guards refused to have an ache or pain at the right grave mound, or would choose to sit facing the only eroded grave in the vicinity.'

It was also extremely risky. Ancestor worship was practised not only by the Chinese, but also by the Japanese, and the theft of bones, implying disrespect, would have been punished with the utmost severity. Impressively, however, by the end of three months they had all the main bones – except for the ulna. 'Try as we might we always seemed to bring out the radius rather than the ulna, and ... collected no fewer than four in our attempts.'

In the summer of 1944 a major upheaval in the camp nearly closed the medical school for good. Five prisoners escaped and as was the Japanese way, savage reprisals were wrought on those who remained. Nineteen men who had shared a room with the escapees were taken away and tortured, among them a lad a year older than Ron called Louis who was also studying medicine. Three of the men never returned from their interrogation and the medical student was so shattered by having been tortured that he gave up on his education and dropped out of classes. Escapes always led to hut by hut searches and the fledgling medical students were worried their stash would be uncovered. 'We hid all the bones and equipment we could. The Japs, however, put the hut, in which our animals were, out of bounds before we could get at them, and for about five months they stayed there undiscovered in a tub under a pile of wood. All through the rest of that hot summer and the beginning of the winter, we thought of our animals getting higher and higher. Besides the usual animals we had just acquired some foetal pigs and foetal goats from a farm we had just started. The preservative would only keep them for about a month, so you can imagine the cheating that went on when lots were drawn to select the burial party when we finally did get to them.'

Ron's unusual training was good enough not only to win him a place at Cambridge after the war (where his tutor turned out to be Dr Cater), but also to allow him to finish his BA in two years instead of the customary three.

In Weihsien in northern China there was no shortage of teachers as the staff of Tientsin Grammar School had been interned with many of its pupils. There were also a few teachers from Peking, as well as mission teachers who had been teaching Chinese at mission stations. The problem was lack of materials and suitable premises. Tientsin School had been seized by the Japanese on 8 December 1941 and prisoners had entered camp with no textbooks and very little in the way of paper, pencils and pens. Ron Bridge, who was interned as a nine-year-old with his mother, father and baby brother, says, 'It was chaos at first, but by June classes were started. In summer they were often held in the open. We didn't have anything to write with, so, when it came to Latin, we wrote out our verbs in the dust with a stick. When it was too cold or wet to be outdoors we had lessons in the church. One form would occupy a couple of rows of pews, while another age group would use the spaces two or three rows back.'

The plight of the older children, who were reaching the age when they should be taking public exams, began to concern the teachers in Weihsien. Nothing was organised for 1943 because the British adults in camp expected they would be repatriated, as so many American and Canadian internees had been. But by 1944 they had accepted that there would be no early end to their imprisonment. Following contact with the camps in Shanghai they decided to set and mark their own exams, trusting that the relevant authority would accept them post-war. By the time this plan was adopted the child population of Weihsien had been increased by the arrival of the staff and pupils of Chefoo School in September 1943. Chefoo School had traditionally taken the Oxford Matriculation Exemption school-leaving exams, which were sent to England by ship for marking. When war broke out in Europe the teachers feared there would be a risk of valuable exam papers being lost through shipping being sunk and had presciently hidden away extra copies. Estelle Cliff, a Chefoo pupil, was interned in Weihsen at fourteen, with her sixteen-year-old sister and eighteen-year-old brother.

'With all the disturbances in our lives we got behind. My sister had been ill before we went into camp and had dropped a class. Then there was further delay caused by going into camp. Her class eventually sat their exams in May 1945. We were due to take our mocks' in June 1945 and the exam itself in October.' The end of the war, however, triggered a change of plan. Concerned that his sixteen-year-olds would miss the boat the headmaster of Chefoo School P. A. Bruce, known as Pa, recommended they take the exam straight away. They were given a week to prepare and found themselves taking exams in the middle of the upheaval of liberation.

'In order not to miss the action, planes going over dropping food parcels,' Estelle recalled, 'I sat outside – under a tree for protection from stray parcels. When there was no action I sat on the bank of the little stream that flowed past the front gate. As we sat the exam, the cicadas were buzzing, planes flying over and goodness knows what we were missing. But we managed to shut all that out and concentrate on the job in hand.'

Pa Bruce personally took the papers to Oxford when he finally arrived in Britain. Estelle and her sister received their results in April 1946. They had both passed and went on to study pharmacy. Some former Weihsien prisoners became teachers themselves. One man who had his first Latin and French lessons sitting on a cabin trunk instead of at desks became a Latin teacher and took pride in being able, decades later, to say the Lord's Prayer in French.[15]

At Yangchow C camp, hidden away in the interior of China, education was also taken extremely seriously. Children started French at six and the boys started Latin at eight. The teaching of Latin was initially hampered by a lack of a dictionary, put right when the Red Cross sent one in. In addition to the whole range of academic subjects time was also devoted to vocational training – shorthand, accountancy and book-keeping, as well as anatomy and physiology for those planning a medical degree. Among the internees were two teachers from the two top schools in Shanghai and they took on the boys and girls respectively. There were also some very bright pupils. At least two went to Oxford and three became doctors.

Education in camp was run by a man called P. C. Matthews, an unmarried Anglican clergyman in his late forties who had run the Shanghai Cathedral Boys' School. With his ubiquitous pipe and sporting the thick glasses of the chronically short-sighted, Matthews, who had a first-class degree in Classics, was a cartoonist's dream. A teacher of the old school Matthews ordained that the boys in the top form sat in the classroom in order of achievement.[16] Domineering and not suffering fools or slackers gladly he was not universally popular, but he was a dedicated teacher. Before internment he had instructed his boys at the Cathedral Boys' School to take textbooks in with them and one boy took Kennedy's Latin primer and some mathematical tables.

From the start the shortage of paper in camp posed serious problems. Neil Begley was one of PCM's younger pupils. 'The camp committee issued a notice that no piece of paper was to be used for any purpose until it had been written on both sides. Coarse toilet paper called Clo Pah in Chinese, was available and this was used for exercises and homework before being put to its original purpose.'[17]

Matthews expected anyone with a degree to volunteer for teaching, whether they had experience or not. One father, who had an arts degree, was press-ganged into teaching English literature and history to the senior boys after parents complained about the standard of teaching in those subjects.[18] The science teacher was a Canadian evangelical Christian missionary who made regular references to the Genesis version of the creation of the world in his lessons – until forbidden to do so by outraged parents.

All this high-powered, and on occasion eccentric, teaching took place in the most spartan conditions. Cyril Mack, who was eleven when he was interned, says they were always desperately uncomfortable in their makeshift classroom, which was a room about 18 feet by 14 feet, the floor of which was inadequately covered with small broken concrete tiles laid directly onto the earth. 'In the summer the floor became a dustbowl and in winter the damp seeped up from the ground. A skylight let in extra light but leaked profusely in wet weather. There were three window frames, in which all the glass panes were missing. The blackboard was a thin sheet of iron, pitted with indentations, nailed to one wall ... chalk would slip and slide across the surface and it was always difficult to discern what had been written.'

In the summer the children were tormented by biting insects that swarmed in through the broken panes, but winter was worse. 'Icy winds whistled in and snow floated into the room. The students sat at desks clad in coats. Woollens, balaclavas, gloves, mittens and two pairs of socks, shivering from the cold and each taking turns to go into a corner to do the "postman's slap" in an effort to warm up. Eventually the window frames were taken out and dozens of fragments of glass, of all sizes and shapes, were cobbled together with tiny bolts and nuts and washers to fill the frames.'[19]

Not a man to let standards slip merely because conditions were tough, Matthews behaved in camp as he would have done in the classrooms of the Cathedral Boys' School in Shanghai. Any boy who made a mistake in a Latin unseen was expected to redo the entire exercise – even though the 'exercise book' was paper peeled from old cans.[20] A disciplinarian of the old school Matthews believed that the cane was the best punishment for growing lads. Neil Begley was caught throwing a tennis ball at a pecan tree to dislodge a nut and was sent to PCM for a highly ritualised six of the best:

> Matthews: 'Why are you here, boy? Speak up boy. Speak up like a man.'
> Begley (nervously): 'I was sent to see you Sir.'
> Matthews: 'Do you know what you're here for boy … well do you? Speak up boy, speak up!' The lips moved as he spoke but the teeth remained clamped firmly onto the pipe stem.
> Begley: 'Yes Sir.'
> Matthews: 'You know you've broken the rules boy?'
> 'Yes Sir.'
> 'You know what the penalty is?'
> 'Yes Sir.'
> 'Well take it like a man. Bend down and touch your toes.'
> Then PC checked your shorts for any padding.
> 'Y'ready boy?'
> 'Yes Sir.'
> There was the swish of the cane and the sting of the first cut.
> 'One' you'd count under your breath, biting your lips in case you let out a cry, 'three, four, five,' then finally 'six.'
> It was over and you hadn't cracked.
> 'Stand up boy,' PC was saying, 'stand up and rub it. Rub it boy. Get the circulation going that's the ticket.'
> While you fought back the tears he'd go over to the little table and from his thermos pour out two precious rations of tea. Somehow, we never knew how, he'd conjure up a couple of biscuits, invite you to sit down on the bed and serve you a cup with one of the biscuits. He'd talk to you about general matters and then, when the tea was finished, dismiss you. As you headed for the door, he'd shake you by the hand and say,
> 'You broke the rules boy, you've taken your punishment like a man. I'm proud of you boy. This will never be raised between us again.' And he meant it.[21]

The dedication of so many teachers throughout the camps is never more evident than when it came to the setting and marking of exams.

Two pictures that evoke the seemingly eternal charm of ex-pat life in China before the war: (*left*) Bill Macauley (on the right) in Hangkow in 1937; and (*below*) in the Diocesan Boys School First Eleven cricket club in spring 1941 (back row, second from right). He was separated from his parents for the whole of his internment.

(*Bill Macauley*)

Neil Begley in his mother's arms in Peking. His parents were Salvation Army missionaries.

(*Neil Begley*)

Four school friends pose together in Singapore before the war. Ralph Armstrong, whose entire family would die in the lethal camps of Sumatra, is on the right.

(*Ralph Armstrong*)

Ron Bridge was interned at the age of nine with his mother and baby brother in Weihsien camp in northern China. His family, like all 'enemy aliens', were obliged to wear these identity badges when Japan entered the war. (*Ron Bridge*)

Children at Lunghwa camp near Shanghai.
Lunghwa had one of the biggest populations of child internees. (*Greg Leck*)

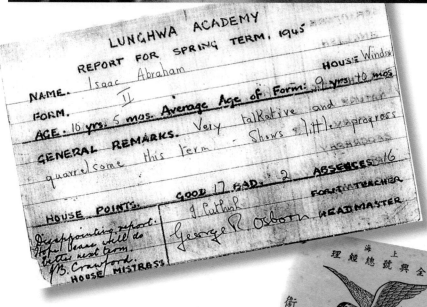

LUNGHWA ACADEMY

REPORT FOR SPRING TERM, 1945

NAME. Isaac Abraham   HOUSE Windsor

FORM. II

AGE: 16 yrs. 5 mos. Average Age of Form: 9 yrs. 10 mos.

GENERAL REMARKS. Very talkative and quarrelsome this term – shows little progress

HOUSE POINTS.   GOOD 17 BAD: 2   ABSENCES 16

FORM TEACHER.

Disappointing report. Hope Isaac will do better next term. M.B. Crawford. HOUSE MISTRESS

George R. Osborn HEADMASTER

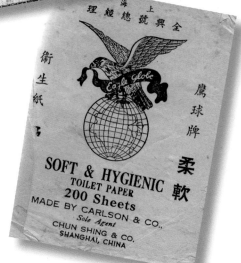

Top: As this classroom in Lunghwa
camp shows, education in the camps
was often of a surprisingly high standard.
Teachers were demanding in their
reports (*above*) and resourceful in finding
equipment: toilet paper (*right*) was often
used for writing exercises, before being
consigned to the latrines.

(*Victoria Morley; Isaac Abrahams; Barbara Tilbury*).

Adults devised endless entertainments to prevent children from running wild in the long, unstructured days of internment. Here children play old-fashioned games in Weihsien camp, and a young girl is crowned Queen of the May in Ash camp in Shanghai. The 2nd Chefoo Girl Guides Company simply reformed in Weihsien camp. Its members included Joyce Kerry (back row, second from left), Estelle Cliff (sixth from left) and K Strange (front row, far left).   (*Japanese Ministry of Foreign Affairs, Diplomatic Record Office; Joyce Storey*)

Father Thornton, the inspirational Roman Catholic priest who taught Form Two at Yangchow C camp, called the boys 'little heroes' for the stoical way they put up with hunger and cold. Neil Begley is on the far right with a bandage round his leg; Cyril Mack is second from left on the front row. (*Neil Begley*)

Left: There were few toys for children in camp. This toy version of the chatty (or stove) that loomed so large in camp life, started out as a tin of instant coffee. (*Barbara Tilbury*)

Right: The poor quality of fuel made fires hard to light. Here two children in Lunghwa use a bamboo fan to light a chatty made from an old food tin. (*Barbara Tilbury*)

Sylvia Williams washing up with her parents. Her father weighed fifteen stone before he was imprisoned and only nine when he came out due to the scarcity of food in their last year in Santo Tomas camp. (*Sylvia Williams*)

Queuing for unappetising and inadequate rations of SOS ('Same Old Stew') dominated camp life. (*Neil Begley*)

An emaciated young woman in Stanley camp, Hong Kong, shows a portion of rice that had to feed five people. (*IWM*)

The water in the Indonesian camps was often polluted. Thirsty children regularly contracted dysentery through drinking unboiled water. (*IWM*)

In some instances, as in Weihsien, they had kept copies of the actual papers. In other camps teachers pooled their mental resources to set questions, mark papers and then, as Pa Bruce had done, carefully save them until the end of the war. In their unusually communal environment some teachers felt the need to mount a twenty-four-hour guard over the papers.

In Stanley, where two sets of Matriculation papers were taken with excellent results, and a third only prevented by liberation, the exams were set by interned members of Hong Kong University. After the war they were sent to the University of London, which recognised them. The last exams were written on toilet paper. One of the co-opted examiners recalls the hazards they were up against. 'You should have seen us typing those question papers! Instead of doing them behind the locked doors of the University Examination Room, we enjoyed the privacy of the cubicle shared with others. We had only one small table and when both were working at the same time, I typed sitting on my bed, with the machine on my knees. Until the registrar collected those papers, because I had no means of locking them up for safe keeping, I sat on them by day and slept on them by night.'[22]

Over and over again the results were accepted by the various examination boards in England to which they were faithfully sent. PCM sent Yangchow's School Certificate results – written on tin labels from Red Cross parcels carefully bound into book form – to Cambridge University after the war. Eleven passed their School Certificate and five won Matriculation Exemption.[23] At Lunghwa, fifty pupils passed their School Certificate of which twelve obtained Cambridge Matriculation Exemption. In Chapei six teenagers sat the Oxford and Cambridge School Certificate. All passed and one boy got to Oxford on the strength of his 1944 result. In Weihsien, where the whole of Chefoo School had been interned with their teachers, pupils sat the School Certificate in 1943 and 1944.[24] The papers were submitted to Oxford after the war with several gaining Matriculation Exemption.

Internment represented an unprecedentedly harsh time in these young lives, but there were benefits. And some would last a lifetime. Among the children's volunteer teachers were men and women of quite extraordinary dedication and charisma, whose influence on occasion would leave a permanent impression on the lives of their young charges. Father Thornton was one of these. James Thornton was an Irish-American Jesuit who was interned in Yangchow C camp and was a rather unlikely cleric. He had only been ordained a year before war broke out and had left his native Ireland for America specifically to avoid having to teach, which Irish Jesuits are required to do. Father Thornton rattled through Mass in record time and rarely wore his cassock round camp. Energetic and ebullient he was known for his loud and unmistakable laugh and his fondness for softball and bridge. Ironically the priest, whose thick Irish brogue was matched only by his passion for English literature, soon found himself pressed into teaching English to a group of young girls and boys. Thornton was a demanding teacher. In this world where books were a precious rarity he was able to recite entire scenes from Shakespeare plays, and expected his pupils to read a Scott or Dickens novel every week. He regularly set them chunks of text to learn by heart – '32 verses of Gray's Elegy or 21 of Shelley's Ode to a Skylark'.[25] Far from resenting it many of his formal pupils take pride in the fact that they can still recite them today.

Neil Begley, who had been caned by PCM, was in Father Thornton's English class.

'He recited to us in chunks and we learnt it that way. We had to be able to quote Mark Anthony's speech over the body of Caesar, Tennyson's Brook or Shelley's Skylark, Wordsworth's Daffodils and Upon Westminster Bridge; Thomas Gray's Elegy Written in a Country Churchyard and The Ancient Mariner from beginning to end.'[26] Learning by heart has fallen out of fashion among today's teachers, but Neil Begley believes Father Thornton did him a great favour. 'They were all learnt, never to be forgotten and how grateful I am to him for the rich memory of those words that have kept me company through seemingly endless sleepless nights or on long trips or during times of quiet contemplation.'[27]

Cyril Mack was another pupil for whom, in a Spartan Chinese prison camp, Father Thornton unlocked the magic gates of English poetry. Cyril stood next to the priest at roll-call, where he towered, not only over the young schoolboy, but over most of the guards as well.

'[He] brought some softness and beauty and laughter into our lives with his stories and his poetry. His voice used to grip us and draw us into the poems – we sat in Thomas Gray's country churchyard and we were the ploughman plodding homeward in the evening light. Each one of us was the Ancient Mariner with the albatross around his neck floating in a "painted ship [up]on a painted ocean".

'Father Thornton understood us better than anyone. We worked with him and for him and in return he read to us stories like *Treasure Island* and *Kidnapped*, acting out all the various characters, assuming all the different voices and the variety of accents. You cannot imagine what it all sounded like mixed in with his own heavy Irish-American accent. But it was magic to us and we loved him for it. Sitting in that classroom in the gloom of late afternoon, in that final frigid winter, we were held spellbound by the sound of his voice. We were very cold, very hungry, and very tired and he gave us sunshine, magic and romance. He would take us out of our surroundings ... we would be on this beautiful tropical island or in the raging waters off the Scottish coast. We would sit huddled for warmth in our coats and balaclavas and scarves ... Often he could barely see the words on the pages because by then we had no electricity so he would sometimes stand with his back to the windows to find some reflection from the snow lying outside and would continue to act out each character until it was too dark to see the writing on the pages. Then he would say, "Sorry boys, goodnight and God bless you", shut the book and stride off into the snow.'[28]

What Cyril Mack describes so eloquently is a gifted teacher. And yet, had it not been for the war no one would have ever known that Father James Thornton was born to teach.

7

A Healthy Mind in a Healthy Body

T he same group of dedicated adults who insisted that children
be educated were equally determined that they should not be
deprived of artistic stimulus. The sheer variety of callings, professions
and cultures represented by the internees and the unusual amount of
time they had to fill combined in many camps to create a pool of
remarkably creative artistic endeavour. This at least was the case
during 1943, which for internees in China was the first year of
internment. Morale was high – many adults still believed the war
would soon be over and they would be freed within months; food
was adequate and families were still able to buy the extras that made
life bearable and people's health was on the whole still good. As the
adults directed that summer's Shakespeare or composed amusing
coded songs which mocked their captors, they had no idea that by
the middle of the following year the children they happily dressed in
makeshift costumes run up from curtains and tablecloths would be
ransacking dustbins for food and that many of their number would
be too weak from lack of food to take any interest in art or entertainment. It is all the more impressive that such varied efforts were
doggedly sustained and upheld against a background of random
violence where men and women were liable to be viciously slapped
for the most trivial of offences.

But this was a talented and resourceful generation used to creating
much of its own entertainment. Almost everyone had a skill. They
could play the piano, or paint a backcloth, knit and use a sewing
machine. Shortages seemed to trigger greater inventiveness. One
camp had a man who was an accomplished sign painter. He made a

red paint from ground bricks and a black ink from coal dust and used them to paint scenery for plays, to dye costumes and to paint toys for the children at Christmas. As with art, so with music. If you couldn't play a bona fide instrument you used a comb and paper.

In the unlikely setting of a prison camp some children watched, heard and participated in concerts, dance shows, plays, operettas, pantomimes, music hall, skits, recitations, sing-songs and record recitals with a frequency that, even in those pre-television days, would have been unlikely in peacetime. Some children recall being read aloud to. Mary Hill was one of them: 'One wonderful man in the summer evenings would read to us. A tremendous crowd of children would gather and sit as quiet as mice, about the only time we ever were. I remember *Children of the New Forest* and *The Cloister and the Hearth* particularly.'

These cultural events were pointedly performed on festival days imbued with patriotic, morale-boosting significance – Empire Day, May Day, Easter. Listening to recitals or comedy sketches in the velvet darkness of a tropical night, with a multitude of stars overhead and fireflies flitting among the audience, constitute, for many former internees, memories of real happiness. For some, a lifelong love of classical music began in an internment camp.

Young girls who dreamed of becoming dancers benefited from the presence of high numbers of Russian women in camps, some of whom had reached the top of their profession. Margaret Blair, whose mother had been beaten by a Japanese guard for being late for roll-call in Yu Yuen Road, was taught ballet by a woman who had danced in and choreographed several silent films. 'We regarded her as a rather exotic person, to be respected. She taught in a very professional manner. In the concert hall she put us through our paces with a Von, Two, Tree. We had no barre equipment. On good weather days we practised our back bends on the grass ... I was never able to do a back bend. One day Mrs Edwards watched me as I tried and said, "If I could have you when you were tree, then I could do something with you."'

Despite her lack of suppleness, Margaret was selected to lead the corps de ballet onto the stage at the right moment during concerts. The girls spent much of their time practising for the various ballet shows that were put on during their internment.

A special modern dance show, devised to celebrate Easter, was nearly wrecked when stage fright overtook the younger stars. 'I was a (relatively) large rabbit standing beside a big Easter egg made of two large baskets covered with brown paper. When I whispered through the brown paper that it was the right time, some small rabbits (three or four years old) were to burst through and do a dance. We were just about to open the stage curtains when one little rabbit said, "I want to go to the bathroom." This feeling was infectious. Soon there was a chorus of, "I want to go to the bathroom." The mothers had to unpick and re-sew almost all of the costumes before we could open the show.'[2]

Drama played an important part in many camps in China. In Yangchow C camp, with its unwavering emphasis on the importance of high culture incarnated in P. C. Matthews, the 'school' held an annual speech day. This culminated in a production of a scene from a Shakespeare play, one performed by the girls' school, one by the boys'. In 1943 the boys did *Twelfth Night*, with Keith Martin playing Malvolio in traditional yellow stockings, while the girls did some scenes from *As You Like It*. The following year the boys did the trial scene from *The Merchant of Venice*. The sixth-formers tackled Shaw's *Androcles and the Lion*. A sign of the relatively good relations between the internees and their captors is that the camp commandant presented the form prizes at speech day. Even at Yangchow C, however, it was not all highbrow. They put on pantomimes, which were very popular. Aladdin, in which one of the sixth-formers played the slave of the lamp, was a great morale-booster. It was performed early in the winter of 1945, when conditions were at their worst and the prisoners were starting to despair of ever being freed.

Other camps held regular art exhibitions, Saturday night dances, lectures, displays of national dancing, and even 'best-decorated hat' contests. Teenagers in Yangchow B camp, where David Nicoll was first interned, made a 4-foot-long cardboard model of the camp based on sketches of all the buildings. Children there celebrated May Day with a display of country dancing to a fiddle accompaniment and a dance round a Maypole. Empire Day was celebrated with a Hat Parade, a display of country dancing accompanied by bagpipes and ending with a 'camp fire', which was in fact a light bulb at the end of a lead instead of a real fire as fuel was becoming scarce.[3]

At Easter 1944, despite the deteriorating conditions, they set up a Children's Theatre. This, David Nicoll recalls, consisted of 'a short play set in the time of Charles 1; various dances; a skit written by a Dutch boy and performed by him and me; Pyramus and Thisbe from *A Midsummer Night's Dream*; and as the finale 'Wooden Soldiers' danced by five girls to music hummed by us boys on comb and paper ... After the last performance each of us was given an Easter Egg, a hard-boiled hen's egg with the shell painted in a decorative design.'[4]

In many of the camps music played an even bigger role than drama. In Weihsien, in the far north of China, they set up a choir, directed by a woman missionary from the China Inland Mission. It gave a varied programme, which ranged from Gilbert and Sullivan to Bach. Major performances featured the *Messiah*, Sir John Stainer's *The Crucifixion* and J. H. Maunder's *Olivet to Calvary*, the latter two relatively new sacred works that were very popular at the time. Among the internees in Weihsien were some entertainment groups which had formed part of the Western community in the big cities in north China. This included a black jazz band, which provided a vibrant contrast to the largely religious music favoured by the choir. David Michell, who had been a pupil at Chefoo School, a school run by the China Inland Mission, had led, as he admitted, a very sheltered life in the missionary compound and had never seen a black person before, never mind heard jazz performed.[5]

In Singapore Mel Bruce learned the basics of guitar-playing as other nationalities began to join the British in internment – French, Hungarian and Russian. Many of the newer internees brought musical instruments in with them and eventually a twenty-strong orchestra was formed. Mel palled up with a musically gifted Jewish lad who played the guitar, saxophone and accordion, and he taught him the basic chords so that he could join in and strum along with the band.

They also had a choir in Yu Yuen Road camp in Shanghai, conducted by the former headmaster of Tientsin Grammar School. There was already a piano in camp and the accompanist was the wife of one of the missionary doctors. They sang a similar selection to Weihsien – but they had a secret reason for choosing *The Crucifixion*.

Maureen Collins was interned at fifteen in Yu Yuen Road with her parents and brother, who was three years younger than her; her father was chief architect to the Shanghai Municipal Council. She says, 'We liked that [*The Crucifixion*] because it contained the phrase "fling wide the gates", which was a sort of code. The Japanese guards used to attend our concerts. They always sat in the front row. They understood a bit of English – some of the officers had even been to England – but I don't think they understood that.'

Children in Yu Yuen Road saw some good performances of Shakespeare. People produced bits of material which the women turned into costumes and someone painted a highly professional backcloth. As with all amateur dramatics, however, there could be snags. Hope Lee, a Quaker missionary, was one of the driving forces behind the staging of several Shakespeare plays, playing Olivia to her husband's Malvolio in *Twelfth Night*.

On the second night Mrs Lee was on stage calling for Malvolio – but Malvolio did not appear. 'Thinking that my voice had not carried backstage, I called again – still no Malvolio ... so I paced the stage with impatience, examined my rings, walked round my seat exhibiting much annoyance and once more called "Malvolio!" At last he appeared smiling a rather stupid smile ... and so we proceeded, with me in quite a tantrum.'

There had been a crisis backstage. Neighbours had heard the Lees' baby crying and had gone in to see what was the matter. One of the camp cats had got into their hut, climbed on top of the baby's mosquito net and made a puddle, which had dripped onto her and woken her. The neighbour did not know where to find dry clothes and bedding and sent her husband backstage to find the parents.

'He found Kenneth as I was on stage and was in the middle of explanations when Kenneth heard a desperate call for Malvolio coming from the stage. He just managed to get over to Mr B what to do ... as he rushed back onto the stage. He conjured up this frightful smile in order to reassure me!'[6]

The Red Cross worked tirelessly to improve the comfort and morale of the internees. Food parcels, though eagerly awaited, were not the only items they provided. Their provision of cultural nourishment, such as books and musical instruments, were much appreciated. But they could never have imagined how much the gift of two pianos to Chapei camp in the summer of 1945 would delight one young boy interned there.

The concert was a tour de force in itself. It was to be a dance display to be set to Beethoven's Fifth. The whole symphony had been transcribed for two pianos. David Nicoll sat in on rehearsals. 'I had never heard music remotely like this, to me it sounded fantastic ... especially the opening sequence of the Second Movement which I reckoned had the most wonderful tune in the world.' Eventually the concert was announced on the notice board in a flyer featuring Peace, Hope and the Future under a picture of searchlights criss-crossing a night sky. David attended all four of the performances and suspects he was the only child to show such commitment. He says he has never heard a performance of the Fifth that outshone that first thrilling performance.

'For me the music of the pianos will never be equalled because each note was distinct and given due value, a thing I have always found lacking in subsequent hearings of the symphony played by an orchestra.'

Nourishing the spirit was important, but exercising growing bodies was considered no less vital. There was a crushing feeling of claustrophobia about internment – evidenced by the well-beaten track just inside the perimeter fence where the prisoners walked like the caged beasts they were.

Neil Begley recalls the track they walked in Yangchow C: 'Around the perimeter of the camp ... there was a well-trodden track that you'd walk when you needed to be alone, or if you needed company, or if you needed to think, or you couldn't bear to think any more. Inmates would walk round and round, singly, in pairs or in groups, hour after hour, day after day. It was the major camp occupation. Some folk played bridge, some chess, some played board games like Monopoly, or sat around and yarned, but everyone walked.'[7]

The natural energy of the children needed channelling and sport injected an element of structure into the long otherwise empty days. Plenty of sport was played, at least during the first year. *Mens sana in corpore sano* (a healthy mind in a healthy body), as the old adage decreed, and the adults did their best to promote it. By the close of 1944, though, in many camps the children were too weak through hunger to run about. In some the playing fields were dug up and turned into vegetable patches to supplement the meagre rations. Most of the camps in China were sited in large compounds which before the war had either been missions or educational establishments and therefore had considerable space for playing fields at their disposal. The most popular sport was softball, an American version of rounders, but football, rugby, hockey and cricket were also played. Many camps held 'school' sports days, featuring old favourites like three-legged races and sack races, as well as 100-yard sprints, long jump and putting the shot. Leagues of softball were organised in Weihsien, where, in the early days, the Catholic priests fielded a keen team, as well as in camps in Shanghai including Chapei, Ash Camp, Lunghwa and Pootung. The Japanese enjoyed sport and often put themselves forward as opponents. Sometimes the commandant presented prizes at sports day. Pootung camp held baseball matches against the guards and used the occasions to tease them. In Lunghwa camp the three boys who won the 100-yard sprint were summoned to the office of Mr Hyashi, the commandant, and given a bag of sweets as a prize. In Yangchow C, where P. C. Matthews ran the closest thing you could get to a British public school in an internment camp, competitive sport and daily exercise were considered an essential part of the curriculum. The boys did football, rugby and boxing, and the winner of a boxing bout earned an extra loaf. The girls played hockey in winter. In summer both sexes played softball.

Many adults in Yangchow camp worried about the risk of the children becoming feral with so few constraints and so much time on their hands. In a bid to avert this it was decided that the boys would do early morning gymnastics and body-building with a man who had run a gym in Shanghai. His initials were LPQ, which the boys translated as Low Pee Koo, the Chinese for 'old backside'.

Neil Begley enjoyed those sessions, despite the early start. 'At 5.30 in the morning he'd assemble us in a corner of the camp grounds and put us through all sorts of physical training. We did arm, leg and stomach exercises. We did push-ups and chinned the bar on tree branches. To strengthen our stomach muscles we'd take turns sitting on a bench with someone holding our feet, then bend back till our heads touched the ground then forward to bring our head between our knees. For dumbbells and weights we used bricks. In spite of our poor diet we became surprisingly fit and very strong. He set us objectives then he forced us to attain them: 100 push-ups, 100 chin-ups of the bar, 200 sit-ups. We took great pride in our muscles and had competitions, taking turns punching each other to see how much punishment we could endure.'[8]

Children in Weihsien camp arguably had better sports coaching as internees than they would have had if they had remained free. Interned with them was every boy's hero in those days, the 1924 Olympic gold medallist Eric Liddell, whose 400 metre triumph was immortalised in the film *Chariots of Fire*. Liddell had gone out to China shortly after his sporting victory to work on behalf of the London Missionary Society. A modest man, he was popular with the children and helped organise athletic events and sports days.

David Michell, a missionary's son who was ten when he went into Weihsien, recalled the kindness of the man behind the legend. 'I remember him as umpire of our soccer games which we used to play barefoot on the athletic field by the church. He tore up the sheets he had brought into camp so that he could bind up the field-hockey sticks ... he always inspired enthusiasm as he found ways to keep the sports side of camp life going. To all of us young people in camp he was known as Uncle Eric ... he stood out as kind and friendly with his ever present smile and gentle ... manner. He was a true Christian gentleman.'[9]

In most camps entertainment committees worked hard finding ways to fill the time. Teenagers found the long evenings particularly boring. In Lunghwa, where no one was allowed out of their own block after 9 p.m., Irene Duguid recalls adults reading or playing games – mah-jong, bridge and patience. As they prepared people for internment the British Residents' Association had asked everyone to bring three books into camp with a view to building a camp library but there were a lot of duplications. There were at least 150 copies of *Gone With the Wind*, the bestseller of the 1940s. There were also a few wind-up gramophones, but again, a limited number of records. 'We knew every word on the records by heart by the time the war ended.'[10]

Younger children were often better catered for than the teenagers. The adults played tennis, attended lectures or held jam sessions, where musicians got together to give impromptu concerts on instruments they had brought into camp. While they did this the children had officially sanctioned letting-off-steam game evenings 'when youths and we younger ones could play active games like chasing one another round a table while blindfolded'. One Hallowe'en there was a fancy dress party. David Nicoll went as a newspaper boy, 'cap on at an angle, cigarette dangling from my lips and newspapers under one arm'. They could have been leading a normal childhood, but for the fact that there was no slap-up party tea, just a cup of cold mint tea each.[11]

Many of the children became Cubs, Scouts and Guides in camp, diligently passing their badges, learning the camp fire songs and enjoying being in the open air. In the summer holidays of 1944 three Scout troops were set up in Chapei camp. David Nicoll was eleven years nine months and was not officially allowed to join until he was twelve but was admitted on special licence as all his friends were Scouts. 'Every Sunday morning after Roll Call we met by the Water Tower and erected tents under the shade of the trees and remained there all day, learning Scout lore, playing games, foraging for wood for our fires, cooking our Tiffin ... In the early evening we would take down our tents and return home.... before evening Roll Call.'

Eventually the Japanese allowed a permanent hut, provided two sides were left open so that they could ascertain that no anti-Japanese activity was taking place there. The older boys built it themselves. '[They] made the hut and its roof out of branches, leaves and mud, and part of an old pram formed a window frame. The Kitchen staff were kind and used to give us rather more than our proper ration of meat and vegetables and on occasion we were given sweet potatoes which we baked in the embers of the fire.'[12]

8

Fun and Fatigues

I t is the central paradox of internment. On the face of it they were prisoners, held in by fences, gates and watch towers. Yet despite this, many children found in camp a freedom that they had not tasted in their pre-war lives – to play and wander, to be hectically active or to dream. The adults chafed at the lack of space, longed for news from home and loved ones, grew sick of the sight of their neighbours, worried about their final fate, but a child's world is smaller and programmed to optimism. To them a tree, a pond, a shed, a dead insect can open the door to a magic kingdom. Colonials had never been the most possessive and solicitous of parents. There had been amahs for that. In camp, as in their old lives, they were to a great extent preoccupied, with their chores, with their games of bridge and mah-jong. And of course in camp, unlike in a louche and inviting city like Shanghai, the children were – relatively speaking – safe. On top of this in many camps there were huge numbers of children so that even the shyest only child always had a gang of pals to play with. And so, outside school hours, the children were free to roam the camp and amuse themselves.

Although living quarters were crowded, many of the camps had been built as schools and campuses and had spacious, attractive grounds. They had been planted with exotic plants and trees by their former owners and to children they constituted perfect places to climb or hide in. In other circumstances these would have been extremely pleasant places to be and many of the children, especially those from the cities, derived great pleasure from the beauty of nature during their internment. In Singapore, where families were split along gender lines, fifteen-year-old Mel Bruce looked forward to the start of the rains after the long, wearying days of intense heat, knowing they would cause the countryside to explode with colour.

'The rainy season began in earnest towards the end of September and the rain when it came, literally sheeted down, flooding the pathways between the huts, and the main monsoon drain within the camp became swollen with torrents of muddy water. When the rain ceased, and the sun shone again everywhere was beautiful, the hibiscus hedges were covered with blooms all dripping wet, and some bougainvillea behind the northern main gate was really a picture ... everyone was out in the rain ... bathing in the pure soft water, and having a good clean up. After one of these downpours, one could hear the bullfrogs in the valley croaking away after dusk till well into the night.'[1]

The grounds in Yangchow C camp had been planted as a garden and in spring and summer were leafy and full of flowers. In spring there was the blossom of the white snowball tree and fragrant lilac. In summer roses bloomed round the porches of some of the guards' houses while vivid blue Morning Glory rambled over the wall of the church. Pink and white cosmos and orange-red zinnias bloomed in the beds. The compound hosted several fine trees – two immense gingko trees (*Ginkgo biloba*) and an ancient *Magnolia grandiflora* with its giant, fragrant cream flowers. And it wasn't all ornamental. There was a magnificent mulberry tree from which the women made jam,[2] a large Chinese walnut tree, a couple of big pecan trees and, near the guardhouse, a couple of pomegranate and persimmon trees.[3]

In those days when hand-held games consoles would have seemed as outlandish as a semi-detached house on Mars would today, the games boys played were old favourites long vanished now – Crack the Whip, Kick the Can, Sardines, Cops and Robbers, leapfrog. They were energetic, imaginative, not infrequently dangerous and generally of a type to give nightmares to the Health and Safety tsars of today.

The tall trees in Yangchow C provided a haven for birds and bird-nesting was a favourite hobby for the boys. The camp committee did their best to prevent it, but to little effect. 'In an attempt to preserve the extraordinary variety of the camp's birdlife the committee passed a rule that disturbing birds at nesting time was forbidden, but that didn't stop us . . . In the very early morning while the adults still slept and the air was filled with the calls of courting doves, the cry of cuckoos and the liquid warblings of golden orioles, we'd sneak out from our rooms into the spring semi-light to climb trees and rob the nests where we'd observed birds sitting during the day.' With a nod to conservation the boys imposed a rule that no boy ever took more than one egg from a nest – but that didn't limit the number of boys who each took an egg from the same nest.[4]

Another favourite among the Yangchow boys was cricket fighting. 'We'd catch male fighting crickets – and keep them in cages that we made from pieces of bamboo with tiny bars to give them ventilation. We fed them on grains of boiled rice that we saved from our meals. To train them we'd tease them with ticklers that we made by splitting fine stems of grass. The crickets would mistake the ticklers for the antlers of other crickets and attack the grass. When our charges had become sufficiently aggressive we'd place two of them in a bowl that we'd fashioned from clay and coax them around with the ticklers until their feelers touched. They'd then set upon each other with opened jaws and fight until one surrendered and ran away.'[5]

The physical freedom was something even very young children benefited from. Toddlers, ironically, had far greater freedom than if they had been free citizens growing up in a city. In Yu Yuen Road camp Hope Lee liked to let Marion, the little daughter she had given birth to shortly before internment, run free. 'As soon as I was through with my chores I would let Marion loose on the field and follow behind with my knitting. She was happy if she could race away on her own . . . she moved so quickly as a little thing that I could not take my eyes off her for many minutes. I well remember one time stopping to chat to someone in the middle of the field. We talked for a while and then she stooped down to say hello to Marion. Marion was no longer there. She was not even in sight! I hurried off to look for (her) . . . She was nowhere to be seen . . . It took me three quarters of an hour to track her down. She had crossed the campus and climbed three flights of stone stairs to the top of G block where she was playing with the McClellan children.'

Even winter didn't deter the energetic little girl. 'When the cold winds started I would bundle her up and off we'd go: she racing ahead, me following, trailing knitting wool, my fingers numb with cold which didn't worry me as long as I could see Marion happy with her rosy cheeks and bright smile. I had to keep knitting as she had grown out of her baby garments and needed warm things for winter, especially socks. When all my wool was used, I pulled my sweaters undone and knitted them up for her.'[6]

The bigger girls also loved the freedom of being outside. In this area of long hot summers everyone loved the rain. Grace Harvey, one of the youngest children in Yangchow C, liked going out to play after a downpour.

'We delighted in playing in the watery pools which lay under the trees after a violent thunderstorm .... there was the fine fresh smell of deliverance from the thunder and lightning. After the downpour, pools of water – twenty or thirty feet across – formed under the sycamores. Out we went to gather up the cicada shells found among the leaves. These too we gathered, to serve as boats for our cicada passengers. Grownups forbade us to wade in the water; they threatened us with nameless diseases if we disobeyed. The temptation to cast aside our battered sandals, roll up our ragged garments, was too great. We pushed the leaf-boats across the bays.'[7]

On occasion the freedom to be inventive verged on disaster, as when Margaret Blair and two friends in Yu Yuen Road decided, on the basis of a book they read, to become a team of girl detectives. The plan was to hide under the bed in each of their rooms and note down anything they saw or heard. The first room they chose belonged to the Hunts, the parents of one of the other two girls. They all crawled under the girl's parents' bed and waited.

'The first half hour was extremely boring as no one came into the room, and we were almost giving up ... when suddenly the door opened and in came Mr Hunt. He wandered about, preparing for some camp task he had to perform by putting on a pair of overalls. At least that's what we guessed he was doing, as all we could see was his feet and ankles. We had a school exercise book with us to take notes of any conversations; but being alone, he didn't say anything...'

At this point Margaret's conscience began to prick and she whispered to the others that they should come out and let the girl's father know they were there. The others disagreed furiously and they remained hidden. 'After Mr Hunt had left the room we crawled out and agreed it wasn't as good an idea as we had thought. Then Mrs

Hunt entered and saw us all there, so we decided to tell her what we had done.' Fortunately the girl's mother had a sense of humour and the three were sent off to play more conventionally.

Boys preferred boisterous games full of risk. Crack the Whip was a favourite among David Nicoll's friends in Chapei. The boys all linked hands, with the biggest boy acting as anchor. The boy next to him would start running slowly, the third ran faster 'and so on down the line until the small boy at the end would be running at full pelt finally flying through the air'. Another even more physical game was Willy Willy Wagtail, which meant David having to seek a safe place for his glasses. This game involved one team jumping from a tree onto the backs of the other team, who were crouched in a row. On summer evenings or wet days they chased each other noisily in and out of buildings, bumping into people and infuriating adults trying to listen to classical music on a gramophone. On winter nights they played the old favourite Squashed Sardines.

'We would form pairs, one pair would hide among the trunks lining the corridors and the rest would go in search of the first pair; once found the new arrivals would squeeze in and be joined by other pairs until the last pair found them, not too difficult with the noise this writhing mass of bodies made.'[8]

What is striking about the way children played in camp was their readiness to be satisfied with so little. When the weather was bad everyone was confined to their rooms. This could prove trying for the adults, but tapped reserves of ingenuity in the young that would astonish many modern parents. William Sewell, a missionary teacher, sharing a cramped room in Stanley camp in Hong Kong with his own three young children and several other adults, was intrigued by the children's adaptability.

'In our tiny room one wet afternoon eight-year-old Ethel Dale and Guy were playing with a toy train which had been found in the camp. Backwards and forwards the engine ran over the line, from below the window under the table and round to the door. Joy was sitting on her bed with Joan Corona ... sewing dolls' clothes from bits they had found in a dustbin. They were using as thread some fine strands unpicked from lamp wick the Welfare had given them. Vee was up on the daybed reading a story.'

Sewell saw with sadness that many of the imaginative games the children played were inspired by the inhuman conditions they were living in. Trying to stay alive and healthy became part of the fibre even of the very young. The children gathered pine needles on the way home from school to make tea to provide vitamin C. They killed flies to reduce the risk of dysentery. Even their play was dominated by hunger.

'There were endless games of cooking and eating. Every story we read to them, whether Peter Rabbit, Kipling or Hans Andersen seemed to have some description of food or feasting which was discussed and dramatised by the hungry actors. Surrounded by sickness as people fell ill with dysentery and deficiency diseases they invented a new game – hospitals.'

'A fly sits on your rice and then you get that toilet sickness,' announced Dr Guy. But when Guy himself was the patient it was Vee who painfully penned his chart-name: 'Guy. Sicknes: Disenterie. Room: 10 people. Bed: matres on floor. People in family: five. Tempricher: 103 point six. Food: Rice water, soop, tea.'[9]

In some camps the outside world seemed tantalisingly close and the air of danger lured children into thrilling games of risk-taking. In Lunghwa camp there was an area outside the main part of the camp which was less robustly fenced and less well patrolled by the guards. Dubbed by prisoners the 'New Territories', it housed the camp school and only schoolchildren and teachers were allowed access to it. Beyond the New Territories lay freedom and normal life. Fired up by knowing that escapees faced execution, the children deliberately tempted fate.

Ann March explains the rules: 'We would take it in turns to dare each other to crawl out under the wire and pick up a stone or a twig – something identified beforehand – and then rush back with it before we were shot. We also swam naked in the creeks and did all kinds of things that my parents would have been quite horrified about if they had known.'[10]

Boys will be boys and in the absence of over-vigilant adult supervision some games were inevitably less wholesome than others. One aspect of internment that the class and caste-conscious British found particularly hard to adjust to was its egalitarianism. The Japanese lumped everyone with a British passport together, irrespective of racial origin or social class. The result was that the camps were a melting pot of cultures and mores. This caused ongoing friction among the adults. The children, however, loved it. They sought out the ones their parents deemed bad boys, who responded by telling them weird versions of the facts of life and introducing them to bad habits. In the old days Chinese amahs would have kept their charges from mixing with children they deemed undesirable. Now the parents had little alternative but to accept that in an internment camp the reins of control were loosened and children chose their own friends.

In Yangchow C the children had a den which they had created from the space underneath the dining hall and which they used as a secret place to speculate about sex and to experiment with smoking. Most of the time the cigarettes were an experiment in themselves as tobacco was unobtainable, but some children got their hands on genuine Chesterfields after the Americans began their airdrops.

Cyril Mack was a junior member of the gang. 'Access to the space was gained through a vent which was easy to remove at the far end of the dining hall and was out of sight of the general public ... We had to crawl along the earth floor in filth and dust into the bowels of the hall to get away from the opening and there we could crouch or lie in the grey darkness.'

The boys had to whisper because the adults in the hall were only inches above their heads, showering them with dust as they moved around. There they enjoyed their first drag, on 'cigarettes' made from whatever they could find – toilet paper, dried tea or a selection of grasses. However, all too soon the game was up. Wisps of smoke rising from between the floorboards gave them away and the maintenance department was asked to block up holes leading to the church and dining hall 'in order to stop the children getting into mischief in these places'.[11]

The undisputed leader of the 'mischief' was a boy called Joey. Joey, known as the King of the Kids, was the quintessential bad boy. He was every mother's nightmare, the Bad Influence made flesh – and the younger children worshipped him. Reputed to be half Japanese, his parents had separated and he was in camp with his British mother. Joey was only twelve when he went into camp, but had a switch knife, had seen all the latest films, been everywhere – and, best of all, knew the mysteries of sex.

Neil Begley was always present whenever the King was holding his secret court. 'About a dozen of us used to congregate in the semi darkness under the floorboards, hanging on Joey's every utterance. He told us that he had been a member of one of Shanghai's most notorious street gangs and that his gang would wait around outside the brothels to watch the American Marines go in to do something he called rooting. When they came out, he told us, they'd walk with a curious stiff-legged gait which he tried to demonstrate in the confined space of our hideout. "That's how men walk after they've done rooting," he told us. After they'd been rooting they couldn't run away, which made their wallets easy prey for the gang.'

Joey went further. He imparted details of the female anatomy and taught his spellbound audience how to masturbate. 'He told us that when we got older, spunk would come out. He'd seen men do this often and that the spunk was black.'

Neil's parents, who were missionaries, urged him to keep away from Joey, saying he wasn't a nice boy. But their pleading fell on deaf ears: '... nice boy or no, nothing would have kept me from those rendezvous under the dining hall'.[12]

While the younger children spent their free time playing or being led astray, the older ones were expected to help with chores. Internees were responsible for everything to do with life in the camp and in many places everybody between the ages of fourteen and fifty-five was required to serve in the labour squads. Children worked on vegetable gardens, gathered firewood, dug wells, and even dug graves. They pumped water, they worked as stokers, the worst job of all as it meant an early start and was so hot. They worked in the kitchens, where they were entitled to extra rations, they worked in bakeries if there was one and delivered bread. They picked the weevils out of rice, they helped in hospitals. In camps lucky enough to have them, they tended animals.

In all these areas girls and boys played their part. In Lunghwa sixteen-year-old Irene Duguid (later Kilmarnock) was expected to help with chores as soon as she had finished her School Certificate in the last year of internment. 'Water was rationed and was handed out at various points round camp morning and evening. I volunteered to work at the water boiling station handing out their ration to the people queuing up with their Thermos flasks. Because there were so many people they queued for hours. The water was brought into camp daily by Chinese coolies on water carts. (The doctors insisted that all had to be boiled for at least half an hour to make it safe.) It was boiled in huge tubs on fires built from wood which had to be gathered every day by teams of young men.'

As a young teenager Irene soon found this work 'dead boring': 'It wasn't too bad in summer but in winter it was jolly awful standing there hour after hour getting colder and colder.' There was a shortage of people to look after children while the parents did their camp fatigues and so Irene offered to do that. 'I helped a mother who was suffering from pellagra, a severe deficiency disease caused by the poor diet. I chopped wood and collected coke for the chatty, the little stove that heated our room, and did the washing. My mother was a cleanliness fanatic and she even insisted on having sheets on the beds in winter which no one else in the dormatory (sic) did and they had to be washed and dried in the freezing winter air. Over time things wore out and I spent a lot of time mending things such as our two camp chairs, my camp bed and homemade table.'[13]

Irene had her own vegetable patch towards the end. 'I grew melons and lettuce which was very good for our vitamin level. I worked jolly hard at my vegetable patch but some of the other internees used to pinch what I'd grown.' In Lunghwa, in contrast to other camps, the doctors forbade the prisoners to adopt the oriental practice of using human waste on the gardens on health grounds. Irene also worked in the camp dispensary. 'It sounds rather grand for an internment camp, and I only handed out things the doctors had prescribed, but in Lunghwa we were lucky, considering some camps didn't have any drugs. Kind people from nationalities which were not interned, who were still living in Shanghai, sent things into us. We didn't have much, just things like aspirin and stuff to stop us getting malaria.'[14]

In some camps the Japanese allowed the prisoners, who otherwise were not getting any calcium, to keep goats to provide milk for babies, young children and the sick. Albert Nissim was interned in Yangchow C when he was nine. He shared a room with his parents and his two younger sisters, his uncle, aunt and their three boys and his sixty-nine-year-old grandmother. Albert's father had been a successful estate agent in Shanghai, specialising in commercial property, and Albert had had a totally urban childhood. In camp, however, his job was to look after the goats, of which he became very fond.

'There were about seven to ten fully grown animals, including one billy. During the entire time, there were just two billies, one replacing the other when he got old. There was a special fenced area that was used to house them, which included a shed with stalls or partitions. We fed them with kitchen slops and milked them twice a day. All children were given about 3 to 4 ounces of milk maybe twice a week. After milking we took them out to where the grass was usually long, tethered them with a long rope and let them feed. The nannies were often not tethered but the billy was or he would have wandered off.'

The children, most of whom were innocent of the facts of life, even became involved with birth. 'Once or twice a year we had a bunch of kids – sometimes twins. Even though we were barely aware (speaking for myself anyway) of sex, we assisted in the births – usually by pulling the kids out.'[15] In the final days the goats were slaughtered to make a goat stew for the protein-starved inmates. Albert and the other children who had helped with the goats, despite their hunger, were too upset to eat it.

Children liked working with animals and made good goatherds. Lunghwa camp also had a flock of goats, which had been donated by the wife of the Italian ambassador. They provided milk for the babies and children under five. It was Ann March's job to look after them. When the goats were first milked the guards had tried to take all the milk for themselves. An ingenious solution was devised. 'Our man in charge of the goats peed into it, then gave it to the Japanese and they took it off. They came back saying that they didn't like it. I think they'd been really sick – and so it was available for us to use.'[16]

As the food rations were cut back further and further the prisoners created vegetable gardens, and children, especially boys, were expected to lend a hand. 'It was very stony soil and hard to dig,' remembers Albert. 'The older ones dug while the younger guys picked out the stones, helped sieve the soil, planted seeds and carried off the debris to another area. We also sometimes helped around the kitchen doing menial jobs such as carrying vegetable peelings to the plots to use as fertiliser. We planted flowers around the buildings. When our families needed water it was often children who carried the heavy buckets from the well to our rooms, which could be quite a walk.'

Yangchow was one of the camps where water was a major problem. The pumps that brought water up from the wells caused endless problems and in 1944 the prisoners decided on the ambitious plan of building a reservoir. Albert and some of the other children helped. 'It was just like a large swimming pool, measuring approximately 150 feet by 50 feet and maybe 4 to 5 feet deep. It took several months to complete. It had an impressive filtration system. Water circulated through four rectangular compartments at one end, each filled with filtering materials of graded sizes, the first large pebbles, the last fine sand to filter out impurities. It was a joint effort. The men did the digging and we children carried away the stones and spoil.'

The project improved the internees' lives considerably as now the water could be distributed round the camp – to the kitchen, the laundry and the bakery – instead of having to be carried there in heavy containers. 'Now we could get a quick shower rather than a cold sponge bath and water for laundry flowed slowly out of a tap. We could now carry water from the laundry back to our rooms, which was nearer.'[7]

Not all the children chose manual work. After taking his School Certificate in the summer of 1944 Colin Palmer volunteered to help as an orderly in the camp hospital. Medical standards in Yangchow C were high. This was due to the excellence of the staff, which was headed by two experienced missionary doctors, and to the fact that they had providently brought significant quantities of medicines into camp with them, including anaesthetic. Colin's job as a sixteen-year-old was to mop out the clinic, which doubled as an operating theatre when necessary, and to assist with the odd operation. Conditions were far from ideal. There was no proper system of running water in camp, making difficult the vital scrubbing up, which prevents infection. And, of course, no surgical gloves.

The doctors were resourceful, however. 'They had built a wooden frame and on this stood an oil drum filled with 5 gallons of water. A tap had been fixed to the bottom of the drum. The water in the oil drum drained into a crude basin. They had rigged up a system whereby the tap was opened and closed by a foot pedal. This meant the doctors could wash their hands in the stream of water without having to touch the tap to turn it off.'

On two occasions the doctors performed operations on the Japanese. One involved taking out an appendix and required a general anaesthetic. 'I don't know if the Japanese thought the doctors would take the opportunity to kill the patient while he was helpless, but a group of them with rifles came into the theatre with him. The surgeons weren't going to operate at gunpoint. They told the Japs they were making them nervous, which was not ideal for the patient, and asked them to withdraw. They did.'

Colin's first operation as theatre assistant was when a Japanese guard came in to have a large cyst removed from his forearm under local anaesthetic. 'I did feel a bit queer when they made the incision. There seemed to be a lot of blood. But one of the doctors gave me an instrument to hold and that helped.'

There was one final operation. After the end of the war the internees left the camp in batches to return to Shanghai. Colin's batch was within two days of leaving when his father developed a painful abscess, which needed to be cut open and drained under general anaesthetic. Colin was selected to assist the surgeon. 'It was a baptism of fire though I didn't feel as queasy as I did when the Jap had his cyst removed. There was no injection. They just poured chloroform onto a rag and held it over Dad's nose and mouth . . . and carried on with the operation.' Colin's father was not deemed fit to make the arduous journey back to Shanghai, which involved lorries, barges and an uncomfortable overnight train journey. In the end the Americans sent a plane to transport the three or four sick people left in camp. Colin helped to carry his father's stretcher from the lorry to the plane.

In Sime Road camp in Singapore, where internees who had started off in Changi prison were transferred, boys were billeted with the men. There were two hours of classes in the morning, but in the afternoon boys were expected to help with chores like tending the vegetable plots where the men grew tapioca and sweet potatoes to supplement rations. The huts were lit by generators and Mel Bruce, parted from his mother, sister and younger brothers, was deputed to help the electrical engineer. He liked the work, which involved learning how generators and transformers worked. He used to go on repair trips with his boss – to the hospital and occasionally to the women's camp. This meant he could see his mother and other brothers and sister – although the Japanese forbade them to talk to each other.

From the age of fourteen boys were allowed to accompany the men on the wood-cutting parties which went out from the camp each morning and afternoon to cut wood for cooking fuel. The camp was surrounded by extensive rubber plantations. The trunks would be dragged back to the camp on a hand-hauled lorry chassis (the guards riding on the chassis with the logs) to the camp where other men with axes and two-handed saws would chop them into suitable lengths for cooking. The boys did the lighter tasks such as trimming the branches off the trunks. Wood-cutting was popular because it got the prisoners out of the claustrophobic confines of the camp, and brought them into contact with local natives who were often ready to trade with them. If they were lucky, and the guard was one of the more friendly ones, he would look the other way. 'We could not wait to be detailed for this job as we had the chance to barter for extras like eggs and sometimes even cigarettes, or the odd packet of tea or coffee outside.'[8]

9
Boils and Malaria

———

Camp diet was lacking in almost all the nutrients necessary to build healthy growing bodies and this hit children hardest. The bulk of the calories the children ate came from cheap carbohydrates such as root vegetables and rice. In a regime which, towards the end, amounted in many cases to less than 600 calories a day, proteins, fats, minerals, notably calcium, and vitamins were almost totally lacking. In addition, many of the camps had little in the way of medical supplies. Some doctors, especially in Shanghai, had managed to take medical supplies in with them, but over the course of the war necessities such as anaesthetics, disinfectant, syringes, bandages and serums simply ran out. And not only medical supplies – toothbrushes and toothpaste did not last; spectacles broke or became inadequate. In many instances vital supplies sent in by the Red Cross, which would have saved lives, were withheld by the Japanese. It is not surprising, therefore, that many children were ill while they were interned. These were not the normal childish ailments such as measles and whooping cough, though they had these too. These were illnesses they would never have encountered in a normal cared-for childhood; illnesses that were a direct result of the primitive nature of camp conditions – malnutrition, overcrowding, poor hygiene and lack of medicine. A great many former internees experienced health problems during the years they were in camp – jaundice (caused by drinking water contaminated by sewage), dysentery, boils, painful septic sores on feet bare through lack of shoes, skin problems, infected eyes, violent attacks of malaria that had to be endured because there was no quinine, tooth abscesses for which there was no relief except painful extraction. Broken bones could not be set properly because there was often no plaster for casts. In a few cases toddlers' jaw muscles failed to develop properly, leaving them as adults with a permanent dribble, because they couldn't be weaned onto solid food at the right stage of their development. Towards the end of the war, the amount of illness among children disrupted their education. Teachers grew to accept that every day the ranks in the classroom would be thinned by pupils who were in hospital. Many former internees have inherited a life-long legacy of health problems. Girls who were interned just before puberty, or who reached the age of puberty while in camp, have experienced an above-average level of fertility problems, while others attribute troublesome teeth and osteoporosis to the years without calcium.

In contrast to the tragedy of this man-imposed and highly avoidable suffering was the magnificent example of dedication and high-mindedness set by the doctors and nurses in the camps. Their inspired and inspiring behaviour mirrored that of those who kept the flame of learning alight in the camps. Working with minimal equipment in primitive conditions, medical staff tapped into unsuspected reserves of ingenuity in their determination to uphold their calling. Over and over again their efforts saved or ameliorated young lives.

The harshness of the conditions endured by these young civilian prisoners cannot be overstated. One sixteen-year-old boy, doing the heavy work of a full-grown man, came close to dying from a condition brought about by the combined pressures of overwork and under-feeding in the first summer of his internment. Ron Huckstep, the boy who had braved roadblocks in Shanghai to take an exam, was interned in Lunghwa camp, 8 miles outside Shanghai. 'I was building roads and digging ditches in the camp. As a result ... due to dehydration and malnutrition my intestines became paralysed, a condition known as paralytic ileus.'

The doctors in the camp felt it was beyond their limited facilities and said his only hope was an operation. Because of his youth the Japanese were persuaded to allow Ron to be taken into the Country Hospital in Shanghai to be operated on by a Chinese surgeon. 'I was opened up by a large incision extending half the length of my abdomen. He said there was nothing that could be done ... that there was no hope of survival, and closed up the incision without doing anything further.' Because he could not eat or drink, salt and water was injected into muscles in the front of both thighs, an excruciatingly painful procedure. He remained flat on his back, becoming more and more emaciated, for several weeks. Back at camp prayers were said for him as they awaited the inevitable. And then a miracle happened. 'Perhaps destiny had plans for my future which I did not know ... for some unknown medical reason, the paralysis suddenly started to recover. In about three months, weak and ema-ciated, I returned to the camp, and to manual labour.'

With so little in the way of drugs and equipment to treat the sick it was regarded as a bonus when patients were granted permission to leave camp and attend hospitals. What the internees didn't realise, however, was that hospitals which catered for foreigners before the war were now being run by Japanese and Chinese staff with very different ideas about hygiene. A little girl in Yu Yuen Road camp contracted diarrhoea and, without the necessary drugs, the camp doctors found themselves helpless. Finally her mother got permission to take her to a German doctor who was a child specialist. Another mother, who was a neighbour of the couple with the sick child, describes her 'treatment'. 'He put her on an extraordinary diet of protein and nothing else ... However, her condition did not improve and the doctor said she must go into hospital. After about two weeks a message came through the Commandant that Cilia had contracted measles in hospital and would have to remain there another three or four weeks.'

Measles was a serious illness in the 1940s and the girl's mother was very worried. But she was not allowed to see her daughter or to get in touch with the doctor. Eventually they relented and the mother was escorted to the hospital. She was directed to a small ward with three beds but couldn't find her daughter. She was told Cilia was in the far bed by the wall. She went back and realised that the child in the far bed was Cilia. 'She was so changed she had not recognised her own child. Cilia at first did not show any signs of recognition, but after a few minutes she did and began to cry weakly.'

Neglected and ignored, the little girl was sitting in a wet mess, so thin and emaciated as to be unrecognisable, and covered with sores. The mother reported that the state of the hospital, which had been the Country Hospital, with an almost exclusively ex-pat clientele, was shocking.

'When Margery came back to camp she was nearly demented and Johnny [her father], who doted on Cilia, was beside himself. Poor Margery came rushing into our hut and flung herself on the bed sobbing wildly.' The parents tried everything they could to get their daughter brought back into camp but the German doctor initially forbade it. After about ten days, however, the child did return. Her appearance shocked everyone. 'The first time I saw her,' Hope remembered, 'I nearly cried. Her little back was almost raw and she was nothing but skin and bone.'[1]

Many children suffered problems with their teeth, due both to the lack of calcium and to the absence of toothbrushes and toothpaste. There was no shortage of dentists among the internees but standards of equipment varied enormously throughout the camps. Some had only the most basic pliers and no anaesthetic, while others deployed state-of-the-art technology to rival the world beyond the wire.

Such was the case in Chapei camp in Shanghai, as David Nicoll discovered. 'I got a surprise when I entered the dentist's room off a murky corridor in the East Building: it was fitted just as a proper dental surgery with special tilting chair, an electric drill and even a cabinet with rows of drawers ranging from shallow to deep ones ... the dentist must have brought in all his equipment by special arrangement.' This dentist, arguing that his service was still as good as it had been before the war, actually wanted to charge his patients. The matter was discussed by the camp committee who decided to accept his request, on the understanding that 'he be charged an equivalent amount for all the services everyone was contributing towards his wellbeing'.[2]

But Chapei was the exception and many children suffered agonies with abscesses. Barbara Bruce, interned in the women's sector of Changi jail in Singapore with her mother and two younger brothers, developed an infected milk tooth. 'When you had toothache you were sent to the men's camp. I was sent there and a chap sat me down and just pulled it out with no anaesthetic at all. The pain was so bad I fainted.' Barbara had to have all her teeth taken out at the age of forty and blames the camp diet for this. She also didn't start her periods till the relatively late age of fourteen, several years after the war.

In many of the camps the equipment the dentists had brought in became damaged or wore out. In Yangchow C the dentist had brought his electric drill with him from Shanghai but it had been wrecked on the journey. Engineers in camp rigged up a crude manual version cranked by an assistant, which proved surprisingly effective, although people approached it with dread. This system was later updated by connecting it to the treadle of a sewing machine, enabling the dentist to operate it on his own. Internees thought it less like a piece of dental technology than a 'Wright Brothers prototype trundling down the paddock gathering speed for the take off'.[3]

The dentist was a kindly man, but the children still went in fear of him and his primitive engines. There was one thing stronger than their fear of a visit to the dentist, however, and that was their hunger for something other than the monotonous camp diet. The arrival of food parcels from the Red Cross was an event awaited with excitement that approached pressure-cooker intensity as the presumed delivery date approached. In March 1945, when rations were at their most meagre and internees at their lowest ebb, a rumour flew round Yangchow C that a consignment of Red Cross parcels was imminent and that there would be enough for every internee to have half a parcel to him- or herself. Cyril Mack, interned with his parents and older brother, had never had a parcel and was beside himself with delight. Unfortunately, even as he fantasised about the parcel's mouth-watering contents his jaw began to swell and to ache with paralysing pain. How would he enjoy his parcel with an infected jaw? Faced with having to forgo his food parcel he decided a visit to the dentist was the lesser of two evils.

'I crossed the compound to Dr Riddell's surgery, every jarring step of the way sending an extra stab of pain through my aching jaw. Dr Riddell ... guided me gently to the chair, carefully probed into my mouth and confirmed that I had developed an abscess on the tooth he had filled some months earlier. I told him to pull the tooth but he quietly explained ... that it was not such a simple exercise, as he first had to press down on the tooth in order to facilitate breaking the ligaments holding the tooth in place. More importantly he did not have anything to use as an anaesthetic so it would be an extremely painful extraction.'

The dentist tried to dissuade the boy, suggesting he wait a few days as he was expecting some supplies. But Cyril was worried the parcels would arrive first. He told him that he had never had a food parcel and was determined to enjoy it. The dentist understood.

'Without a word he picked up his extractor, propped himself beside me on the edge of the chair, put his arm around me, held me close, said that he would be as quick as he could, gripped the tooth and pushed down hard. The pain was indescribably excruciating and I struggled to break free but his hold on me was like a steel band, and he continued to press down, maintaining the pressure for, what seemed to me, an interminable time. And then, with a flourish and a cry of triumph, he held up the tooth ... "Now you can enjoy your parcel!"'

Cyril had not been alone during his ordeal. 'A small cheer went up from the three or four patients in the Men's Ward on the other side of the partition. Distracted by my tooth, I had quite forgotten that they would have heard every word that had passed between Dr Riddell and myself. The parcels arrived about a week later, on 2nd June, and I was overwhelmed with excitement as I crossed the compound clutching tightly the small, heavy, cardboard box.'[4]

In summer the heat and the primitive hygiene waged a merciless war on bodies whose resistance was lowered due to their numerous deficiencies. In Lunghwa camp seven-year-old Barbara Tilbury's mother pricked her finger while she was sewing and it went septic. The only treatment was to immerse it in boiling water. Barbara remembers her mother sobbing with the pain. They had pets in Lunghwa and Barbara had a baby butcher bird, which was like a shrike. It ate meat and Barbara would be sent off to the kitchen to find scraps for it. Some time later she broke out in huge blisters all over her body. The condition was diagnosed as pemphigus, and was attributed by the camp doctors to an infection acquired handling meat.

'I was only about seven but I was put in an adult ward in the hospital. I suppose there was only one women's ward. They covered my blisters with a mixture of gentian violet and mercurochrome, which was red, but before they did it they pulled the skin off. It was dreadful. It hurt so much I screamed and cried. Mum couldn't be with me very often as the hospital was in an out-of-bounds area of the camp. As food for us was so scarce I suppose the meat they gave me for the bird was unfit for human consumption, really rotting . . . and that's how I caught the infection.'

Dick Germain's fifteen months of untrammelled freedom roaming the streets of Shanghai had finally come to an end in June 1944 when he was interned in Lincoln Avenue camp with his uncle and ailing grandfather. This was the last camp to be set up and housed the elderly and sick, with about eight children, including Dick, who was now eleven. Because he and his grandfather had different surnames they were housed separately, and Dick found himself in a room with seven men. They showed so little interest in the young lad that no one showed him how to put up his mosquito net. To this day, he remembers the misery of being eaten alive that first night in camp.

Shy and self-conscious, Dick was reluctant to behave like the men, who kept cool by stripping off their shirts. Instead he stuck it out through the hot sweaty day, only stripping off in the cool of the evening when it was dark. As a consequence he went down with pleurisy. His condition was considered so serious that the Japanese allowed his parents, who were interned in different camps, to be transferred to Lincoln Avenue to be near him. 'I was put in the camp hospital and my mother started working in the hospital kitchen to try to see I had adequate food, but there wasn't any treatment.' Eventually Dick began to recover, but the illness left its mark, causing chronic bronchitis and leading to an attack of whooping cough so severe that he had to be hospitalised again.

Children interned in Malaya, with its malarial climate, and where the regime was invariably harsher than in China, suffered from repeated health problems, including ulcers and boils that became infected, as well as dysentery, pellagrous dermatitis and malaria. Medical supplies from the outset were minimal. During the first two years of internment the only supplies prisoners received from the Japanese was a bale of cotton wool.[5] Barbara Bruce's family were transferred from Changi prison to Sime Road camp, based in what had been a British army barracks. Barbara's brother Mel was constantly ill. He had typhus, dengue fever, blackwater fever, recurrent attacks of malaria and dysentery, which developed into amoebic dysentery. There was a medical centre at the rear of Mel's hut where three doctors and a dentist ran a clinic. Patients suffering from dysentery were isolated in the camp hospital. There were no anaesthetics. Anyone who cut themselves had to endure having their wound stitched with a needle and cotton, painted with iodine and bandaged with 'whatever strip of material was available'. All bandages were washed and returned to the dispensary for reuse. Luckily for those in Malaya the treatment for malaria – quinine – was derived from a local tree. The drug was extracted from the bark and taken in liquid form. The effect of the treatment was to reduce the incidence of shivers and shakes that characterise malaria until eventually the patient's temperature reached normal. But the sufferer was left totally drained of strength until the next attack. Mel escaped beriberi, which was starting to claim victims as a result of the preponderance of white rice in the diet, only because the Japanese introduced rations of red palm oil, which is rich in vitamins B1, B2 and C, and which were stirred into all cooked food.[6]

The extremes of climate in many parts of the Far East added to the toll of ill health. When wounds weren't turning septic in the humid heat, children's bodies, inadequately clad and fed, were suffering the effects of the extreme cold of a Chinese winter. A large number of children in camps in China suffered from the agony of chilblains. Irene Duguid, an older teenager in Lunghwa, describes how people's health began to break down.

'When the second winter came on we were beginning to get a bit desperate. It was a very cold snowy winter and the weather began to take its toll . . . . those like myself who had suffered all summer from malaria were at a pretty low ebb and it was a terrific effort struggling against the constant ailments of winter – colds, chilblains on hands and feet and various skin and eye problems brought on by malnutrition. My mother had frequent bouts of dysentery, infected eyes and sores.'[7]

Children with poor eyesight suffered severely as in many camps either the means or the will to help them was lacking. Margaret Blair, interned in Yu Yuen Road camp in Shanghai, suffered when the camp acquired a new, harsher commandant. 'In the early days sick internees were able to leave camp to have medical attention in hospitals in Shanghai but after the arrival of Hyashi all this ceased and beatings for infringement of the rules became the norm. Prisoners were not allowed access to dental or eye care and renewal of prescriptions was forbidden.'

Margaret was found to be short-sighted and could not see the blackboard during lessons, but had to go up to it instead. The strain of trying to focus on objects she couldn't see gave her blinding headaches. She, too, contracted dengue fever. She suffered several bouts of jaundice and on one occasion was in bed for three weeks. The cooked food in camp nauseated her so her mother tried to get her strength up by feeding her bread and margarine. But then she became ill as well with an inflamed gall bladder. The condition was agonisingly painful and confined her to bed. A woman in an advanced state of breast cancer was also suffering extreme pain but there were no painkillers for either of them. On top of all this, by the spring of 1945 they were getting only one meal a day, 'a ladle of watery congee'.[8]

Because of her frail condition the doctor suggested that Margaret and her family move out of the ground floor dormitory they were sharing with other people to an upstairs room. But this room had wide cracks in the plaster and the cracks were home to hundreds of cockroaches. Margaret's sight was too bad for her to see the cracks but her brother told her about the cockroaches. One day, by now aged nine, she lay ill with another bout of dengue fever, shivering under a mound of blankets and coats, even though the weather outside was blazing hot. 'During these fevered times the cockroaches became even more bold than usual and I imagined (or really did see) huge ones sitting silently on the blankets of my bed, watching, and waiting. Are they waiting for me to become so weak they will be able to crawl all over me? I wondered.'[9]

Mel Bruce was lucky to have been in Singapore, where the malaria cure grew wild. In camps in China there was no treatment and the children had to live with their condition, which was recurrent.

Neil Begley suffered badly from malaria. The first attack came while he was at school in camp. 'By the time I got to bed my teeth were chattering and I was shaking uncontrollably ... My bed was shaking so badly that my brother sat on it to stop it rattling.' In his delirium Neil's temperature reached 107°F. Lacking appropriate drugs the nurses could only fan him and sponge him with cold water. The fever abated but returned the next day. Thereafter Neil could predict the onset of malaria: 2.45 p.m. every second Friday. His teacher, the popular Father Thornton, was primed: 'At about two o'clock [he] would say in his Irish brogue "Oi tink it's toime ya went home, don'choo?"' In Neil's case the attacks of malaria led to painful outbreaks of herpes. 'The discharge from the herpes formed scabs that glued my eyelids together.' Because he was not able to be treated this resulted in permanent scratching of the cornea.[10] Children like Neil did not receive treatment until liberation when American medics distributed atabrine as a preventive treatment for malaria and emetine – a new drug – which was effective against dysentery.

Many children experienced the embarrassment of bladder problems in camp. The causes varied from stress to the rigidity with which the Japanese imposed roll-call.

In Shanghai, David Nicoll started bed-wetting in the winter of 1944. There was snow on the ground and the school closed because the classroom was too cold. The fact that he and his parents shared a room with twenty-four other people and that it was impossible to hide the wet sheets the next morning caused him deep shame.

'We felt the cold more this winter as our constitutions were less robust and although I did not understand the reason at the time that was the probable cause of my wetting the bed . . . all I was aware of was my embarrassment, especially among two dozen people. I avoided drinking during the evening and Mum would shake me awake gently in the middle of the night to get to the lavatory but as I slept heavily it took a long time for me to surface without the whole room being roused.'[11]

The Japanese were extremely strict about any type of assembly. Once assembled the internees were required to remain there, often forbidden even to talk, with no concession for emergencies – people often fainted as a result of waiting hours in the blistering sun – until the guards or commandant had finished with them. In the case of Neil Begley, interned in Yangchow C camp, this gave rise to an embarrassing condition.

'I found the long parades particularly trying as I'd always had what the kids at school called a Japanese bladder. I could barely last through a class at school without having to leave the room. These roll-calls were agony. I'd twist and turn and squirm. There was no being excused from parades, so when I could no longer control the urge I'd put my hand in my pocket and squeeze the end of my dick as hard as I could. After an hour or so of this the pain around my kidney region was almost unbearable. When, after an eternity, the roll-call was over, if I hadn't already wet my pants I'd rush to the nearest toilet block to relieve the pressure. The ache in my kidneys was excruciating and for the rest of the day I'd continue to widdle in dribs and drabs every few minutes.' Years later Neil had an X-ray that revealed a very large extrusion on the side of his bladder: '... an urologist told me [it] was probably caused by the abnormal pressure to which it had been subjected on those tortuous roll-calls'.[12]

One of the most universally observed characteristics of the Japanese was their fear of infectious diseases. Before the war British children recall Japanese wearing gauze masks covering the nose and mouth while outdoors. Visitors wishing to enter the Japanese district of Shanghai were subject to health checks. Those unable to produce satisfactory certificates would be given an injection on the spot, 'perhaps using a non-sterile needle'.[13] Their anxiety about catching disease from prisoners constituted a weakness that internees were quick to exploit. It meant that people were often able to smuggle items – information or valuables – in anything that looked like phlegm. Neil Begley's mother, imprisoned initially in Stanley internment camp, hid her and her husband's wedding rings and watches in her handkerchief when the Japanese were confiscating everybody's valuables, coughing and sneezing and keeping the handkerchief to her face as they passed.[14]

In Yu Yuen Road camp in Shanghai a Chinese coolie delivering food spat out what looked like a lump of sputum, which the Japanese guards avoided. A quick-witted prisoner picked it up and found that it contained an important message warning prisoners that a secret radio had been discovered in another camp and that there had been very severe reprisals.[15]

This fear of infection meant that in some camps, which often had little in the way of drugs themselves vaccinations were permitted against typhoid, smallpox and cholera early on in internment. Overcrowding and lowered resistance to infection, however, meant that when a disease arrived its impact was devastating.

An epidemic of whooping cough in Yu Yuen Road, in which some elderly adults died, caused prolonged misery for already weak children. Hope Lee, a Quaker missionary who was in camp with a small baby recalled: 'It swept through the camp like wildfire ... Many of the children and most of the adults were very ill indeed. There were no drugs or anything to alleviate it . . . At night we would hear one child after another all down the corridor retching and choking.' A family with a small baby who lived opposite the Lees all had it. Hope worried about the poor baby. 'It used to have terrible spasms when it couldn't get its breath and one wondered if it was ever going to breathe again. I remember the intense relief when one heard it start gasping. The poor mite looked like a little skeleton. Most of the children were looking pretty terrible and there was nothing nourishing to help them pick up. Many residents had eaten through their iron rations.'[16]

Adversity often brings out the best in the human spirit. The more the Japanese refused to help or sat on vital supplies, the more the doctors rose to the challenge. Parted from most of their instruments and nearly all of their drugs, the interned doctors performed miracles of ingenuity.

A surgeon in Yangchow B camp performed an operation on a girl suffering from mastoiditis, a highly painful condition arising from an untreated middle ear infection. In the absence of the correct instruments the doctor used carpenters' tools. He improvised the self-retaining surgical retractor he needed to hold the incision open by making one from a piece of a child's Meccano set.[17]

Children's toys were requisitioned on other occasions. In north China an eight-year-old boy was called on to sacrifice something very precious to a child locked up in an internment camp with very few toys – his lead soldiers.

Ron Bridge and his family had lived in Tianjin. His father, a businessman, had been arrested at the start of the war, but was released after a few months. Ron went into camp with his family in March 1943. 'My mother told me there was only room for food, medicine and essential clothes in the few bags that we could carry. I did not want to be parted from my favourite lead soldiers, so I crammed as many as I could into my trouser pockets, as well as sneaking a few into my baby brother's pram.' In the summer a baby was born in camp with a cleft palate. Finding a doctor who knew what to do wasn't a problem. Among the internees in camp was a man who had been a plastic surgeon at the University Hospital in

Peking. The problem was finding metal with which to create a false palate.

Ron Bridge remembers, 'A British GP and surgeon from Tientsin, who lived in a hut near our family, told me, "There is a little baby girl who has just been born and is very sick and I would like some of your toy soldiers to make her better."' Ron was deeply reluctant to part with his precious soldiers and was relieved when he was assured that broken ones would be perfectly acceptable. The lead was melted down to form an artificial palate and sewn into the roof of the baby's mouth. When the family returned to England at the end of the war the child underwent more conventional reconstructive surgery at Great Ormond Street Hospital. More than sixty years later Ron met the 'baby' and her mother again. Susan Dobson, a retired nurse, now in her sixties, only learnt about the role played by the lead soldiers at that meeting.

'Like many parents, my mother rarely spoke about camp and I was too small to have any memories. I had heard stories of my sister helping my mother to feed me; it was a very slow business and apparently they would put the food in my mouth and it would come out my nose. I knew I had had an operation in camp when I was only a week old. My mother and I went to meet Ron Bridge, who was the head of ABCIFER (Association of British Civilian Internees Far East Region), to discuss something quite different – some aspect of our compensation claim – and he told me the full story. I found everything about the story moving: the ingenuity of the doctors – thinking of the lead in the first place, and then being able to melt it, operate and suture in what was a very run-down setting ... And I was touched at the generosity of the little boy who in a prison camp didn't have much in the way of toys to play with. I had had a very uncertain start in life, and yet here I am, all these years later, and Ron is part of my story. He assured me he only volunteered the soldiers who had lost their heads, but I am very grateful to him nonetheless.'[18]

Occasionally the equipment, worn out through being endlessly reused and never replaced, let everybody down and there were accidents. David Nicoll's sister Ella contracted dysentery and sprue (an intestinal malfunction) as a result of the starvation rations. She had been receiving injections into her hip to treat the condition from the camp doctors. They had the correct drugs but were having to reuse needles. One day a blunt needle broke leaving a one-inch portion of needle inside her. In Chapei, which was one of the most humane of the camps, a taxi was made available once a week for internees needing outside medical treatment. Ella was operated on, under local anaesthetic, but the Chinese doctors couldn't find the broken needle and the girl returned to camp two weeks later with the needle still inside her.[19]

Equipment and drugs may have been in short supply, but the camps had no shortage of medical expertise and many children certainly benefited from this. This was particularly the case in Shanghai where there had been a certain amount of cooperation between the Japanese and the British Residents' Association over the organisation of internment. The BRA did its best to distribute people with vital professional skills as equally as possible among the camps. In Yangchow C camp, for example, there were four doctors and one dentist for the 620 prisoners, a ratio which, as one former internee has observed, compares favourably with the ratio of doctors to patients in contemporary Britain.[20] The relatively good state of health of the Yangchow internees at liberation was put down to regular medical examinations, injections against typhoid and cholera and the high ratio of doctors to patients.[21]

On occasion some internees received better medical care while they were interned in a prison camp than would have been available in their everyday life, where surgery was expensive. Billy Spencer was a boy who had gone into camp in Yangchow at the age of fourteen with deformed legs. He walked with the aid of two sticks and was unable to run about with other boys his age. One of the older men in camp was a retired Harley Street surgeon who had become caught up in the war when he decided to visit relatives in Shanghai in March 1943. He thought that an operation could help Billy and, though he felt too old to perform the surgery himself, he offered to supervise it. The operation took place and was successful. After that Billy was able to take exercise and join in his friends' games. 'Yangchow and its surgeons transformed Billy's life; he and his parents may have been some of the few who thanked Providence for internment.'[22]

Many of the doctors were touchingly aware of the fears and sensitivities of children and went out of their way to take the sting out of being ill. Cyril Mack went down with a fever that baffled the doctors in the summer of 1944 when he was twelve. He was too weak to walk from his billet to the hospital and so it was decided he should be carried there by stretcher. As a self-conscious teenager he was mortified at the idea of being exposed to the gaze of all his peers in his enfeebled state and wanted to walk over – something he was too ill to do.

The doctor thought up an ingenious solution. 'Through our opened windows I was soon able to hear Dad's voice calling out for stretcher bearers. I knew that other men would be collecting and would be trotting back with him. They waited on the veranda ... as the stretcher was too long to be negotiated up the space of the narrow, confined stairwell. As I slipped on my kimono Dr Bolton, wearing a huge smile, turned his back to me, crouched, and told me to hop on. We were off, laughing and joking ... The stairwell was always a dim area and I was terrified that he would stumble or lose his balance and that we would both pitch headlong down the stairs. But Dr Bolton had much practice and success with his own personal mode of trans-porting patients so we soon quickly and safely descended. As we emerged onto the veranda ... about fifty well wishers had gathered but all the attention had embarrassed me and I could only smile shyly back at them.'[23]

10

Nobody's Child

Children are natural optimists. They can put up with a surprising amount of hardship provided they feel surrounded by people who care for them. For the majority of children who endured internment, recollections of cold, hunger and illness are softened by memories of family life – its rows, its jokes, its good night kisses, its scoldings – continuing much as normal. But some children were deprived of this comfort. Almost 200 spent the whole of their internment separated from their parents and some didn't see them again for nearly five years. Usually these were children who were stranded at boarding school, hundreds – sometimes thousands – of miles from home when the Japanese attacked. Others were separated for other reasons, such as death or illness. The amount of surrogate care these 'orphans' received from other adults in camp varied widely. In situations where the very necessities of life – food, water, fuel – were disappearing, the survival instinct often choked off more altruistic impulses. The boys, especially, were expected to grow up overnight. Deprived of the comfort of unconditional love they had no one older and wiser to tell their troubles to, no one to praise them when they did well at school ... Shut out from the warmth of the family circle they suffered the ongoing ache of loneliness and of being unwanted.

Up to the autumn of 1942 Jose Chamberlain was a happy little girl with two parents who adored her. Then her world began to collapse. On 5 November her father was arrested by the kempeitai. In February mother and daughter were ordered into an internment camp in Shanghai. Two months later Jose's mother became ill and was sent to a hospital outside camp. Jose never saw her again. In August she was told by the camp authorities that her mother was dead.

In just over six months she had effectively lost both her parents and found herself a virtual orphan – at nine. Apart from two brief visits to his prison and a shared outing to her mother's funeral, she did not see her father again for two years and eleven months. 'They didn't say what the problem with my mother was but I think she must have had a nervous breakdown,' Jose says. The emotional burden of worrying about a husband who was almost certainly being ill-treated combined with packing up a house and preparing for internment alone would take its toll on anyone and Jose's mother had never been particularly robust. As for how she died Jose has not received a credible explanation. 'The cause of death was given as organic brain lesion with heart failure given as the secondary cause. I have asked several doctors about this over the years but they all say that this is not medically recognised terminology.'

A collection of letters, treasured for more than sixty years by Jose, chronicles the family's ordeal. Jose's mother, who was known as Ciss, wrote to her husband from camp saying that she was being treated for nerves and insomnia. She added that Jose was attending school in camp but was proving 'rather difficult over food'. Helpless in a prison where men were being tortured and ill-treated on a daily basis, Jose's father Harry Chamberlain wrote a harrowing note to his daughter:

> I am writing to ask you to please be a good girl while Mammy is sick. She will soon come back and if you are good she will not worry and will get better and strong again. I hope I shall see you soon.
> All love
> Dad

Jose was interned in Yu Yuen Road camp, which was composed of two former schools and their extensive playing fields. She was allowed out of camp to attend her mother's funeral accompanied by the wife of a former colleague of her father's. She has sketchy memories of that sad day. 'I remember being at the cemetery, Dad and I standing with a big hole in the ground and Mum down there with a coffin near some trees. Dad had a Japanese guard with him and so did I. There are no trees there now, but there are trees in the photo that was taken at the time.' (There is a post-war photo of Jose next to her mother's grave, wearing a smart tailored suit. 'Before we went into camp Mum sent some clothes up to the dairy owned by our friends, hoping she would be able to retrieve them after the war. They were packed into a couple of boxes and hidden under bales of straw. After we were liberated an old overcoat of Dad's that Mum had kept was cut down and turned into a nice brown suit for me.')

After his wife's death Harry Chamberlain addressed an emotional appeal about Jose to Mr H. J. Collar, the camp representative where his daughter was interned:

> With reference to the recent death of my wife I have to state that I am gravely concerned regarding my daughter Lilian Jose, aged nine years, who is in Yu Yuen Rd Civil Assembly Centre.
>
> The child is very advanced mentally for her age and I could see when I saw her at the funeral, that the news of her Mother's death has shaken her tremendously and I fear that the knowledge that she is separated from both her Mother and Father and in the charge of comparative strangers, will have a detrimental effect on her health.
>
> Mr Collar, will you please request Lt Honda and Colonel Odera to sympathetically consider my transfer to Yu Yuen Road Civil Assembly Centre to take care of my Motherless daughter ...

Harry Chamberlain's request fell on deaf ears. He then turned to the woman who had accompanied Jose to her mother's funeral, whose husband he had worked with, and asked them to become Jose's guardians. But the arrangement did not leave Jose with happy memories. Jose found no special kindliness from any women in camp, either while her mother was ill or after her death. While her mother was in hospital Jose remained in the room she had shared with her. Its other occupants were a woman whose husband was also imprisoned in Haiphong Road prison and her son and daughter. Her memories of that time are not happy ones.

'The son was two years older than me and used to tease me a lot. His mother was very fierce and I was terrified of making her angry.

I hadn't eaten my food one day and had left the plate under my bed where it had gone rotten. She told me off dreadfully. She made it very clear she didn't want me.' The couple who eventually became her guardians evidently felt the situation had been forced on them. The woman was so far from being motherly that one of Jose's most painful camp memories specifically features her. 'It was very cold the second winter. We didn't have enough clothes. I didn't have any gloves. I was on my way to school across the football pitch. My hands hurt so much I was crying. I went to find Mrs Toon [her guardian] to see if she would comfort me, but instead of taking my hands and rubbing them she told me to go and hold them under a cold tap.' The woman subsequently suffered bereavement in her turn when her husband died in the camp hospital.

Trying to act for the best from a prison cell Harry Chamberlain had had little choice when selecting someone to look after Jose. But he remained the only one who knew the misery his wife and his daughter had suffered after his arrest. He put his anguished feelings into words when he submitted an emotional claim to the China War Damage Office after the war:

> ... anyone who was in Shanghai at this very difficult period knows that the times were very bad for a woman with a small daughter (aged 8 years who was sick after my arrest) left to fend for themselves. I last saw my wife on February 7th 1943 when she was allowed to visit Haiphong Road camp prior to her internment at Yu Yuen Road camp on February 8th 1943. She seemed quite well but nervous and appeared to be putting on a good face for my benefit but the ordeal of seeing her husband pulled from his bed by a gang of ruffians, being turned out of her home with a young daughter crying for her father, was something from which I am sure she never recovered. She died in Japanese-conducted mental hospital ... and ... I was not allowed to see her. It should be noted that after my wife's death my daughter was left in a camp without any parental care until released.

Jose undoubtedly suffered from emotional isolation in camp. But lack of love was not the only problem. She had always been a fussy eater and hated the camp fare. 'I had never liked stews, preferring my ingredients to be separate and distinct. In Yu Yuen Road everything was cooked up together in a big cauldron and I once a found an eye looking at me.' Consequently, she was always hungry. In her lowered state her health suffered – she went down with a bad case of measles and was isolated for weeks in a darkened room.

One way of countering hunger was to do the camp bread round. 'If you delivered bread you got a crust as a perk. So I did that. And like all the children I hung around the kitchen to scoop up the bits of burnt rice that stuck to the bottom of the cauldrons.' Being hungry brought her into conflict with her guardian. The woman in question had taken a few extra supplies in with her, including a bottle of Horlicks, which had gone solid in the jar. One day Jose ate it. 'I had to clamber up and get it off a shelf, but I devoured it. I got into terrible trouble.' Mosquito bites on her ankles became infected. The only treatment in camp was primitive bread poultices. 'You made them by soaking bread in boiling water, wrapping it in muslin and pressing it against the boil to draw it. It was very painful and I dreaded it.'

At the beginning of 1945 all the prisoners in Yu Yuen Road were transferred to Yangtzepoo camp, which was about 4 miles from the centre of Shanghai, in what had historically been the Japanese area of the city. By now the tide of the war had turned definitively in the Allied favour and American bombing raids were a regular occurrence. Knowing the Americans would not bomb prisoners the Japanese had sited the camp next to one of their own barracks and military bases. The new camp was based in what had formerly been a convent and hospital and was very cramped. Conditions were inferior in every way to those at Yu Yuen Road. 'It was filthy and smelly,' says Jose. 'The sewers were blocked and half the water supply did not work. The lavatories were just a platform over a hole. They were full of maggots and the stench was appalling. There was no running water .... I don't remember washing or brushing my teeth. After the war I was invited to a school friend's house and someone pointed out my teeth. And I said, "I haven't cleaned my teeth for three years."'

Throughout her three years in camp Jose was allowed by the Japanese to write her father a monthly letter of twenty-five words, which the Red Cross delivered. The letters reveal a busy, chatty little girl, heedless of spelling and punctuation, serenely unaware of the grim place her father was being held in. The letters were censored, however, and Jose would not have been allowed to complain.

On 15 June 1943, when her mother was still in hospital, Jose wrote:

Dear Daddy,
I hope you are well. Have you been inoculated? We have We still have school two hours a day I go to Church and Sunday School. We children get an egg every day now We had a party on Angus birthday I write to Mummy every month ... much
   love
   Jose Chamberlain

In November 1943, three months after her mother's death, she described her progress in knitting.

Dear Daddy,
... I am going to see the dentist tomorrow. I am taking cod liver oil and malt. We are reading Black Beauty in the evenings. Have you read it? I can knit properely and cast on stitches now. Will you have a nice Xmas? The Xmas workshop is very busy here. The IRC is sending us children's parcels. Yesterday we got oranges, we got lettice today. I will soon be ten
   love and kiss
   Jose Chamberlain

In February 1944 she wrote about her Christmas, clearly imagining that her father's had been similarly cheery.

Dear Daddy,
Did you have a nice Xmas, I did I had a Doll's bed, with sheet's, and everything, and hanky case, and paints and brush, and a bag. I was very happy on Christmas Day ... Feb 1st I will be ten thank you for your Xmas card ... I wish you were here for my birthday Angus teases me every day Don't get sick I still get my half pint of milk. I hope you had a happy birthday.

Few people's recollections of the past are all bad. Camp life provided a constant pack of other children to play with, something especially welcome to an only child. And the heat in summer meant they spent long hours in the open air.

'Towards the end of the war we had no lights. It was nice, lying on the grass in the middle of the football pitch looking up at the millions of stars with the other girls. I liked lessons – we did English and arithmetic and Latin, which I particularly liked. And we had plenty of time to play games. I liked skipping and roller-skating and leapfrog. I broke my wrist playing leapfrog. One of my most vivid memories is of a boy called Reid, who must have been about fourteen at the time, while I was only ten. On New Year's Day 1945 he stood between the goalposts on the football pitch in full Scottish regalia and played the bagpipes.'

On 11 October 1945, almost three years after Harry Chamberlain's arrest, Jose's guardian took her to the Bund in Shanghai to meet the ship bringing her father down from Peking. Harry Chamberlain wrote in his diary that day that 'Jose and Mrs T came to the ship ... Jose looks well but needs some school poor kid. I can see she's had a rotten time.' A few days later he wrote sadly, 'Mrs T is not a happy woman for a young girl like Jose to live with.'

Fifteen-year-old Keith Martin was another camp orphan. Keith's father had died in 1940. His mother worked in a reserved occupation and was not able to leave Hong Kong, so she sent Keith and his younger sister to stay with their aunt and her family in Shanghai. They stayed there from July 1940 to March 1943 when they were interned in Yangchow.

In camp Keith and his sister shared a crowded room with his aunt and her son, two of their friends and another woman and her two daughters. A rope strung across the room on which hung a curtain gave the illusion of privacy: 'You couldn't see what was happening behind the curtain but you could hear everything – it was a difficult time.'

Keith says, 'I was fond of my aunt, but she had just lost her husband who had been killed at the start of the Pacific War and was grieving for him. I missed my mother a lot. I missed being hugged and being reassured that I was doing well with my schoolwork.' Keith was an academically gifted and hard-working student who was always top of the class. There were a number of educated men and women in Yangchow, many of them missionaries or priests. Under the cogent persuasion of the Reverend P. C. Matthews, many of them became teachers for the duration of internment. The result was that the standard of education was high in Yangchow C camp.

Because of his age Keith was expected to help with camp chores, even though he was still going to camp school every day studying for his Cambridge Senior School Certificate. He chose the toughest job of all, stoking. There were no gas stoves in isolated, backward Yangchow. All the water for the breakfast congee and the evening meal had to be boiled by lighting fires in a bank of eight primitive stoves. The morning shift began long before dawn at 3.30 a.m. The men began by fetching water in heavy wooden buckets from huge storage kongs and filling the cauldrons. The filled buckets were estimated to weigh a ton and a half. When the cauldrons were full the fires were lit and kept going while the water boiled.[1] It was hot, sweaty and tiring. 'I didn't really want to be a stoker,' said Keith, who recalled the heat and flames of the kitchen as like a scene from Dante's Inferno, 'but any job in the kitchen meant the possibility of coming by an extra bit of food and I was so hungry.'

All the children who were separated from their parents were lonely. There was one day in Yangchow camp, however, when Keith Martin felt particularly in need of older, wiser counsel. Suddenly he found himself expected to make a decision, the outcome of which would have implications not only for his own happiness and wellbeing, but also for that of his younger sister and his mother. 'Our camp representative told me that Mr Hashizuma, the camp commandant, wished to see me. I was ushered in and Mr Hashizuma said, through an interpreter, in Japanese: "If you and your sister wish to go and see your mother in Hong Kong you may do so, but if you do you must go today."'

Keith was stunned. 'I told the commandant I needed time to think over such a momentous decision. But he replied that there was a Japanese ship leaving Shanghai for Hong Kong the following day.

'He told me: "You must take the train to Shanghai today or you will miss it."'

Keith's head was in a whirl. 'On the one hand I and my sister ached to be with our mother. But I was worried about the risks of travelling by sea during a war. I knew that Major Begley [Neil Begley's father], a Salvation Army missionary in camp with us, had been interned in Stanley camp so I decided to ask him what he thought.

'He told me: "This camp is better for you youngsters than Stanley." We had been able to take three boxes of things and a bed into our camp, while the Hong Kong residents had had to flee their houses with just a suitcase.'

The other thing that weighed on Keith's mind was the importance of keeping up with his education, and standards in Yangchow camp, considering the circumstances, were high.

'I knew that in our camp I would be able to take my Senior School Certificate in a year's time, which was vital for my future employment. We had a small number of textbooks, some of which we had brought with us, some of which the Red Cross had sent out from Shanghai.'

In the end, after much heart-searching, Keith took the toughest decision of his young life. 'I decided we should stay put and so I told the commandant, through the interpreter, "We prefer to stay where we are." To his surprise Mr Hashizuma replied, "Mr Martin has made a wise decision."'

Sixty years on, Keith says he now realises how much he must have hurt his mother. 'It was a selfish decision. I was thinking of my School Cert. and of the fact that the Americans were sinking Japanese ships off the Chinese coast. Other children from our camp who had been separated from their parents did travel and the ship we would have travelled on did in fact make it. My decision must have upset my mother. She had lost my father in April 1940 and then in July she had lost me and my sister. As a child you don't imagine your parents suffering.'

There was another factor in Keith's choice. He had learned via a Red Cross letter that his mother had remarried while she was in Stanley. Her second husband was an old family friend who had been an officer in the Hong Kong police. 'So I knew she had someone to look after her.' Looking back Keith thinks it was just as well the commandant told him to decide on the spot. 'Otherwise I would have spent days agonising over what path to choose.' The decision by the Japanese to unite families may seem surprising in view of their reputation for heartlessness towards prisoners but there were other cases in China and Hong Kong where families who had been split up were offered the chance of reuniting.

As far as his own education was concerned Keith's decision paid off. In the summer of 1944, despite the fact that by then rations were very meagre and many of the pupils were weak and sickly, Keith Martin was one of five teenagers in Yangchow C who scored so well in their School Certificate that they were eligible for a university place. He took five subjects and gained a distinction in four of them.

Tucked away in the Chinese interior Yangchow camp's exact location was not initially known to the Allies. This meant its inmates were among the last to be liberated. After leaving Yangchow by barge they made the rest of their journey from Chingkiang to Shanghai by rail as the Japanese had mined the Yangtze River. The journey, on hard seats and without food or water, was arduous, but the young people enjoyed pushing off the Chinese boarders who climbed on the sides of the train trying to snatch a free trip to Shanghai whenever it stopped at a station.

When the train pulled into Shanghai Keith's mother was waiting excitedly with her new husband. To her horror she couldn't pick her son out among all the children. And then her husband whispered, '"That's because you are looking for a twelve-year-old and Keith is seventeen now." She hadn't expected me to look so different.'

Keith Martin rejected the offer of joining Stanley camp, but Bill Macauley had had no choice. After being driven out of his boarding school in Kowloon by the Japanese invasion of Hong Kong, he had been sent there, with almost 2,000 other equally unprepared civilians, at the beginning of January 1942. He was separated from his entire family. His parents and younger brother were stranded in Canton when the Pacific War began, while his older brother Jim, whom he was especially close to, had sailed for England the month before Pearl Harbor. Stanley was a far less orderly camp than Yangchow C, where adults felt a keen sense of responsibility towards the young people sharing their fate. There were nearly four times the number of internees and a feeling of every man for himself. Like Jose Chamberlain, Bill found his fellow internees too preoccupied with their own fate to have much compassion for a teenage boy.

The first shock he had to deal with was when he learnt his parents had left China. 'We were allowed one Red Cross letter and I sent mine to my father's address in Canton. I received a reply months later, in November 1942, saying the whole family had been repatriated.' He showed the letter to a young woman he had made friends with in camp and she asked him how he felt about it. 'I told her, it's good and it's not. I'm here and they're thousands of miles away. I was pleased for them, to know they were safe, but I did feel a bit bereft. I didn't cry, though. I never cried through loneliness.'

Bill's experience of camp was that, since there was no one in charge of him, his childhood was deemed over and he was treated like an adult. A handful of people tried to keep an eye out for the orphaned youth, who at fifteen and a half was no longer a child and yet still not a man. These included the matron from his school, who was a childless widow, and various Christian ministers, notably the dean of Hong Kong Cathedral, Aleric P. Rose, whom Bill had met while sheltering from the battle in the Church Hall. But, however kind, these remained figures of authority, stiff and formal as was the British way in colonial times. Few were parents themselves. For what remained of his boyhood the intimate, warm-blooded, rough-and-tumble of family life was denied to him.

One of his first tasks as a newly fledged 'adult' was the harrowing one of taking Matron's dog to be put down. Missie was Matron's Scottie dog, and since her husband's death, her dearest friend. Initially the camp was crowded with cats and dogs. The animal-loving British could not bear to leave their pets to a fate which in the east was highly doubtful. But within six months a decision had been taken by the camp authorities that there was not enough food to feed animals as well as humans. The camp committee decreed that all domestic animals were to be put down. Bill volunteered to take Missie up the hillside. 'I don't know how they did it because drugs were in short supply for humans. I imagine they thumped them on the head with the head of an axe or a hammer. Matron was very upset. Along with all the humans buried in the cemetery there must be scores of pets buried on the hillside.'

With no one to help him Bill had to become self-reliant. Objects once regarded as humdrum assumed a wildly inflated value in camp and could be bartered for extra food. Nothing was thrown away.

Shortly before the surrender of Hong Kong, Bill had bought some food at a shop known as the Dairy Farm. The toothbrushes given him by the Portuguese sales assistants there 'soon became luxury items so I sold them to buy soya sauce and brown sugar to make the tasteless rations a bit more palatable'.

The consequences of being classed an adult was that Bill was expected to work. His first job was in the cookhouse, which cooked for 500 to 600 people three times a day. Here he worked alongside three former colleagues of his father in the Chinese Maritime Customs. All kitchen work was coveted because it brought with it valuable perks. 'You got access to hot water, an extra bowl of rice, five cents and half a cigarette payable every ten days of the Japanese calendar.'

The work was hard and involved going back to the basics of survival. The men started by going out to collect firewood and, when the firewood ran out, grass, to light the furnaces. 'The next job was collecting the rice rations and dividing them up for the camp's three kitchens. Then you had to cook it – the rice, the sweet potatoes and the soya beans that we lived on for three and a half years. Everything was cooked in giant woks that looked as if half a dozen people could sleep in them. For a while we got a small portion of fish or meat once a week; the fish was usually going off and stank and the meat was buffalo. A week's ration was the size of four postage stamps and it had to be eaten in one go as it wouldn't keep.'

At first they used to boil the meat until it fell off the bones and then leave the bones in giant tubs and tell people to help themselves. 'But then we realised that the marrow inside the bones was valuable protein and so a chap who had been in the Merchant Navy developed a makeshift pressure cooker. We put the bones in the pressure cooker, cooked them until they were soft and turned them into a paste and gave everyone a small spoonful of the bone paste with their rice.'

Bill was a conscientious boy with a well-developed sense of right and wrong. While he was working in the kitchens at Stanley his honesty put him on a collision course with some of his colleagues. His determination not to be brow-beaten shows courage and a maturity beyond his years.

'With rations so low people began to suspect that kitchen workers were getting more than their share of food. We were entitled to an extra bowl of rice as the work was hard and lots of people in camp did no work at all. After a while the camp committee decided that our extra bowl of rice should be consumed in front of everyone. This seemed perfectly fair to me. One of my colleagues, however, felt differently. His plan was that we would eat an extra bowl of rice before we left the kitchen and still partake of our extra rations. Despite this he took umbrage at the suggestion that we were untrustworthy. He told us we were on strike and there would be no food for the internees. I disagreed and went to work as usual and cooked the rice and the sweet potatoes. As we marched out with the rice to the distribution point I heard the man call me a scab. I had only just turned seventeen but I wanted to fight him.'

In 1943 Stanley Civil Internment Camp came under military control and was designated His Imperial Majesty's Military Internment Camp. At that point all meat and fish rations ceased. Bill had no money to buy extra rations through the black market and from now on his only source of protein was soya beans. 'The hunger was the worst part of the last two years. Teenage boys are always hungry. We were people who had been used to breakfast, tiffin, tea and dinner and all we were getting now was two meals of boiled rice a day, and rotten rice sweepings at that. I thought about food constantly – English crown roast of lamb with all the chops topped with little white frills, and dishes we had in Hong Kong: wun tun, which is like ravioli, fried rice, lap cheung, which are Chinese sausages.

'To take my mind off the hunger I used to think back to the happy times at home in Canton with my family. On a snowy winter's day I would eat a full English breakfast – porridge, bacon and eggs, toast and marmalade – and then go to the servants' quarters where our Chinese cook would be waiting with delicious parcels of sticky rice wrapped in a special Chinese pastry. And off I would go on my skates to school with the snow whirling around me.'

Bill felt very low in 1943. Henry White, the school friend with whom he had been through so much during the battle for Hong Kong, was an American citizen. He was among a big group of American internees who were repatriated that spring so he lost one of the few people he called a friend. In September his hopes rose that he, too, might be repatriated, when the Canadians went home. 'A family friend from pre-war days who was sailing said she would write to my family in the hope that an uncle who had emigrated to Canada, would claim me. If he had I would have been on that boat and on my way to freedom, but my uncle never knew I was interned.'

Living on a subsistence diet Bill's health began to suffer. 'I got malaria very badly. I don't remember anything about it because I was delirious. They told me that at one stage they found me outside the hospital rolling around on the grass saying "I'm on fire." There were no quinine tablets to treat me with, only the actual bark of the cinchona tree. It was absolutely horrible to chew – it was very bitter and dried your mouth out instantly. I had a five dollar note given to me by one of the Americans who was going home and I used it to buy some wong tong, or raw brown sugar, on the black market so that I could chew the wretched stuff.'

For young people whose feet were growing, shoes had been a problem right from the start. Bill had mended his as best he could, by 'scrounging a few nails and bits of string'. In the later years he went barefoot and experienced, like so many others, the ordeal of an infected cut. 'Just before Christmas 1944, I was in hospital with a septic leg. I had no shoes by then and had cut my foot. The whole leg was swollen and extremely painful. There was no anaesthetic. The only treatment was to open it up. The Sister, who was 6 feet tall and towered over me, told me to hang onto the bars of the bed. The pain as the doctor dug in was murderous. I screamed but I didn't cry. All this stuff poured out. Afterwards there was no disinfectant, not even salt. They just washed it with water and hoped for the best.'

One thing that worried some parents in Stanley was that as a result of internment their children would become feral and amoral. There was some justification for this. The scarcity of food and fuel turned the honest into thieves; stealing from the Japanese was regarded as an act of patriotism, and the most obvious role models for children were the survivors. Stanley operated a thriving black market and, provided one had money, the black market was a short-cut to survival. Black marketeers stood out through their new clothes and plump waistlines. British agents working with free Hong Kong Chinese smuggled in life-enhancing extras – duck eggs, lard, brown sugar, salt – and sold them at extortionate prices to their starving fellow prisoners in return for post-dated cheques and IOUs. In Stanley the black market operated by prisoners ran alongside a rival system operated by the Japanese.

When Bill was approached by a black market 'godfather' and offered a franchise covering his area of the camp for a lucrative cut, he had to make up his own mind as to whether conscience should prevail over expediency. 'I thought the black marketeers were exploiting their fellow prisoners. The profit they were making was exorbitant. They were charging twenty dollars for a duck egg, which represented a profit of 400 per cent. The Japanese guards would sell you a duck egg for between two and four dollars. I could never afford a duck egg.'

After Bill turned it down the franchise was accepted by another prisoner who had been a prison warder. Bill sailed home on the same ship as him in October 1945. 'He was boasting that he wouldn't have any difficulty finding his feet in Britain as he was carrying £2,000 in post-dated cheques and IOUs. That was a huge amount of money in those days. I thought it was loathsome.'

Happily, Bill's reputation for integrity led to a promotion of which he could feel proud. Towards the end of the war the quartermaster in Stanley was taken away by the Japanese as part of a group of hostages. A replacement was needed and Bill got the job. Once again his honesty was tested. 'There were random spot checks to be sure you weren't pinching anything. We managed to get hold of some bran one day, which contained vitamin B. This was vital for preventing beriberi, which was sweeping through the camp by now as people were living on rice. The committee decided to weigh my bran and it came out to within half an ounce of what it was meant to be, which showed I hadn't been pilfering.'

As quartermaster, Bill's job was to measure out the rice and soya beans for more than 500 people and collect the rations of sweet potatoes that made up their diet. He admits that on occasion he did help his fellow prisoners – but not for profit. 'I'd bring the potatoes back in a big wheelbarrow and on my way I'd pass a nice young woman with young children and just flip a couple of sweet potatoes in through her open window. In return she gave me a razor blade, which I sharpened on a piece of glass. It lasted six months.'

Stanley was liberated in September 1945 and soon after Bill set out on his journey back to the family home in Northern Ireland. But when the ship put in at Gibraltar he received news which would upset him more than any of his experiences in camp.

Joyce Kerry (later Storey) was already separated from her parents when the war began. Joyce's parents were both missionaries in West China. They lived in a mission compound in Luchow, the main city of Szechwan province. Joyce's memories of childhood are of happy times where the weather was always warm, of playing with her dog Ramsey and her younger brother Brian, and climbing mulberry and fig trees with the children of their Chinese servants.

'We were bilingual and used to love escaping from the Mission House to the servants quarters where the food was delicious.'

Joyce didn't go to school but was taught at home by her mother, a well-read woman who had been educated at grammar school in England. Severely short-sighted all her life, photos of Joyce at this time show a girl reading with her head almost touching the page. 'My mother could be quite a severe person and my father was very busy with his mission work but we were a very close, loving family.'

In 1939 just before her eighth birthday Joyce learned that she was to be sent away to be educated at a highly regarded school for the children of missionaries in Chefoo (now Yantai) in north China. The 3,000-mile journey included a plane trip, a train journey through Indo-China to Haiphong, a boat to Hong Kong and, finally, a week-long steamer trip from Hong Kong. In those days the mammoth trip took eighteen days. Joyce was very homesick in Chefoo, suffered from the unfamiliar cold of the north China winters and missed the delicious rice-based food of Szechwan. Because of the huge distance she was not able to go home for holidays. After eighteen months her parents came to Chefoo with her younger brother Brian. Her parents stayed in the Mission House, which was dedicated to visitors, and for the Christmas term of 1940 Brian and Joyce were allowed to stay with their parents and be day pupils. Then one day in January 1941 their parents took them both out for the day. On their return they were, in Joyce's words, 'popped into boarding school'.

'When I realised what had happened I was distraught,' she says. 'I woke up in the night down the wrong end of the bed, crying. I got up and went and found a teacher and asked her for a hankie. She was the strictest of the lot and, far from sympathising, she told me she would "give me something to cry for".' Joyce was even parted from her brother as the girls' school was separate from the boys' school. The only time she saw him was when they went to church on Sunday.

For Joyce camp life began in September 1943 when the staff and 245 pupils of Chefoo School were ordered onto a very cramped and dirty steamer that took them to Tsingtao and then by train to Weihsien. The school had very little notice and had spent the last year operating in temporary accommodation after the Japanese occupied the main school building. This meant that they went in with little to make life comfortable: bedding, a few saucepans and bits of china, but very few clothes. Joyce was one of 114 children separated from their parents in Weihsien. She took in with her a few possessions that formed a precious link with her faraway family: 'I took two toys, a brown golly doll, whom I had been given on board ship on our last journey back to England, and a teddy bear. The books I took were my *Alice in Wonderland*, the Prayer Book Mum had given me and a book of the lives of the composers, which my grandfather had given me.'

One of the reasons Chefoo School were interned in Weihsien was that the Pope had been applying pressure to the Japanese to release the Catholic priests and nuns in the camp, who numbered several hundred. His efforts were eventually successful and the children were sent to take their place.

The camp had been an American mission compound with an excellent well-equipped hospital. The mission had been the scene of a battle between the Japanese and the Chinese and when the first internees arrived they found in one of the yards a 5-foot-high pile of books, tools and laboratory equipment that the victorious Japanese had burnt. Conditions were physically harsh. There were no beds for the pupils as the nuns and priests had taken theirs with them when they left. Insufficient fuel supplies meant they were cold in winter; they grew out of their clothes and shoes. Joyce fell ill with hepatitis and jaundice and was given special food from the diet kitchen. 'But I couldn't keep even that down.'

When they arrived the pupils were billeted in the block the priests and nuns had occupied. They had their own plates, which they washed after meals and kept the entire time they were in camp.

Joyce's 'plate' was an oblong frying pan. 'We slept together in a dormitory and laid mattresses on our trunks. Bedbugs were a terrible problem. We all got bitten all over. Every week we had blitzes where we went round our mattresses with knives digging them out and killing them. The bugs used to hide in the trunks in the day and come out at night.' In the icy winters, when the temperature went down to -22°C the dormitories were supposed to be heated by big metal stoves, fuelled by coal, but the coal supplies ran out and the makeshift coal balls did not give out the same heat.

As in all the camps the food was lacking in most of the vital nutrients and no Red Cross parcels reached this camp till 1944. 'We were always hungry. Breakfast was porridge made out of millet, which I liked, or a north China grain called gaoliang, which I hated. We ate it plain with no milk and we drank black tea. We didn't get any milk. We got the occasional egg.' Concern about the lack of calcium meant Weihsien was one of the camps where the adults ground up eggshell and made the children drink it mixed with water. Like all the others Joyce detested the gritty beverage – 'I used to cough and scatter it when it was my turn.' Dinner was a ladleful of vegetable stew. Instead of rice, which was not eaten in north China, the children were given tough, dry bread. 'If there was any left over it would be placed in a bin and cooked up the next day with water and served as a kind of porridge.'

At the age of fourteen Joyce started her periods, a time when a mother's presence would have been comforting. She only knew what to expect because an older pupil had explained the facts to her. There were no sanitary towels in camp so she used rags, which had to be reused. 'For the sake of privacy I used to hang, them on the bedstead in the headmistress's bedroom to dry.'

Education for the Chefoo School pupils in camp failed to reach the standards for which it had been famous before the war. Lessons took place in the dormitories with the girls sitting on their 'beds'. The teachers tried their best to keep the girls' education going but there were gaps and when she returned to England Joyce was found to be way behind her peers. 'The curriculum was limited by the lack of textbooks and paper. We hardly did any science.' In fact, lessons were often curtailed to make time for clothes-washing – a colossal task in view of the fact that there were nearly 250 pupils. 'The girls' school did theirs on Monday so we were too busy washing and pegging out to have much in the way of lessons then. The boys' washday was Tuesday and the Prep school's was Wednesday.'

As the months dragged by Joyce began to run out of clothes. 'At school our best dresses had been white. Keeping them perfect was not a problem before with servants, but in camp we dyed them green so they lasted longer between washes. We made pyjamas out of tablecloths and dresses out of curtains. I had an overcoat, which kept out the worst of the winter cold, but I had no shoes. That was fine in summer, but in winter there were puddles on the ground and my feet were cold and wet. Shortly before we left camp I was given some black Oxfords, which had belonged to someone's son. They were hardly feminine, but they kept the water out.'

All the children suffered physical discomfort in Weihsien, but most recovered their health quite quickly after the end of the war. The emotional privation suffered by sensitive teenagers like Joyce who were on their own bit deeper, however. 'The teachers did their best, but teachers in those days were pretty strict. They encouraged respect, not friendship. They were much more ready to criticise than to praise. I went without physical contact for years. My brother was my best friend in camp. I don't know what I would have done without him. I missed my family dreadfully. As a result I became very self-contained, almost withdrawn. I don't know that I ever made up for not having the support of my family in those vital years.'

Weihsien camp was liberated in September 1945 and Joyce arrived in England in December. After a separation of a month short of five years she was met by her parents and two new siblings who had been born while she was interned. She found blending back into her family extremely difficult.

Fifteen-year-old Iris Krass had no idea that she would spend her time in internment apart from her mother, younger sister and brother. By the time she was sufficiently recovered from the typhoid she had contracted soon after arriving in the Philippines to be discharged from hospital and sent to camp, the family had already been separated. Her mother and her sister Pat were billeted with other mothers of young children in a former convent, a bus ride from Santo Tomas internment camp. It would be two years before they were together again and six months before Iris's mother even knew where her daughter was. In Santo Tomas the sexes slept in separate quarters and her brother Peter was billeted with other men in a building some distance away. When Iris arrived she was directed to a room on the first floor of the main building. There were no British women in the room and no one she recognised from the ship. The women were not welcoming and their behaviour loutish.

'I was a very young fifteen-year-old and they were all years older than me. They were either American women or Hispanics who lived in Manila. Their favourite pastime was bed-pushing, surreptitiously moving their beds to try to increase the space between the beds. It caused daily rows, with accusations and counter-accusations escalating until the women were screeching and shoving and hitting each other.' One might have expected that out of so many women some would have shown a young girl separated from her family some motherly concern. Like Bill Macauley in Stanley, however, Iris found none. 'There was nothing, no introductions, even.'

An out-and-out refugee, Iris arrived in Santo Tomas with only a few items of clothing. There were no plates in camp so she was unable to eat until someone gave her a 'dish'. 'There used to be a brand of dried milk we drank in those days called Klim. Someone gave me a Klim tin which had had a piece of wire inserted in it to make a handle. Twice a day I had to queue up for food with my tin and a spoon to eat with.' Like many young people Iris was shy about undressing and hated the showers, which were communal and had no doors or partitions. 'I used to wait till midnight and go when no one else was there.'

Iris's health, like that of so many other children, suffered as a result of the meagre diet and overcrowding. She had no money and had to survive on the basic camp rations of corn mush for breakfast, with vegetable soup containing tiny pieces of meat for the other two meals. Occasionally, one of the other women would offer her a bit of Spam from their extra rations. 'I got amoebic and bacillic dysentery and I got dengue fever, which is a complication of malaria. They put me in the little camp hospital for a couple of weeks. You get blinding headaches and can't bear the light with dengue. I used to put my head under the pillow to blot out the light.' Iris's periods started in camp and she, too, had to wear rags, made specially for all the young girls by some of the women. But after a year, due to the lack of food, the periods stopped.

Iris developed a technique to protect herself from the loneliness and anguish she felt in camp. She missed her mother dreadfully at first. She tried to deal with this pain by not engaging with other people. She also made a conscious decision. 'I felt that the way to survive was to go with the flow, not think about things too much, keep busy ... so I got involved in various tasks. The third-grade rice we were served was full of bugs, so I joined a team of women who spread the rice out on big picnic tables and tried to de-weevil it. I helped with the weekly de-bugging of the beds, when the men dragged the beds out into the sun and we poured hot water on the joints. I helped in the kitchens, mainly so that I could get some of the scrapings of rice or cornmeal mush that stuck to the bottom of the pans.'

She was determined not to neglect her education and to keep her mind busy. This was particularly challenging as in camp she was not offered any tuition tailored to her youth. There was no attempt to set exams. 'Various classes were pinned up on the wall as being available, but these were aimed at adults. You could take Spanish, French or German, but there was no English literature, no history, no geography.'

There was, however, an American professor of mathematics in camp. Iris joined his class and found herself using higher mathematics to study structural engineering. 'We used calculus to calculate the various forces on bridges.' Where there was no teacher, she taught herself. 'In the basement of the main building I found a book which contained a chart depicting the evolution of the heart, digestive and nervous system, from amoeba to man. I decided to copy it out onto some brown paper I managed to find. I found it fascinating. We had had a very charming family doctor in Shanghai who had helped me with my First Aid badge for Guides and I had been interested in medicine from then.'

In the last year and a half of internment conditions deteriorated starkly. The civilian commandant who had been in charge at the beginning was replaced by a thuggish regime run by the military. Bowing was aggressively enforced and several women in Iris's room were slapped round the face until they fell down for failing to show respect. There were room searches at gunpoint in the middle of the night when the women would be required to stand by their beds in their night attire while the Japanese went around shouting. Some men who were on the camp committee complained about the rations and were removed from the camp. Their trussed bodies were found after the war shot through the head in a shallow grave.

The lack of food affected every activity. 'I wasn't conscious of hunger, though my poor brother was,' Iris says. 'Your stomach shrinks in a starvation situation. Everything stopped. Sport stopped. Classes stopped. You didn't feel like reading. You felt listless. Young as you were you lay on your bed, or on a bench, and slept.' By this time Iris's mother had been moved into camp, but she was ill with heart trouble and beriberi and spent her days in the hospital. Now it was the turn of Iris's twelve-year-old sister, Pat, to feel bereft of a mother. Towards the end of their internment the famine was somewhat relieved by the arrival of two consignments of Red Cross parcels. 'The Japanese took most of the contents. We were left with a teaspoon of jam, two cigarettes and two squares of chocolate each. I swapped the cigarettes for a tin of corned beef, which I shared with my brother. Mixing the jam with the corn mush made it rather tasty.'

Iris's response to the nightmare that surrounded her was to become detached. 'I felt I had become anonymous, that I had no identity. Although I functioned and appeared all right I didn't relate to other people. I closed my head to what was going on all around. I wasn't bothered. I became rather blank. I decided, for example, that if I wanted privacy I simply closed my eyes.'

II

The Enemy

———

The Japanese emerged from the Second World War with one outstanding stain on their reputation: the cruel and often sadistic way they treated their prisoners. Death rates among civilian internees were nothing like those that decimated the ranks of prisoners of war. However, the men, women and children who found themselves herded into internment camps from the start of 1942 soon found that their civilian status offered them little protection. This was an enemy who despised the very notion of surrender and was committed to overthrowing European empires. As their behaviour in camp would show, the Japanese were no respecters of either women or old age.

The Japanese eagerness to resort to casual and random violence towards the defenceless came as a profound shock to those British families. It wasn't just a question of punishment for serious offences such as escaping or possessing forbidden radios. In camp after camp men and women, old and young, were slapped and punched on a daily basis for trivial or trumped-up misdemeanours – failure to bow, talking during roll-call or failing to call out their number fast enough, being in the wrong place, stealing food. Face-slapping first on one cheek and then on the other was so violent that the victim often collapsed and continued to be beaten while on the ground. Sometimes other guards would hurry up and join in. Not infrequently rifle butts or swords would be used and the victim would have to be carried to hospital for medical treatment.

In most camps children were seldom the direct victims of this violence, though this was not the case in the Netherlands East Indies, as we shall see later. Paradoxical as it seems, as much a part of the Japanese character as their propensity to brutality was their fondness for children, particularly the youngest ones, to whom they liked to give sweets and ice cream. Some adults in fact believed that the presence of children in camp protected them from even worse treatment. 'There are no enemies under the age of eight' was the way one man put it.[1] Children may not often have been hit themselves, but hundreds saw their parents and other adults beaten and were distressed and terrified by it. Margaret Blair, in Yu Yuen Road, was so upset by seeing her mother punched by a Japanese guard that she began wetting the bed. They hated it, too, when the Japanese were cruel to animals – tormenting dogs was a favourite pastime. In many camps there was always some sort of punishment going on. Somebody would be sent to jail for a minor misdemeanour, rations would be cut or stopped altogether for several days. Entertainments would be forbidden.

All former internees describe the Japanese as being unpredictable. According to Ron Huckstep, interned as a fifteen-year-old in Lunghwa camp near Shanghai, 'the Japanese mentality was always difficult to understand. Sometimes they would be quite civil, and then suddenly a truck load of secret police would tear into camp in the middle of the night and take some poor chap for no apparent reason, and torture and perhaps kill him.'[2]

The ever-present, unpredictable threat of violence created a climate of fear in which children felt worried and insecure. They dreaded the shouting and yelling, the clatter of boots and clunking of swords on the ground that heralded a slapping and learnt not to look the guards in the eye.

The degree of brutality varied from camp to camp, the worst being those run by the military. On the whole internees in camps in China endured the least violence. Some children never saw any mistreatment and there was one camp (Chapei) where even bowing was not enforced. The reason for the more civilised behaviour in China is thought to be because the Japanese had never fought the British there but had merely occupied the treaty ports in the eastern section of the country in a series of peaceful takeovers. This meant these civilians were not perceived as conquered enemy aliens to be abused and humiliated in quite the same way as they were in Hong

Kong and Malaya. In addition, the China camps tended to be run by civilians with commandants recruited from the diplomatic corps. Some had been interned in Britain and America and had been impressed by their own ethical treatment. The prisoners who suffered the most savage ill-treatment were those in jungle camps in what had been the Netherlands East Indies, now Indonesia. Here it wasn't only adults who were ill-treated, but also boys whom the Japanese classed as men from as young as ten. Most of the camps there and in Malaya were run either by the army or the navy. In some camps the regime alternated between military and civilian. Takeover by the military always heralded a deterioration in conditions and an increase in punishment. No matter how hard successive generations try to explain the reasons, the sheer sadism of some of the incidents remains beyond most people's comprehension.

Many who experienced the violence of the Japanese believe there was a racial element to the brutality. The Japanese soldier was not very sophisticated or well educated. Many were barely literate. Before the war the Japanese military machine had devised a crude propaganda programme designed to whip up hatred of European colonials. The Indonesians, in particular, were targeted with films and posters designed to inflame hatred of the Dutch. One of the avowed aims of the Greater East Asia Co-Prosperity Sphere was expressed by the unabashedly racist 'Asia for the Asians'. The newspaper editorial published after the fall of Hong Kong proclaiming that the white races had 'melted like butter' left no doubt about the writer's distaste for the vanquished. Now, after more than a century of being looked down on by Europeans, who in those days regarded all Orientals as inferior, it was payback time.

But it was more than a simple question of revenge against the overbearing colonials. The Japanese soldier had been bred to cope specifically with pain from the start of his training. In contrast to Western tradition, which emphasised stamina and endurance in the building of a tough fighter, Japanese military training used pain and humiliation to toughen up its troops. Officers would slap student officers, who would then hit NCOs to see how much they could take. Then NCOs would hit privates, who, in turn, hit prisoners. Bushido, the way of the warrior, was their rallying cry. It was a code handed down the centuries from the universally feared, bloodthirsty samurai of old, committed to fight to the death for honour's sake. Many children saw evidence of this brutalising behaviour and were shocked by it.

In April 1945 Margaret Blair had been transferred with her mother and brother from Yu Yuen Road in central Shanghai to Yangtzepoo camp, a much more cramped site in the industrial suburbs. Because it was next to one of their military bases the Japanese assumed they would be protected as they knew the Allies would not bomb their own prisoners. The camp was sited in a former convent. Looking over the wall Margaret watched convalescing patients in the Japanese military hospital being drilled by their officers. 'We could see all Japanese military patients who were not confined to bed being drilled at early morning exercises until some of them collapsed. The drill-master shouted and kicked at the fallen men until they fainted or somehow managed to stand up again. These exercises took place twice a day.'[3]

Interned on Sumatra in what was then the Netherlands East Indies, thirteen-year-old Ralph Armstrong regularly saw women being beaten and slapped and was slapped himself for not noticing a Japanese was passing and failing to bow – 'a thunderous slap, which would send your head spinning'.

'If they [the Japanese] felt slighted while making a speech ... they would send the guards into the crowds to bash the prisoners with their rifle butts, truncheons or their fists. People fell down, women shrieked and screamed ... we were left to help the injured back to the dormitories, some of them so badly hurt they had to be carried back.'[4]

Ralph saw a link between the dehumanised way the Japanese treated their prisoners and the way they were treated in their own ranks.

'If a soldier tried to argue with a higher rank he was instantly slapped hard across the face. He had to stand to attention while being slapped and shout "Hai", meaning "yes" to whatever he was being told. If the officer was a little man and the soldier resisted, some others would come to the aid of the officer, and hit the soldier with their rifle butts till he fell to the ground.'[5]

One of the triggers for outbursts of violence was loss of face. The Japanese were highly rank-conscious within their own society and thin-skinned where their dignity was concerned. This could lead to acts of what to the internees was proof of the barbarous nature of their captors.

The prisoners in Lincoln Avenue camp, where Dick Germain was interned with his grandfather and uncle in June 1944, had an Alsatian dog. During an official visit, a sergeant of the guards, keen to prove how relaxed and friendly the atmosphere was in camp, called the dog, but instead of trotting over the dog kept his distance and began to bark. This was passed off with a laugh, but after the visitors had left, the guards were instructed to find the dog and bring it to the sergeant major. The dog was eventually found and all the internees were summoned to an open space and the sergeant major appeared with his sword. 'The dog was tied up with ropes so it could not move and then the sergeant major proceeded to beat the living daylights out of it with the back of his sword.' The guards then tried to decapitate the unfortunate animal but one of the camp doctors intervened and was allowed to give the dog a lethal injection.[6]

It was a distressing scene for children to witness. 'We children were fond of these dogs. We used to feed them scraps of the food that we found too disgusting to eat. There was another dog in camp and we were all so terrified that it would meet the same fate that in the end it was smuggled out of camp in one of the food carts.'

In another camp the bravery of an animal-loving little girl saved a dog from an agonising death. Helen Ford was interned in Lunghwa at the age of nine with her mother and father. One day she saw some guards with a small dog. 'They had tied a rope round its neck and were about to hang it. I adored animals and I was absolutely furious. I rushed over to them, trampling the internees' vegetable plots in the process, and told them they couldn't do it, that it was horrible and cruel – all in English of course. I spoke fluent Shanghai-ese, but not Japanese. They thought it was really funny that I was so angry, but I managed to stop them and the dog ran off. They were just doing it for fun, because they were bored.'

The Japanese were at their most savage where a prisoner's refusal to capitulate caused a perceived loss of face. Neil Begley's father, a major in the Salvation Army, had left his mission base in Peking when war broke out to go and help the people of Hong Kong. He ran a soup kitchen for refugees before being interned in Stanley.

Begley was Australian and the Japanese had mapped out a role for him as an Australian version of Lord Haw Haw. He was to make propaganda radio broadcasts to the Australians, ahead of the planned invasion, telling them of the Japanese goodwill towards them and suggesting they welcome the invasion instead of offering resistance. In return he would be released from camp and installed in a luxury apartment in Shanghai's top hotel. Major Begley refused. He was subjected to a savage beating and when he still refused he was led outside, in front of his horrified wife, for execution by firing squad. But this was all part of the torture. He was led back into the guard-room and beaten again before being led out once more to be executed. This ordeal was repeated three times. Major Begley would undoubt-edly have been killed had not a less scrupulous Australian woman internee, hearing of the commandant's proposition, volunteered for the assignment in his place. His two sons, who were at boarding school in northern China at the time, learned of it when the family were reunited in Shanghai, before being interned together.

Violence inevitably followed wherever the kempeitai made their appearance, and children were not always shielded from it. On occa-sion the Japanese explicitly demanded their presence. One of the worst examples of atrocity towards civilian internees of the entire war occurred in Changi prison where Mel and Barbara Bruce were interned. On 10 October 1943 the Japanese arrested and tortured fifty-seven prisoners in the prison. The raid, which became known as the Double Tenth, occurred because the Japanese had been the victims of a series of audacious attacks of sabotage in Singapore, culminating in the sinking of six of their ships in the harbour. They suspected the internees of complicity in the attacks. The inter-rogations were so severe that fifteen of the men died under torture. The prisoners in fact knew nothing of the sinkings, which were carried out by a team of British and Australian commandos. Mel Bruce, who was fifteen at the time, was present when the Japanese began the hunt for the radio they believed was responsible for coord-inating the attacks.

'The whole of the men's wing in the prison was turned out into the main exercise yard and made to stand in rows in the boiling heat all day, whilst the Japanese Kempeitai did a thorough search of the entire prison ... During this time many prisoners, including youngsters, fainted and fell to the ground, but the guards insisted that they should remain where they had fallen, and we were not allowed to assist anyone.'[7]

Changi was the scene of many brutal punishments. For the Japanese, cowing and frightening children by making them witness savagery, was the most effective way of enforcing discipline.

Mel had to do his share of fatigues in camp and for a while this involved going out of camp to cut wood for the kitchen fires. On one of these trips the prisoners came upon a village which had recently been visited by the kempeitai. One of the village women had been suspected of stealing from Japanese food stores and selling the goods on the black market. 'The unfortunate woman had been tied to a stake in a clearing in the village, her hands tied to her sides, her head had been severed as a punishment and the gruesome sight left as a warning.' The sight was so shocking that almost everyone in the working party was violently sick – including the Japanese guard.[8]

Despite the stated aims of the Greater East Asia Co-Prosperity Sphere – it professed to be an alliance of Oriental races against the European imperialists – Japan's ultimate plan was to run Asia itself, with all other Oriental races subordinate to its empire. The Japanese regarded the Chinese as inferior and they were frequently the victims of Japanese cruelty. Many Shanghai children saw Chinese mistreated in the city before internment began. This continued in camp. In Lunghwa a young internee called James Ballard, later to become the best-selling writer J. G. Ballard, author of *Empire of the Sun*, actually witnessed a murder. It occurred towards the end of the war in front of a large crowd of prisoners. Two Japanese had returned from Shanghai and, for no reason, turned on the rickshaw coolie who had brought them. The terrible scene took place within 30 feet of the boy. 'As the desperate man sobbed on his knees the Japanese first kicked his rickshaw to pieces, probably his only possession in the world and sole source of income, and then began to beat and kick the Chinese until he lay in a still and bloody pulp on the ground.'

The boy noted that none of the adult prisoners watching the attack tried to prevent it: 'I ... understood why none of the British ... had tried to intervene. The reprisals would have been instant and fearsome. I remember feeling a deep deadness, which may have been noticed by one of my father's friends, who steered me away.' Ballard offered an original explanation for the brutality that seemed endemic in the culture of the enemy. 'In some way, I think the Japanese soldier assumed unconsciously that he had already died in battle, and the apparent life left to him was on a very short lease.'[9]

In the women's wing of Changi prison Barbara, then aged ten, was likewise not spared from witnessing brutality. 'With us in camp was a lovely woman we all liked. She was in her forties, was Canadian and worked for the British Red Cross, which was why the Japanese interned her. She was a very tall woman and always very positive and optimistic. She had a tiny radio, which she kept in a matchbox. She used it to keep in touch with the progress of the war and used to tell us not to worry, that things were going well and it wouldn't last much longer ... One of the other women split on her in return for extra rations and the Japanese took her away. We heard that they'd tortured her. I dread to think what they did to her.'

Barbara was playing on the lawn in the centre of the prison when they brought her back. 'I saw the empty, glassy look in her eyes as they walked her down the steps. She was a pitiful sight. She had lost her mind. She couldn't hold a normal conversation any more. She was such a wonderful person, it terrified us all. All she did was sing at the top of her voice – patriotic songs like 'Rule Britannia'. It infuriated the Japs. They put her in a padded cell. Her singing seemed to intensify when the moon was full.'

One night when the woman was singing loudly a Japanese guard went up to her cell and poked his bayonet through the bars to shut her up. 'They say that mad people are capable of superhuman strength. Instead of quietening down she grabbed him round the throat with both hands and squeezed. He was short like most Japanese and she lifted him up so that his feet left the ground. He let go of his rifle, which fell to the ground with a clatter. This alerted the other guards who ran up and prised her hands off his neck. He was gasping for breath and if the guards hadn't rushed up when they did I think she would have killed him. Strangely, they didn't punish her any more.'

From the start prisoners in Singapore received very little food. In their desperate search for vitamins they grew vegetables, but the general hunger meant that the crops were often stolen. The internees stealing from each other provided the Japanese with a fresh excuse for refined cruelty.

Barbara Bruce remembers the occasion two sisters stole vegetables from the vegetable patch because they were so hungry. 'They were a family of five children called Harris and they shared the same hut as us. The Japanese found out who the culprits were and then went to the men's camp and fetched Mr Harris who had been a prison officer. They brought him to the fence dividing the two camps and made him kneel on the sharp stones in the full midday heat. They then brought the girls out and made them watch while they hit him over and over on the head and shoulders with their truncheons. The girls were sobbing and crying but the more they cried the more the guards rained blows down on their father. He pleaded with them not to cry. In the end he passed out and the guards called a couple of the other prisoners to take him away.'

In many of the camps children were left in no doubt that there could be a worse fate than a beating. In Stanley camp in Hong Kong, as in Changi, radios were discovered and this invariably meant the death penalty. One group of teenage boys, to their shock, found themselves witnessing the Japanese version of summary justice. John Stanton was eleven when he arrived in Stanley. The family, his father a British businessman and his mother a Norwegian, had been separated for six months as the parents had taken their son up to school in Tientsin in northern China shortly before the outbreak of war. On their return to Hong Kong they were interned. Their son was one of a number of European children whom the Japanese allowed to be reunited with their parents and John had arrived in camp by launch in June 1942.

On his arrival he palled up with three other boys the same age as himself. They called themselves the four musketeers and were dedicated to adventure. One day they got more than they bargained for. 'The four of us decided to go up to the church and have a good look round. All of a sudden we heard voices and footsteps just the other side of the perimeter fence – we ducked right down and watched. There were three Japs with swords and five men ... digging their own graves. They made each man in turn bend down and chopped their heads off, the next man had to fill in the grave so that the last man the Japs had to fill in. The blood from one man spurted out within two or three feet of us.'

Escapes were viewed by the Japanese with the same severity as communicating with the outside world, and Stanton was lucky not to find himself in seriously hot water when he assisted an escaper. He was walking back from his job of looking after the chickens when a young man asked him if he knew the best place to get out of camp. Stanton and the three other musketeers, like children in other camps, used to scramble under the wire regularly to pick guavas to eat. Their places were well chosen, hidden from the eyes of the guards by bushes. He gave the would-be escaper, whom he didn't know, a choice of three places. Being adult the man chose the largest hole. 'He told me he chose to go immediately after tenko [evening] which would give him a chance to get away from the area ... One week later he went, he was caught within two days and brought back to our camp.' The punishment stopped short of execution, but was sobering enough to the teenager who had helped him. 'They gave him a good beating and used the water torture on him. Pumping him full of water and then jumping on his stomach, he eventually passed out, [was] taken to our hospital and survived.'[10]

The following year, also in Stanley, there were further executions. This time the Japanese meant the internees to take note.

Bill Macauley was part of the audience when the whole camp was summoned to witness the men's fate. 'One day ... after I had done a shift as part of a work squad, digging and weeding the Japs' vegetable gardens, we were all told to assemble on the parade ground in front of Stanley prison. They made us stand there for hours and anyone who swayed or staggered got smacked round the face or was jabbed in the back by a rifle butt. Suddenly the Japs moved the front line back and a half-covered truck appeared from inside the prison. Inside were some prisoners, faces I knew. I only saw four, but there were in fact six. They called out "Goodbye boys. You won't be seeing us again. They're going to shoot us." I was thunderstruck. There had been talk of a secret radio having been found in camp and I'd seen prisoners digging for radios watched by Jap guards, but I hadn't realised where it would lead. They drove them down to Stanley Beach. We never saw them again.'

Parents in Stanley, as in all the camps, tried to prevent their children from seeing the punishments. Towards the end of the war a woman prisoner suspected of having tried to cheat a Japanese guard in a black market deal was badly beaten.

Bill Macauley saw the incident. 'One evening I had gone to arrange a bridge party with some fellow players when I heard screaming. I looked up and saw a white woman being beaten by a Jap with a bamboo stick. You could see this pole going up and down rhythmically. One of the women there said to me, "My daughter is up on the roof watching. Can you please get her down." I went up and found this girl, she was only fourteen or fifteen. She was counting the blows out loud as they fell. When she reached sixteen I decided she had had enough. But she was transfixed. I had quite a job getting her down. It must have been very traumatic to be seeing something horrific happening and not be able to budge. I met up with that young girl fifty years later and she couldn't recall the incident. I think the body does that with things that are damaging. It shuts them off.'

The Japanese were at their most savage when they considered themselves unobserved and therefore not judged by the eyes of the world. Running camps hidden in the jungles of Java and Sumatra they felt relatively free of the eye of the Red Cross inspectors. Inside the borders of Japan itself, where there were six civilian internment camps, they felt even less restricted. This goes some way to explaining the petty cruelty with which the Japanese treated the inmates of Fukushima camp, 150 miles north-east of Tokyo. This camp housed 140 men, women and children, nearly half of whom were British. The internees were survivors of shipwrecks whose vessels had been attacked by German ships in the south Atlantic. The camp operated a list of 133 rules, which were enthusiastically enforced. Thuggish guards were given permission to hit at will. No. 79 stipulated that only children may sing; no. 73 ordered 'Must not wrap blanket round body above waist during any time', no. 7, 'Must only wash face, feet and hands daily', no. 36, 'must always do anything any guard orders at any time'. This included admitting a guard to the washroom when the women were using it, and even allowed admission to enter an occupied lavatory.

The women of Fukushima wrote to the Red Cross complaining about the harsh conditions in which they were held. The beatings featured prominently. 'On one occasion a guard unmercifully attacked one of the women . . . he threw her to the ground and kicked her several times in the face. She was compelled to remain in bed for a week to recover from her physical injuries and it was many weeks before she recovered from the nervous shock. Another woman was hit sharply on the head with a key for closing a dining room window. She went immediately to the office to lodge a complaint – the guard followed her and in front of the captain slapped her face. Becoming more and more enraged he followed her out of the office, grabbed her throat, bent her back across a table preparatory to hitting her again. He was, however, pulled off by the interpreter, whereupon he seized a chair and went for her again.'

In this camp children were not exempt. A ten-year-old boy who had been to the refuse pit to empty a bin, paused on the way back to make snowballs. He was made to stand in pouring sleet for one and a half hours. The women were not allowed to give him a coat and his clothing was soon soaked through. He developed a bad chill and later contracted jaundice, which kept him in bed for eight weeks.

A seven-year-old boy broke a pane of glass in a door while playing ball with two friends. The three boys were taken to the office by the guard and their mothers summoned for interrogation by the camp commandant, Captain Wimoto. When the women arrived they found their children trembling with fear and crying. Their clothing above the waist had been pulled up and their hands linked below their bare abdomens. On an open brazier two pokers were being heated. Through the interpreter Mr Midorikawa, the captain questioned the mothers and declared that they were to blame. One of the mothers pleaded with the commandant to show mercy, reminding him that the children had already been through a traumatic ordeal by being shipwrecked. But her plea fell on deaf ears. To their horror, speaking via the interpreter, the commandant ordered the women to remove the pokers from the brazier and burn the children's bare stomachs. One mother burst into tears and refused to comply and her son begged her not to burn him too much. The other mothers also refused; the children were wailing with terror. Faced with mutiny on the part of the mothers Captain Wimoto picked up the poker and brought it so close to the children's faces that it singed their hair.

So outraged were they by the incident that the mothers wrote a report about it, which they addressed to the Red Cross. In conclusion, they wrote, 'the memory of this brutal treatment haunted the boys for several months and had a most serious effect on their nervous systems – and also that of their mothers'. The report is signed with the three mothers' names.[11]

Even in Yangchow, one of the more civilised camps, some Japanese favoured exemplary punishments, often for trumped-up reasons. These would be witnessed by the whole camp, children included. In the bitter winter of 1944 a man called Savage, who was head of the camp Public Works committee, a family man and a devout evangelical Christian, was instructed to convert the bathhouse into billets for a group of Belgians who were being interned. He received permission from the commandant to relocate two doors to give greater privacy in the women's toilets. He didn't, however, seek clearance from another Japanese guard, who was the official supply officer. The Japanese man, a thug, who was widely feared in camp, forced the man, who was recovering from a bad attack of malaria, to kneel for two and a half hours on the snow-covered ground. Grace Harvey, who was eight at the time, and the daughter of a missionary, was morbidly intrigued by this humiliation of a respected adult. 'We children of the church were fascinated. We could see Savage's figure as he knelt alone among the drifting snowflakes. "Come away from that window!" came the curt voice of anxious parents.'[12]

It would be wrong to say that all the Japanese with whom internees came into contact were brutes. It was part of the contradictory nature of the culture that the same guard who would enjoy slapping and knocking down a child's mother would happily give sweets to her child. The number of internees with consistently pleasant memories of their captors is very small, but there were commandants who were widely regarded as decent and humane and that did help set the tone in camp. However, they often had rowdy and thuggish guards under them and were not always in a position to control them. Equally, there were commandants who were harsh but who included in their team guards who were family men themselves and who sympathised with the interned families.

In China many of the commandants were former diplomats to whom the violent 'way of the warrior' credo was as alien as it was to the internees. Used to mixing as equals with people of other races, they lacked the racial paranoia of their less cultured subordinates. Tomohiko Hyashi, commandant of Lunghwa camp, was one of these. He had spent four years in London with his wife and young son. Interned on the Isle of Man, he was repatriated in the first exchange of internees.* An honest man, Hyashi tried to protect the internees from exploitative dealers. He was also a kind man. He lent his private car so that a prisoner could visit his mother, who was in another camp, on Christmas Eve 1943. Winners of junior sports events at Lunghwa camp's sports day would be personally rewarded by the commandant with a packet of sweets. He extended the curfew by one hour on New Year's Eve. Mr Hyashi could be said to have been too kindly for his own good. He extended the camp's boundaries, which made it more difficult for the guards to patrol. This resulted in a series of successful escapes, which led to Mr Hyashi being demoted in favour of a tougher replacement.

Ann March, who was in Lunghwa camp from the age of ten, discovered Hyashi's gentle nature for herself. The commandant had some terrapins which were kept in a large earthenware bath, or kong, and it was Anne's job to look after them. But she thought that their living conditions were cruel and decided to rectify the situation. 'I got very worried about them swimming all the time so I tried to build up a platform for them to sun themselves on, and, of course, completely forgot that they could easily get over the edge. One day, when I came to feed them, they had all gone and the guard was called out and searched for them and not a single one was found. I think probably someone had caught them and eaten them and I quite thought I was going to be shot, but he [the commandant] was very sweet about it and let me off.'[13]

It seems extraordinary that in places where men were being tortured to death guards were being nice to children, but even in Changi prison, the youngest internees occasionally experienced kindness. Barbara Bruce remembers that in the evening, when they were allowed to play on the lawn in the centre of the compound, the sentries patrolling the ramparts above them would throw sweets

* Hyashi's son was the Japanese Ambassador to London from 1997–9.

down. On one occasion a guard treated her less like an enemy alien
than like a daughter.

'One night when it was really hot and I was sleeping on the veranda
in my camp bed I woke up feeling something was biting my head.
I was screaming in agony. The lady next door had got hold of some
palm oil, which was highly nutritious, and it had attracted red ants.
They had invaded her bed and had spread to mine. The Japanese
guard who was on duty at the gate came rushing over with his torch
to see what the matter was. I wore my hair in long plaits and this
guard gently undid my plaits, got a fine comb and combed through
my hair until the last ant was gone.'

Like many children Barbara was happy to exploit the Japanese
fondness for children to get her own way. 'At one stage my father
was very ill with beriberi from the poor diet and was in hospital in
the men's camp. There was a guard on duty and visits were not
allowed. But I had learned the Japanese anthem and I sang it to the
guards. They were so impressed that they let me speak to my father
through the window.'

Barbara's older brother Mel, in the men's prison, found similar
humanity on occasion. Some Japanese, like soldiers in any war, were
less interested in fighting and killing than in getting back to their
home and family. When they turned fifteen, the boys were allowed
to go out with the men on wood-cutting parties. Mel spoke Malay,
which was useful when they wanted to barter with the natives. One
guard was happy to turn a blind eye while the internees conducted
their 'business'. 'On one occasion he sat on a log enjoying a cigarette
and showed me photographs of his wife and family in Kyoto, and in
sign language conveyed the fact that it had been two years since he
had seen them. I wonder now if indeed he ever saw them again.'14

On occasion the kindness would appear more like kidnap to suspicious parents who believed their captors capable of any cruelty.
Myra Scovel, the wife of an American doctor, was interned in
Weihsien camp when she lost her little boy. He was missing for
several hours and his mother got other internees to help her comb
the camp, and the environs, looking for him. Just before dark he
was seen leaving the Japanese commandant's headquarters eating an
apple. 'He had had a wonderful day. The officers had taken him

home with them, shown him a cow and some new puppies and had given him sweets and the apple.'[15]

Some of the children in camps report individual acts of kindness from guards who clearly felt sorry for them – and particularly for the fact that they were so hungry. Dick Germain, in Lincoln Avenue camp in Shanghai, was one youngster who experienced the sympathy of a guard. Before the war Dick's father had been Assistant Secretary of the Chinese Maritime Customs. The boy was growing tomato plants from seed in the camp vegetable plot when, to his dismay, a guard who was passing, nipped out the heads of the plants. He then signalled to the boy to follow him and they walked to the garden behind the guards' house. 'There, in a cold frame, were a number of tomato plants, which were four times the height of mine. He indicated that I should take the bigger plants to replace mine. He indicated that mine would take too long to produce. I didn't realise that he was telling me that the war might be over soon.'[16]

In most camps internees regarded their Japanese guards with suspicion, adopting the habit of expecting the worst. When a Japanese guard did show sympathy, it was sometimes mistaken for something more sinister. In Yangchow C camp, tucked away in the interior of China, there was one guard who was always kind to the children. Yamamoto was plump, jolly and rather scruffy and often showed the children photos of his own children with their mother. With the exception of camps in the Netherlands East Indies, the numbers of children who died during internment compared with the adults was low. One of the most tragic events to occur in Yangchow was the death of a thirteen-year-old boy. Sonny Rees was the son of a widowed mother and had been a pupil at the Cathedral School in Shanghai, where he sang in the choir. He had been in the same class as Neil Begley and the two were best friends. Sonny died in the camp hospital on Neil's eleventh birthday of what many believe was diphtheria, but was described somewhat vaguely as 'constriction of the throat'.

The funeral in the mission church was already underway when 'the service was interrupted by the tramp of boots and the clank of a sword as a Japanese guard came into the church. Father O'Collins stopped the ritual ... We were all alarmed and outraged at this intrusion. But it was Yamamoto who stood in the doorway. Slowly he removed his cap, then to our amazement he unbuckled his sword and laid it on the table inside the door ... with bent head he moved quietly up the aisle, bowed to Sonny's coffin then sat down beside Mrs Rees. We could see his shoulders shaking with the heart-rending sobs that racked his body.'[17]

Very occasionally a Japanese guard was prepared to put his life at risk to help them. Such a man was Kiyoshi Watanabe, known in Stanley camp as Uncle John. Watanabe was a Buddhist who had converted to Christianity. Trained in America as a Lutheran pastor, he spoke English and in 1944 worked as an interpreter. The Japanese treated their internees here appallingly – feeding them starvation rations and depriving them of all medical supplies. Their excuse – that they themselves didn't have enough food or drugs – was exposed at the end of the war when the stores were broken into and found to contain undistributed food parcels from the Red Cross and medical supplies in abundance. The humane Watanabe was shocked at the way his fellow Japanese were treating the prisoners and did his best to help them, smuggling in letters, money, food and vital drugs.

William Sewell wrote of Watanabe: 'He did not tire in trying to help those who had friends or relatives missing in Hong Kong ... He always had a pleasant smile on his face, while in his pocket were biscuits for David and George, [children in camp] to whom he tried to teach a few words of Japanese ... he was the only Japanese, who had lived in the camp, upon whom no suspicion of cruelty fell.'[18]

His obvious lack of hatred for the enemy was noted by his fellow officers who suspected him of treacherous activity and regarded him with ongoing suspicion. Despite this Watanabe took huge risks with his own life to show compassion. In so doing he saved the life of at least one young internee. 'When he heard of extreme cases of need he would use his own money and smuggle in special food and drugs which saved or alleviated many lives. We had a youth in his teens who came into camp with diabetes. The doctors had a stock of insulin to start with and were occasionally able to get some more until none was left. It seemed certain that the lad would die. One of them was able to have a private word with Watanabe and he bought a supply on the black market in the city (he must have paid a wicked price).'[19] The boy survived the regime in Stanley but sadly died on the ship taking him home, due, it is thought, to not being given sufficient time to get used to normal food after years of a near-starvation diet. Malnutrition affected the eyesight of a lot of internees and when one boy's eyes started to give trouble they asked Uncle John if he could help – and he did, knowing that he faced execution if caught. 'He was a very brave man.'[20] Watanabe was not supposed to fraternise with the internees but in 1944, as a fellow Christian, he attended the Sunday School Christmas party and sang Japanese hymns to his fellow guests.

The kindness of this good and courageous man brought comfort to many. It was not, sadly, to bring him any reward. In one of the bitterest ironies of the war the atom bomb dropped on Hiroshima destroyed Watanabe's home and killed his wife and one of his daughters. All that remained of his marriage was a metal fitting from his wife's handbag and a distorted piece of metal that had been part of her sewing machine.[21]

12

Baiting the Enemy

The way prisoners viewed the Japanese depended to a large extent on what camp they were in. In camps that witnessed executions, beatings and torture they were regarded with a mixture of fear and hatred. In others where no one escaped and no radios were found, where internees were treated with decency by civilised commandants, hatred was replaced by a wary mutual tolerance. What united the two groups, however, was the common view that 'the Jap', as the enemy was invariably referred to, was ridiculous. Children, with their reduced sense of danger and their irrepressible taste for mischief, were quick to pick up on this. In many camps the guards were accompanied on their rounds by crowds of young children, parodying their movements and exploiting their lack of English to tease them. Older boys, with a nose for danger, took incredible risks to annoy the oppressor. Humour is a powerful weapon and even the most cowed internee took secret delight in anything that made fun of the enemy. They mocked their shortness. This meant that their curved swords often bumped along the ground as they walked, that European women of average height towered over them and that they often had to resort to boxes to stand on when making announcements, or even to hit people. Women interned in women-only camps in the Netherlands East Indies made fun among each other of their smooth legs, comparing them unfavourably with the hairy calves of their own men; they found their strange rubber boots with the separate compartment for the big toe ridiculous, they mocked their obsession with solemn ritual and bowing.

Most of the time, the mockery was secret and internalised. But occasionally it broke cover, creating irresistible bubbles of mirth and schadenfreude that united everyone in camp and made them forget, for a moment, the bleakness of their situation. Entertainment provided a perfect cloak for communicating secret messages of hope which, enjoyably, were lost on the Japanese authorities sitting in front row seats. In Santo Tomas in Manila an American comedian, who was one of the internees, kept his audience up to speed on the island-hopping advance of US forces by a series of coded messages, which the Japanese politely and uncomprehendingly applauded. 'Better latey than never' was his punning way of telling his audience of just how far the tide had turned in the Allies' favour — and how close they were to rescue. The Battle of Leyte Gulf in October 1944 had been one of the largest naval battles in history, and had caused crippling losses to the Japanese navy.

In Stanley camp, despite the lack of food the regime prided itself on its civilised treatment of prisoners. During a camp show, which the commandant and his staff usually attended, photographs were taken by a Japanese photographer to show how well the Japanese treated their prisoners. To the fury of the Japanese, who banned all entertainment as a result, the developed photographs showed some of the children making V for victory signs as they smiled for the camera.

Many of the pranks involved stealing, but one can't help feeling that in the relatively unsupervised atmosphere of camp, the search for kicks was at least as powerful a motive as hunger. In Sime Road camp in Singapore Mel Bruce and a gang of other teenagers took the colossal risk of raiding the Japanese food stores. They had noticed a large storm drain, which began within the men's camp and ended as a grill-covered manhole right outside the door of the Japanese cookhouse, and became intrigued as to where it led. 'Some of us lads explored the drain, crawling all the way along up to the grill, and found that the grill simply lifted off and gave access to the yard next to the cookhouse, and boys being boys, we decided it would be a simple matter to raid the cookhouse under cover of darkness, and see what could be found.'

A raid was duly planned. Lookouts were positioned at various vantage points, and when the time came two of the boys went underground to see what they could find. Mel and another boy were lookouts. About half an hour passed, the lads were beginning to wonder what had happened, 'when suddenly our two raiders emerged from the drain dragging a small sack with them. We scurried off and, when well away from the scene, stopped and shared out the contents, which included rice cakes, a coconut, some bread and a few oranges ...'

Astonishingly, the boys repeated the escapade twenty-five times, coming within a whisker of getting caught. 'On one occasion I was lucky to get away with a slight bayonet wound to my left knee when we were discovered by a Japanese soldier ... It caused quite a shindig, but as it was dark they put it down to local natives ... Little did they suspect that we had relieved them of quite a lot of foodstuffs, also some of their bottled beer and sake which the men in our hut enjoyed thoroughly.'[1]

In Yangtzepoo camp Margaret Blair's brother Gordon, now thirteen, had a similar taste for mischief and risk-taking. His energy is all the more surprising as the internees were moved here from Yu Yuen Road in the spring of 1945, at a time when many adults were weak and ill. Gordon's reign of terror started with a childish prank. 'At about sunset every evening the Japanese guards took a bath in very hot water contained in congs [very deep tubs in this case made of metal] heated from below by fires. They lit the fires, left them to heat the water and then returned to have baths when the water was hot, first extinguishing the fires. The 'Gang of three' [composed of Gordon and two other boys of the same age] had the bright idea of stealing into the bathhouse when the guards were away and playing a trick on them. I saw the boys creep in carrying handfuls of mud which they threw into the heating water. They then hid upstairs with me and we watched to see the result ... Along came the guards. They looked forward to their baths after a day working in the hot and humid Shanghai weather. The Japanese stripped and settled gratefully into the hot water – only to realise that something was in there with them. They jumped out, saw the mess they were in and went wild. Clad in towels the guards rushed out looking for the culprits.'[2]

As time went by the gang of three grew bolder until they dared each other to climb over the convent wall into the Japanese barracks next door and steal equipment from them. The Japanese soldiers used little portable cookers to heat up food, which were far simpler – and safer – to use than the electric burner owned by the Blairs' mother, which had to be connected to the light socket. They referred to these cookers as 'Canned Heat' and decided to steal a box of them. Their escapade sounds like something from the Just William stories.

'That night the Gang of Three stole away from their rooms when everyone else was asleep, found a box of Canned Heat and tied a rope around it. Between them they had no trouble carrying the box to the wall and positioning themselves before starting to haul it over. One boy was on the camp side of the wall pulling. Another sat on top of the wall guiding the rope and the third (Gordon) pushed the box up from the outside.' All went well until they had the box about halfway up. Suddenly the boys heard a guard coming. They froze in mid action. Gordon, who was on Japanese territory, silently slid behind a bush. But their luck held and the guard paced by without noticing. 'When the boys finished they fell about, doubled over with suppressed laughter. This was the best raid yet.'

The boys so enjoyed the idea of cheating the Japanese that they continued to steal supplies of Canned Heat long after all internees had more than they needed. On the last occasion they managed to evade a carefully laid Japanese trap and returned with their booty – only to find they had nowhere to store it. They hit on the idea of hiding the cookers in a barrel of pig's swill destined for a pig donated by the Red Cross.

Margaret woke early the next morning to see one of the gang entering their room with an anxious look on his face. 'He shook Gordon awake and beckoned him to come out. As Gordon pulled on his clothes Ronnie whispered that he had just been to check on the cans – and had found them floating, bobbing around on top of the pig's swill. Gordon and Ronnie rushed out along the corridor and down the stairs ... I rounded the corner to the sty just in time to see (them) putting straw ... over the cans just as people were beginning to wake up and walk about.'[3]

The pranks proved infectious and nearly led to disaster. As a way of upping the stakes an older boy stole three bottles of spirit from the commandant's office. The commandant was furious and ordered the camp representative to hand over the culprits, threatening severe reprisals. It was touch and go. The commandant ordered a full camp assembly for the next day. The boys were saved by the announcement of the end of the war.[4]

It was at their former camp in Yu Yuen Road that one of the boldest, and most risky, teases of the Japanese was hatched. Possessing radios was a capital offence. That didn't deter a brave and resourceful electrician in Yu Yuen Road. Mr Kawasaki, the camp commandant, who had the reputation for being a fair man, had a radio contained in a cabinet that needed repairing. The electrician who volunteered to help innocently requested more parts than he needed. Eventually he had enough to build a short-wave radio to obtain news of the war. An ever-changing group of internees would plug the radio into a hidden spot which housed a map of the world, and tune in, covered with blankets to deaden the sound, for news of the war. Other prisoners acted as lookouts. They were able to receive KGEI (a short-wave radio station broadcasting to the Far East) from San Francisco as well as Australian stations. Knowing how the Allies were progressing kept spirits up in the later stages of the war.

The Japanese never found the radio. Yet it was on full view most days. The electrician had disguised it in a pull-along toy, which his child often played with in full view of the guards. During searches the boy would be sent out to play with it under the very noses of the guards.[5]

One of the Japanese customs internees found irritating and risible was bouts of noisy, highly ritualised traditional fencing. The weapons they used for this sport were either bamboo fences or dummy wooden rifles with the bayonet tip protected by a rubber guard. In Yangchow C camp the Japanese insisted that the internees watch these contests, where, to their fury, the prizes were taken from Red Cross parcels which had not been distributed. Occasionally, however, the tables were turned. One day the Japanese had finished competing with each other when one of them swaggeringly challenged the internees to take him on. He was, as tradition demanded, fully armed with heavy leather body protection – bamboo ribcage armour and shoulder pads.

A huge crowd of men, women and, particularly, intrigued children gathered to watch this unprecedented scene, wondering what the outcome would be. Cyril Mack was one of them. 'At first no one moved and there was total silence. He started to sneer and jeer at us and the others laughed ... Our men were put in a very difficult position and the atmosphere became very tense. None of the men moved ... But Mr Denton seemed to have had enough and he stepped forward into the circle, quietly picked up the dummy rifle and adopted the en garde position. What the Japanese did not know was that Mr Denton was, I believe, ex-Royal Norfolk Regiment. The Japanese, still in all his protective gear, circled Mr Denton, making the usual guttural sounds but there were no such niceties written in the British Army training manual. Before the Japanese could do anything Mr Denton was on him, as he had been taught: strike first, boots, butt, rifle and jab. He used them all, and the Japanese went down from the sheer weight of the onslaught.

'There was a wary silence and a worrying few moments of pause. But then the other guards started to laugh, we relaxed, and they stood up and quietly packed up their equipment and our Red Cross parcels, and returned to the guard house.'[6]

A moment of surreal comedy occurred as a result of the decision of internees in Yangchow C camp to observe Remembrance Day. This time no less a figure than the guard commander found himself the butt of the joke. It had been decided that the customary two minutes silence was to be signalled by the ringing of the meal bell. Cyril Mack's father was deputed to ring the bell and did so when the guard commander happened to be in the middle of the recreation area. 'There was an instant silence, and all the people rose from their chairs; those standing or lounging straightened, the few carrying buckets put them down, and the whole camp came to attention. Because we had all been watching the commander's progress through the camp, when we came to attention most of us were facing him and to him it would have appeared that whatever we were doing was focused on him.'

The commander came to a standstill. All he could see was hundreds of internees, men, women and children, all standing silently at attention, looking at him. 'He was completely nonplussed ... His guards were nowhere to be seen. It was obvious that he thought it was some sort of demonstration, but against who or what? Him? The rations? The Japanese?'

Before he could summon his men to break up the incipient mutiny the bell rang again to signal the end of the two minutes, the camp came to life and everyone started to go about their normal business.

The commander, clearly discomfited, turned and stomped back to the guard house.[7]

The black market was one obvious way the internees could beat the enemy and many camps carried on a brisk smuggling business with the Chinese. This was often conducted under the very noses of the Japanese, a fact which doubtless procured the inmates added satisfaction. Usually the goods were thrown over the fence or wall, but occasionally the traders behaved with greater boldness. In Yu Yuen Road camp the commandant arrived every day by rickshaw. Hidden under his own seat, in a specially constructed compartment, were eggs, tinned food, cigarettes, milk and other items to be sold to prisoners.[8]

Some camps were better favoured than others for maintaining a lucrative black market. Weihsien was one of these. Surrounded by farmers who had plenty of produce to sell for cash the camp's geography and recent history lent itself to illicit contact with the outside world. The perimeter wall was too long for the guards to patrol effectively and was in addition endowed with earth mounds placed at regular intervals along its length, which the Japanese had used as firing steps when they had occupied the compound.

War produces unlikely heroes and at Weihsien the most prolific smuggler was a deeply devout Australian Cistercian monk, Father Patrick Scanlan, a kind man who became a hero to the children because of his courage. The priests' quarters were, conveniently, close to the south-east wall of the compound, along which there were Chinese houses. There were several hundred Roman Catholic nuns and priests in Weihsien, most of them old China hands with an extensive knowledge of Chinese dialects. To the delight of the children the pious Father Scanlan took to smuggling like a duck to water and was not slow in recruiting children to the cause.

Faced with the daily over-the-wall offers of eggs, groundnut oil to fry them in, sugar, jam, honey, fruit and chicken, to boost the meagre camp rations, many internees defied the Japanese edict of not fraternising with the Chinese and bought freely. However, after a while it became clear that too much individual enterprise increased the risk of getting caught and Father Scanlan found himself volunteering to be senior buyer.

At first the priest made it a rule only to buy for children and the sick. But as other people had to stop buying because of the increasing vigilance of the guards, and hungry people kept appealing to him to get things for them his business expanded until he was buying for people all over the camp.

Other internees joined the team and on some nights several thousands of dollars worth of foodstuff, clothing and general items were coming into camp. Despite being an unworldly man Father Scanlan enjoyed the risk of smuggling and the pleasure of outwitting the Japanese. 'We had to be very quick – one or two received the goods over the wall, at least another carried them into the house nearby, and several were on watch for the guards . . . I received many a pleased and knowing smile when I happened to walk through the camp in the mornings, and saw and heard the eggs I had bought sizzling in the peanut oil on the small stoves.'

Even after he was nearly caught Father Scanlan continued to buy over the wall. In one close shave he had to fall back on the dignity of his habit in a very literal sense. 'One evening I alone received a box of eggs over the wall when I heard the guards coming. I put the box back against the wall of our hut, put the eggs into it, and then sat on top with an open breviary in my hand. The two guards were in good humour. "You can't read by that light," said one. "You will ruin your eyes," said the other.

'"Oh no," I said, "my eyes are exceptionally good." I am sure that they were slightly suspicious. They half-guessed the breviary was only a hoax.

'"Go on," they said. "Let's hear you."

'The light was fading fast, and I really could not read the small print. I fitted the breviary before me at a correct distance from my eyes and began to read slowly and distinctly, line after line. But it was a psalm that I knew by heart. The guards departed and I removed the eggs to a safer place.'

In the end the priest was caught red-handed, with a 10-pound pack of sugar in one hand and a box containing fourteen tins of jam in the other. He was sentenced to two weeks in solitary confinement and was held in the Japanese part of the camp. The punishment was regarded with amusement by his fellow internees, who knew that for a Cistercian, whose life is dedicated to silence and prayer, it was not punishment at all. Father Scanlan was held in great affection by the internees for his bravery and was looked up to by the young boys in camp, three of whom took it upon themselves to visit him secretly while he was in prison, with one acting as a lookout for the other two. At considerable risk they took him food and carried letters between him and other internees. Now the tables were turned and it was the priest's turn to admire the bravery of the young.

'They enjoyed the danger, but in my eyes they were little heroes. Had they been caught by the Japanese, they would have been well beaten. Dennis was seen and chased a few times, but he managed to get away. It was forbidden to go into the part occupied by the Japanese [where the priest was being held]. The youngest of them used to climb a tree just inside the Japanese compound, and there, hiding in the thick branches, would give an agreed sign to the other two coming along as to whether or not there were Japanese about.'

To while away the long hours Father Scanlan sang Latin plainsong from his cell. This so irritated the Japanese that they agreed to release him four days early, provided he stopped singing. He was cheered by the entire camp on his release. But he did not forget the three boys who had braved the guards to visit him. Drawing on the extra rations provided by his black market activities he invited the hungry boys to the kind of slap-up tea they had not seen since their internment. 'I had prepared a really good spread, some friends in camp having made up some special dishes for us. I myself prepared three pounds of plums, which I had bought the evening before I was caught.'

There was so much food that the boys' stomachs, used to the gruel of normal camp fare, couldn't cope. 'I never saw boys so gorge themselves in my life. When they could eat no more, they lay about the room puffing. They simply could not swallow any more. After a rest they went for a walk about camp and returned in the evening and again helped themselves. Dennis had one sister, older than himself . . . The day after the feast I asked her how her brother was. She answered rather crossly, "The little animal! When he got into bed, we had to tuck him in, or he would have rolled out onto the floor."'[9]

Teenage boys have always thrived on testing the boundaries and playing with fire and internment did not deter them. In Stanley during the summer months internees were allowed to go swimming on the beach, escorted by Japanese guards armed with rifles. John

Stanton had palled up with three other teenagers, styling themselves the four musketeers. Suspecting that the Japanese were less than confident in the water, they decided to put the guards to the test, 'to see if they would really shoot ... We were all Hong Kong boys and were good swimmers so out we went and swam under water to get out of range.' As good as their word the Japanese fired at them. On their return they were given what John describes as 'a good talking-to Japanese style'.

There was probably not that much difference in age between the guards and the teenaged prisoners and on occasion they sparred together almost as if there was no war on and they were friendly rivals rather than enemies. Sometimes the water-shy guards would join the British lads in the water and they would tussle together the way boys do the world over. But there was a war on and it told when they wrestled. 'We drew a circle in the sand and one Jap and one of us would wrestle until you got him out of the circle ... Needless to say they always won, we were only boys and under-nourished.' But the prisoners, who had been raised by the sea and were in their element in the water, had a secret weapon. 'If we all decided afterwards to have a swim we got our own back by ducking them.'[10]

PART THREE

Dark Days

13

'These children will bear the brand of camp life as long as they live'[1]

They had gone in with their camp beds and stocks of tinned food thinking it was an adventure. Their parents, too, were upbeat, utterly convinced the tiny, backward Japanese nation could not possibly prevail over the combined might of the British and American forces. The universal belief was that everyone would be out again by Christmas 1943 and for many the first year of internment was not too unpleasant. But as 1944 dawned, with no sign of rescue, conditions began to deteriorate. What had started out looking like a holiday became a nightmare. Far from being overwhelmed the Japanese seemed invincible as they pressed ahead with their planned invasion of Australia and India. As they commandeered the lion's share of food supplies for their war machine, rations in the camps were savagely cut. People grew thin and went down with deficiency conditions. Death rates rose. In January 1945, thirty-two people died in Santo Tomas in the Philippines. Children scavenged in dustbins for any scrap of leaf or peeling, increasing their risk from disease. Supplies of everything required in a normal life ran out – soap, paper, toilet paper, candles, matches, razor blades, shoes and clothing in general. Coal supplies ran desperately low and in some camps the electricity supply ceased. To keep warm, or cook whatever extra rations they could come by, prisoners first stripped the grounds of any wood they could find and then turned to furniture, floorboards and even the doors of their rooms for fuel. In Shanghai the winter of 1944–45 was the coldest since 1871 with the temperature remaining below freezing for seventy-nine days in a row.[2] Children, lacking nutrients vital for developing bodies, growing out of clothes and shoes (in some cases growing out of beds), lacking warm bedding and generally ill-prepared for an imprisonment which would last not months, but years, suffered, if anything, more than adults.

By the last bitter Chinese winter many who had started the war as smartly dressed colonial princelings from centrally heated homes were as ragged, cold and hungry as street urchins. Biting winds penetrated every corner of the dilapidated run-down buildings they lived in, snow blew in through broken windows; they developed painful chilblains which itched and bled. They wore every stitch of outdoor clothing they had – hats, scarves, mittens – to sit through lessons in freezing classrooms. Many of them were frequently ill – with malaria, dysentery and eye and skin problems. By June 1945 many camps were only serving one meal a day and that was often simply watery rice or bread and vegetables.

One man noted in his diary that summer (May 1945): 'Our lunch today consisted of onion and beetroot and for dinner we had braised cabbage. There is still no rice.'³ That last summer internees were fed the flesh of some of the 1,000 greyhounds from the Canidrome, Shanghai's famous dog track.

In June the Swedish legation in Shanghai warned that high numbers of internees were facing death from starvation. Life in the camps had virtually come to a standstill. All the active games the children had so enjoyed – the bird-nesting, the cricket-fighting, the hide-and-seek – died away. Sport stopped and playing fields were dug up to grow vegetables in a frantic search for nutrients. In many camps classes ceased as teachers and pupils became too exhausted to concentrate. On a few hundred calories a day children no longer had the energy to play together. Instead they retired to bed early. But even here, knees curled up to chins, under inadequate bedding, many were never warm and were thus deprived of nature's best restorer of hope and energy – sleep. Even the bravest cried. Some even welcomed the idea of death as a relief from suffering.

A group of mothers interned with fifteen children in a camp in Fukushima in Japan became so desperate that in the spring of 1944 they wrote a letter to the Red Cross describing the harsh conditions in which they were being held, pleading for more food. They listed their daily rations, which were almost completely lacking in fats, calcium or vitamins:

Breakfast 1 bun (six oz) 1 cup of weak tea (no milk or sugar)
lunch 1 bun (1 cup weak tea)
supper 1 bun, 1 cup weak tea, 1 small plate of stew consisting of
a little meat, rice or barley and vegetables.[4]

A small issue of milk was reserved for the young and the sick, but
if a doctor prescribed milk for a patient, it was taken from a child's
ration, instead of the camp ordering more.

In Yangchow the bitter cold of the winter of 1944–45 added to the
general misery. To quell the pangs of hunger the children took rusks
spread with lard to school for the mid-morning break. The rusks
were made from stale bread and scrapings from the oven, tables and
floor of the bakery.

'These would be rationed out to us, usually at breakfast time with
our maggot-riddled cracked wheat porridge, with a dollop of greasy
lard to help them slide down ... it didn't taste that good – but it did
help to stave off a few hunger pangs.'[5] The cold caused uncomfortable
chilblains for many children including Neil Begley, who had already
suffered from malaria so badly in Yangchow.

'First our ears were attacked. They became red and itched and
burned, then formed scabs which bled and oozed. Then our fingers
and toes swelled until the skin split and burst. Like our ears the splits
wept and oozed and the pain was excruciating. We found that we
could get temporary relief by rubbing our chilblains with snow.'[6] On
one occasion when he was eating his evening meal with his family in
their room twelve-year-old Neil was so hungry he began to cry. His
father responded by instantly offering him his own portion. The
memory is still so painful that in recounting it sixty years later Neil's
eyes filled with tears.

Neil was not alone. Cyril Mack, who had had his throbbing tooth
extracted in order to be able to enjoy his Red Cross parcel, succumbed
to the same despair. 'The long, depressingly cold, black nights of
that final bleak winter was when hunger hit us hardest of all. The
snow lay on the ground up to our knees for months, we had no
electricity, we were frozen to the marrow, and we were very hungry.
After our evening meal we had no alternative but to retire to our
rooms. So we shivered ... huddled under our bedclothes in an
attempt to conserve energy and to keep warm, but that only made

the nights even longer and the hunger stayed with us through the darkness.'

Weak and in poor health by now, Cyril cried silently, knowing that nothing could be done to improve their situation. One night he even asked God to let him die. 'After I said my prayers, the Lord's Prayer, Hail Mary, followed by the popular children's prayer which ended, and if I die before I wake, I pray to God my soul to take, I spoke to God seriously and asked Him to make sure that there would be breakfast for us in the morning but that if it was not to be, then I would like him to let me die in my sleep … I only asked for breakfast and not for more food because I felt that the chances were that if we had breakfast then we would probably have a tiffin and a dinner and we could get through another day.'[7]

In the camps in Shanghai the situation was just as bad. In Yu Yuen Road the kitchen staff were given 2 pounds of meat to feed 300 people. Margaret Blair, who had gone into camp aged six, was living on grey watery soup with a bit of cabbage. Throughout 1944 food became even more scarce. Children who could drank extra water to try to assuage hunger pains. By the spring of 1945 food rations were cut further, to between half and two-thirds of the 1,100 calorie ration the Japanese had originally allowed them. Many children stayed in bed in the evening through lack of energy.

In Chapei camp, also in Shanghai, where supplies had been initially quite generous, rations were pared to the bone by 1945. David Nicoll queued up with his two enamel bowls to collect food for his family. He didn't need the second bowl. 'The rations for all four of us was a watery mixture with a few slices of onion and a suggestion of mince, all contained in less than half of one bowl.'

In Weihsien camp the major enemy for the children that last winter was the cold and they felt it more because they were always hungry. Kathleen Strange (later Foster), known as 'K' at Chefoo School where she was pupil, recalls the bleak menus of that last year. 'Breakfast was a small bowl of bread porridge, no milk no sugar; lunch stew; supper stew, and tea without milk. There were some veg in the stew and not much meat. A notice went up: Whatever the meat the Doctor says it's good.' By now their clothes were inadequate and outgrown. Curtains were turned into dresses and blankets into trousers. The girls, most of whom in those days of domestic science classes were already competent knitters, unravelled their peculiar beige stockings 'knitted in fairly large stitch wool,' which had gone into holes, and reknitted them as ankle socks. Like so many of the children, the cold gave K painful chilblains on her feet. The only warm shoes that could be found for her were too small, so, to see that at least the soles of her feet were warm, the toes were cut out.

The Chefoo schoolchildren had had a shock when one day in August 1944 they had witnessed the death of one of their number. The boy, a young lad of about seventeen, had reached up and touched a sagging electric cable that fed a searchlight mounted on a corner guard post. He had been electrocuted in front of his mother and many of his fellow pupils.[8]

Red Cross parcels would have made all the difference to the hungry children in Weihsien, but although they were conscientiously sent, they were never distributed promptly. This was not so much because the Japanese were keeping them for themselves but because the Americans in camp insisted that they were intended only for them and were reluctant to share with others. Estelle Cliff recalls that the first of these parcels only arrived in July 1944. They had been posted ten months earlier. On that occasion Estelle earned herself a tin of condensed milk from an American missionary in return for a good deed. She had unravelled a pullover of his and reknitted it as a sleeveless tank top.

The second lot of Red Cross parcels arrived at Weihsien in January 1945 when the prisoners were in a desperate state. Estelle Cliff remembers: 'Again the Americans claimed it was all for them. Even the Japs were unhappy with that and refused to distribute them until the matter had been discussed further. Finally they put their feet down and said all or nothing, and we got one whole big parcel each.' When the parcels were opened it was plain that the packers believed they would be being delivered every month to prisoners, as each was divided into four smaller boxes, designed to last a week. 'We eked out our parcels for as long as we could. They were literally a lifesaver. We girls were not as hungry as the boys, whose community job was to pump water all day.'

Added to the cold and hunger for the children in Weihsien was the misery at being separated from their parents for so long. K Strange had not seen her parents since 1937 when she started as a boarder at Chefoo School. Estelle had not seen hers since 1940. K only received three Red Cross postcards from her mother, although she wrote many more. As Estelle says: 'The worst thing of all was not knowing how long it would last. It seemed forever.'

Even in camps where cold was not a problem things were no better. In Santo Tomas in Manila the first year had been relatively civilised, but conditions deteriorated, as they invariably did, when the military took over early in 1944. Not long after that Sylvia Williams, who had been interned with her parents on her eighth birthday, was facing starvation.

'After the first year hunger affected every aspect of life in the camp. People fell ill, diseases swept through the camp population and people started to die. My father got beriberi. As the months passed lack of food made the adults listless. Banana trees grew round our shack, but my parents couldn't wait till the bananas ripened. They dug them up and ate the roots. The adults seemed to stop caring where we children went or what we did. It wasn't their fault. Starvation affects the mind and they were being slowly starved. Many were giving their children the lion's share of their rations and they had no energy. The classes petered out and the school collapsed. The teachers were exhausted and ill. My memory of the latter half of internment is of long unstructured days.'

In Santo Tomas the Japanese did not supply fresh meat or fish for six weeks from November 1944. Even the supply of the tiny crisp salt fish, which were occasionally served with the daily rice, ceased. Sugar ran out and salt was scarce. There were a number of babies born in the camp (some of which occurred more than a year after internment, despite the separation of the sexes). To give the newborns a better start doctors took the drastic step of stopping the supply of milk to children over three. Before that, milk – from carabao, or water buffaloes – had been provided for all children up to ten. By now inmates were eating almost anything – weeds from the vegetable gardens, boiled and served over rice, the bulbs of canna lilies, the roots of banana palms, the leaves of hibiscus plants. Cats were caught and eaten and young dogs were seen as a delicacy.

Frederic Stevens, an American businessman who had been a prominent citizen of Manila before the war, elaborated: 'The people who ate dogs usually tried to get the puppies. These were skinned and cut up into small pieces and boiled till tender. Then a gravy was made with rice flour and the meat added and cooked. This was served over roasted rice.'

By the end of the year the internees were completely at the mercy of the Japanese. Galloping inflation meant that food could no longer be purchased and sent in from outside. By January 1945 the average man in camp had lost nearly a third of his body weight. Frederic Stevens drew a graphic picture of life in camp at this stage.

'The internees presented the appearance of an army of walking skeletons. Pipe-stem legs seemed scarcely able to bear the bodies above them; arms were thin and scrawny; the skin wrinkled, without elasticity, hung down in folds; the men wearing no shirts showed prominently a corrugation of ribs like washboards. They walked about with a listless air, staring at the ground, scarcely giving a glance at those who chanced to pass them.'[9]

Like a tourist passing through the notoriously poor quarter of a major city, Stevens noted the pathetic response of mothers and children. 'Inability ... to withstand ... a comparatively empty stomach led to the highly dangerous and disgusting practice of salvaging condemned vegetables and other decaying matter from the camp garbage. After camotes (sweet potatoes) were peeled or vegetables cleaned ... numbers of women and children arrived to pick up and carry away the refuse. Children hung about the food processing shed in the hope of picking up a stray camote or piece of squash.'[10] In the end refuse collection was discontinued – because there was no rubbish to collect. It had all been harvested.

Iris Krass, interned in Santo Tomas without her mother, who was ill throughout her internment, says that over the last year there was hardly ever protein, fat or calcium in their diet.

'There were only two meals a day. Breakfast was served at about 11 a.m. and was corn mush, a mixture of cornmeal and rice. The evening meal was served at five or six and consisted of watery vegetable broth with small pieces of talinum, a local leaf vegetable, added and a bit of salt.'

Knowing how desperate the prisoners were, Swiss civilians in Manila sent meat into the camp. 'It happened twice. They sent in three buffaloes and four pigs. It added a bit of flavour to our soup for one day, and even a bit of meat, if you were lucky with your portion, but it didn't go far among 3,000 people.'

In the early days of internment many of the Americans who had lived in Manila had buried tinned food in the grounds of the campus. This proved a lifeline. 'Their servants used to come and throw stuff over the railings but then the Japanese built extra fences and stopped it. I knew a girl who was friendly with an American chap who had buried food. Several times during those last months they invited me to share a tin of corned beef or Spam with them.'

In the end Iris didn't even feel hungry. 'You weren't aware of hunger. Your stomach shrank. You just lost interest in everything. The whole camp stopped functioning. There was no more sport, no more classes. You didn't even feel like reading. You felt listless and tired all the time. If you had a camp duty to do, like de-weevilling rice, or dealing with the bedbugs in the room ... you did it. Then you went to your room and you just lay on your bed.'

In Singapore Barbara Bruce and her family had been transferred from Changi prison to Sime Road, a former British barracks, in May 1944. For three years the prisoners existed on a rice-based diet with virtually no protein or fats. They received no Red Cross parcels, with those nutritious little extras that made such a difference, for the whole of their internment. By 1944 the prisoners were in a bad way. Dysentery, malaria and pellagrous dermatitis, a deficiency skin disease, were rife. Children's arms, legs and feet were covered with tropical ulcers. The sick could not be treated as there were no drugs and even the supply of bandages ran out. The plight of the men and boys was particularly acute because, in spite of the starvation rations, they were forced to carry out manual labour for the Japanese, including working on military projects.

The new camp provided more freedom to walk about than the prison, where they spent hours locked in cells, but the diet was no better.

Barbara says: 'In all our three and a half years we only had two meals a day. Breakfast was a small bowl of boiled rice. Lunch was the same with a bit more water and a few vegetables thrown in.' Once a month they got a banana. 'We regarded that banana as nectar. After we'd finished it some children would fight to get the discarded skins and then scrape off the bitter pith and eat that too.'

Barbara watched fearfully during the last year and a half as at mealtimes her mother gave half her ration to her two youngest children and became matchstick-thin herself. Eventually her mother had a heart attack. She spent two weeks in the camp hospital, just resting, as there were no drugs to treat her.

'I had to look after my two little brothers while she was ill. The other internees called me "the little mother". Mum remained very poorly even after she came out of hospital and I was afraid she might die before we were released.'

Clothing was almost as much a problem as hunger. 'Many people were interned later than us and they had warning. Some of them came in with trunks full of clothes, which they swapped for food. We had just been bundled into lorries and driven into camp. Luckily my mother was a very resourceful seamstress. She was able to draw threads from worn-out cloth to sew with. By the end my dress was covered with patches.'[11]

In Stanley camp in Hong Kong the last year was similarly bleak, with increasing hunger and illness punctuating the weary days. Like those in Singapore the inmates in Stanley had been interned at the beginning of 1942 and here the screw tightened a year earlier than in many camps. In 1943 the camp came under Japanese military control and all meat and fish rations ceased. People like Bill Macauley, the schoolboy who had worked as an ARP agent during the battle for Hong Kong, had no money to buy extra rations through the black market. His only source of protein for the next two years was soya beans. In March the flour allocation ran out and people were thrown back on a rice-only diet, with its attendant risk of beriberi. Babies received 15 ounces of evaporated or powdered milk each day, but five-year-olds and over got no milk. Bill Ream, a Methodist missionary, was particularly concerned about the effect of the deficient diet on the older children. 'Young children were often sent milk in the rations and seemed to do reasonably well. Children over the age of eight and especially teenagers suffered most and have probably been suffering in one way or another since.'[12]

For the majority of children the dish of the day was rice with whatever vegetables were in season – turnips, water spinach, boiled lettuce leaves, pumpkins . . . or 'dustbin stew', a concoction of cabbage stalks, carrot tops and turnip tops.[13]

As people became too weak to play sport the playing fields were dug up and turned into vegetable plots. In the end even this exertion proved too much effort for many. People became ill with beriberi, dysentery and malaria. Men and women who had enjoyed perfect health before the war began to die. The Chief Manager of the Hong Kong and Shanghai Bank died of beriberi and his second-in-command died of starvation.[14]

At the beginning, internment in Stanley, a popular beach resort before the war, had seemed almost pleasant. One adult prisoner described swimming with his children in Tweed Bay, catching crabs, collecting shells and looking for jellyfish. To him, in those early days it had seemed an 'internment de luxe'. Two years later he and his family were too weak from lack of food even to make the journey down to the beach.[15]

As the rations shrank the children's minds and bodies became dominated by the thought of food. The Bartons were the largest family to be interned in Stanley – the family totalled thirteen. John Barton, who was thirteen when he went into camp, describes how food overtook even sex as a preoccupation among teenage boys. He had pictures pasted to the wall next to his bed, not of scantily clad girls, but of food, taken from advertisements in magazines.

'The conversation was always about food. We used to eat the skin of the banana as well as the banana itself. It tasted awful. The Japs gave us chrysanthemum leaves instead of vegetables to go with our small bowl of rice. We had no meat for months on end and I remember searching the dustbins outside the communal kitchens for something to eat. I never found anything. One night when I was 15 years old I walked into an adjoining veranda at 2am and ... cried out of sheer hunger.'

Everything fell into decay. John woke up on the floor one night because the canvas base of his bed had rotted away. There was no mattress, so from then on he was forced to sleep on two 12-inch boards placed side by side and supported by a chair at each end. The children found, to their horror, that the lack of thrown-away scraps was turning them into prey for pests like cockroaches who normally relied on garbage. 'I would wake up in the morning to find my finger tips on both hands eaten away to the last layer of skin making it almost impossible to pick anything until new skin grew again.'[16]

William Sewell chronicled the deterioration of life in camp and watched with dismay the effect on his family. In the last year there was no coal and the camp had no electricity. Fuel for cooking was at such a premium that people burned the doors to their rooms and their floorboards. 'Every morning there was the continuous noise of hammering all round us as floor-boards, furniture and doorposts were split to tiny pieces for the day's cooking.'[17] The low yield from the barren vegetable patches forced Europeans to adopt the abhorred oriental practice of putting human waste and urine straight onto the land as a fertiliser only to see the vegetables wither through water shortages. At one stage they were getting water in the taps one day in five. The black market was an alternative to starvation if you had money but by the last year prices had soared to £5 for an egg and £20 for a pound of sugar. Dried egg and powdered milks fetched £25 a pound. Sewell, who had no money, had to exchange things like cigarettes and garden produce.

At this low point Sewell described a 'special treat' he cooked for the family. The Japanese had supplied, the day before, some putrid salt fish. He had carefully saved the bones, which he fried in a little oil. 'A friend had received a parcel from town containing bananas ... The bananas also had been eaten, but with the bones I ... fried thinly-sliced skin seasoned with curry and some scraps of onions and ginger.'

Sewell and his wife watched helplessly as their once boisterous children became more and more languid.

'Vee was not well, though she never uttered any word of complaint. She was pale, always tired and would lie long hours on her bed reading, without much desire to romp and play. Joy was still active, but was content to sit singing to her dolls ... Guy ... had festering sores that would not heal.'

A thoughtful man, Sewell reflected that he and his wife were going through what so many other parents throughout history had suffered. 'Stanley parents tasted a small part of that crushing anxiety felt by those in so many lands who had helplessly to watch their children starve or suffer because of war and destitution.'

Death, inevitably, became a familiar presence to children in many camps. In Stanley the frequency of deaths, and the fact that the deaths were often of people they knew, led to children developing a

startlingly pragmatic attitude to the subject. In the topsy-turvy world
of camp where wood was worth as much as gold they had grown so
used to the idea of the one coffin with its false bottom that was used
and reused that the idea of the dead keeping their own coffin struck
them as wanton extravagance.

'"Do people each have a coffin and are they left in it, outside the
camp?"' Vee asked in surprise.

'"What a waste of wood; think of all the meals a coffin would
cook," said Joy. "That will mean that this coffin won't be wasted
when the war is over: whoever dies last will be able to keep it."'[18]

One of the distinguishing aspects of life in Stanley was the mean
spiritedness shown to children by many adults. William Sewell was
not the only person to be shocked by the hostility of many middle-
aged internees to suggestions that children should receive extra
rations. The Pope had sent relief money into camp and the camp
representatives decided that the money should be divided equally
among all those over eighteen. This provoked an outcry among
Catholic families who protested that they tended to have more
mouths to feed.

Sewell told how one middle-aged woman reduced a young mother
to tears by telling her: 'It would be much better for your baby to be
in the cemetery instead of some of the older people who were leading
good and useful lives and now through no fault of their own have
weakened, died and been buried here.'[19]

As time went on, however, Sewell's children began to learn the
law of the jungle for themselves and give as good as they got.

'One day at the leaky hydrant in the road Joy was filling a tin.
"Move off: get out of here! I want some water," said a man putting
his bucket down in the road.

'"I have as much right to get water as you," replied Joy. "Besides
as I am only a little child, if you were nice you would help me instead
of being so cross." "I didn't mean to be rude," she said to us later,
almost in tears, "but unless you speak like they do, they don't understand."[20]

In Stanley people burned floorboards and furniture as fuel. In
other camps grubbing for coal became a daily chore at which children,
with their ability to worm their way into small spaces, excelled.
The coal was used in chatties, homemade native stoves, which the

prisoners knocked up from containers such as biscuit tins. They used them to warm up precious tinned food to eke out meals provided by the kitchens. There can have been few sights more symbolic of the reversal in fortunes between whites and Orientals than that of ragged and dirty European children scrambling among ash heaps for scraps of sought-after fuel. The irony was not lost on Chinese onlookers who laughed when they saw European children stealing precious lumps.

The coal was destined for use in the kitchens and boiler rooms and internees were forbidden to take new coal. In Chapei camp in Shanghai the larger throw-out of ashes came from the kitchen in the morning before roll-call. The men and boys would follow the bin until it was tipped out, then the free-for-all began. Because the ashes were still hot, most people used tongs made from a piece of sheet metal bent over, although with time the children developed burn-hardened skin on their fingers.

According to David Nicoll the children were nimbler than the men. 'We boys would worm our way between the men often succeeding in grabbing ash-covered lumps which might turn out to be coal ...' In this fight for survival people fought with each other over pieces of spent coal and the camp leaders were obliged to impose a regulated queuing system. In future the ashes would be dumped only after roll-call and distributed in different heaps about the yard. 'Two queues were formed, one for adults and a priority one for children, so we could get to school on time, and then, at a signal we would advance in pairs to a heap.'

Occasionally, David and a pal would steal new coal. On one occasion they watched as sack after sack was carried in by Chinese coolies. Suddenly a very large lump landed on the ground in front of them. A split second was enough to convince David that it was worth the risk. 'I dashed across, picked up this wonderful find and sped away to our room, leaving the coolies laughing at my action.'[21]

What, more than anything else, kept internees alive, and prevented the guttering flame of hope from dying completely, were food parcels, but in most camps deliveries were few and far between. Many camps received none. When they did arrive they triggered a mini celebratory feast, but the goodies were soon gone and they had little impact on the general hunger. They came from two sources: those from the

Red Cross and those sent in by friends or relatives who were not interned. The difference was that Red Cross parcels were delivered to everyone while private parcels only came to a few. People in isolated camps like Yangchow or Weihsien never received private parcels nor did people who had no money or contacts outside. Those who were able to make arrangements with people who had avoided internment were the lucky ones as these parcels were a lifeline. But of course this led, just as the black market did, to gross inequalities among families. Margaret Blair and her family (in Yu Yuen Road camp) received a parcel from her father's secretary at Christmas 1943 containing bacon and chocolate. In Lunghwa, Irene Duguid and her mother arranged for a friend to send them one small parcel a month for three months. The parcels contained salami, cheese and bacon. Irene's mother agreed to pay £60 per parcel – a truly staggering amount for those days – after the war. The bill reached the Duguids in London in March 1946 and Mrs Duguid faithfully paid up and sent off a cheque for £180. 'Those parcels, small though they were, pulled us through the winter,' said Irene.[22]

Where Red Cross parcels were concerned there were often problems. Some camps received them monthly; others only received one or two in the whole of the internment. Some got none at all. In many instances they were looted by the Japanese – and the Chinese – or simply withheld. But when they got through they caused outbreaks of euphoria that lasted for several days. The parcels, which came in boxes of uniform size, were packed as neatly as pieces of a jigsaw to economise space and contained a wealth of foodstuffs, packed in anything up to thirty miniature tins to enable them to fit into the restricted space. Parcels contained among other items tea, coffee, margarine or butter, sugar, tinned meat and fish, pâté, cheese, jam, biscuits, tinned vegetables, cigarettes and a selection of tinned puddings.

One eyewitness described the excitement which greeted a delivery of parcels to Chapei camp in Shanghai: 'The arrival of the three trucks, each flying the Red Cross flag, and piled high with cartons and bulk supplies, was always the event of the month, eagerly awaited and partaking of the nature of a holiday, especially for the children in the Junior and Senior schools, whose yells of joy on their release from the East Shed, their schoolhouse, which would be needed for parcel inspection and distribution, were a most effective signal to the whole camp that the long expected moment had arrived. For the next few days after parcels there will be a marked improvement in the general morale and cheerfulness of the camp, an increase in the activities of home cooking, preparing bacon, sausages and noodles, and a corresponding decrease in the numbers in the breakfast and supper queues.'[23]

In Santo Tomas in Manila internees received just two parcels from the Red Cross in three years. According to Iris Krass the first contained about thirty tins of food. 'I got one and so did my brother, who was housed separately from me, with the men. Poor Peter was very hungry and gobbled up the contents of his parcel straight away. He came over to me to see if I would give him some of mine. By that time my younger sister had joined me so the three of us shared a tin of corned beef.' The second parcels arrived just before Christmas in 1944 when people were at their lowest. They had all been looted by the Japanese.

In Yangchow C camp only one consignment of Red Cross parcels was received and by the time they arrived, in March 1945, the families had nothing to eat apart from what was served by the kitchens. Cyril Mack, who had insisted on having an inflamed tooth extracted so that he could enjoy his goodies, was beside himself with excitement. In the event the Mack family received one parcel from the British Red Cross and one from the American. 'The Brits included more meals and we decided to hold them back for later in case an emergency should arise.'

None of the Mack family was tempted by the sugar and syrups in the parcel. 'We had not had sugar for such a long time we had lost the craving for it and it was too sweet for our palates so we saved it for another time. Butter, margarine, chocolate and chewing gum were favourites ... coffee was a real treat.' The American parcel contained a tin of Spam, which Cyril had not tasted before. It triggered a fondness for the stuff that continues to this day.

In Chapei camp in Shanghai meals in the early months had been quite palatable. Chapei internees had access to comfort loans from the British Government, which enabled them to buy extras like eggs and milk. As the months passed, however, the funds ran out. The problem was made worse by spiralling inflation, which meant that money bought less and less.[24] David Nicoll attributed the decline in camp to the drying up of comfort money in the December of 1943. It soon affected his health. From being a carefree, healthy boy, he developed chilblains, which caused his fingers to swell and split. The following winter was so cold that on some days they closed the school. 'We felt the cold more this winter as our constitutions were less robust.'

David's family were now completely dependent on camp rations. The differences between the haves and the have-nots became striking here too. The other hungry children queued for 'seconds', which were merely the rice scrapings from the cooking pots, and pretended they were popcorn. In their deprived state, where the staple was 'grey damp stodge' masquerading as bread, they came to relish foods they would have spurned in normal times. One of these was 'magic' persimmon jam. 'When issued the jam had been most welcome, thick reddish brown and sweet, but with the summer heat it turned sour quickly and fermented which was great for we kept on using it to scrape onto our bread, or toast, yet overnight its level would rise, the jam getting more and more sour but what did that matter so long as we could add any flavour to the bread.'

David's mother took to washing clothes in return for food. A widower with a son gave the Nicolls a tin of jam for having his laundry done. People began scavenging. David and some other boys collected cigarette butts discarded by other, wealthier internees for their fathers to smoke in their pipes. A neighbour scoured the rubbish tip in search of discarded tins that still had bits of food adhering to them. From this he would make a broth which he offered to David's father. David worried as his mother's health declined.

'One day Mum happened to be bending over the chatty in our cubicle and in her loose low-cut summer dress I could look down her front and saw her ribs sticking out. I got such a shock, I had never thought of Mum being skinny, she was the plump one in the family. I stood back a little and took a careful look at her face and figure and realised that she really had lost a lot of weight, then I remembered her having joked over the months that her clothes were now so loose on her. Mum was always so reliable, always willing to help, lighting the chatty every morning and carrying out all other household chores ... she was never ill ...'

In this atmosphere it was hard for the hungry children not to envy those who got private parcels and were still eating well. David thought about this a lot. With a maturity that belied his years he tried to adopt a mental stratagem to stop him minding about the situation. 'One girl came back to our room crying because she had not received a parcel that month. As the idea of receiving a parcel was novel to me I tried to think about the girl's reaction and reasoned within myself on the basis of a graph: everyone in Chapei was going about his daily life irrespective of getting parcels, so, to that extent we were all on an equal plane; however, if a person who normally could expect to receive a parcel failed to get one he would be sad and would fall to a lower plane – I would not because I had no expectation; if, on the other hand, I were to receive a parcel I would soar to a higher plane than the person getting a parcel. Whatever the logic of it I found it sustaining.'

David was lucky, for in Chapei there were some generous families who were happy to share the contents of their parcels with their less fortunate neighbours. One day David was sitting by himself when a girl a couple of years younger than him walked up. 'She appeared almost staggering at her age of 10 years carrying a carton of tinned goods and other food and asked if my mother was in . . . Even though (they) were in receipt of parcels regularly it could not have been easy to part with vast quantities of food. Another benefactor was . . . one of my teachers, he called me over a few times to hand me a tin of meat or dried fish from his family's parcel.' Every offer was accepted, even when it was the dregs of someone else's tea. 'Mrs Beith would of a late evening call over the counterpane offering us leftover tea in her thermos flask, so rich and flavourful in contrast to Camp tea.'

And then, one momentous day, David's longings were fulfilled. In January 1945 the Red Cross announced that they would be sending in, not one, but four parcels per prisoner.

The reason so many arrived at once was that a consignment of parcels destined for prisoners further east had been torpedoed. The Red Cross decided to distribute the salvaged parcels, rather than risk losing them to further raids. David couldn't believe the plenty which now lay before him. 'A person would be hard put to carry all four of his parcels at one time. Many people had to get others to help carry the parcels to their rooms but I was determined to carry as many as

I could and struggled up the stairs with three parcels ... we had so much chocolate ... each person had eight bars, i.e. 64 cubes of dark chocolate all to oneself!'

No one knew if there would be any more parcels and everything had to be made to last. David decided to limit himself to one cube of chocolate a day. 'Sometimes after school I would lie on my bed reading a P. G. Wodehouse story or one by Conan Doyle, at the same time scraping my daily cube with my teeth to eke it out. Chewing gum was also plentiful for a time ... and once I chewed one stick for a whole week.'[25]

Chapei was not the only camp where there were gross inequalities between families. Hope Lee, who was first in Yu Yuen Road and latterly in Yangtzepoo camp, was distressed by the role money played in determining the health of families. 'Many families with young children suffered terribly. They had nothing to supplement the camp food except the extra soya bean milk supplied to children under 7 and a small piece of extra bread ... the mothers went without and so suffered from awful deficiency complaints. A family I knew well, both parents were doctors, were in a bad way – they had come from inland China and had no connections with Shanghai at all – the mother had pellagra on her hands and the children were covered in boils and ulcers ... yet in the next room the family ... lived in relative comfort with parcels coming in regularly and the children having tinned milk and other supplements to their diet.'

One of the major problems with the younger children in the last year was that they found the food served by the kitchens so disgusting they were not eating enough. All the things vital to the development of young children – fruit, eggs, fresh milk – were lacking. Hope Lee experienced at first hand the difficulties of getting her toddler daughter to eat the camp fare. 'We were down to one meal a day now; tea twice a day and usually an issue of congee or bread once a day ... I was breaking into iron rations for Marion as she could not tackle much of the kitchen stuff. The rice was so very dirty and full of grit and the meat often unpalatable. I would try to get a little meat and vegetable down her and make up with powdered milk and what was left of the honey I had brought in ...'

The problem became so acute that parents protested en masse to the camp representative. He eventually managed to persuade the

Japanese to send in special nutritious supplies for the children, including liver and fresh vegetables. This led to the creation of a special children's kitchen. 'For a while all went well: then there was no more special children's food coming in from outside. All rations were cut. So was the children's milk supply. The kitchen was taken over by the clinic and it was decided ... that each block should run its own children's kitchen.'

Hope, who had a toddler of her own, was one of the instigators of the children's kitchen. But, as in many of the other camps, adults who were not parents resented the idea of children getting better rations. 'The children's kitchen was never a popular idea with the kitchen gangs. It meant fuss and bother setting aside the children's rations and constant grumbling that the children were getting more than their fair share ...'

Hope and other parents stuck to their guns, however, cooking their children's food themselves even after the special deliveries ceased. 'We got our rota going and on the whole it ran fairly well ... what we produced depended a good deal on whose gang was on that day. Some of the cooks tried hard to be helpful and did what they could for us. Others did not care and made things awkward ... I'm sure a lot of them resented having women muddling around ... but we appreciated those who tried to be helpful. I think it was worth it and we made the most of what was issued to the children. They had their food, poor as it was, prepared and cooked with a good deal more care than that in the main kitchen.'[26]

Nothing illustrates the decline in conditions more starkly than the way Christmas was celebrated in the camps. In 1943 there was still a sense of optimism, a feeling that the situation was temporary. There was also, relatively, a feeling of surplus. By 1944, however, everything had run out – materials to make toys, extra food rations and, above all, the will to celebrate.

In Yu Yuen Road camp, for Christmas 1943 there was a tree and plenty of material still available to make Christmas presents. The pillowcase overflowing with toys that had greeted Margaret Blair and her brother Gordon on Christmas Day 1942 had given way to one present each – a knitted scarf for Gordon and a dolls' bed for Margaret, made from a cardboard box covered with material. A neighbour made her a bag, which she used to carry her books to school, and she embroidered a handkerchief for her mother. The children performed a nativity play in which Gordon played one of the three Kings, wearing his mother's bright blue dressing gown, topped with a turban made from a towel. The monotonous camp fare was cheered up by a parcel from their father's secretary containing bacon and chocolate. Christmas 1944 was a far less festive affair. There was no tree, no special meal and no presents. All they received to mark the season was a hand-drawn Christmas card from their father, held in the grim kempeitai prison of Haiphong Road, where men died under torture. The card was a thin, anxious-looking self-portrait and included a poignant couplet:

> Our craft, dear ones, is sailing on,
> Through mists today, clear seas anon.

In Chapei camp, Christmas 1943 had been made jolly by the local Red Cross who sent in food, games and presents. Every child received two mandarin oranges. David Nicoll's presents were a jigsaw puzzle and a comic book. There was a traditional nativity show which took the form of tableaux. A year later his only present was a pencil wrapped in Christmas paper from a girl in his class. At least in Chapei they had a reasonable dinner as some of the camp pigs were killed to provide roast pork for tiffin on Christmas Day. The children were allocated to tables of ten and asked to devise a theme for their table. Knowing how much they owed the tirelessly committed organisation David's chose the Red Cross and all put on armbands featuring the famous symbol. Appropriately, the table decoration was a ship laden with Red Cross 'parcels' – made from matchboxes. The entertainment was a performance of part of *A Christmas Carol*. But the élan of previous shows was absent. 'It was a bleak production. I do not think the customary care had been devoted to this effort. Because it was too cold to put on the play in the customary venue of the east shed it was presented in the Lobby with the minimum of décor.'[27]

Not long before that Christmas (1944), David had celebrated his twelfth birthday. The adults in many camps did their best to make birthdays as special as possible given the circumstances. The camp band came to his room before roll-call and played 'Happy Birthday'.

Children in Yangtzepoo Camp in Shanghai carry their tiffin tins back from the kitchen. Rodney Stableford, brother of Maureen Collins, is on the right. Like many children he had been ill in the last months of the war and was severely underweight. (*Rodney Stableford*)

There were no eating utensils in many of the camps. This mother and son in Santo Tomas used old food tins. (*Getty*)

Overcrowding was a major source of strain and friction in the camps. Several families had to share a room and privacy became a forgotten luxury as these photographs of Stanley camp (*above*) and Banjoebiroe camp on Java (*below*) show. (*IWM; Museon*)

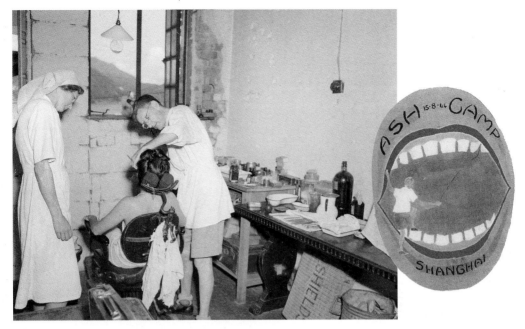

With few medical facilities and no toothpaste or toothbrushes, internees suffered endless problems with their teeth. Makeshift dental surgeries were set up, such as this one in Stanley camp. The same spirit of cheerful enterprise is evidenced in this dentist's card from Ash Camp. (*IWM*)

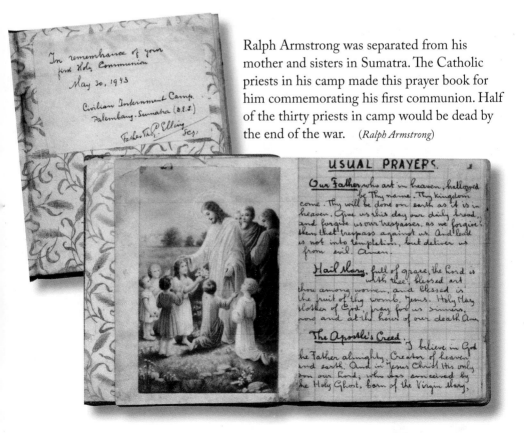

Ralph Armstrong was separated from his mother and sisters in Sumatra. The Catholic priests in his camp made this prayer book for him commemorating his first communion. Half of the thirty priests in camp would be dead by the end of the war. (*Ralph Armstrong*)

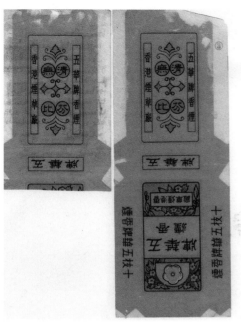

Bill Macauley's school matron wrote him these letters on cigarette packets while they were both interned in Stanley camp. The second letter was written just days before the war ended. Sadly, Matron never saw freedom again as she died of beriberi a few days leter. Its poignant words read: 'Just to wish you all the best – which I sincerely hope will be the best for you and before long – also to send you a small remembrance – a sign of unending interest in you and your future. God bless you, Matron'.   (*Bill Macauley*)

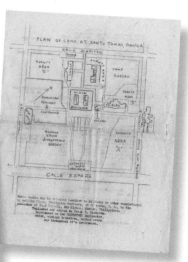

Some of the camps had paper, and published magazines and bulletins, such as this one, produced by internees in Santo Tomas to celebrate their daring rescue by the US cavalry.

Smiles at last as freedom comes for these internees at Ash camp in Shanghai (*above*) and Stanley in Hong Kong (*below*). Note the forage caps adorning the heads of two lads in Stanley, donated by liberating troops.   (*IWM*)

British internees, newly released from Stanley camp, climb aboard the lorries that would take them to the docks where troopships were waiting to carry them to England. (*IWM*)

A minority of children were separated from their parents during internment. These youngsters who had been in Weihsien in northern China are about to be reunited with their parents after four years apart. (*National Archives and Record Administration, Washington, D.C.*)

This five-year-old boy spent eight hours in the water when the ship that evacuated his family from Malaya was torpedoed. His mother was killed in the blast. He and his father were interned in Sumatra for three years. (*IWM*)

Jose Chamberlain stands by the grave of her mother who died during the first year of internment leaving Jose effectively orphaned as her father had been imprisoned by the kempetai in 1942. (*Jose Chamberlain*)

Excited children, recently released from two and a half years in prison camps, look up in amazement at the giant 'diver' at a party on board HMS *Belfast* in October 1945. Those who attended this party still remember the copious amounts of food, which made them sick at the time. (*IWM*)

Homeward bound for this three-year-old, who was born while her mother was interned in Singapore. Rations there were meagre and milk for babies almost unobtainable. (*IWM*)

David Nicoll and his sister Ella after the war. Although Chapei, where they were interned, was one of the more humane camps, both youngsters were very poorly when they were released. Ella still gets pain from a worn-out needle that broke off inside her body in the course of an injection in camp. (*David Nicoll*)

But it wasn't a normal birthday for a boy on the threshold of teenage life. Not only did he weigh just 68 pounds (average weight for a twelve-year-old is 87 pounds), but he was also aware his stamina was declining. Now if he ran up the stairs he had to lie on his bed to get his breath back.

The preoccupation with food among the children is revealed in the childish verse composed by his sister Ella in the birthday card she had drawn for him:

> Best wishes for your birthday.
> We hope you'll soon be free
> Then you can eat to your content
> And make real gay whoopee.

In Yangchow C the Christmas meal of 1943 had been so splendid that Cyril Mack can almost savour it more than sixty years later. 'Our camp committee put in a request for a special ration of food for Christmas and surprisingly and unexpectedly the Japanese granted their request; an extra ration of pork.' As Cyril stood in the tiffin queue and saw the 'unimaginably huge portions' other people were bearing away he became anxious that the supply would run out before it got to his turn. 'When we eventually arrived at the serving table I could not believe the amount of meat which was ladled into our bowls: inch cube chunks of delicious pork cooked in soya sauce, so tender that they almost fell apart in your mouth, with boiled rice and a variety of vegetables, and for once all served separately and not in a stew ... It ... proved to be the highest point of the food situation in Yangchow.'[28]

The following year the camp committee again requested extra rations to make a festive Christmas dinner. Parcels had been promised, but never materialised. By now, however, the resources for a lavish feast were no longer there. The International Red Cross sent a donation but it was only enough to buy about 1 pound of lard and 1 pound of pork, a paltry amount for 650 people. 'We got the lard and apparently the Japs sent in some ribs and one or two scrawny shoulders and hams – not what we had hoped for.' A few weeks later the Swiss Consul told the Yangchow internees that the IRC funds had run out.

In Manila by Christmas 1944 things were as bad as in any camp. Internment here had begun in 1942, more than a year earlier than in China. That first Christmas, parents interned in Santo Tomas camp had pulled out all the stops to ensure that the children should have as happy a time as possible. Determined that internment was not going to deprive the children of presents at Christmas they made them. It was a titanic effort and took weeks of work. Everyone who had a skill – carpenters, needlewomen, handymen and hobbyists – were pressed into service and, in the absence of funds, urged to use their ingenuity. People who did not regard themselves as artistic or practical were encouraged to have a go by a camp toy show held in November 1942. This featured 300 wooden toys made by men and women in camp and was seen by 1,100 internees. In a splendid spirit of make-do-and-mend scrap-boxes were provided for people to contribute unwanted materials.

'Out of these rolled odds and ends of all descriptions; old clothes of silk, cotton and rayon ... worn-out sofa pillows, bedding and torn mosquito nets, handkerchiefs, ribbons and scarfs (sic), old curtains, buttons and beads, papers wrapped with brightly colored thread and yarn, pieces of wood, small cans of paint and enamel with fine paint brushes, scrip and money in all denominations ...' When donations began to run low, and cotton and kapok to stuff toys were in short supply, self-sacrificing women took the padding from their mattresses and pillows. Men who had never tried woodwork before joined a hastily set-up workshop and learnt to make wooden toys. The heroic effort was a huge success. By Christmas Day an impressive 1,963 toys had been wrapped and distributed to the children. The novices 'turned out trains, hobby horses, kiddy kars, scooters, metal and wooden boats, jig-saw puzzles, rulers, stilts'.[29]

Christmas 1944 could not have presented more of a contrast. There had been a delivery of Red Cross parcels shortly before Christmas, but the Japanese had looted them and kept the best of the contents for themselves.

Sylvia Williams recalls the desperation of that time. 'The last Christmas our great family treat was three tiny squares of chocolate, carefully broken up and handed out by my father.'

Frederic Stevens recorded the menu of 25 December 1944.

Breakfast: one ladle rice mush with sweetened chocolate and cocomilk. One cup of coffee (of sorts)
Lunch: one ladle vegetable stock thickened with soy bean meal.
Dinner: fried rice with tiny shreds of canned meat
Double serving of camotes (sweet potatoes) and rice.[30]

It wasn't just the children's bodies which suffered in the camps. The conditions had other, psychological effects, some of which would be permanent. As the idle, hungry days succeeded each other the dynamic of family life was altered, with preoccupied parents withdrawing from their children. James Ballard, interned at the age of twelve, observed this in his own family in Lunghwa. At first he had enjoyed the unaccustomed intimacy with his parents which camp life imposed – eating, sleeping, dressing and undressing together. Colonial parents tended to leave displays of affection to the amahs and James liked watching his mother reading in bed behind her mosquito net, enjoying the feeling that he could reach out and take his mother's hand – 'though I never did'. Sadly, as their physical intimacy grew, he felt the emotional distance between them increase. He put this down to the fact that as prisoners his parents had suffered a loss of power and found themselves reduced to the same status as himself. 'A gradual estrangement from my parents, which lasted to the end of their lives, began in Lunghwa camp ... One reason ... was that their parenting became passive rather than active – they had none of the usual levers to pull, no presents or treats, no say in what we ate, no power over how we lived or ability to shape events ... '[31]

The moral norms of the old world broke down in other ways too. The starvation conditions created a new, brutish ethic in which stealing came to be seen, not as a social evil, but as a survival skill. Vegetable plots, tended at great physical cost by weary people whose own energy tanks were running on empty, were looted. Tinned stores were raided. Anything left out by mistake was commandeered. Many parents looked on with dismay as they saw children all round them turning into precociously streetwise urchins.

This was what William Sewell found happening in Stanley. 'The children developed a kind of repressed excitement and urgency which came from the life they were leading. Patience and humility are the virtues of a secure society, but not of an internment camp, where to sit back in patient apathy would be to wait for death ... The child has to be out in the street on the watch, gathering chips of bark as the men chop the firewood, or rice which has leaked in the gutter from the sack. The struggle was very real, and so, like any children of the slums, they struggled with each other in rivalry.'[32]

Hope Lee in Yu Yuen Road found the situation much the same. 'Stealing went on all the time everywhere. It affected even the decent folk. Little Tony Corner, nine years old, after five weeks of camp life says to his mother, "Someone's left a broom out on the field – there's no one there now. I'll just run and get it." If you saw something belonging to you in someone else's hut, it would not be camp etiquette to mention it ...'[33]

The suffering of the internees, children as well as adults, especially in the latter months, was intense and widespread. And the worst part about it is that it was avoidable. The Japanese blamed the shortage of food on the war but that argument does not stand up. None of the Japanese running the camps was ever short of food. Neither were the black marketeers. Over and over again when camps were liberated stores of food and medicines were found which would have alleviated suffering and saved lives. In many camps the Japanese army simply stopped ordering food for the prisoners. The evidence suggests at best utter indifference, at worst a policy of deliberate starvation. Expert students of the Japanese policy with regard to civilian internment stress that from 1943 civilians were not given the rations they were entitled to under international and Japanese regulations. 'Nowhere had war conditions, shortages of food and transport caused such scarcity and want as to justify to any extent conditions prevailing in the camps. After the Japanese capitulation sufficient supplies could immediately be sent to the internees.'[34]

After the war Cyril Mack learned via a US Army report on Yangchow C camp that for the last five months of the war (from March 1945) the commandant had not received any funds from Tokyo for the purchase of food for the prisoners. As Mr Hashizume was also the Japanese consul for the Yangchow area he drew on consular funds to feed them. 'Had he not done so we would have indeed been in a very parlous situation. This might give some credit to the credence of many people at the time that if the Allies had landed in China and the Japs were facing total defeat, their intention was to execute us and one of the most economical ways to do this would have been to abandon us and let us starve to death. Maybe they had already started to put the plan in motion.'[35]

As 1944 dragged to an end rescue of the boldest and most unexpected kind was imminent for some internees. The majority of prisoners, however, were going to have to wait another seven hungry months.

14

'They have to grow up like beasts, your children'[1]

By 1944 conditions in most camps were pretty grim, with supplies of everything – food, fuel and clothing – running low and the health of prisoners deteriorating. But in another region of Japan's Greater East Asia Co-Prosperity Sphere thousands more European civilians were not merely being starved. Men, women and children interned in the islands of what are now Indonesia, but were then the Netherlands East Indies, were being systematically beaten and mistreated by a succession of thuggish regimes. The story of the starvation and frequent deaths of 20,000 civilian prisoners on islands like Sumatra and Java is less well known than the suffering of the military prisoners who built the Burma railway, but the stain it leaves on Japan's reputation is no less lurid. In this part of the globe for the three years that spanned the autumn of 1942 to the autumn of 1945 humanity hid its face.

The experience of internment in the Netherlands East Indies differed profoundly from even the worst stage of incarceration in camps elsewhere in the Far East. The death rate here from starvation-related disease was double that in civilian camps elsewhere. The suffering was so bad young children saw their best friends die of hunger. They became so used to it that it no longer upset them. The cruelty of the punishments in these camps, invariably witnessed by children, was savage. Occasionally children were the victims. One lad had been caught leaving the compound to search for food and was locked in an underground cell for a month.

The smooth and largely bloodless invasion of the islands in February 1942 gave little clue of what would lie ahead. As Japanese forces landed first on Sumatra and two weeks later on Java there was none of the blitzkrieg that accompanied the attacks on Singapore and Hong Kong. Well before the start of the war in the Pacific, General Wavell, commander of British troops in India, charged with seeing that British territory was protected against a Japanese attack, had warned that Java's defences would not hold out for more than a month. In the end it was five days. Japanese troops advanced stealthily on foot from all the coasts, marching through mangrove swamps and rubber forests, over mountains and through tobacco plantations. European families awoke to find the enemy had arrived – on push bikes or motorcycles.

On 9 March the Dutch and Allied forces surrendered. The news reached thousands of trapped and apprehensive families via the wireless. The announcement of the surrender was followed by advice as to how the vanquished colonials should behave towards their conquerors. This included a deep bow every time they met a Japanese man and a blackout of all domestic lights at sundown. The last instruction was directed at women. It warned that when a Japanese man addressed a woman, she was not to look into his face but should keep her eyes fixed on the ground while she listened or spoke.[2] This was to prove the cause of much violence and misery in the coming years.

Physical amenities in the camps in the Netherlands East Indies were primitive in the extreme. Accommodation consisted for the most part of crowded bamboo huts where prisoners slept on narrow shelves, tormented by insects and vermin. Latrines were primitive ditches which overflowed in tropical rainstorms, flooding the camp with a brown ooze of lethal human waste in which the younger children often slipped and fell. Aspects of civilised life, which were accepted by the authorities throughout the majority of camps, were expressly forbidden here. In the overwhelming majority of camps prisoners were not allowed to practise their religion or to educate their children. Anything that might afford spiritual nourishment was banned – books, pen and paper, games – as was anything that reminded the prisoners of home or homeland – photographs of loved ones, coins or paper money or anything bearing a national emblem. They were deprived of anything that makes life liveable, from soap and toothpaste to medical supplies. Lack of drugs led to terrible suffering. 'Yesterday there was a stomach operation without anaesthetic. Local anaesthetic which gave out after two hours, while the operation lasted four hours,' one woman in a camp on Sumatra noted.[3] Unlike internees in other parts of the east, where eventually a form of modus vivendi was achieved with fellow internees and with the enemy, prisoners here were rarely allowed to remain in one camp very long; instead they were subjected to repeated, life-sapping journeys – on foot, on boats, in trains. Some moved as often as nine times. In the vile conditions – the majority had dysentery and if there was a lavatory were far too weak to reach it – many died. They were either thrown overboard or given a perfunctory burial beside the railway track. Harrowing scenes arose when a child died and its mother refused to part with its body. All this was witnessed by children.

The majority of prisoners in these camps were Dutch, but included in their number were more than 1,000 British women and children. Here the contradiction between the Japanese fondness for children and their willingness to see them suffer was at its most marked. They did not often physically abuse children (though there were exceptions), but there are other ways of causing pain, and their captors showed a callous disregard for their emotional or intellectual welfare. Not only were families not allowed to live together, but also at the age of twelve boys were sent off to men's camps to work. This age reduced as the war progressed until ten-year-olds came to be classed as men.

But it is through the treatment of their mothers that the Japanese caused most suffering to children. In all-women camps, safe from the threat of physical resistance that was always present in a men's camp, the Japanese had carte blanche to bully. Total obedience to the guards, who had the power to 'hit at will', was compulsory, even if it meant admittance to an occupied lavatory.[4] Casual beatings for minor misdemeanours were commonplace in most Japanese-run internment camps. The violence children witnessed in the Netherlands East Indies was on a different scale. The tormentors were invariably primitive, uneducated men, far removed from the consular staff who ran the camps in China. Anything warranted slapping and beating in these camps. On one occasion women were ordered out of their houses, made to stand to attention and required to listen to a speech by a Japanese officer who told them their plants had died because they were thinking bad thoughts.[5]

The captors felt no shame at bullying women as a casual comment uttered by a Japanese officer made plain. 'Dutch women ... you pick them up and smack them down. You wound them, you bruise them ... but they are like rubber balls. Hit them against the wall ... pht ... they come back again and stand before you again.'[6] By revealing his own brutality the man was in fact acknowledging the courage of so many of his victims. The violent tableaux enacted before the eyes of children were relentless. One group interned in a prison were made to watch a hanging and had to close their eyes in horror. In the camps women were beaten within the hearing of other prisoners so that horrified children could hear their screams. Often they were beaten in public, creating in some children a fascination which even at such a young age they knew to be unhealthy. The wretched women were then paraded, bloodied, bruised, shaven-headed and often wearing only their underwear, through the camp as an example to others. The most common reason for the beatings was smuggling, as mothers parted with anything tradable – wedding rings, blankets, even children's clothing – in their desperation to find fat or protein to prevent their skeletal children from dying. The natives who acted as their middlemen were punished even more harshly, as helping the whites was the worst of crimes in this brave new world. An Indonesian who tossed a bunch of bananas into the camp was thrashed and made to stand for six days without food or water with a sign round his neck saying 'I gave bananas to the rotten Dutch.'[7] He only survived because grateful women gave him food and drink while the guards were asleep. The Japanese liked to punish all for the sins of one and, with an additional twist of the knife, when they caught a smuggler they cut off food to the rest of the camp, often for days at a time. For many of the weakened prisoners these 'hunger days' proved the last straw. Many died during them, children included.

It was not only the beating of their mothers that affected the children. All the women in these camps had to work. Working entitled them to pathetic amounts of extra rations. But underfed, and in many cases giving half their rations to their children, the mothers collapsed and fell ill. This not only left very young children responsible for caring for their mother and younger siblings, but also deprived the children of the desperately needed extra rations. In many cases seriously ill women would insist on being dragged from their sickbed and propped up by friends in the queue for extra bread so that their children could get the much-needed calories. The fact that they had to work, often outside the camp boundaries, meant that their younger children were left unsupervised all day. In the tropical climate the children were thirsty. The only access to water was from wells or puddles. The children knew that well water was dangerous and that all water had to be 'cooked' first, but without being there to stop them, how could the mothers know that they would not drink something deadly?

There could be no pretence here that shortage of food was the result of the war. From the very beginning the internees' diet consisted of the cheapest rations to sustain life – simple carbohydrates. The Red Cross sent parcels, but they were hardly ever distributed. In some camps the Japanese played what to them was an amusing little game – they kept the parcels, but made the prisoners fill in a form claiming to have received them, even to the extent of listing the contents. And, even if they had had any money, there was no canteen here, offering life-sustaining extras. Many lived on flour thickened with water and flavoured with sugar, if any could be obtained; others ate bread soaked in water. There was hardly any protein and practically no calcium. If the prisoners needed fat for frying they melted candles, but as one child observed, you had to eat this food while it was hot. Cold it tasted revolting. In many camps no vegetable matter was served and, terrified of getting beriberi, the prisoners tried to grow their own in dry, uncooperative soil. They ate anything – dogs and cats, snakes, if they could catch them, worms, slugs and plants they picked at random in the jungle, not knowing which was edible and which toxic. Some desperate children stole the food destined for the cherished Japanese Koi carp, which turned out to be poisonous to humans. One young boy paid with his life.

Illness ravaged the camps. Unlike the situation in China there had been no advance warning here of internment. People had been herded into camp with a day's notice at most and many had been parted from even their small suitcases on the way. There were doctors but few drugs – no anaesthetic and not even disinfectants for the cuts which, on malnourished people in a humid tropical climate, turned dangerously septic. With no tools it was like a return to the stone age. Bandages had to be endlessly rewashed, but only in water as there was no soap, the scabs and pus of the former user scraped off with twigs and sticks. Doctors in several camps were forced, like battlefield surgeons in a barbarous earlier age, to perform operations on patients who, without anaesthetic, had to be held down. The patients were sometimes children who would otherwise not have survived. One young boy, diagnosed with septicaemia, owed his life to being smuggled out of camp, at huge risk to all involved, and treated in hospital.

Death became a hideously public presence even to young children. In a prison cell that had contained thirty-three women and children, only thirteen were still alive fourteen weeks later, the rest having died of dysentery or starvation. Children died and children were orphaned when their mothers died. Boys and girls as young as eight found themselves taking on the role of parents to very young brothers and sisters. One eight-year-old boy whose mother was gravely ill, looked after his four siblings, the youngest of whom was two, insisting that they say their prayers each night as their mother had taught them. Little girls who should have been skipping or playing hide and seek found themselves cooking, baking, washing clothes, looking after younger children and tending the sick. Older children were obliged to dig graves because they were sometimes stronger than adults. Over-familiar with suffering they began to feel indifferent to it, their own and others. Tragically, some young people, who should have felt that they were on the threshold of life, longed for death.

And at the end one comes back to the fact that it was all deliberate. Why was the suffering of people interned on Java and Sumatra so much worse than elsewhere? Why were the Japanese here so particularly lacking in humanity? We may never learn the answer. The Japanese foot soldiers who found themselves in the Netherlands East Indies had certainly been subjected to an intense indoctrination programme which promoted hatred of white colonialism. The local Indonesians would also be targets of the same crude anti-colonial propaganda. This proved so effective that, by a grim irony, at the end of the war the newly liberated Europeans had to be protected from mobs of murderous natives – by their erstwhile captors, the Japanese.

Methods of discipline in the Japanese forces were tough and brutal, as we have seen, with each rank sanctioned to assault the man one rung below him. To the unsophisticated subjects of Hirohito surrender was shameful and the status of prisoner contemptible. As far as women were concerned in Japanese society they were regarded as beasts of burden, lowly creatures created to wait on men. It is possible that men who regarded themselves as living by a warrior's code found the work of guarding female prisoners supremely degrading. Now even the humblest private had someone to slap. Perhaps it was anger at being deprived of a more glorious war that explained their cruelty.

In the Indonesian camps the Japanese never lost sight of their long-term aim, which was to destroy the colonial superiority of Europeans through stunting the intellectual growth of the next generation. In the great majority of camps they imposed and enforced a ban on education. Atlases and history books, or anything that promoted pride of homeland, were ruthlessly rooted out. Regular book raids were organised by the guards with boys being ordered to collect books in wheelbarrows and dump the 'useless paper' on lorries, which they drove away. In a camp on Sumatra the Japanese discovered an atlas in a room in which children had been being covertly taught. In his rage the commandant laid bare the philosophy that lay behind this crusade against self-improvement, screaming at the women: 'They can eat and drink and nothing more, like beasts. They have to grow up like beasts, your children.'[8]

Happily, in this campaign, too, the Japanese were ultimately unsuccessful. But the damage they inflicted was profound. Starvation affects brain function, and in particular memory. High numbers of children who had been interned in the NEI were found to have poor memories and needed two years of recovery to catch up.

15

What, All Dead?

———

'I t was miserably cold and raw weather. Weedy children, their enamel plates and cups in their hands waiting barefoot and dressed in inadequate clothing, waited for the breakfast bell to be sounded. These young were not playful and lively; they were like old men as they strictly waited for the meal bell.'[1]

When thirteen-year-old Ralph Armstrong first set eyes on the *Vyner Brooke*, the ship that was to take him, his mother, his two older sisters and his toddler cousin Marc away from the horror of burning, blazing Singapore to a new life in Australia, his heart swelled. 'To my eyes, as she stood off-shore, she looked lovely. The nicest-looking ship of the lot.'

The Armstrong family were prosperous Brits who loved the life out east. Ralph's father had been the manager of Robinson's, the well-known Singapore department store, and had decided it was his duty to stay behind and fight. His two grown-up daughters Gracie and Dixie, smiling out from the sepia pre-war photographs, possessed film star glamour with their white teeth and tanned legs. Little did Ralph know, as he looked back at the black smoke that blotted out the once-seductive city, that the journey he was beginning would take him within an inch of death and smash this happy family forever. As they sped out by launch towards the veteran luxury liner, built in 1927 in Leith, Scotland, Ralph's attention was caught by a group of fifty Australian army nurses, happy at being homeward bound, who were singing 'Waltzing Matilda'. At that moment no one could have imagined that within days twenty of those vital young women would be dead, massacred in cold blood by Japanese soldiers.* It seemed equally unlikely that the stately *Vyner Brooke* with her Chippendale chairs and crystal chandeliers would be lying at the bottom of the sea. As Singapore burned, dozens of ships loaded with frightened women and children were playing cat and mouse with the Japanese air force in those island-dotted waters leading to the Java Sea. Many didn't make it and ended up as prisoners. The *Vyner Brooke*'s captain tried valiantly to dodge the bombers by sailing at night and zig-zagging, but at about 2 p.m. on 14 February the ship was attacked by half a dozen planes, one of which scored a direct hit.

Ralph and his family jumped into the nearest lifeboat but it refused to pull away and the ship was about to tip over on top of them. 'There was a shout, "Abandon lifeboat. Jump – jump quickly", and we all had to jump into the water and get clear. I swam away blindly, not really knowing where I was headed but trying to stay near our family ... all of a sudden life rafts were bobbing all around us. We reached one and scrambled on.' The Armstrong family found themselves on different rafts. On Ralph's raft was the daughter of an English Singapore Municipal Council officer, aged nine, a Russian woman and a badly burned Malay seaman from the engine room, which had received a direct hit. Paddling furiously the Armstrongs tried to push the two rafts together so that they could get onto the same raft. A sudden wave smashed the two rafts alongside each other. The little girl who had been holding on over the edge of the raft had a finger chopped off at the top knuckle. 'She screamed and rushed over to me, clinging to me with her head in my lap and sobbing.'

The Armstrong family remained drifting at sea for three days and nights with nothing to eat or drink – no milk for Marc – and no shelter from the sun, which inflicted horrific burns on their fair skin. They forced each other to keep awake so they wouldn't fall over the edge of the raft. On the fourth morning they found they had drifted towards what turned out to be the northern coast of Sumatra. They

---

* After being shipwrecked and drifting at sea for several days the nurses came ashore in a lifeboat and were ordered into the sea by Japanese soldiers who then machine-gunned them, finishing off the wounded with their bayonets on Radji beach on Banka Island near the town of Muntok.

managed to scramble ashore through a mosquito-infested mangrove swamp and were eventually taken across to Banka Island. After George's mother and sister recovered from their burns they were imprisoned in the jail at Muntok on the north-west coast of the island. There the beds were sloping concrete slabs and their meal a small cup of watery rice porridge. For Ralph, the most degrading aspect of life in Muntok prison was the very public native-style lavatories – ten for 600 prisoners.

'In this place everything was built of stone or concrete and the lavatories . . . were no exception. They comprised ten oval-sized holes cut into the stone, on each side of the room. The prisoners had to squat on these openings, native-style, facing five other people on the other side. I don't know where the excrement went, but it must have dropped down into a hidden drain and been flushed off somewhere. With my upbringing I found this routine daily opening of the bowels an incredibly difficult thing to do . . . . But eventually the force of nature . . . regardless of personal feelings, caught up with me and I had to rush in there and do my business quickly.'

A doctor treating Ralph's sister warned that the island was very dangerous for Europeans, harbouring lethal tropical diseases like cerebral malaria and beriberi. And so, for the Armstrong family, as for so many others, it would prove. The family did not stay long in Muntok prison – at least on this occasion. It was part of the plan of the Japanese occupation to keep harrying prisoners with moves, pointless, draining, degrading . . . each marking a new low in their victims' health. The sea off Muntok was shallow and to facilitate shipping it was equipped with a mile-long pier. During the war Muntok pier would become infamous, a symbol of suffering as, under a lethal tropical sun, successive waves of wretched civilian prisoners shuffled and stumbled up and down it, loaded with baggage, carrying babies, dragging children, supporting the sick and dying. People collapsed on Muntok pier, people died on Muntok pier, all under the eyes of guards who, as so many chroniclers noted, for all their compassion, might have been carved from stone.

The first time they made the trip down the pier and into the boats that would take them across to Palembang in the southern part of Sumatra, the prisoners were still reasonably fit. Ralph and his family ended up in a camp called Irenelaan in a fenced-off area of what had been a Dutch residential area. It was a small camp, consisting of between 400 and 500 women – Dutch, British, American and Eurasian. The treatment of internees here was reasonably civilised.

Then, one day in April 1943, came the moment that changed Ralph's life forever. Some unfamiliar Japanese officers called at the house. 'The soldiers came in first and stood at the door waiting for the officers to enter. They then shouted "kiri." We all had to bow. It was either that or get your head bashed in. All the boys were made to take down their trousers in front of everyone while the officers walked around nonchalantly inspecting their privates. One of the officers pointed at certain boys who were then separated from the others. I was one of them.

'Then the announcement came. These boys have matured. They are now men. They will be transferred to the men's camp.'

The boys were taken to the guardhouse immediately, allowing their families only the briefest time to say their goodbyes. Thirteen-year-old Ralph put on a brave face in front of his mother and sisters, telling them he was sure they would all meet again after the war. The women's tone was more sombre – and more practical. His mother said, 'If anything should happen to me ... promise to remain cheerful.' Grace's thoughts were for her young son. She told Ralph, 'If anything should happen to me promise to do your best for Marc.'

The 'men' were taken to the guardhouse while the women were left standing outside.

'We all got into lorries with boards mounted above the front camp which read Dai Nippon. As usual one of us tried to make a joke of it, but nobody laughed. The lorries moved off ... and the tears came.'[2]

Ralph was taken to the men's camp at Palembang where he and the other young boys were treated with kindness by the men. Each one was allocated a guardian to show him the ropes. In this camp, unusually for the region, the authorities were not opposed to education. There was even a library of about 1,000 books built up through bartering with a Chinese trader. There were many priests in the camp and they taught him maths, geography, science, history and nature study. But there were many things about camp life he found hard to get used to. The first was public showering. Ralph had already found defecating in Asian-style lavatories a problem and now found himself expected to strip off in front of strangers. He tried to get round the problem by keeping his shorts on, but then found, as the shorts failed to dry in the humid air, he was running out of clothes.

'The man who was supposed to be my guardian said, "Why don't you go and bathe?" I told him I felt a bit embarrassed. He stared at me. "You should not be ashamed of being naked. It is the men with their misshapen bodies who should be embarrassed." I thought to myself, I'm not Charles Atlas, but I made the effort to go and bathe with the others.'

At Palembang prisoners soon began to fall ill with beriberi, dysentery and malaria, and death became almost a daily event. Ralph's guardian became too ill to look after him. Successors were appointed, but they too fell ill and died and much of his education petered out. 'The first one was an architect who started to teach me perspective and line drawing for a few weeks before he died. He was succeeded by a cabinet maker who taught me quite a lot of wood working and wood carving before he too died.' The priests, who showed outstanding dedication to the young and the sick, took him into their dormitory. But their ranks were thinning out too. Of the thirty Catholic priests in camp at the outset more than half were dead when liberation came three years later. Ralph had to dig their graves.

In the autumn of 1943 the prisoners were moved back to Muntok jail a second time. Here they slept on bare concrete floors with only thin mats to protect them from the seeping damp. 'We tried putting other materials between the mats and the concrete floor, but these could not be used for long, as they attracted vermin, and had to be burned. The mats themselves attracted bedbugs but we solved this problem by pouring boiling water over them and drying them in the sun.'

Ralph fell ill with blackwater fever, a serious complication of malaria, particularly in the absence of drugs. 'I was taken back to my spot in the Priests' dormitory. I quickly developed a high fever and could not swallow. All eating and drinking was difficult. One priest came to my aid, Father Elling. He sat by me and every now and then tried to get teaspoons of soup down my throat.'

While he was mortally ill Ralph had a nightmare in which it appeared that death was calling him but he was resisting. 'I saw people in the dark corner of the room beckoning me to come to them. I said no. I became semi-conscious, then slipped into the dream again, and they were there again at the far end of the dark room, beckoning ... I said, I am not coming.' He heard the priest appealing to him to take 'just one teaspoon'. He tried to refuse, 'but my head was tilted back, and the soup was forced into my mouth until I couldn't help but swallow.'

Eventually the priest managed to get a whole cup of soup down Ralph's throat, and after having been semi-delirious for more than seven days he began to feel normal. The first thing he did was to ask for the cat he had adopted in camp. To his horror the priest replied, 'You've eaten it ... we had to make some soup ... otherwise you would have died.'

Once he had recovered Ralph grew adept at hoarding food, allocating himself tiny quantities of vital nutrients on a daily basis. 'It made sense to cut things into tiny pieces ... if you got a piece of ginger, say a half inch cube, you could make it last for a week ... by cutting it into four portions and storing them in your closed biscuit tin. Then each time you got a small cup of miserable tasteless soft boiled rice, you could add a few of these bits to it, and it would improve the taste remarkably .... Having a tiny piece of lettuce or kang kong (Chinese green leaf vegetable) a day was better than eating the whole leaf and having nothing the rest of the week.'

Meanwhile, more and more people were contracting dysentery and beriberi. Conditions in the stinking sick wards, which were run by dedicated Catholic priests who were fearless about exposing themselves to deadly infections, resembled a cowshed. 'As the sick were lying on concrete platforms on either side of the centre passageway ... it was possible to hose out the run twice a day, and clean up individual patients too. The same thing was done in the beriberi ward. The patients were individually cleaned every morning and then the platforms were hosed off so that they had a clean bed to start the day.'

Ralph was particularly distressed by the beriberi ward where normally healthy people were dying for lack of vitamin B. 'Beriberi starts with a build-up of fluid in the legs, and the legs get very swollen. It was noticeable that when you pressed your finger on the swollen portion of the leg, it didn't spring out again quickly. The dent remained for some time. Slowly the fluid builds up higher and higher in the body.'

What was particularly gruesome was the noise these unfortunate people made. 'When the beriberi patients got worse they started making a sound ... It was somewhere between a humming ... and a moaning wail. The sound seemed to rise and fall and it went on for hours. Once one person started, the others would follow suit one by one, until they had all joined in.'

At Christmas 1944 the men tasted protein for almost the first time in two years when they were allowed to kill a pig, but for Ralph the best treat occurred at the end of the first week in January 1945 when they were told that they were being allowed to visit their mothers and families. After two years apart they were to be allowed ten minutes together. Ralph was beside himself with excitement, although in the end he saw only his married sister. It was a highly charged moment.

'When we arrived, we stood waiting on the grass outside, for them to come out. Suddenly the gates opened and out they came ... my sister Grace came out smiling as usual. We ran to each other crying with joy. She said Mum and Dixie could not come out because they were still in the sick ward. I asked, "How is Marc?" She answered, "He is fine, he is a big boy now."' In no time the ten minutes visiting time was up. The siblings clung to each other as long as they could. Then the Japanese guards separated them and led the women back inside.

No sooner had the happiness and hope generated by the brief reunion faded than the prisoners learnt that they were being moved back to Sumatra again. They were taken to Muntok pier in lorries and left to walk or drag themselves down the mile-long pier – the elderly, the sick and the dying. Ralph was shocked by the heartlessness of the guards. 'They watched our progress without reaction. People fell, sick stretcher-cases died – but the guards did not budge an inch nor blink an eyelid.'

And as if this spectacle of the wretched colonials humbled was not entertaining enough, when they reached the end of the pier the order was changed. It was decided that they would wait for the next day to sail. The dead were dumped over the side of the pier into the sea. The living were ordered back to the shore and had to repeat the process all over again the next day. They sailed towards Sumatra but anchored overnight in the mouth of the Moesi River. With so many suffering from dysentery the stench and mess was appalling.

When they arrived back at Palembang they had to march to the railway station. They were herded onto a train – some in carriages, some in goods wagons – headed for Loebok Linggau (and Belalau) on the west coast of the island, but the train did not leave until the next morning, so they were locked in all night. When they arrived in Loebok Linggau on the evening of the third day they were given some boiled rice and locked in the carriages again. In the putrid air, reduced to the level of a beast, Ralph was on the point of collapse. 'Details of what was happening were becoming a blur. I had reached a state where I just did not care anymore whether I lived or died, propped up, semi-conscious between two others.'

The new camp, set deep in the jungle, seemed like paradise after the stone prison walls they had come from. A crystal stream ran through the camp, while the air was filled with bird calls and the ceaseless chorus of cicadas. The beauty of the setting seemed to mock the prisoners' plight. 'Along the stream were hundreds of butterflies. Their colours were exquisite. I thought, how can such beauty exist in a place like this where people are dying daily from disease and starvation?'

The beauty of the surroundings made no difference to the Japanese fondness for punishment, however. It was strictly forbidden to leave the compound, but the boys discovered a way, by crawling through a storm drain. Ralph tried it once and was lucky. He had to take food to a boy who had been caught and the punishment – being locked in an underground cell in solitary for a month – put him off. 'On the two or three days I had to take the food to him I was shocked at what I saw. Eyes bulging, staring about wildly, the prisoner came out to take the tin plate when the guard unlocked the door. He must have been living in the room in his own excrement. The sight was too horrible to behold. The guard quickly pushed me away.'

The end came unexpectedly. The camp was summoned to hear an address by the commandant who told them peace had been declared. Overnight, rations increased threefold and no more rotting food was served. Ralph and the other boys were offered several sets of dark green jungle uniform by the Japanese and told they could go and visit the women's camp, only a few miles down the road. As spick and span as they could make themselves in their new uniforms, they set off. The camp was thronged with people asking where their families were. Ralph couldn't wait to see his mother and sisters and Marc. 'At last I got to the right hut. There was the usual walkway down the centre and platforms on both sides with all the ladies on their bunks. Marc was pointed out to me and I went to him. He recognised me immediately and came straight to me ... We gave each other a big hug.

'"My, how big you've grown," I said. "Where's your Grandma?"

'He said, "She died in Muntok."

'I was shocked. My mother, dead? "Where's your Mum? Where's Gracie?"

'"Dead," he answered.

'"Dixie?"

'"Dead."

'My heart sank. "What! Are all of them dead?" I said. "Who is looking after you?"

'Marc pointed to the lady next to him. I turned to her and she explained that all my family had died in the last year of the war, Gracie and Dixie only a few months before, in April. Gracie and Dixie died within a week or ten days of each other. Dixie just before they left Muntok and Gracie very soon after we got to Belalau.'[3]

The woman who had been caring for Marc gathered together what little there was of the family's personal effects and bundled them up with his clothes. She kissed him goodbye and told him to be a good boy. Ralph and Marc started back for the men's camp. Ralph was still struggling to take in the implications of what he had been told – that he would never see his mother or sisters again.

The little boy was quite excited about going to the men's camp, where he was able to bunk down next to his cousin, now that so many men had died. Ralph, who had been considered a man for the last three years, had not wanted to give way and lose control in public. 'I thought I would do my crying in the night, when all had gone to sleep. I stared hypnotically at the wall for some time ... then I tried to pull myself together. I couldn't cry here. Although it was night, and many bunks were empty, there were still people around. I got up and went out to the toilet, and then slowly made my way down to a grassy patch beside the fast flowing stream. There I lay, and sobbed my heart out.'

After a few days planes came and dropped supplies on the camp. Ralph and Marc walked to Loebok Linggau to see the huge Allied force arrive to take back the island. To their astonishment they found that Sumatra had been wrested from the Japanese by a force of just twenty men, led by a South African Royal Marine, Major Gideon Jacobs. They also learnt that the location of their camp, and the women's camp, had only been known of due to two survivors of the Bangka Island massacre who told the Allies that there were a number of civilians still unaccounted for.

Ralph and Marc were collected from camp in lorries driven by British and Dutch troops and taken to Loebok Linggau station and thence to an airfield. Along the way they noted with satisfaction columns of Japanese soldiers 'obeying the orders of Major Jacobs, bowing to whites and carrying their baggage'. They flew to Singapore by Dakota and were taken to the Alexandra Hospital for a week where they were treated for malaria. Once they had recovered they were put up in the luxurious Raffles Hotel, which had been requisitioned as a transit camp for prisoners of war returning home. Ralph still didn't know whether his father had survived the war and was sadly expecting to be flown to England when the Red Cross again worked its miracles and found him. He had escaped internment for the duration of the war, having been hidden by a Malay family.

It was a deeply emotional reunion as Ralph's father had already learnt of the deaths of half his family via the Red Cross. 'We went to the place where he was staying and threw our arms round him. We couldn't stop hugging each other and we all cried.'

Ralph then had to make an agonising decision. As ex-prisoners if he and Marc travelled to England it would be on a free passage. His father, however, would have to pay and didn't have any money. 'One idea put forward was for us two to go to England first, establish ourselves, and then send for my father. We thought about it long and hard, but to go now, so soon after we had been reunited, would have broken Dad's heart, so we decided to stay.'

Fifteen-year-old Olga Geel (later Moss) began her internment in an overcrowded Javanese prison containing dangerous native criminals. The daughter of a Dutch bank manager and a Russian mother, Olga shared a cell with thirty-three other Europeans – nine children and twenty-four women. These included a family of five children, four boys and a little girl, whose mother was in a camp hospital, dying. The eldest, Jonathan, was eight. The youngest was two. Another inmate was a partially paralysed woman with a small boy. There were no beds or blankets. The prisoners had to sleep on the earthen floor, which by morning was running with water. Large rats infested the cell at night. The lavatory was a fly-infested hole in the corner, which all had to visit with no privacy. Conditions here were so atrocious that after fourteen weeks, when the prisoners were finally released to go to a camp, sixteen of them had died – publicly, in front of horrified adults and wailing children, where they lay. One woman had gone mad.

Before being herded onto the waiting lorries that came to wrest them from their old life in Bandung, Olga and her mother had given their pet dogs to their Chinese neighbours to spare them a cruel fate. 'It was the custom of the Japanese, when they picked up people, to lock up any dogs, cats, birds inside the house and shut the doors of the house with a Japanese seal. So the poor animals just starved to death inside the house.'

They were driven to Bantjeuj prison, an institution built to house Indonesian convicts. The first night the prisoners decided they had no choice but to remain standing up. 'There was an inch of water on the floor, coming out of the ground. As we had no mattresses, nor blankets, we looked in despair at the wet floor and decided we could not possibly lie on it. So we started by all standing together, close to each other for warmth and comfort. But as the hours went by, we could not keep it up and we sat down, leaning against one another. Towards the morning we were all lying on the ground and woke up when we heard the rusty sound of the key in the door. We were all wet and had to try to dry ourselves by walking in a little narrow strip outside our cell.'

Even worse than the cold were the rats, of whom the Indonesian warder had warned: 'Don't move when [they] come, otherwise they'll bite you which will give you a fever.'

'While I was lying on my stomach towards the end of that memorable first night ... I felt a rat walk over my legs ... the thoughts raced through my head, don't go mad, just remember even a rat is made by God. And it helped me. I noticed it had a soft warm body and could feel its little webbed feet on my skin. I tried to forget what it looked like.'

Every morning the inadequate lavatory was blocked and one of the native convicts would be sent to fix it in front of the gagging prisoners. 'Many flies were on him and followed him. He would start poking the toilet with his crooked stick to try to unblock the system. That usually did not work, so he would stand with both feet in the toilet hole and start stamping up and down. Then he would proceed to go on his knees to put his arm in the toilet right up to his shoulders. At last he got it unblocked.'

The white women's humiliation was complete. They were filthy. They stank. They had no change of clothes, no toothpaste, tooth-brushes or soap, no books to while away the empty hours. Their meals comprised one spoonful of boiled rice with salt. In the long weary hours the prisoners talked about their fears of what might happen to them. With wisdom beyond her fifteen years Olga ana-lysed each prisoner's weak points.

'Some of us could cope with broken sleep, but not with hunger. Others managed the interrogations but suffered deep depressions caused by the uncertainty of our future. We were all being trained in endurance, patience, and the will to fight against all sorts of fears, despair and anger.' Her own secret fear was that she would go mad.

The plight of the younger children in the prison was pitiful. The situation of the eight-year-old responsible for his four younger siblings was particularly harrowing. Despite his extreme youth he insisted that they all said their Hail Marys every night, just as their Mummy had taught them. 'As the days dragged on, the children got weaker and weaker. Jonathan became very sad, and every time someone died in our cell or in any other cell, he sighed, "wish it was me! I'd rather be with Jesus than here." It was caring for his three brothers and little sister that made him so weary. He told us that his ninth birthday was approaching. That particular day a whole string of awful things happened, and not one of us remembered it was Jonathan's birthday. And when the evening came he said, "It was my ninth birthday today." All of us were stricken with guilt for having forgotten it.'

An even younger boy of five had to look after his mother, who was partially paralysed having contracted polio when he was a baby. He helped her get up with her crutches and brought her plate of rice. Olga was moved by his devotion. 'He never sulked or complained and he was an amazingly independent, calm character. In spite of being only five years old, he seemed to have already an inner source of strength. He never turned to any of us for help. It never entered his mind that he had a lot of capable adults in the cell who could give him a hand; instead he considered his mother to be his responsibility.'

Just before Christmas 1942 the woman with three small children started coughing up blood. The rest of the women were convinced that she had contracted TB from the contaminated tap water. On Christmas morning they found her children crying. Their mother was dead.

'Suddenly the doors opened ... and the warden was there with a Japanese officer next to him. The Japanese looked at the woman and the sobbing children and pointed towards their mother, asking what was the matter with her. Before any of us could answer him one of the women jumped up and screamed at him, "She is dead! She is dead and it is all your fault, because the water killed her!" The Japanese officer took out a short whip which was stuck in his belt and he raised his arm to whip her. But the woman shouted to him, "Oh whip me, whip me! You are not scared of me, but out there is One of whom you should be scared, that is ...", now she pointed with her finger upwards, "Allah", the Islamic God. He stopped in mid-air ... and slowly he brought his arm down with the whip. Then he turned on his boots and walked away. The woman sat down and wept.'

The plight of the orphaned children led to one of the few acts of humanity Olga witnessed throughout the terrible years of her internment. The Japanese officer had ascertained that the children's grandmother had not yet been interned and gave his personal authorisation for them to remain with her, not interned, for the rest of the war.

The prisoners were constantly reminded that a terrible fate awaited anyone who failed to submit to the new regime. The Japanese took delight in intimidating the women by forcing them to watch acts of violence. On one occasion Olga was forced to watch an execution in the prison. She was waiting to see the doctor when she saw a young man being led between two Japanese policemen. 'His eyes were full of agony and his face was deathly white ... I looked at the Kempeitai officers . . . they had no expression either in their eyes or faces . . . To my horror they turned into an open court-space opposite us and from a pole lowered a noose. We gasped and closed our eyes. The anguish on the young man's face was terrible . . . We don't know what he had done but he was slowly tortured to death in front of our eyes and, while we did not want to watch, we were forced . . . to stay where we were with closed eyes, weeping.'

Interrogation sessions were another part of the control process. To maximise the women's terror the interrogations took place in the middle of the night, when individuals would be woken by torchlight and taken from the cell alone. Teenagers like Olga were not exempt. One night it was her turn. Sweating with terror she followed the guard who had come to collect her. 'My legs felt weak . . . the uniformed warden . . . led me to an enormous hall. At the end of the hall was a platform on which a table was set with four Japanese officers sitting round it. Huge whips lay across the table.' As she entered the hall Olga saw a face reflected in mirrors which flanked the room '[I] did not recognize myself at first. I looked on the verge of death, scraggy with very large hollow eyes. The thought struck me: I haven't got much longer to live.' In her terror Olga prayed to God to help her. Almost at once a change came over her.

'It was as if an invisible wall was formed circling around me. It seemed as if I was lifted an inch from the ground and instead of walking, I seemed to be gliding over the floor towards the Japanese. Their voices seemed to be coming from a distance, faraway . . . I felt protected and the spirit of fear left me, giving way to a spirit of rest in my soul. It was as if I was in a little house in the midst of a raging storm, like Noah's Ark in the flood.'

When she reached the end of the hall one of the Japanese officers came down from the platform and started to walk towards her. He held a whip which was made up of many strings, each ending in a cork to increase the sting of the blow. As he advanced he whipped the air menacingly. The Japanese began questioning Olga in an incomprehensible mixture of Japanese, Malay and English – pointless questions she could not answer, like the names and dates of birth of grandparents she had never met.

Suddenly everything seemed clear. 'I had to remember not to look in his face when I answered him, as I was a woman and he would slap me in the face if I did ... I tried to understand what he was asking me and quite definitely I was guided by someone, an angel perhaps, who knew more about the Japanese character than I did, because I was made to understand by an inner voice. Thus I could answer the Japanese officer without letting him wait or making him repeat his question. He should not be made to feel ... his inadequacy at speaking either Malayan or English ... if I gave the wrong answer to his question, that gave him an opportunity to call me stupid ... By myself I would never have hit on this solution.'

Later in the session the officer returned to the identities of Olga's grandparents. As she couldn't remember what she had said before she made up new names and dates. She felt no fear – 'His voice came from afar, although I knew he was shouting at me. I knew what to say: "I did not know their names nor birthdates when you asked me before." He replied: "Why did you give false names and dates?" And I replied calmly, looking at his boots, "Because I did not want to offend you with my ignorance."'

Eventually the questioners tired of the interrogation. As the warder was told to lead Olga back to the cell the invisible protective 'wall' left her. 'I seemed to drop down and could feel the ground again. Sounds came rushing towards me. Then I knew for certain; God truly helps people in their distress.'

Feeling she was being protected by God helped Olga endure the suffering of internment. Later, in her last camp, she received what she believes was further proof of God helping the helpless. Conditions in Kampong Makassar, a primitive jungle camp, near Batavia, now Jakarta, were appalling. On her first night in camp Olga woke up, suffering from diarrhoea, like most of the prisoners, and needed to go to the lavatory. Half asleep and trying to find her way in near-total darkness, she slipped on the sticky reddish-brown clay and found, to her horror, that she had fallen into the camp's cesspool. Exhausted and in failing health after so many months of near-starvation, she decided to allow herself to drown in the stinking slime which covered her face and hair. Suddenly she heard a voice ask: 'Do you believe in God?' When she answered 'Yes' the voice reminded her that she did not have the right to take her life. Sobered, she struggled to get out but it proved impossible.

'My hands grabbed the edge, but I could not hold on as it was all slimy. Then my feet tried to touch the bottom so that I could take a jump and throw myself out of the pool and onto the ground. But as my feet searched the depth, I felt only thick slime, no hard bottom to rest on and to push myself up from. There was no way of getting out. If I tried to shout no one would hear me. I was now very aware that I might drown ... and I prayed intensely: Oh God, God, help me ... And suddenly I felt two hands underneath my elbows lift me up as if I were a feather and lay me on the ground.'

Sobbing and shaken Olga forced herself to get up and stagger back to the barracks where her mother and sister were fast asleep. She woke her sister up. 'I could not speak, I sobbed ... she saw this strange muddy phenomenon and smelled the stink and understood at once what had happened. She jumped up from the bamboo bed and put her arm round me and wept. Never will I forget the love of my sister ... she managed to lead me to the bathroom, her arm firmly around me, supporting and comforting me. In this camp ... we had an enormous communal bathroom where we had running water gushing down from a bamboo holder. She stood me underneath it, and told me to wait there as she was going to search for the kitchens to find cooking-salt to scrub me with.

'How long she stayed away I don't know. I just let the cold, strong running water gush over me, through my hair, over my face and cried ...'

After the prisoners were released from Bantjeuj prison they were taken first to Tjihajit camp, which was formed from a fenced-off district of Bandung. Here Jonathan and his brothers and little sister were at last reunited with their mother. 'As soon as we clambered down the truck, the waiting Roman Catholic nuns who lived in the camp embraced ... Jonathan and his three brothers and sister and took them quickly to the hospital to see their dying mother. She had been told that her five children had been put in Bantjeuj prison and she had struggled in those past one hundred days to keep alive in the hope of seeing them.'

The joy on the mother's face when she saw her children again made everyone who was there weep. She stroked the little boy's hair and whispered to him. She died later that day.

On her first day in Tjihajit, Olga, who had been living on rice for three months, was given something 'nice' to eat with her rice and cabbage and discovered with horror that it was dog meat. She noticed that there were few cats or dogs in the camp. 'The women told me that the boys tried to catch them when the owners were not watching, so as to kill and eat them. We had several outbursts of tears from women who could not find their dog or cat and feared that they had been killed and eaten by the boys.'

Like Ralph Armstrong and so many other children, Olga Geel experienced the horror of an arduous journey, crammed together with the sick and the dying. They were given only a day's notice to prepare for the move from Bandung to Batavia. They walked to Bandung railway station with only a flask of water and a bread roll each for a journey that would last thirty-eight hours. The walk was hard for the children and the elderly and the streets were lined with Indonesians watching the humiliation of the once-proud whites in silence. They were loaded into cattle trucks and the ventilation shutters closed. The sick lay on the floor. In the airless conditions people began to die. The horrified prisoners pulled the communi-cation cord whenever this happened.

A Japanese officer would go from coach to coach to find out who had given the alarm. The dead body was then lifted up and passed over the women to the door. Japanese soldiers hurriedly dug a shallow grave alongside the railway track before the train moved off again. Children died alongside adults.

'It was hell when a child died as the mother refused to part with the dead body of her child and some mothers became hysterical. Then a tug-of-war would ensue with the women trying to wrench the child's body from the mother. All this wrestling was conducted with shouts and screams, pleadings and furious shouts from the Japanese telling us to hurry up.' Olga, who was not well herself, lost consciousness from the horror of it. Occasionally the train would stop and the women would be ordered out to relieve themselves in front of curious villagers. Their degradation was deliberate and total. 'We had no toilet paper or water. Most of us, like myself were suffering from diarrhoea, so one can imagine the smell in our cattle trucks.'

The new camp, Kampong Makassar, was far more primitive, with bamboo huts and ditch latrines. There were no mattresses and the bare bamboo sleeping platforms were uncomfortable. 'As we were all very thin, they were very painful to lie on, and one tried to find a position between two bamboos with one's hipbone in between.' Rations were just enough to sustain life, 'rice with a spoonful of cabbage and a teaspoon of sugar a day'. They lived on what the Japanese threw away. Some women made a broth from pig tripe that the Japanese discarded. Others retrieved the loaves of mildewed bread and rotting veg the Japanese put in the dustbins. The hunt for protein was desperate. The doctors urged the prisoners to eat frogs, snakes and slugs. They had been struck by the sound of frogs croaking when they arrived. Within three days all the frogs had been caught. The Japanese had fishponds located outside camp, which were constantly guarded. The fish were fed on dried food called 'bunkil', which came in the form of round flattened cakes 'full of holes and worms'. Many of the women worked outside the camp – Olga's job was cutting the grass round the fishponds. Some of the other women begged them to smuggle some of the bunkil back in for them to eat but the women doctors in the camp warned against it, saying it was poisonous. Some women did smuggle some in and gave it to their friends. The results were horrific. 'People who had eaten it woke screaming in agony, their stomachs swollen and sweat running down their faces.' Some even died.

In this camp doctors had to undertake the appalling task of performing operations without anaesthetic. In both cases the patients were children. When two boys developed symptoms of appendicitis, the doctors warned that they would need to have their appendixes removed or peritonitis would set in and prove fatal. But there was no anaesthetic. The mothers had to make the terrible decision whether or not to consent to the operation. 'One mother hugged her son ... reassuring him that he was not going to be operated on ... he was so relieved ... telling her how much he loved her for her decision. The other mother wrestled herself free from the arms of her son and said to the women, "Take him to be operated on."' Out of earshot the mother collapsed weeping. 'Nobody dared to come near her ... and many wept with her. I was only a teenager at the time and did not know what motherhood was. It took twelve women. There was no anaesthetic and only primitive instruments. His mother walked as far as she could so she could not hear his screams. But he recovered from his ordeal. Some months later, as the doctors had predicted, the other boy began to feel pain. It was peritonitis, and the doctor was unable to help. He died in great pain.'

The women in the camps in the Netherlands East Indies were never able to understand the Japanese mentality, particularly where young children were concerned. They saw that their captors were attracted to their children, particularly the blondest, cutest ones, whom they liked to spoil with sweets. Sometimes they would take them off to their houses and give them treats such as bananas and chocolates, things that their mothers hadn't tasted for years. And yet these same men were happy to rough up their mothers and stand by while the children died of hunger.

'One little girl with long fair hair was a great favourite with one of the Japanese officers. She was about nine years old. One day she fell seriously ill with bacillaire dysentaria, which is curable if you have the medicine. Her mother rushed to the gate to tell the Japanese officer, who followed her quickly to the barracks and then peeped in to see her lying listlessly there. Can you imagine the amazement of the mother when he refused to bring any medicine for the little girl and just let her die when it was within his means to have saved her? It was this mentality of the Japanese we could never penetrate and which frightened us deeply. It was as if you were not dealing with humans, but another species.'

In Kampong Makassar the Japanese pursued their familiar policy of punishing a whole group of women prisoners – publicly – for the transgression of one. A favourite torment was making them stand out in the burning tropical sun with their arms stretched above their heads. The sight horrified Olga. 'Whenever I saw some woman being punished in that way, a sickening feeling in my stomach would well up with tears pricking behind my eyes. A Japanese soldier with a bayonet would stand guard close by and as soon as one of them would lower her arms, he would start yelling and shouting, waving his bayonet very close to their stomachs … many fainted and got sun-stroke through it.'

When, towards the end of the war, one of the more humane guards told a group of women that a men's camp, which housed some of their husbands, was being moved close to theirs, some of the wives planned to sneak out and meet them at night. Three of them were caught as they tried to slip back. 'The Japs made them walk through the camp with a placard on their chest and back on which their crime was written in bold letters. All their hair was shaven off and they were put on a severe food ration. They all slept in the same barracks and the Japs punished the head of that hut and all the women (about two hundred of them) had to have their hair shaven off. So they were all bald and this was a warning for us.'

By the time the atom bombs were dropped Olga was so weak from starvation that she had been granted permission to stop working and lie on her bed all day. Her companion was a little boy called Bennie whose mother, the widow of a war pilot, was dangerously ill in the camp hospital. 'Bennie was weak from starvation and the two of us would just sleep most of the time.'

When the end came, there was little of the anticipated euphoria, just weak tears of relief. They learnt of the surrender from the commandant, who made a speech in which, grotesquely, he appealed for forgiveness. 'He started to talk about different religions and that the faith of a Christian is in Christ, who has given us a shining example of forgiveness and who teaches us that we should pray for our enemies and now he ended, "I want to remind all of you to act like Christ in whom you believe. The war is over and the Japanese have lost the war." Instead of rushing out of the gates towards freedom we quietly walked back towards the barracks.'

Not long afterwards a plane flew over the camp to drop crates of food by parachute. As so often happened, one parachute did not open and crashed through the hospital roof killing several people. The famished prisoners could no longer digest sugar, after being without it for so long. 'We all developed sugar-heads and had big swollen faces ... As our bodies were so thin we looked like frogs and the doctors forbade us to eat any more sugar.' Tragically, peace came too late for many of the prisoners and people continued to die. 'It seemed worse when they died when the war was over than for those who died during the war.'

Little Bennie survived, but only just. 'If peace had come only a few days later, he would have died.' Olga noticed that one of the effects of starvation was that children like Benny had stopped growing. 'After the war their bodies ... tried to catch up with the lost years. People marvelled at this, saying how wise nature is to put a stop to their growth so as to preserve their strength.'[4]

*

Ernest Hillen was seven when he was interned with his mother and older brother Jerry in the first of four camps on Java, where his father had run a tobacco plantation. For three years he played no sport, was not allowed to read or write and received no education. His experience of internment included being parted from his brother, watching his mother's health decline through malnutrition and overwork and seeing his best friend die from hunger. He saw women being beaten so frequently he stopped discussing the incidents with his mother.

At first boredom was the major problem, but by the last camp this no longer seemed to matter 'because heat and hunger and dying got so bad ... everyone's daily-life circle grew tighter and tighter – food, work, rest ... I made no new friends. Sameness flowed on. It was as if I was half asleep. My eyes felt like glass; I saw only what was close, anything far off was blurred. I walked with my head down, but not, as before, looking for things to play with, only for what might be edible: snails, unripe fruit, spoiled greens from the camp kitchen's garbage ditch ...'

What was truly inspirational, in this world of cruelty and fear, was the way the courageous women were prepared to risk the worst violence to help each other. Before long Ernest's mother became ill. Helplessly he watched her one night drag herself out of their room and crawl on all fours to the outside toilet. Her job was loading furniture looted from Dutch houses and transporting it on carts to houses the Japanese now occupied. As a worker she was entitled to extra bread, but that extra ration was only given to the worker herself. A neighbour named Zuseke Crone came to the rescue.

'It was Mrs Crone who every morning would half-carry my mother to wherever their team gathered. [She] would hide my mother in an already emptied house nearby, where she lay on the floor until the bread was delivered. Then Mrs Crone would fetch her, prop her up in the breadline, and later sneak away to help her home again.'

It was not long before the courage of the women saved Ernest's life. In their malnourished state the internees were vulnerable to infections and there were no drugs in the camps. One day Ernest cut himself while digging in the earth. Nurses in the camp diagnosed blood poisoning and a plan was hatched to smuggle him to a hospital run by Dutch nuns who were still at liberty. They concealed him on the step of the wheelchair of an elderly woman who had got clearance to leave the camp.

'I climbed between the old woman's legs, the blanket came down, and the wheelchair began to move. It bumped out of the door and the bumps shot into my arm. It was hot under the blanket. We rolled along and no one said a word. We stopped and men's voices started shouting. There was a clank and a squeaking and the chair rolled on again and then it stopped. I felt us swing through the air and thump down.

'We started off. It was an old truck ... its shaking shoved the chair around and at corners the old lady pressed her hands down on my head ... In the blackness I squeezed my eyes shut against the pain ... I didn't move a muscle – there might be a soldier in the truck. We stopped. Outside I could hear only women's voices. "Careful, careful," said the old lady above. The blanket was lifted and my nose was in a long, wide, fresh-smelling white dress. I looked up. It was a tall woman wearing a huge stiff white cap that hid her hair.'

Ernest spent seventeen days in the hospital. He was cared for by Dutch nuns, who were not yet interned. For those few days he ate a normal diet, took vitamin pills and soaked his infected finger in agonisingly hot salt baths before he was smuggled back to camp in a lorry full of civilians being interned for the first time. He never saw the old woman who had smuggled him out again.

While they were in their second camp the Japanese announced that boys of thirteen and over were deemed a 'danger to the state' and would be removed to a men's camp. The age continued to fall until boys of eleven were removed. The Japanese gave the families minimal notice, announcing at midday on one day that the boys had to be ready with their luggage at the gate at 6 a.m. the next morning. All too soon it was Ernest's brother Jerry's turn. The older boys were touchingly brave.

'The tailboard of the first truck was slammed shut; standing pressed together, the boys waved, some crying, most not. Mothers screamed and surged against the hard rifles. As the truck rumbled out of the gate, a second one hastily backed in, its engine left running. Boys were hoisted into the back with speed. I couldn't spot Jerry at first but then he was clambering up, too, one of the last. He stood on his toes, his eyes searching for us.' Jerry acted brave, but he evidently feared the worst. His mother found a piece of paper in her purse. On it Jerry had written, 'herewith I Jerry John Hillen bequeath all my personal belongings to my dear Mother and my little Brother.'

Ernest, used to the protectiveness of Western males towards females, was upset by the violence meted out to the women – and the older children – by the guards. Many things could trigger a beating, particularly smuggling objects that in these camps were forbidden. These included anything that reminded the prisoners of their former nationality or identity: Dutch coin or paper money, anything featuring the Royal family, family photographs, cutting tools, books, paper, pen and pencils. Whenever there was a move the prisoners would have to submit their belongings to the most thorough of searches. Frequently culprits were discovered. During one move Ernest heard yelling at the front of the crowd. 'When we got closer to the gate I saw two young women standing to the side, straggling hair falling over puffy, bloodied faces, their clothes streaked with red earth – the soldiers had been mad enough to beat them to the ground. No one, of course, dared approach the women or call to them, and they didn't look up ... The whole day the two would shake and sway there trying to stay on their feet. We heard later they had collapsed a few times and been kicked upright again.'

One soldier, dubbed Johnny Tomato, was particularly vicious. He acquired his nickname from the way he stole ripening tomatoes being grown by the prisoners. During one beating Ernest witnessed, 'Johnny Tomato got off his bike and wheeled it yelling up to the woman who was still bowed and rammed the front wheel between her legs and hit her with the flat of his other hand, and then with the back of it, many times on the side of her head, on her ears, until she crumpled onto the road. Then he climbed back on his bike and pedalled around the corner. 'I ran over to where the woman lay. Two old women were helping her sit up. Her head was wobbling, blood dripped from the left ear, her eyes stared, not even crying.'

What disturbed Ernest about the violence was his own reaction to it. He was shocked, but he was also, in some dark way he hated, attracted. 'I wanted to turn and walk away from the beatings I saw, but I couldn't: I sweated and watched. I saw every slap, punch, and kick, heard every yell, shriek, and cry. When Japanese rage erupted, the air quivered; strange anger, dark, their eyes giving no hint of it

... The women, or teenage girls, were rag dolls with no feelings, with no parts of their bodies special. They could moan and whimper and scream ... that didn't stop the military men.'

One dreadful day it was Ernest's friend Mrs Crone who was caught with forbidden contraband when they were preparing to move camps. Zuseke was the woman who had helped his mother get her extra ration of bread when she was ill. She had grown especially close to Ernest in camp, allowing him the unusual privilege, in those days of formal politeness, of calling her by her Christian name.

Mrs Crone's husband was a sea captain who had been away at sea when the Japanese invaded and his whereabouts were unknown. Suzeke Crone was a tall (a head taller than her husband), strongly built, no-nonsense sort of woman. She was respected in camp for her gritty integrity expressed in a wealth of pithy sayings highlighting the foibles of human nature. ('That helps as much as a mosquito peeing in the Rhine,' 'Whores and crooks are always talking about honour.') As their baggage was being thoroughly searched in the customary manner a guard named Tesuka found a photograph of Mrs Crone's husband, and, wrapped in a twist of paper, a silver Dutch coin worth ten cents. This crime provided the excuse for an exemplary beating in front of everyone.

'Tesuka ... kicked the suitcase shut, stepped over it, and yelled something in Japanese at Zuseke, thrusting ... the picture and coin under her bowed face. She shook her head no ... Then Tesuka slapped her face, snorting with the effort, and the things in his hand fell to the street. He slapped her again, so hard that big as she was she staggered. But just the once: she parted her feet for a better grip. He beat her several times with his left hand. Each time flesh struck flesh he snorted. But he favoured his right, hitting, then swinging back with the nail side. That hand just streaked back and forth, landing all over Zuseke's face. With each blow sweat sprayed, her hair jumped, blood drops flew from her nose, but her body and head hardly moved. Tesuka was sweating too. And then, just as the beating began to take on a rhythm, Zuseke slowly came out of her bow and straightened to her full height. Head up, chest out, she towered over him.'

The guard now had to reach up to hit the woman. He stood on her suitcase to be able to reach her better. He continued to hit her and then eventually stopped and went back to his luggage-searching. Only after the beating did the brave woman collapse. She was tended to by her sobbing daughters and other shocked prisoners.

One would have thought seeing a woman he was deeply fond of brutally assaulted would have traumatised a nine-year-old boy. But Ernest saw Zuseke not as victim but as victor, a heroine who had stood up to the most cowardly bullying the empire of the rising sun could deliver and, by her courage and dignity, defeated it.

'On my hands and knees beside her, I blew into her hair. The pounding hadn't shaken me up: I'd seen worse. I felt no pity, just pride. Near her head still lying on the street was the crumbled picture of Mr Crone. I picked it up and slipped it into her still hand. "Zuseke," I whispered . . . "What would Mr Crone say if he ever met Tesuka?" "Say?" she croaked through thick, cut lips. "What would my husband say? 'Here's my hand,' he'd tell that Jap. 'You did what I haven't managed to do in twenty years'."'

To reach their last camp, Ernest and his mother had to make the same terrible train journey that Olga Geel made. In peacetime the trip from Bandung to Batavia took three hours. This time it took twenty, during which the women and children were crammed into blacked-out carriages without food, water or sanitation. When they arrived at Batavia the floors of the carriages were slimy with urine and excrement, in which the wretched prisoners and their wailing children staggered and slipped. As the lorries taking them to the new camp moved off Ernest noticed the corpses of those who had not survived the journey – the 'still figures and a broken suitcase . . . left on the platform'.

Conditions in the new camp were atrocious, but at least here the lonely Ernest made a new friend, a boy his own age, called Hubie. Hubie owned a precious toy, a helmeted soldier, mounted on horse-back, probably dating from the First World War. Ernest coveted the soldier but Hubie refused to swap it. He and his mother shared a sleeping platform 44 inches wide. His mother worked all day in the vegetable garden, where, despite the blazing heat, they were only allowed water at noon. The prisoners were fed twice a day. Breakfast was a slice of bread or a cup of thin sago gruel, weak tea or warm water, with on occasion a spoonful of sugar. The other meal, served in the late afternoon, was a cup of the lowest-grade rice with sometimes a few peanuts or tiny salted fish, and a cup of vegetable-scrap soup. Once a week they received a spoon of salt, and occasionally a teaspoon of hot-pepper paste. An hour after each meal hunger returned. Ernest tired easily, suffered from dizziness and often felt shivery, symptoms he knew to be the result of hunger.

The beatings here were worse. The camp commandant, Tanaka, was a sadist. When he punished in person a woman was unable to work for days, so her children went without her extra rations. Smuggling was savagely punished because it suggested that his rations were inadequate.

One night two women were caught smuggling. 'Two or three hours later that same night beating sounds and screams welled up from the stone house. They didn't stop until just before the six o'clock roll call for which the commandant himself came by. Beside him walked the interpreter and behind him, wearing only panties and brassieres, stumbled two trembling young women, each held up by a soldier; their bodies were blotched with welts and black bruises, and smeared with blood, even their bald heads.'

As usual the punishment was extended to the whole camp. For the next two days the prisoners remained in their huts and there was no food for anyone. Many people died during those dreadful hunger days. One of those was Ernest's friend Hubie. Maddened by hunger the boys had stolen some bunkil, a form of animal feed based on soya. It turned out to be poisonous. Hubie was in a different hut from Ernest and Ernest didn't discover his death until after the hunger days were over.

In Makassar camp Ernest saw so much death that he felt he was becoming desensitised to suffering, a tragic situation for a child. 'I could think about other people dying ... I could think about it ... people living beside and across from us in the barrack. I could see them dead, and it didn't make me sad: dead was dead ... People got sick, went to hospital, then disappeared out the gates on stretchers. I could walk down our barrack ... past women and children with broken teeth and bleeding gums, hair growing in tufts ... faces and stomachs and legs bloated from hunger edema and beriberi, boils ... and oozing tropical ulcers for which they had no bandages ... and not let myself really see them: pain was pain.'

When the war was over and the camp was being disbanded one of

Hubie's sisters came to offer Ernest some of her dead brother's belongings. At last, in the saddest of circumstances, the toy soldier was to be his. 'She handed me a soft wool cap ... the riding boots that had hung from the rafter, and the soldier on horseback. The boots, she told me, her mother had carried all those years so Hubie could wear them to run to his father when he saw him again.'

The effect of the Japanese surrender was less euphoric in the Netherlands East Indies than elsewhere as it coincided with a bloody uprising by Indonesian nationalists violently opposed to the re-imposing of Dutch rule. The prisoners had to stay in camp, protected from the rebels by the British and, ironically, their former captors.

Ernest had difficulty adapting to the new world. When the father he had not seen for three and a half years, whom he had adored in that happy, far-off life before the war, walked into camp, their greeting was bizarrely formal. Surrounded by a nightmare of suffering and death, the boy had suppressed his emotions. Now they welled up. Grief for his dead friend Hubie overwhelmed him. One day he was playing fighter pilots on a rooftop in camp with his brother Jerry. 'We had turned and were swooping back – when I put my arms down and started to cry .... it was real crying, sobbing and coughing – Hubie was so alive in my mind. I kept saying his name. Why was he dead? And why, if he was, wasn't I? Jesus, how could Jesus have let him die? It happened again, during a meal, and I left the table and sat down on the floor in another room facing the wall I thought of Hubie ... as I cried, and of all the others who ... had gone into the mist.'[5]

Richard Dobson was seventeen when he was arrested by the kempeitai. It was 1942 and internment was already underway on Java, where Richard had grown up with his family – his British banker father, his Dutch mother and three sisters. Academically gifted, Richard had taken his Matric a year early and had left school. Women's camps were being set up and his girlfriend was already interned in a camp in Surabaya. He began smuggling food into the camp where she was. 'It was a game of dare really. I used to go right into the camp under the noses of the guards and then leave again.' A younger boy he knew, who was only fourteen, thought it sounded fun and asked if he could join him. Richard agreed. It was a decision which would resonate down the rest of both their lives. The boy, called Wim, was caught by a Japanese guard. He was arrested, taken to a prison run by the kempeitai and tortured. Under torture he named his accomplice. Richard was arrested about two weeks later and taken to the same primitive prison where a mixture of prisoners, white and Indonesian, were packed ten to a cell.

He too was repeatedly tortured. The Japanese believed the boys were spies working for the Allies. 'One of the things they did to me was to make me kneel while they beat me repeatedly on the back of the neck with a wooden sword. It was agonisingly painful and I lost a lot of blood.' The pain was all the harder to bear because there was nothing that Richard could tell his torturers. But to his surprise, he found that throughout his many ordeals his mind remained highly alert.

'The thing about torture is that even while you are screaming and begging for forgiveness because it hurts so much the mind is very clear. It thinks. My mind suggested that it was pointless to tell the truth at once as the Japanese wouldn't believe it. I decided to start by telling them a total lie and then slowly tell the truth. I began with a cock and bull story naming a fictitious Indonesian who had been selling paraffin, saying I didn't know him, and then slowly let the true story be squeezed out of me. And that was, not that I was acting in a political manner, but that I was simply trying to help my girlfriend who was in camp and who was hungry.'

Richard says being tortured was so terrible that it left him with no fear. 'Nothing could be as bad as that. Whenever I have met with difficulties in life I have thought back to those interrogation sessions with the kempeitai and said to myself, you have seen worse.'

The boys were separated to prevent their colluding. A number of things, however, gave Richard the strength to keep going during those terrible weeks. 'I was being returned to my cell after a beating one day and as I passed another cell on the way I looked in and saw a white man who from the state of him was obviously going through what I was. He didn't say anything. No one spoke in front of the Japs. It was too dangerous. All he did was to discreetly jerk his chin in a defiant chin-up gesture.'

The other thing that gave him courage while he was being inter-rogated were thoughts of his mother. 'I adored my mother. I was only seventeen, still not quite a man, and during those dreadful interrogation sessions I imagined her standing smiling with her arms open wide calling to me, "Come. Come." I had had a very happy, secure childhood and as a little boy whenever I hurt myself I would look for her and she'd be there sitting in her chair. She'd fling her arms wide and I'd bury myself in her embrace and everything would be all right again.'

After about four weeks the kempeitai gave up, realising they were dealing, not with Resistance fighters, but just with two lads playing with fire. The boys were sent to a normal prison run by more humane Indonesian guards. Wim was shattered by the experience of torture and by having betrayed his friend.

'In the car taking us to the new prison he turned to me and said, "Richard, I'm so sorry to have given your name." There was an Indonesian detective sitting between us and I reached across him and shook him by the hand. I said there was nothing to forgive and that if I had been interrogated first I would have spilled the beans too. He was only young and he was frightened. I told him to think of his dad, who loved him.' Richard and Wim remained together for the rest of the war, with Richard acting as the younger lad's elder brother.

After being held a few weeks in a holding prison, Wim and Richard were transferred to Der Werfstrat, the main prison in Surabaya. It was full of young Dutch entrepreneurs and a headmaster Richard knew from the outside world. He had been choirmaster at a church Richard's family frequented and he started a choir in prison. 'Once a week our relatives were allowed to come to the main gates. One of the walls of our cell was an outside one. The choir would strike up with that powerful American hymn 'Whispering Hope, How Welcome Thy Voice'. We would sing at the tops of our voices to let the relatives know that we were still fighting.'

After about a month they were loaded onto transports for Bandung, at the opposite end of Java. By now Richard was very ill with gastroenteritis. 'We were taken to the railway station and loaded into third class railway carriages. I could hardly walk. They put me in the luggage rack so that I could lie down. The blinds were down and the carriages were guarded by Japanese at either end. The journey would normally have taken a day but this time it took forty-eight hours. I was pretty well out of it and just remember they moved the slats at the window to try to let in some fresh air. When I woke up I was in a hospital ward.'

The camp was a former Dutch army barracks in a suburb of Bandung around which the Japanese had placed a fence. The earlier internees had been housed in the officers' billets, the later arrivals in the brick-built barracks. Initially living conditions seemed a relief. Walking down a street with houses on either side felt like freedom after a prison cell. Bandung was high up in the mountains and therefore much cooler than sultry Surabaya, which is on the plain. As more and more people arrived, however, space shrank until internees only had a 2-foot-wide floor space on which to sleep.

While Wim and Richard had been in Werfstrat they had received a small parcel of a thin bedroll and a change of clothes. Richard says, 'I put away the only decent outfit I had. It was a white shirt, white shorts, white socks and shoes. I kept them for liberation. In the meantime I wore only a loincloth and went barefoot.'

Breakfast was boiled tapioca and a mug of water. In the early days the lunchtime meal was rice with watery soup containing a little water buffalo meat, but after a while the meat disappeared. The prisoners ate snakes if they could find any. The evening meal was a little loaf of bread, which was divided between three people. It had to be divided exactly equally or fights would break out.

Richard took up smoking. 'I used to see dots of red in the barracks at night. The men said it helped to deaden the hunger pangs. We got issued with tobacco by the Japanese, long stringy stuff like pipe tobacco.' They used pages torn out of the Bible as paper. They set up a shop in camp where people could buy extras if they had any money. Richard had no money but one day a young Roman Catholic priest came up to him and said, '"We know your father. We've been collecting for you. Here is five guilders. You can pay it back after the war." Suddenly it seemed as if my father was standing there in front of me, helping me. There were two retired soldiers in the camp. They stopped me one day and asked, "Your name, are you the son of Dobson the banker?" When I said I was they invited me to share a precious cup of coffee with them. "This is a thank you for what your father has done for us," they told me.'

Those five guilders became Richard's capital. 'I used them to start trading. I'd find out that one man had a jacket to sell. I'd buy it from him and sell it for a little bit more to another chap who wanted one. I sold my tobacco ration and used it to buy sugar. I put it on the tapioca, which made it taste better, or in my coffee, or just ate it neat.' With what flowed from the five guilders Richard bought himself protection from sunburn. 'I managed to get an old army jacket and a British pith helmet, which protected the back of my neck. I also used the money I earned to help Wim. He was younger than me and I felt responsible for him.'

Richard dug wells as part of a never-ending search for water, which was very short inside the camp. In addition, prisoners left the camp to work outside most days. A major project Richard worked on was the building of a railway line, which the Japanese planned to use as an escape route. 'The Japanese were convinced that when the Allies landed, they would attack from the eastern end of the island. Hence they began to shift all camps to the western end of Java. The plan was for the prisoners to build a railway leading west, on which they could retreat when the moment came. We built an embankment, on which the rails could be laid, across paddy fields.' The railway was never completed.

Richard also unloaded heavy sacks of rice and sugar from goods wagons and carried them on his back to storage warehouses. He became adept at removing rice and sugar from the sacks, smuggling the booty home under his shorts. 'It was dangerous. You risked a beating if you got caught. Luckily I never was. I learned in camp to keep a low profile. At roll-calls or in parades I always chose a place in the middle, never at the end, where I might attract the Japs' attention.'

One of the things that the fastidious Richard found most degrading about internment was looking dirty and scruffy, all key aspects of the humiliation of the colonials. 'When the commandant addressed us he would stand on a platform. I would look up at him. I would look at his immaculate white shirt folded out over the collar of his uniform and at his highly polished black leather boots and then I would look at my own bare feet, filthy legs, filthy shorts. I thought to myself, when I'm free again I will wear a white shirt and my shoes will always be perfectly polished.'

Thanks to an indoctrination programme created and reiterated by the Japanese, many Indonesians now felt extreme hostility towards their former masters. Every day as the Heiho (Japanese Indonesian Army) marched past outside the camp fence Richard and his fellow prisoners could hear their chants, '*Inglis kita lingis, Amerika kita strika*' (The English we will spear, the Americans we will iron flat). A scene connected with this remained etched in Richard's memory.

'The Indonesians used to hitch free rides on the trains, hanging on the sides, crouched on top ... When they saw us toiling away, building the new railway, they used to shout and jeer. It was quite dangerous and on one occasion some of them fell off and were badly injured. Among the men working on the railway were doctors – Dutchmen, naturally. They immediately went to the aid of the injured Indonesians. I thought how ironic it was that the masters who had become objects of such hatred were still willing to do something to help.'

One of the few upsides of life in camp was that it contained many highly qualified and educated men. Richard had decided he wanted to build ships. It was lucky for him that among his fellow prisoners were the former head of the academy of the Merchant Navy in Batavia and several master mariners. At night, in conditions of extreme secrecy, Richard was taught seamanship. 'They had one or two books on navigation and, without the aid of a sextant, they explained how navigation worked using the stars.' The professor of mathematics from the University of Batavia gave him lessons in advanced mathematics. Richard wrote his calculations down on paper from cigarette packets or on a slate with a stone. 'I learned to write very small.'

The old boy network of the camps worked to the advantage of some boys starting out on a career after the war. It helped Richard Dobson too. 'Eighteen months after the end of the war I applied for a bursary to study at the nautical academy in Delft. I walked into the room for my interview and there was that same professor.'

As it became obvious that the Japanese were losing the war, the ad hoc nautical academy in camp decided to set exams for the course they had been teaching. One of them was a Lloyds Register surveyor called Frowess. 'This man said he would tell me what subjects would come up so that I could prepare. At the end we received a certificate signed by prisoners who were well known in the Dutch maritime industry. When I applied for jobs in London, they saw Frowess's name on my certificate and I was in.'

For Richard Dobson the end of the war meant liberation from imprisonment by the Japanese and an emotional homecoming. But before long he would be a prisoner again.

'All our family made their way to our old home from our different camps. My father from his, and my mother and my sisters from theirs. We had all survived.' They were lucky. Two of Richard's friends who had been military POWs had been caught escaping and had been beheaded. Indonesia was now in the throes of a bloody nationalist revolution in which many newly freed Dutch, including some of Richard's school friends, would be slaughtered. Surabaya was a highly dangerous town for Europeans at that time. When Richard arrived home the couple that had been the family's head servants as long as he could remember came out to greet them. They had tried valiantly to protect the house from looters and were courting danger from the nationalists by showing affection to the now hated colonials.

'Our major domo was an elderly Indonesian lady. When word spread that I was coming home our old servants were all standing in the road in front of our house, which was a very brave thing to do at that time. This small lady wearing her traditional tight sarong, said to me, "Wait here." When she came out of the house she was carrying a bowl of water into which she had put rose petals. She knelt down in front of me, removed my shoes and socks and washed my feet. Then she stood up and said, "In order that you may never have misfortune in your life again." I took her in my arms and kissed her. It was a very moving moment. She was an Indonesian and a Muslim, I a Catholic and a European, and we loved each other.'

The streets of Surabaya were becoming more dangerous by the minute. The town was filled with Indonesians, armed with traditional bamboo hunting spears and wanting to murder all colonials. Richard was arrested by the Indonesians and found himself back in the Werfstrat prison, this time with his father. The prison was surrounded by a lynch mob and two of Richard's friends were beaten to death by the crowd as they were being taken there. From their police prison they were transferred to the old and now deserted women's camp, where he had been caught taking food in to his girlfriend over three years earlier. Eventually a truce was negotiated in which the British guaranteed to evacuate the prisoners.

'At the beginning of November British officers came to the camp and told us to prepare to leave Java. Those who had relatives outside were told to go and fetch them. We went to our house and came back with my mother, sisters and a handful of their women who had found shelter in our house on their return to Surabaya from their various camps. It was too dangerous to bring luggage so they just had to wear anything they wanted to bring with them. The next day lorries arrived manned by troops armed with rifles, British officers and British Indian troops. We climbed up and were told to keep our heads down. We made a run for it to the harbour where frigates took us out to waiting troop ships.'

In Singapore Richard's family were once again put into a camp as the city had nowhere else to put the hundreds of freed prisoners. He himself had to be hospitalised because of an outbreak of tropical sores on his feet, the result of prolonged malnutrition. When he came out he declined to join his family. 'I went to the port and found a ship flying the Dutch flag. It was a hospital ship. It turned out that the crew were Dutch and the medical personnel British. I waited till the master came ashore and asked if I could join his ship. I had had enough of camps. I was twenty-one by now and desperate to start life.'

Elizabeth Macnamara was nine when she was interned with her mother and her six-year-old sister Bridget in Sumatra. In their three and a half year imprisonment they moved from camp to camp suffering the same horrific ordeals as other prisoners across the Netherlands East Indies. There were no drugs and no Red Cross parcels in their camps and all three were frequently ill. Bridget was in hospital five times, Elizabeth three times, her mother twice. When the camp was liberated her mother was close to death due to dysentery and weighed 3 stone.

Despite the imminence of an invasion in 1942, Stella Macnamara, the girls' mother, a doctor's daughter from London, had been unwilling to leave their father, who ran a tobacco plantation near Medan in northern Sumatra. Their last desperate attempts failed, however. 'Father rang to see if he could get us on a flight,' Elizabeth recalled,

'But there was nothing leaving. He packed us onto a train instead and we tried to reach Padang, on the west coast of the island to see if we could get a ship. While we were on our way father rang again to say it was too late and we had better come back.' In those last tense hours in the first few weeks of February the headmaster of Elizabeth's school rang all the pupils and offered the women and children his hospitality. They remained there till the Japanese arrived.

Their first camp was at Brastagi, where they formed part of the group of twenty British internees in a camp of 2,000 Dutch. This camp, which was in the hills, was for some time regarded as better than the jungle camps down in the stifling plains, where tropical diseases killed prisoners by the score. As conditions deteriorated, however, they began to suffer from cold here. In Brastagi even young children had to work. At first the girls' work was unloading the sweet potatoes, the staple food they came to detest, as they were delivered to the camp. Boys had to do wood-cutting. 'When the faggots arrived the carts had to be completely unloaded onto the street so that it could be seen that nothing was being smuggled in under the wood. Then the boys on wood-chopping duty came with barrows and took the wood back to the kitchen.' Later, as food became scarcer, all available land was turned over to the growing of vegetables and children as young as Elizabeth Macnamara were expected to lend a hand. In a memoir written after the war when she was fourteen, and a pupil at an English boarding school, Elizabeth described the daily struggle to survive.

'We dug up parts of the golf course in Brastagi. Planted it with obies (sweet potatoes) and maize. We did not dig for the first ... year. Then only adults had to dig, but later on children over 10 had to dig too. When there had just been a harvest of obies the children under 10 would go out to try to find any small ones that were left. We had to dig for an hour every time we went which was two days a week. Later on we would dig for three quarters of an hour and then be allowed to go and look for wood.'

The language is somewhat stilted and cryptic, evoking a child whose educational level lags behind her real age – not surprising considering conditions in camp. The grammar is sometimes odd, due to the fact that in camp Elizabeth spoke Dutch most of the time.

If anything, however, the baldness of the words serves to increase the pathos of the physical decline she was evoking.

'The first 18 months Mummie taught country dancing ... .She gave two big shows. Every child that had lessons did something in both shows ... .She taught a boy and girl to tap dance on a table ... Then we did not get enough to eat so it stopped and she was in the transport ... work for some months but the Japs would not let her because she was a Britisher. Then she worked in the kitchen mixing the nassie tun (rice and vegetables mixed) but she strained her back and then she cleaned the vegetables and minced the chillies. Sometimes she had to work from 6 or 7 till 4 or 5 in the afternoon. Bridget and I had lessons for a few months and then it would be stopped. There were only about 10 English children and only 2 had school. Our teacher was English but married to a Dutchman. She was always getting headaches and then we were free from school. The Japs took many of the Dutch textbooks away.'

As time wore on conditions deteriorated. Boys of ten were removed to men's camps, the mothers, overworked and underfed, fell ill, and the little girls had to take on ever more tasks. When Elizabeth's mother fell ill she became responsible for her younger sister. It was the same in many families. An Jacobs, a Dutch internee, paid tribute to children like Elizabeth who became adults too soon.

'The little girls ... cooked and baked and did the wash, that was to say they rinsed the clothes in well water without brushes – with a brush the remaining clothes would too quickly be slit – and without soap, of which there had long been none. They looked after the small children if the mother was sick, they looked after the sick older people. They knew all about wounds and ulcers and the bearing of pain. They could dig and cut tree bark to fibre. They could knot together flax threads for spinning ... they could clear away filth and clean up blocked cesspools.' In Brastagi, as in so many of the camps, the commandant was a man who liked small children. Unlike many who kept to their own quarters, he was regularly to be seen walking through camp 'laughing, grinning with many gold teeth, his skull gleaming as smooth as a mirror in the sun ...'.[6] The mothers ground their teeth in loathing at the way Mulassai bought their children's affection with sweets. The apparently genial officer was always surrounded by tots. 'The children, especially the very smallest, were hanging on his arms.

They kicked towards his boots and shouted Jap – Jap – Jap ... The commandant laughed and stroked the tight blond hair of a five year old tot which she found funny, noisily telling him to stop. He growled unintelligibly back. He rummaged in his pockets and took something out. Then he walked further on his camp round, his steps regulated by the queue which sauntered on either hand.'

Faced with such strong competition in the form of sweets, the mothers couldn't make their children dislike the man. 'When the mothers were doing ... their duties he always had time for them, and he always had sweeties. They were stubbornly unable to understand that this man was a "Jap", a bad, evil man for children. If they got a scolding, they looked with great pensive eyes at the peppermints they had received and said, "But that is not a Jap Mummie, that is an 'uncle'," (the common word for an adult a child was fond of in those days) and so quickly Mulassai became nicknamed Uncle Molly, a part of the camp.'[7]

The purge on books and the illness of the teachers put an end to education in camp. For a while dancing and PE took its place as a way of occupying the children during the hours when they weren't working. Elizabeth's mother taught dance classes and put on shows two years running, until the collapse of her own health prevented her from continuing. The first was the *Pied Piper of Hamlyn*, the second *Copelia*. These shows had a huge morale-boosting effect on the prisoners. 'Uncle Molly' and several other high-ranking Japanese officers insisted on attending the shows and for a few moments it must have seemed as though the war was a bad dream as prisoners and jailers were transported by the charming efforts of the children. An Jacobs described the emotional effect of captors and captives watching Stella Macnamara's *Copelia* in the harsh setting of a prisoner of war camp.

'They took their places ... twenty Japanese in full dress uniform, above which were twenty grey, sweating Asiatic heads ... Out of their slanting eyes they stared friendly and kindly at the black satin curtain with silver paper stars ... The lights were switched off, the floodlight flashed on; two drab brown dwarfs pulled open the curtain ... The dolls' shop still slept ... As behind the wing the high keys of a piano struck twelve sharp staccato sounds there came a stirring in the rigid dolls' group. The elves danced hand in hand, brought to life by the magic wand, and Snow White skipped out of her house so as to sweep the dance floor with her dwarves. As through a secret spring a black suited curly head moved out of a rough wooden cube. Now the children danced right out of their shop in front of the invited Japanese, where Molly, friendly and laughing, tried to steal a smile from the youngest.'

But even while Uncle Molly and his friends were applauding the young actors, rations were shrinking and prisoners all over Sumatra were suffering – even the children Uncle Molly found so appealing. Many found themselves orphaned as a result of conditions in camp. One day a group of prisoners who had spent two years separated from their families arrived at Brastagi, having come from other camps (at Kota Radja and Lawe Segalagala). Among them were three children whose younger brother and mother had died in Lawe Sega- lagala, which was described as 'hell' by prisoners. The children were now effectively orphans, as their father had been missing since the beginning of the war. The prisoners at Brastagi were horrified by the appearance of the children. '(They) ... were skin and bone, with swollen stomachs and thick feet. They had a large spleen, were underfed and showed after examination to have a completely ruined blood picture.' The two older children were found to be dangerously ill with malaria. Two small boys aged three and five had arrived without their mother, who had also died in the other camp. The children's heads had been shaved against lice. Their mattresses and bedding were full of vermin.[8]

As rations shrank ever further the women were forced to smuggle in vital extras. As Elizabeth put it, 'After the first year we did not have at all enough food for about a whole year. In that year we smuggled a lot. Then we had many Ambonese police and they were all on our side. You could trust them because you would give them a ring and they would take it and have it valued by the Chinese. Of course they made a lot of profit by it. In the middle of the night they would come laden with rice, native sugar ... and many other things under their big raincoats ... '*

---

* The Ambonese are the indigenous population of the south Moluccas, centred on the tiny island of Ambon. Predominantly Christian they were fiercely pro-Dutch during the war and afterwards.

In total darkness, with guards patrolling regularly, this was a hugely risky business and there were plenty of near misses. 'One night Mrs Den Nieuwenboer told one of the police to bring some rice and put it in one of the windows where it would come on someone's legs. This police went and put it in another window instead and 30 or 15 kilos of rice arrived on another woman's head and she got so furious and she let out a stream of Malay words. All the other people tried to stop all the noise in case it should be found out.'

Many women did get caught, however, and the punishments were invariably witnessed by everyone, including children. Usually the women were locked in bamboo cages and starved for days. Elizabeth remembered other women making pancakes and sliding them under the door to the captive when the guards weren't looking. On another occasion all the people in one building were kept in and only children under five were allowed food. As fires were forbidden, anyone who had any food had to cook on candles. But the Japanese were capable of worse punishments.

For Elizabeth's sister Bridget some scenes remain branded on her memory. 'On one occasion . . . some women were made to kneel on the ground at the front of the camp with a pole behind their knees and holding another pole over their heads, being beaten if they dropped their arms. Also women being tied to a tree and left there all day without water or food under the hot sun . . . Another horrific sight that is still with me is of a woman who had gone completely raving mad and how she was chained to what seemed like a concrete plinth . . . she used to scream and moan.'

The sisters' last camp was Aek Pamienke, a primitive camp in the jungle, surrounded by rubber plantations. They were taken there in July 1945, a month before the end of the war. Here their mother worked in the kitchen, cooking the endless rice and sweet potatoes, before she became too ill to work. They had made the bulk of the journey by rail. But when they arrived at their destination they were herded off the train and made to walk the remaining 11 miles to the camp. Exhausted, barefoot and laden with luggage, they trudged along the plantation road through pouring rain, while Japanese soldiers and native guards lashed at them with bamboo sticks to keep them going, impervious to the crying children. Many were seriously ill with beriberi and dysentery and only the sick were allowed transport, but this was no ambulance, merely an open lorry. Stella Macnamara, Elizabeth and Bridget's mother, had to make the journey three times, despite her frail condition, when the Japanese sent a group of women back to the station to collect a piano. Many of the prisoners who dragged themselves along that road would not live to see the end of the war, which although they did not know it, was only weeks away. The scene was one of indescribable wretchedness.

'The rain dripped on our odd assortment of clothing, our naked feet, the old soldier's cape and jute sacks which some had placed over their children as protection. It dripped on our tired babies asleep in their careworn mothers' arms. Over the stretchers with the sick. Over the mad Mrs A ... Mrs B on the arm of a nurse ... Mrs C ... who had nothing else than an evening dress ... which she held tightly against her breast, her only baggage ...'[9]

They had hardly arrived at Aek Pamienke when a group of prisoners arrived from another camp, many of them children. They too had had to walk the long, weary miles. Their condition horrified the women in the camp. Some were ill, some had lost their mothers in camp. 'Crying, whimpering children, with the eldest, the five-year-old dragging the youngest ... They walked on the insides of their feet, their cheeks red and swollen from crying. "Aunty?" said a youngster of three, as one of the leaders took him in her arms ... and felt over her face with hands trembling from tiredness, "Are you an aunty?" and the older sister, suddenly again a youngster of five ... hobbled after them, took her by the point of her skirt, "where is mummy?"'[10]

News of the dropping of the atom bomb took weeks to reach the prisoners in the jungles of Sumatra and it was not until 24 August that Elizabeth and Bridget Macnamara heard peace had been declared. One of the first things the Japanese did was to cut down the hated barbed wire. As in all the other camps, the food improved immediately. Elizabeth, who had grown very competent over the course of internment, celebrated her twelfth birthday in camp by cooking a chicken which, in the absence of a barrier, had wandered into camp. 'I plucked it, gutted it, cut it up and then cooked it on a native stove we called an anglo.'

Gradually the fathers began to appear in the camp. Many of the very young children no longer remembered these men. Some, who had only seen head-and-shoulders photographs, ran round exclaiming that their Daddy has legs.

The children struggled to reconcile the well-built smiling men whose tattered photographs their mothers had clung to in camp after camp, with the haggard, sunken-eyed strangers who now embraced their mothers. 'Little Marina . . . looked with great eyes to the agitated man's face then again to her mother who in the last two days had done nothing else than laugh and cry . . . . With eager, earnest eyes she looked at the two, "Are you now my daddy?"

'"No," denied the mother and pulled the girl to her. "You know it, think of the daddy in the photo," whereupon a friend replied: "Oh but I also have two, one from the photo who we have long had, and . . . a thin one who came yesterday."'

To Elizabeth and Bridget Macnamara's delight their own father arrived in camp one day on foot. So, too, did the girls' old baboo, or nurse. In defiance of the widespread anti-white feeling raging through Indonesia at that time, this woman still felt deep affection for her former employers and hoped to work for them again. Alas, it was not to be.

The prisoners were instructed to remain in camp for the own safety. When the time came, in mid-October, it was the small contingent of British prisoners who left first. 'Our parents weren't happy,' remembered Elizabeth. 'They didn't want preferential treatment. They took the view that they had all shared the same ordeal. They wanted to return to the tobacco estate and take up where they had left off. The British insisted that as the British had liberated the country it should be British subjects who were freed first. As for going back to the estate it wasn't an option.'

On 20 October 1945 Elizabeth and her family left Medan by Dakota for Singapore. Two days later they sailed for India en route for England.

PART FOUR

—

FREEDOM AT LAST

16

Prisoners No More

The end, when it came, mirrored the diversity of conditions in the camps. For some it came with a bang – loudly and unexpectedly; for others, who believed themselves forgotten by the world, it came with a belated whimper that was almost an anti-climax.

The vast majority of civilian prisoners were freed as a result of the Japanese surrender on 15 August 1945 and simply walked out of camp unimpeded by their captors. In many cases these had already left in the night. To most of the internees the end did not come as a total surprise. Many camps had hung onto secret radios, defying searches and the threats of beatings, for the length of the war. Some even had access to Japanese newspapers from which they could piece together the Allied advance. Prisoners in Shanghai and Hong Kong had seen American planes flying over on bombing raids.

A lucky few, however, were freed in a daring operation that took the prisoners entirely unawares. These men, women and children were dramatically liberated six months before the end of the war. In a state bordering on starvation and with death already claiming substantial numbers, they were saved – literally – by the US cavalry. Hearing that thousands of American prisoners in the Philippines were being systematically starved by the Japanese army, General Douglas MacArthur fought a heroic race against time to rescue them. He overcame the objections of the US Navy, who wanted to bypass the Philippines and take Formosa instead, as their route to the invasion of Japan. In so doing MacArthur, Supreme Commander of US forces in the Southwest Pacific, led a bold and bloody island-hopping campaign northwards through the Western Pacific, virtually annihilating the Japanese navy and reaching the Philippines in just four months. Undeterred by fierce resistance from Japanese forces, and unable to reach Manila from his chosen route in the south-west, MacArthur instructed a relatively small unit of the 1st US Cavalry to take the city from the north. In a dramatic rescue as risky as it was bold, US tanks cut through enemy lines, storming their way through a city held by heavily armed Japanese, to reach the prisoners. In fact, the Japanese held out for another month and by the end casualties in the battle for Manila topped 100,000.

Sylvia Williams, who had turned eleven a month earlier, was still up when the Americans arrived on the evening of 3 February 1945. 'It was about 8 p.m. and we were in our huts because now that the Allies were starting to get the upper hand we were forbidden to leave them after that time. It was pitch-dark because the Japanese had imposed a blackout. Suddenly there was a tremendous commotion with the sounds of shooting. Everyone in our building got up and rushed out into the compound. Small children like me couldn't see what the cause of the commotion was as all the adults rushed past in front of us. But everyone was shouting that the Americans had arrived to rescue us and that American tanks had driven through all the barbed wire and come right into camp.'

The euphoric rushing-out by the internees, understandable though it was, in fact placed the whole mission in jeopardy as it prevented the Americans from shooting the Japanese as planned. The Japanese retreated to the education building, where the men and boys slept, taking with them as hostages a number of terrified internees, who had fled there to get away from the shooting.

To Sylvia it looked as if the Japanese had planned their response to the American onslaught. 'There were Japanese look-outs posted at each corner of the compound and as soon as they saw the Americans they all ran and hid in the buildings where the men and boys were housed. I learned later that Lt Abiko, one of the most feared of the Japanese officers, came out with his sword raised and was immediately shot by one of the soldiers.'

Two days later the Japanese guards who had hidden in the education building were brought out holding their guns over their heads. 'There was a tremendous feeling of excitement in the air. We were told to go back into our rooms. It was pitch-dark because of the blackout ordered by the Japanese. My parents were both ill; my mother had hurt her back and my father had walked into something in the dark and had injured his leg.'

Left to her own devices because of her parents' incapacity, Sylvia went with some of the other children to see the body of Abiko, the Japanese officer who had been shot.

'There was a dark pool of blood round the body and in that heat it was beginning to stink. I didn't feel any pity. None of us did. He had got his just deserts. My mother was horrified that I had seen the corpse.'

Conditions became more dangerous in the days following the surrender of the Japanese guards. Granted safe conduct out of the camp they joined forces with their colleagues in the city and launched an attack on the camp. Suddenly Sylvia found herself in the middle of a horrific battle with deafening shells exploding all round her. 'It was awful. People were being killed and injured all round me. My teacher, who was married to one of the camp doctors, was killed.'*

As the Japanese were shelling the front part of the camp internees were told to run and take shelter in the main building, which was towards the back of the compound. 'For a whole week we sat on the floor in the corridor, as far away from windows as possible, while the fighting and shelling went on all round us. At one stage a large piece of shrapnel narrowly missed my mother. It was very frightening. The noise of explosions and shelling went on for days.'

Being exposed to the serious injuries distressed her. 'They turned some of the classrooms into wards and operating theatres and the wounded troops were carried past us with blood dripping through the stretchers. These boys were so young, late teens and early twenties at the most, and for them to die or be wounded when they had liberated us seemed unbearable. The Japanese guards were made to dig graves for the casualties.'

Gradually the siege ended and life in camp became more orderly. Dances were held where young internees danced with the young soldiers who had liberated them. In the general outpouring of

---

* Seventeen people were killed and eighty seriously hurt in the battle to liberate Santo Tomas Internment Camp.

gratitude which blotted out normal restraint, Sylvia was allowed to go for a ride in a jeep with three American soldiers.

'I'm amazed my mother allowed it. The situation was incredibly dangerous. The battle of Manila was still being fought all round us; the Japanese were resisting fiercely and there were snipers everywhere. And to have allowed me to go off alone with three soldiers who had not seen women for months seems extraordinary. I was eleven and one month old and my breasts were starting to develop. They might have raped me.'

When Sylvia's family left camp they returned to their house in Manila and found it a ruin. There was a huge hole in the roof where a bomb had hit it and a grave in the garden. Before they were interned her parents had buried some of their silver in the garden. 'There were spoons and a cigarette box, which my mother had given to my father as a wedding anniversary present. They went to salvage them but the explosion had heated the very ground itself and the silver was ruined, bent and blackened.' Sylvia still has the cigarette box. The lid is soldered to the base but the poignant inscription, dated May 8th 1930, which by coincidence was also VE Day, remains clearly visible.

The family were repatriated to England via America on board the (*Admiral*) *Eberle*, sailing past Pearl Harbor where they noticed the blackened hulls of burnt-out ships, still there over three years later. The journey was dangerous as the war was still being fought. As they crossed the Pacific the presence of Japanese submarines meant they were battened down at night and couldn't go up on deck. Like US troops everywhere the sailors were boisterous and playful.

'I was walking along the deck, unsupervised as was often the way, when two of them asked me: "would you like a swing?" They picked me up and swung me out over the deck rail. I was absolutely terrified. I thought they were going to drop me. It was a very long way down and the Pacific was full of sharks.'

The crossing to California was very rough, with the ship rolling and pitching on huge waves. Sylvia was thrilled by the sheer quantity of food and the way it was served – 'directly onto trays with special hollowed-out compartments so it wouldn't spill with the rough motion of the ship.' The ship was due to dock at San Francisco. However, because of the Peace Conference which was being held there to plan the post-war era, they were diverted to Los Angeles.

'We got a huge welcome when we docked and were taken to a big hall where we were given second-hand clothes, as we had nothing more than the clothes we stood up in. I was given a coat which had a little bell in the pocket. I still have that bell.' It was when they went to get a meal that Sylvia noticed how thin her formerly well-covered father was – 'his clothes hung off him'. A five-day train journey took them to Halifax, Nova Scotia where they embarked on board RMS *Scythia*. Because of the danger, this time from German U-boats, they crossed the Atlantic in convoy. 'We could see the other ships by day and at night we heard their foghorns. That made us feel safer.'

Iris Krass, who was also in Santo Tomas, was responsible for her younger brother and sister as her mother was still in hospital. The family had to remain in camp until her mother was well enough to leave. Iris, who was now seventeen, recalls the fear that accompanied liberation. 'We were in our building when the Americans arrived and we all ran down the hallway and streamed out to meet the tanks. But the Americans ordered us back into the building as they wanted to take out the Japanese, but the Japanese took hostages so they couldn't. At first we were all at the windows in our room on the first floor of our building trying to see what was happening. But then the Japanese began shooting and we were told to go downstairs and stay at the back of the building where it was safer. I saw a Jap soldier lying on the ground in the hall. Everyone said to keep away as he had a grenade but he wasn't moving.'

A few days after the Americans arrived, the Japanese began shelling the camp from batteries in the town and the camp grounds became a full-blown battle zone. 'For about a week we were the front line. We were cowering at the back of the main building and you could hear the shells exploding really near. There was carnage. One of the shells hit room 22, which was next to ours. Unfortunately it was full of people who had gone back to collect their things, thinking they would be leaving. Four people were killed and some of the others received terrible injuries. One woman had gone up there with her husband, who was an American priest. He was killed outright, while one of her arms was blown off by the blast. Another woman's nose was blown away. We saw her later. She had a plaster over the centre of her face, which was just a hole.'

In the midst of all the terror and pandemonium Iris's younger brother Peter was taken ill. 'He was absolutely terrified. He was lying on the floor of the main building trembling. The Americans had given him coffee, possibly to calm him down, and he had got caffeine poisoning. They took him into the makeshift hospital which had been set up in one of the classrooms, where they were treating the battle casualties. They had to put him on a drip because he was dehydrated.'

The Americans set up pom-pom batteries in the grounds to return the Japanese fire. These had several barrels and fired shells in rapid succession. During lulls in the firing Iris left the main building to visit her mother, who was in the camp hospital some distance away. She saw the guns being installed and on one occasion narrowly avoided being hit by an incoming shell. 'I saw it coming above me but luckily it didn't land in the camp.'

After about a week the situation in camp calmed down as the Japanese turned their attention to destroying the city. There was plenty of food now and prisoners were starting to be evacuated. Iris couldn't leave as both her mother and brother were still in hospital.

It is an irony that after the euphoria of being liberated had subsided, and after the departure of the enemy, the personal safety of two young girls became an issue. 'Pat and I were now alone in the main building. We were there for five or six weeks and it was a scary time. With so many American soldiers roaming around looking for women we felt scared when darkness fell. We were worried about where to sleep as our room had no door – they had been removed before internment, prior to renovation. The Americans were a pretty predatory lot. They held dances in front of the buildings and they pressed themselves really close to you. I wasn't naïve. I knew what they wanted.'

The predatory behaviour was not confined to the troops. After the fighting had subsided a doctor in the hospital where Iris's mother was being treated asked if he could take her out for a meal. It seemed innocent enough. 'An older girl was coming too and we set off in a jeep. He took me back to his billet, which was in the suburbs of Manila. We watched a film on a projector in a big hall with fifteen or twenty other people. I sat on his lap. He then suggested we go to his room for a drink. The girl I had come with seemed to be getting very affectionate with her partner, so I agreed. We sat on the bed, but then he pushed me back and kissed me quite forcefully. I was frightened and told him I thought we were going out for a meal. He was very annoyed and started offering me gifts, bottles of sherry, anything I wanted. In the end I got him to drive me back to Santo Tomas.'

The incident sharpened Iris's determination to find a secure place for her and her sister to sleep. They settled for one of the abandoned palm-thatched huts that had been built so that families separated at night could spend some time together. 'The shanty had a door with a catch so we used to go there at night and lock ourselves in. It was pitch-black in camp at night. No one knew we were there. The former owners had left behind a little charcoal stove and a tin we used to boil water for tea. In the day we queued up for food as usual.'

After about six weeks Iris's mother was deemed fit to travel. The family left Manila on USS *Monterey*. Iris's mother was in hospital for the entire trip and was taken off by stretcher as her legs were too swollen for her to be able to walk. Iris says that all returning US internees were given a dollar a day for every day they had been in camp, but no such arrangement had been made for British ex-prisoners.

'We had to stay in a hotel but we had no money. Mother had to ring the British consulate. They advanced us a loan of £300 to be paid back after the war. Mother was so disgusted, in the light of all we'd been through, that she refused to pay it back.' The family returned to England on the luxury liner *Queen Elizabeth*, which was fitted out as a troopship with three-to-four tiers of bunks on the decks.

It was to be another hungry and weary six months before any other internees were set free. In the women's camp in Sime Road in Singapore, where internees from Changi had been transferred at the beginning of 1944, spirits were very low. In this camp, where there had never been an evening meal, Barbara Bruce's mother had been giving half her meagre ration of rice and soup to her two younger children to try to keep them healthy. Malnutrition and anxiety about the welfare of her husband and two older sons, who were in the men's camp, had taken their toll. Barbara said her mother was 'like a matchstick' at the end. She had suffered a heart attack, but had been prescribed merely rest, as there were no drugs.

The end came as a total surprise. 'In our camp there was no radio and no newspapers – so we had no warning that the war was coming to an end. We woke up one morning and noticed that various things were different. No food had been delivered. The time for roll-call came and went without the usual siren being sounded. Most astonishing of all, the sentry box which separated the men's camp from the women's camp was empty. All the time we had been there it had been manned twenty-four seven.'

In the men's camp prisoners awoke to the same scene. This was the camp in which men had been so brutally tortured that fifteen of them had died as a result, so they were cautious about assuming that the Japanese had left. Nonetheless, the unimaginable seemed to have happened. Barbara says: 'Tentatively they began to approach the barrier from their side while the women walked towards them from our side. Then suddenly people realised that the Japs really had gone. As if someone said "Let's go" everyone surged forward greeting each other. Women rushed off into the men's camp seeking husbands and men surged into our camp looking for wives. People just couldn't hold back their emotions. They were hugging each other and crying and laughing simultaneously. About three or four families did not share the general jubilation. They were the ones whose husbands or sons had died, either of malnutrition, or some disease there were no drugs to treat.'

The Japanese had gone in the night when they heard of the surrender. 'There were not even any left in the sentry box up the hill, where their living quarters were,' says Barbara.

The internees did not have long to wait before the victory they had dreamed of was confirmed by a welcome sight. 'At 10 a.m., just as all this was sinking in, we saw British lorries coming up the driveway into camp. They had broken into a warehouse nearby and found it stuffed with supplies from the Red Cross which the Japs had never distributed – masses and masses of tinned food and medical supplies. British soldiers were throwing tins of food down to us. There were tins of Australian butter, tins of sausages, tins of fruit . . . The snag was we didn't have any tin openers. All we could do was rub the tins on the rough edges of the pavements, but we managed.

The butter was the favourite. We children hadn't tasted butter for three and a half years, only watery rice and vegetable soup. We were so hungry some kids couldn't hold back. They scooped butter into their mouths with their hands as if it were nectar. Of course they got diarrhoea. It was fun opening tins of fruit like this, all the juice poured out all over our hands but we didn't care.'

The prisoners stayed in camp for over two weeks after the surrender. But by the first week in September the army had mobilised a fleet of transports to return people to their homes. Barbara and her family went back to her grandmother's house in Serangoon. Three and a half years earlier her grandmother had clung sobbing to her daughter as the Japanese soldiers dragged the family away onto their lorries. Now the old lady wept again.

'She had avoided internment because her husband had been French. But for three and a half years she had had no news of her daughter and grandchildren. Prisoners and internees in Malaya were not allowed to send or receive mail. Gran's reunion with Mum was very tearful. She couldn't believe how thin and frail we looked. She kept forcing food on us, thinking she could put everything right overnight, but we kept being sick as we were not used to eating normally.'

On 12 September Barbara and her brothers walked into Singapore city and watched Lord Mountbatten, Supreme Allied Commander South East Asia Command, take the surrender of the Japanese at city hall. 'I stood on the steps about 8 feet away from him as the Japanese laid down their swords. I must have cut an odd figure alongside him in his immaculate white uniform. I was barefoot – we hadn't had shoes for years in camp – and my dress hung round me in tatters like a cut-down Cinderella, but I didn't care. I was so proud to be there.'

They stayed on in Singapore for a fortnight and then sailed for England on the troopship SS *Antenor*, sharing the journey with thousands of returning military POWs from all three services. As they docked at Aden the children, who had spent all their lives in the tropics, were given warm clothes to insulate them against the British winter. They received vests, woollen jumpers and cardigans and, in Barbara's case, a duo of unfamiliar garments.

'I was presented with a pair of lisle thread stockings and a liberty bodice. This was a strange top which was padded and which had four little hooks which hung down, two at the front and two at the back. I asked my mother what I should do with it and she explained that the hooks were to hold up the stockings. I thought stockings were things you hung up on Christmas Eve. I didn't realise people wore them. I thought it was quite funny until I put them on. In camp I had been going barefoot for years. Now I was wearing not only shoes, but stockings. I found them really uncomfortable.'

In the Shanghai camps the prisoners had hoped for months that the end was coming. When the years of hope and longing turned to reality, however, many simply couldn't believe the news. The Japanese had ordered blackouts from March 1944, though the first air raids did not take place until July. By the end of the year raids were frequent with B-24s and B-29s – the famous Flying Fortresses – from American bases in China attacking targets in the city.[1] In Lunghwa the camp committee painted POW on the roof of the main building with the cooperation of the Japanese who were worried about their own safety. The mood among internees that last summer had been very low. Food rations had almost stopped and many had malaria, dysentery and skin complaints. They dreaded the onset of a winter many knew they would not survive. News of the victory in Europe and a number of successful escapes had made the Japanese more aggressive than ever. Roll-calls became an ordeal. Irene Duguid, now seventeen, felt the tension. 'No one dared move or we would be shouted at and slapped across the face – they (the guards) started snap searches and took away people's notebooks – diaries were forbidden.'[2]

David Nicoll's older sister was the first to notice that something had changed in Chapei camp. Ella had special dispensation to get up early and wash her clothes at 7 to avoid the rush. On the morning of 14 August she had got up as usual. On previous occasions she had been accompanied by a sleepy guard. This time there was no guard at the laundry. After completing her washing Ella decided to see if there were any guards at all. She walked as far as the gate without seeing any. Sensing something momentous had happened she called

out to the room where her family slept: 'The war's over.' Extraordinarily there was no reaction.

Her brother explained their apathy, 'We had heard this said in jest
so many times over the months that there was not the slightest
interest or reaction, even so, as I lay in bed I tried to work out what
this could mean IF it were true this time but soon gave up as ... no
one else seemed to be interested.' Later on David heard women
running along the corridor shouting that the war was over, but still
no one reacted.

The guards returned later that day and on the morning of 15
August they took roll-call as usual. Afterwards, however, they were
seen removing bundles of files from their office. Word went round
that the camp representatives had been summoned to the Swiss
consulate. It wasn't until their representative returned from the consulate that the dream became reality. 'As he got out of the car people
surged towards him, he did not say anything until he reached the
Porch steps when he looked up beaming ... and announced the end
of the War.'

From nowhere flags of the four nations represented in the camp,
banned and hidden for so long, were produced and hoisted – British,
American, Dutch and Belgian. The whole camp gathered on the
field. An organ was wheeled out to play the four national anthems,
which were rousingly sung. The commandant, who had been
regarded by the internees as a decent man, appeared, his emotional
state highlighting the sudden reversal in fortunes. 'Mr Kawasaki
made a speech in English congratulating us on our freedom, wishing
us well and expressing the hope that we would not think badly of the
Japanese administration of the camp, ending tearfully and causing us
to feel sorry for him.'

The first outside contact the internees had was with Russians who
brought newsreels and a generator into camp to enable the internees,
who had been totally ignorant of the progress of the war, to catch up
with the news. 'In the warm dry evening many sat on the grass ...
in the dusk, stars overhead, watching films of the fierce fighting in
the deep snows of Soviet Russia.' As they ventured out of camp
to buy provisions ex-internees discovered Shanghai was suffering
galloping inflation and had three different currencies. People who
had not been interned poured into camp to see old friends again.

Faithful amahs flooded in seeking to mother their former charges once more. Starved for so long of novelty the children raced excitedly round inspecting new visitors.

'As more outsiders began to come in,' recalled David Nicoll, 'relatives, friends and servants, we boys would be at the gate ready to guide them, ever eager for new faces and for any new experiences. Later, as cars came in, we would rush forward jumping on the running-board for the thrill of moving at speed . . .'

Margaret Blair was keeping an anxious vigil over her sick mother in Yangtzepoo camp when the longed-for news came. She had missed assembly that day. She had not seen her father since he was arrested by the secret police in the autumn of 1942. Now she was terrified that if she left her mother, who was seriously ill with an inflamed gall bladder, she would die.

'Suddenly we heard a great shout. Then people were cheering. Gordon [her brother] burst in to tell us that Mr Roberton [camp representative] had announced the end of the war and the peaceful surrender of Japan and of our guards.' Outside camp the streets were suddenly thronged with jubilant Chinese streaming in towards the centre of Shanghai, telling the prisoners the war was over and urging them to come out.

The food situation remained acute, even after the surrender. Everyone got out their reserves to celebrate. Margaret's mother produced her last tin of corned beef, which she shared with Gordon. Margaret, who had always been a fussy eater, was given a precious tin of fruit instead.

The initial jubilation was succeeded by days of limbo when life seemed, wearily, to go as before. On 21 August, nearly a week after the surrender, Allied officials brought food to some of the camps. A few days later food drops got underway in earnest. Jose Chamberlain in the same camp recalls the day planes appeared overhead and dropped containers full of khaki-coloured tins by parachute. 'The parachutes were so colourful – turquoise, pink and yellow. Various women later carried them off and made them into sun suits, which were very fashionable at that time – shorts with tops tied in a knot.' Relatives of a Chinese woman killed by a drop near Shanghai put the parachute to more prosaic use when they turned it into her burial shroud.[3]

The food contained in the drops was highly nutritious, but too rich for weakened digestive systems. There were bars of chocolate, cereal complete with cream (just add water), cans of meat, dried eggs, honey, vegetables, condensed milk, fruit, jam, concentrated fruit and nut bars and chewing gum. Margaret was one of many who couldn't enjoy the food at first. 'Someone gave me a concentrated fruit and nut bar, which I hesitantly ate and promptly vomited back. Strangely I didn't feel all that hungry. My starvation had gone beyond hunger. My mother had to start urging me to eat all over again, just like before we went into the camps.'

The drops, though welcome, were not universally successful. The noise and violence which accompanied them, with the huge planes with their deafening engines swooping low over the camps, frightened children and adults alike. Often wildly off-target, the canisters would break free from their chutes and plummet violently to earth, exploding on impact. In Lunghwa Ron Huckstep saw several parachutes that failed to open. 'One large container of tinned pineapples burst near one man, half drowning him in the juice. It was the only case I have seen of shock due to fruit juice.'[4]

Soon after the food drops American servicemen came into the camps bringing films, which the internees watched on giant screens in the open air. Chinese businessmen distributed dollars of the new currency issued by the Nationalists Central Reserve Bank and the children bought sweets to eat while they watched *Meet me in St Louis*. The exuberance and informality of the Americans made them hugely popular, especially with children, whom they played with and treated with an endless supply of goodies.[5]

Jose Chamberlain, whose mother had died in camp and whose father was in prison, came out of her shell with the young American servicemen and started to enjoy herself for the first time in years – only to be chided by her kill-joy guardian Mrs Toon. 'The Americans were lovely and cheery and very good to children. Mrs Toon liked the Americans. She used to entertain all the young chaps. There was one young American soldier who always made a fuss of me. He used to talk to me about his little sister and he gave me bars of chocolate. He was the first person to show me kindness since the death of my mother. It was the most innocent friendship you could imagine, but

Mrs Toon put her foot down and said I wasn't to see him. She said it wasn't right.'

As the guards disappeared camp gates opened and many internees, children among them, ventured forth on their own. James Ballard decided to leave Lunghwa camp and walk back to his old home in Shanghai. But the interim between the end of the war and the emptying of the camps was lawless and potentially highly dangerous. The Japanese did not retreat in an orderly mass and pockets of battle-hardened soldiers lingered in the countryside. For them the worst had happened and revenge on those weaker than themselves was one of the few diversions that remained to them. James walked for an hour until he reached the Hangchow–Shanghai railway line, which circled the western perimeter of Shanghai. There were no trains and he walked for a while along the embankment until he reached a run-down railway station. As he approached he saw a group of Japanese soldiers waiting on the platform. Fully armed, they were sitting on their ammunition boxes. The boy could hear an odd sound and as he drew near he saw the cause. Some of them were amusing themselves torturing a young Chinese man. 'The Japanese soldier had cut down lengths of telephone wire and had tied the Chinese to a telegraph pole and was now slowly strangling him as the Chinese sang out in a sing-song voice.'

The boy's first thought was to walk away, but then he decided it would be less dangerous to try to ignore the hideous act that was taking place right in front of him. 'I ... was about to walk past it when the soldier with the telephone wire raised a hand and beckoned me towards him. He had seen the transparent celluloid belt that held up my frayed cotton shorts. It had been given to me by one of the American sailors, and was a prized novelty that no Japanese was likely to have seen. I unbuckled the belt and handed it to him, then waited as he flexed the colourless plastic and stared at me through it, laughing admiringly. Behind him, the young Chinese was slowly suffocating to death, his urine spreading across the platform. I waited ... listening to the sing-song voice as it grew weaker. ... Peace, I realised was more threatening because the rules that sustained war, however evil, were suspended. Ten minutes later the Chinese was silent and I was able to walk away.'[6]

Many children found the transition from camp to 'normal' life unexpectedly hard and some showed signs of psychological damage. Institutionalisation had set in during the years of internment, a form of agoraphobia which could bring on panic attacks. They weren't used to the bustle, the roar of traffic or the dozens of thronging stranger faces; they found sleeping in small 'bedroom-sized' rooms frightening and social rituals perplexing. After years of want David Nicoll found himself overwhelmed by the generosity of his relatives. 'When Uncle Jimmy visited us again he brought a chicken dish specially prepared for us by Aunt Mathilda. I was still run down, a large boil had appeared on my chest and the boil on my cheek had developed ... so all I could do was open my lips a little and sip the super-tasting gravy.

'Uncle Jimmy came out on 16th September, my thirteenth birthday and gave me a box of cakes from New Kiesslings, the cake-shop. I was overcome at getting all these cakes the likes of which I had long forgotten, and I had got so out of the habit of receiving presents that I did not know how to react, and when Uncle Jimmy hugged me and wished me a happy birthday all I could think of was to murmur "Happy Birthday" back to him.'[7]

Jose Chamberlain was overcome with panic while being taken to meet up with an old school friend in central Shanghai. They got to the Customs House and were waiting to cross the road when she froze. 'There was a Commissionaire on the door of the Customs House but I couldn't bring myself to go in. I was scared. I don't know why.'

Hope Lee, the Quaker missionary, knew the transition back to normal life would be hard for her three-year-old daughter, but was shocked at the way she too had become institutionalised. 'We started to go for little walks down the river. The first time I was terrified: the traffic and the noise seemed too much. We tried to break Marion into things gently, so we could get as far as the river and sit and watch the junks ... the trams would go hurtling by and I wondered if I would ever get up enough courage to get on one. Even crossing the road was a frightening experience. It seems strange but ... in those first few days it was a relief to get back through the gates and into the camp again, and upstairs into our own squalid little corner. Here we felt a certain kind of security which we had not yet achieved in the outside world.'[8]

For some lucky children Shanghai liberation was marked by a party to end all parties held aboard the British cruiser HMS *Belfast*. War had changed the old order and now the vast majority of ships in the water off Shanghai were American. The *Belfast* was one of only three or four British ships, but the show they put on for the children dwarfed the American efforts, according to their guests. Dick Germain, newly liberated from Lincoln Avenue camp, says that the Americans toured the camps announcing a party, but stipulated that only three children from each camp could attend. 'The *Belfast*, in contrast, invited all the children.' Transport was arranged from the camps to the Bund and launches took the excited children out to the ship.

'Sailors love children and they gave us an unforgettable day. There was a guy in a diving suit and we were encouraged to punch him. Groans came forth from within when we hit him and we thought it was brilliant. Of course there was no one in there and the groans came courtesy of a microphone. The sailors dressed up and put up swings and slides for us; there was a stall where we could throw nuts and bolts at glass bottles. And the food ... We were given money to go to the NAAFI on board and told we could have as many bars of chocolate as we liked. The problem was that our stomachs had shrunk down to nothing in camp and the food made us very ill.'

Gradually the Shanghai internees began to leave camp to try to pick up the threads of their former lives. But the majority found this was impossible as they had no jobs, no money and no homes. Time after time people returned to their old homes to find they had been trashed and ransacked by Japanese or Chinese occupants. The only exception was the family of Barbara Tilbury, the girl who had developed painful blisters in Lunghwa. They returned to their luxury penthouse flat in the Avenue Joffe in the French Concession. It had been used as a headquarters for Japanese generals and they had left it immaculate. The house plants were better cared for than they were when they left them. The only odd thing was the date on the calendar. Instead of August 1945 the date read January 1942.[9]

As the flat the Blairs had lived in prior to internment was not far from camp Margaret Blair and her mother went to visit it. They arrived to find Nationalist soldiers carrying out the last of their furniture, which they claimed to be borrowing. Jose Chamberlain's father made the same bleak discovery. A Japanese family had occupied their house during the war, but when her father visited it on his release a Chinese family were living there. All their rugs, ornaments, utensils, everything that chronicled his marriage, had vanished. Harry Chamberlain, in his mid-fifties and with a young daughter to raise, was looking at a future of destitution. He tried desperately to gain compensation from the British Government, who had ordered men like him to stay at their posts and defend the Empire. He was not successful.

David Nicoll was one of the lucky ones. He and his family returned to the Custom House, which they had been thrown out of by the Japanese just before Christmas 1941. Their new flat overlooked the Bund, providing David with a bird's-eye view of the stirring moment when the US Navy sailed into Shanghai. They watched as hospital ships arrived to take sick POWs home for nursing and saw how the world order had changed.

'On 18th September the US fleet sailed in to a loud welcome from other ships in port and thereafter we always had an American cruiser moored in the river directly opposite our main bedroom window. That particular mooring had in times past been assigned to the British man-of-war but in these changed days when the British flagship – the cruiser 'Belfast' – and attendant destroyers arrived a week later, they had to tie up to buoys upriver.'

The Nicoll family watched with some emotion, amid much blowing of horns from other shipping, a Chinese river steamer sail up the Whangpoo and moor at the Bund. It was the first ship to complete the passage down the Yangtze all the way from Chingkiang since those far-off days of 1938.

The British warships held Open Days for ex-internees, taking children out by launch to the great vessels moored in the middle of the river. David Nicoll twice went out to the *Belfast*, returning on both occasions with five shillings worth of supplies from the ship's canteen.

Various organisations, including the British forces, put on entertainments for ex-internees and on one occasion they went to a showing of Noël Coward's war classic *In Which We Serve*. On the journey David's mother got into conversation with a sad-looking woman. She turned out to be the mother of Sonny Rees. Sonny was David's pal from the days in 1942 when they camped in the hall next to Shanghai cathedral. He had died the following year in Yangchow.

Soon the only people left in the camps in Shanghai were those who had nowhere to go or whose fathers were still imprisoned. This included Margaret Blair and Jose Chamberlain, whose fathers had last been heard of at Haiphong Road prison. They remained in camp until October, Margaret with her mother and brother; Jose with her guardian.

Losing her mother was tragic enough, but Jose came very close to losing her father too (as did Margaret Blair). In July 1945 her father and the other prisoners of Haiphong Road, many of whom had been tortured and were weak and ill, had been transported by rail up to Fengtai, just south of Peking. Here they had been herded into wooden warehouses where they had good reason to believe they were to be burned alive, a method of execution regularly practised by the Japanese against Chinese civilians. The plan was thwarted by the dropping of the atom bomb on Hiroshima and the end of the war. The men were taken to Peking and handed over to the Allies for medical care and recuperation.

When the men were fit again Jose went to the docks to meet the American ship bringing her father down from Peking. As they had nowhere to live Jose and her father were sent to another former internment camp, Jose's third.

In this camp, which had been a British army barracks, they lived in wooden huts in rooms just large enough to hold two beds and a stove. Fuel was still scarce and Jose made coal balls. It had turned very cold. 'I had a jumper and thick trousers, made from an old suit of my father's.' The room had a clothes line strung diagonally across it. 'At night rats walked along it and Dad used to throw darts at them.'

Jose's father had been freed to find that, with the exception of his daughter, he had lost everything – wife, job, savings. 'He was very preoccupied with money and his future. He was trying to get compensation for the loss of our house.' They remained at Ash Camp until the end of January and on 31 January 1946 they embarked aboard the *Highland Chieftain* bound for England.

Margaret Blair's father was released at the same time as Jose's and joined them in camp, where they waited until Margaret's mother had the gall bladder operation she desperately needed. Margaret was happy that her family was complete once more. However, the cruelty of war, from which she had been largely shielded, intruded on this happy idyll as she found out what sadism men had endured in the prison her father had been in, and the wholesale murder of civilians by the Germans and the Japanese. In bed in camp one night she overheard her father tell her mother of the dreadful death of one of the prisoners.

'When another man, instead of him, was accused of sending messages outside the camp, this man owned up. The Japanese took him to Bridge House jail and rotating teams of guards badgered, and beat him with clubs. When he became maddened, possibly brain-damaged, and unruly from the mistreatment they trussed him up tightly with ropes for four days leaving him out in the sun with no water or food – and kept him awake for days. At last the Japanese soldiers brought him back to Haiphong Road. As he lay on his bed, a sobbing, groaning, bleeding mass, unable to move, he started to sing softly. The scarcely audible song drifted out to the growing group of prisoners gathering silently beside the bed. It was 'When Irish Eyes Are Smiling' over and over ... and then the singing stopped. His name was William Hutton and he died soon after.' The story haunted her. 'I thought it was terribly sad, and his wife and children having to know about it, how their loved father-husband had died.'

A few days later Margaret's mother went into hospital and Margaret and her brother Gordon were told that they could go to the cinema in Shanghai by themselves. They chose the Cathay in the French concession. The film was preceded by an extended newsreel highlighting major events of the war in Europe and the Far East. Suddenly Margaret was confronted with nightmarish images. 'On the screen appeared an image of two children electrocuted on a fence, lying stiff and white like carved wooden figures. One still held a doll in her arms. Walking skeletons with skin stretched over their bones and ghastly smiles on their faces came out of a Japanese forced mining camp. A Chinese girl bound to a chair lay dead after being raped by dozens of Japanese soldiers. A press photo of Nanking showed narrow streets choked with bodies, faces down, hands clawed forward, feet stretched out ready to run even in death ... across China black smoke belched from chimneys of hospitals where Chinese civilians had been subjected to vivisection, without anaesthetics, and their bodies burned.'

Margaret was deeply upset. 'I couldn't pay attention to the movie ... for thinking of the ghastly scenes ... That night I dreamed of Japanese surgeons discussing how many 'logs' (Chinese) they had 'cut' (murdered) that day. In the dream two bright red streams of blood shot up from the neck of a civilian beheaded at random in the street. I woke up screaming.'

At the same time as camps in Shanghai were learning of the Allied victory something strange was happening in Stanley camp in Hong Kong. Bill Macauley describes the uncharacteristic generosity of the guards. 'On 16 August I received the order to go to the distribution point to get some supplies. I thought it odd as we had already received our rice supplies for the month. When I arrived the Japs were handing out vast quantities of American toilet rolls, enough for everybody in camp. This was indeed a luxury. Toilet paper had disappeared from our lives. We either used water, or, if I could lay hands on it, the Japanese newspaper. We named them "victory rolls". They were also handing out fundoshis. We called them "Jap happies" but they were traditional Japanese loin cloths, made from very coarse material. One lady asked if she could have six. The Japs just said, "Help yourself." By the next day she had made herself a blouse. Now we knew something had changed.'

Shortly after, Dakotas flew over dropping medical supplies, food and American cigarettes. Every adult was entitled to four packets. 'I was nineteen by then so I claimed my share,' said Bill. With astonishing swiftness the social order of internment was upended and replaced once more by the colonial system. Chinese coolies came from the city to cut wood and cook for the Europeans. They instinctively resumed their high-handed tone when addressing Orientals, causing one seven-year-old boy to ask his father, 'Why ... do some people speak so crossly to the Chinese and order them about?'[10]

Prisoners in Stanley were less cut off from the progress of the war than many other internees. The Japanese circulated a propaganda newspaper in camp. Despite its ever-optimistic tone, the prisoners could work out from the position of American forces that the tide was turning. Early that year the prisoners had received tangible proof that the Americans were on the offensive, though the relief was two-edged.

Bill Macauley recalls: 'On the morning of 15 January at about eight o'clock in the morning I was making congee when suddenly these single-engine fighter-bomber planes flew low over the camp. They were planes that we had never seen before – Corsairs and Hellcats, with curved wings. They were taking out the anti-aircraft gun on the south side of the island and on their way to bomb the harbour on the north side. We knew they had to have come from an American aircraft carrier. The first contingent was maybe half a dozen aircraft and they flew almost roof high wagging their wings at us. It was thrilling to watch them and to realise that they knew we were there. Two other lads and I rushed up onto the flat roof of our block to watch them. It looked lovely. The bullets looked like silver rain falling all round us. Then it went quiet and I went back to the kitchen to cook rice for lunch. An hour later they came over again. Six hundred planes must have flown over that day. They destroyed twenty-six ships in the harbour and half a dozen aircraft.'

The planes were bombing the bungalows in the hills, which were occupied by Japanese. One of the bombs unfortunately missed its target and came down on the camp killing fourteen prisoners. There was no repeat visit. All the prisoners saw after that was the occasional Silver Fortress, the heavy bomber, flying so high they could hardly see or hear it.

Stanley Fort, which had been the British barracks, stood higher up the hill than the blocks which housed the internees. By 1945 the Japanese were evidently expecting an Allied attack and had started digging tunnels in the hillside. This worried the internees who feared they would be in the front line when the Americans attacked.

It wasn't until two weeks after the Japanese surrender that Bill saw the thrilling sight that convinced him he really would soon be free. 'I was up on the roof of our building when I saw a ship on the horizon. Ships were my hobby. As it got nearer I shouted out, "That's a King George V-class battleship." It was HMS *Anson*. Then we saw an Ark Royal-class aircraft carrier. That turned out to be HMS *Indomitable*. Then we saw the cruiser *Euryalus*. To see the Royal Navy coming to rescue us like that was quite a moment. The American Air Force had flown over a few days earlier dropping leaflets telling us to stay put and, in particular, warning the Japs to feed us and not to harm us. Then a rumour went round camp that the Navy were coming. And it was true! An advance patrol of about thirty men in battle order came down the main road into camp. They looked extremely healthy and handed out cigarettes and chocolate that had melted in the heat. "All right mate?" they asked us. "We're glad to be here."'

The surrender of the Japanese was marked by the raising of the Union Jack over camp. A star-struck Bill was standing near the commander of HMS *Indomitable*, who noticed he was barefoot. 'He asked me very discreetly what size I took and said he'd be back. He returned the following day with a brand-new pair of naval officer's shoes and socks – my first footwear in months.'

As in many camps the noise and sheer invasiveness of the drops, coupled with the uncharacteristically rowdy behaviour of the adults terrified many of the younger children. William Sewell, interned with his wife and three children, contrasted the two reactions: 'The planes came over in ceaseless waves; formations of two, three, four or eight, sweeping down low over the buildings, circling the camp. We waved, we cheered ... we abandoned all else to dash from windows to veranda to get a better view of the roaring machines. Ronnie had retired under his mother's camp-bed, frightened by the excitement and the noise. "Mummy," asked Nancy, "when will peace be over? Can't we have war again?"'

Parents like the Sewells watched as their children grappled with this new thing called freedom. Fascinated by the sailors who befriended them they gradually rediscovered the outside world through trips out to battleships and rides in military vehicles. The sudden abundance of things that for most of their short lives had been as precious as diamonds intoxicated them. 'Joy and Guy sat striking matches until several boxes were exhausted, just for the happiness the experience of prodigality gave them.' On a visit to Hong Kong Sewell's children found great delight in rediscovering humdrum objects they had completely forgotten, rushing about in houses they visited turning on lights and ringing bells. The habits of years of privation were hard to break, however, and table manners proved a struggle. The children had to learn again how to eat using knives and forks. 'It was many months before Guy ceased to lick his plate and Joy refrained from peeping into dustbins.'[11]

For internees like Bill Macauley, who had spent his time in camp bereft of all family, the end came almost as an anti-climax. 'After breakfast on 11 September I handed in my quartermaster's keys, collected my little bag with my few belongings and went down to the jetty. Our ship, the *Empress of Australia*, was anchored off Tweed Bay south of the island. We went out to it by frigate.' Cut off from all news for the last two years of his internment Bill was longing to see his family again, and in particular his big brother Jim who had always been his special pal. As he sailed for England after three and a half years of loneliness, hunger and poor health he never suspected that the worst was still to come.

Just over 1,000 miles north of Hong Kong in Weihsien camp fifteen-year-old Joyce Kerry wrote in her diary on Friday, 17 August 1945: 'An aeroplane came over the camp; it circled round and round to see if it would be shot at but because nothing happened some parachutes were dropped. They brought Major Steiger, Sergeant Tad Nagaki, Lt J Moore, Cpl Peter Orlick, Edward Wong, Lt J Harrow, Sergeant Ray Hanchulak. When the first parachute dropped everybody rushed out of camp beyond the guards. If we hadn't, then the Japs would probably have shot or imprisoned the Americans. We were all very, very excited. Our appetite went. How people ran. Flags were waved.' The seven airmen, one of whom had broken his leg, having come down in a tree, were picked up and carried shoulder high into camp by a wildly cheering crowd. It was a specially exciting moment for the children from Chefoo School. Lt J. Moore of the US Navy was a former pupil. He had been interned, been repatriated as he was American and had enlisted in the Navy.

For the isolated camps like Weihsien the end was much more long drawn-out than in Shanghai. That was even more the case in Yangchow where the inmates, and apparently even the Japanese guards, knew nothing of the surrender until three weeks later.

Adults in Weihsien had in fact known since Monday, 13 August when a Chinese worker had come into camp and spat out a water-proof package announcing that the war was over. The camp leaders had read the message, but as there had been no sign from either Japanese or Allies, they decided they had no choice but to carry on as normal. On the Wednesday Norman Cliff, a pupil of Chefoo School and the brother of Estelle, was one of a crowd standing outside the commandant's office, full of anticipation, while the camp interpreter tried to get the commandant to admit that Japan had surrendered. The response had been non-committal and the crowd dispersed none the wiser.[12] The adults had got good reason to proceed cautiously. Three weeks earlier they had boldly celebrated the end of the war in Europe and had triggered a very dangerous situation. In the middle of the night on 8 May 1945 someone who clearly had access to a radio had rung the big brass bell in the tower of what had been the classroom block of the former mission. What they did not know was that this bell was a signal from the Japanese to the garrison nearby that the prisoners were rioting. Fifteen-year-old Estelle Cliff, Norman's younger sister, was ordered out of her bed along with all the other internees. She put her coat over her pyjamas, pinned her roll-call ID badge to her lapel and went outside into the yard, which was lit up by a searchlight. 'Two little Jap guards were standing in the light beam, their rifles with bayonets crossed to make an arch. We each had to stand before them as they slowly examined our ID and referred to a list they held. No support from teachers or friends: it was every man by himself when his turn came. When they were satisfied, we walked away under the arch, but even I at fifteen was obliged to duck to evade those sharp blades!'

Before long, however, not even the commandant could continue to deny the truth. On the Friday of that week, to the great joy of the inmates, the parachutes appeared. Joyce Kerry recalls the excitement. 'Every day for six days parachutes came down with food, delicious stuff which we had not seen for two years – tinned meat, fruit, chocolate, condensed milk, raisins, anything in packets. We used to mix the milk with the raisins and make a deliciously sweet slurpy mess. We still had very little in the way of clothing. I had an overcoat but no shoes. There were puddles of rain on the ground and my feet were cold and wet all the time.'

It was not thought safe to evacuate the internees immediately due to the fighting in the area between the nationalist and communist Chinese. Trains were being blown up and the situation was regarded as too dangerous for foreigners to travel. In the lull that followed the Japanese were ordered to guard the prisoners. The Chinese set up a market outside the wire and even the strictly guarded Chefoo School pupils were allowed out on trips. Joyce Kerry's diary records that on Monday, 20 August twenty-two more Americans landed at the nearby aerodrome. Joyce, a shy, self-conscious red-head, was star-struck by the dashing American rescuers. Her delighted confusion is almost palpable in her diary entry for Wednesday, 22 August: 'In the morning I joined a crowd round the Major. He sang to us and taught us a song, "You Tell me your Dreams". He wanted us to sing to him, but because we wouldn't Ann suggested to him that I could sing him a solo. He called upon me, but not knowing that he was asking me, I turned round to see who he was talking to. Then the others yelled "Carrots" and Flea who was sitting on my lap got off and I was imbarrassed [sic]. At first I was unwilling but I finally yielded. The crowd was the worst part of it.'

As the parachute drops continued Joyce was proud to be chosen to be part of the team who carried in the supplies. A week after the surrender Joyce wrote a poignant letter to her parents. She hadn't seen them since 1940 and was trying to imagine what they would make of each other after such a long separation.

'What you'll think of our clothes and shoes, when we arrive, I don't know. I'd like to know what you're doing at home. Probably you're having an ordinary day but what's that like. There's a lot to get to know about you and for you all to know about us . . . . I hope that you aren't old yet. We've been barefoot so much, it will seem queer to have to wear shoes all the rest of our lives, and socks most of the time. Please buy me a pair of brown shoes, if you can and don't mind me asking. My foot is about 10 ins long now. We need quite a lot of things altogether.'

Five weeks later a truce was arranged in the fighting between the two Chinese forces and, on 25 September, 580 prisoners, who included the Chefoo School contingent, left Weihsien by train for the seaside resort of Tsingtao. Joyce and her friends had been ready to leave the day before but a heavy storm in the night had flooded the roads and, to their intense disappointment, they had to wait another day. The excited children eventually left the camp in which they had spent two years of their lives in a lorry called the Lousy Louse. 'As our names were called we went out to the trucks which were out of the gates. Our truck ... was quite crowded ... The road was very bumpy but good fun. When we arrived at the station we were checked. Quite a few Americans were on the station. Sgt Levy came with us. (I cried.) The last part of the camp I saw ... was 23 tower.'

The train journey was slow as it had to cross long bridges that had been damaged by the fighting between the Chinese. All along the way crowds of smiling Chinese clapped and waved American flags. When they arrived in Tsingtao British sailors were on duty and a Royal Marines band was playing a welcome. But the famed Chefoo School discipline continued to the last. 'We had to stay in the train for a long time before it was our turn to get out. Some of the sailors came and talked to us at the window and some of them gave us some sweets. We had to put on our coats and hats soon after the train had stopped.'

The former internees spent the next three weeks at Edgewater Mansions, a luxury hotel overlooking the sea, which had been a favourite with Westerners before the war. As the bus drove to the hotel, where they would be guarded by US Marines, Chinese joy in the rout of the Japanese surrounded them. 'Our buses passed a Chinese band and ... everywhere there were posters "Welcome to Our Allied Friends", "The Victory of Allied Nations is the Base for World Peace".'

The weather was hot and the girls spent lazy days gorging themselves on first-class food, writing letters and swimming. Lack of costumes was swiftly sorted. 'The Americans lent us US Army issue khaki shorts and singlets. Growing girls that we were we must have looked quite something in them.' In the evening there was dancing, an activity which fascinated these young girls on the verge of womanhood. Their teachers, aware of the danger posed by so many young American males, forbade them to take part. 'We missionary children led sheltered lives and were not used to seeing people dancing. We gawped in amazement at this glimpse of the high life.'

One girl, however, missed all the excitement of Edgewater Mansions. K Strange had become ill on the journey. 'It started with an achy feeling, as if I'd been sitting on a wet bench. Then my hip became sore. Eventually I was feverish and drowsy and in a lot of pain. It got worse as we neared Tsingtao. It was diagnosed as osteomilitis of the hip, which is an infection of the bone. I was operated on straight away. I don't know if it was linked to camp, but two other girls in our school got it while we were interned and I believe it is quite a rare condition. There was no penicillin so they just had to let their body heal itself. I was lucky. There was penicillin on a ship in the harbour as we arrived and I was the first civilian in the area to be treated with it.'

K was in bed for six weeks after the operation receiving penicillin by injection every four hours. When the time came to embark for Hong Kong, on the first leg of the journey home to England, K's stretcher had to be laid across the top of the seats of a large car as there were no ambulances to take her to the docks. 'They couldn't get me up the gangway, so I was lifted on a crane, which was quite hair-raising, but thankfully I was put safely down on the deck. On board I was nursed by young American sailors who were lovely. They were only eighteen or nineteen. One of them dropped a tray of thermometers and got a good telling-off.'

When the ex-internees from Weihsien arrived in Hong Kong their care was taken over by the British Army who pulled out all stops to see they had a good time. They took them for drives in jeeps (chaperoned by teachers), organised trips to the airfield and tried to fill in the gaps in their knowledge of the war by trips to the cinema. The Chefoo schoolgirls, unused to such heady freedom, either in camp or at school, did their teenage best to evade the ever-vigilant teachers, flirting with young servicemen, going for walks in the city.

In a letter to her parents dated 30 October 1945 Joyce wrote: 'The stay at Tsingtao wasn't as good as this. We're given money each week to spend. I get one pound and Brian being younger receives ten shillings. The teachers three times have taken us over by ferry to Hong Kong. The first time we went to the King's Theatre and saw a number of very interesting newsreels. The next time we visited the Tiger Balm Palace.'

Joyce and her fellow pupils sailed for England on 11 November 1945, sent off by the strains of a band of the British Marines on the quayside. The journey took five weeks and their time was filled with lectures about the war and more films. They sailed up the Suez Canal and visited Suez where the Red Cross gave them warm clothing. To her delight Joyce received a canvas bag full of clothes, which included a silk jersey dress in bright green, her first glamorous garment, and a perfect foil for her flaming red hair. They docked at Southampton on 15 December and took the train to Victoria where the whole family were waiting: mother, father, a sister of five and a brother of four whom she had never seen, and her grandfather.

The reunion, however, was less pleasurable than the one she had imagined for so long. 'As soon as my grandfather saw me he put his arms round me in a spontaneous gesture of affection, but instead of hugging him I froze. I hadn't seen him since I was four and now I was fifteen. No one had touched me in years and I felt uncomfortable and embarrassed.'

Among the last prisoners to be liberated were those who had begun to think of themselves as the forgotten few – the 600 men, women and children in Yangchow. From the middle of August the internees had begun to feel that the behaviour of the Japanese had become more relaxed. They were spending less time patrolling the grounds and were more tolerant of banter during roll-call. They didn't have a radio in camp and were cut off in a timeless world inside the towering ramparts of the ancient city. In fact they remained unaware of the Japanese surrender for two weeks. According to Neil Begley it was a Chinese who broke the wonderful news. 'One afternoon a Chinese soldier walking along the city wall looked down into the camp and asked what Europeans were doing there. On being told that they were prisoners of the Japanese he replied, "But the war's been over for three weeks. You should be free".' To convince them, he rolled a newspaper in a rock and threw it down to them. Neil Begley's father, a Salvation Army missionary, and one of the few people in camp who could read Chinese, confirmed what the soldier was saying. Begley's father and the camp representative went to the commandant and told them they would no longer submit to the daily roll-call. There followed a strange interlude when no one quite knew who was guarding whom. According to Keith Martin, who was seventeen by this time, the commandant suggested they remained inside the compound. 'I think they were concerned about themselves and thought that with us around we were an insurance policy for them.'[13] Still in the precarious situation of being under guard by armed Japanese they were trying to get word of their existence to the outside world when on 28 August a small contingent of American soldiers led by an officer, walked through the gate. To the dismay of the internees, however, the American soldiers, instead of liberating them, surrendered their weapons to the Japanese. It was left to a British officer, who arrived a few days later, to disarm the Japanese. This one-man cavalry, called Captain Martin, who wore a red beret and sported a moustache, 'roared and stormed over to the guardhouse where he disarmed the guards, gave the Americans back their weapons, flung open the gates and ordered that we raise our flags immediately and leave them up'. It seemed that Captain Martin arrived in the nick of time. A thorough search of the commandant's residence revealed plans for the extermination of all the internees.[14]

Captain Martin recommended that the internees remain in the compound and used the radio belonging to the American officer to order food to be sent up from Shanghai. A couple of days later they received a message telling them to make two large POW signs. One was to be placed on the roof of one of the houses, the other on the parade ground. The next day, 5 September, three B-29 Super Fortresses flew low over the camp greeted by waving, cheering prisoners. As was so often the way with the Americans the drop was not very accurate and many of the parachutes landed beyond the city wall, damaging Chinese houses and obliging some of the men in camp to rush out and carry the heavy drums back in.[15]

To many of the internees, totally unused to the noise of war in the isolated backwater of Yangchow, the din and confusion of the drops was terrifying. Some, thinking they were being attacked, ran away trying to hide from the onslaught. The young boys, who included Neil Begley, were fascinated. 'As we watched ... their bomb bays opened and tiny black dots fell towards us. As the dots became closer, some changed colour and started to drift, but the others kept coming, getting bigger and bigger ... they were 44-gallon drums, some single, some welded together, which contained pork and beans and cling-stone peaches or spaghetti. Others had powdered milk, chocolates, cheese, coffee and biscuits. The coloured ones were attached to parachutes which opened and took them drifting off into the distance where no doubt some lucky Chinese put them to good use. The black ones were drums that had ripped away from their chutes and rained on us like bombs. Exploding on impact they spewed peaches, spaghetti and pork and beans in all directions.'

Two shocked women on the third floor watching the drop from their window were all but killed when a 44-gallon missile made a direct hit through the loop of the P for 'prisoner' on the roof above them. 'Bursting on impact it ripped straight through the roof, landing on a bed a couple of feet from where they were seated, proceeded on down, taking the bed with it to the second floor where it gave a repeat performance and so on to the ground floor spraying a mixture of pork and beans and peaches in its wake.'[16]

As in so many of the camps the first drop made many of the prisoners ill as they ate too much of the fat-rich food they had been deprived of for so long. A second drop a week later was more accurate and as more of the parachutes opened, caused less waste.

Many of the children were in poor health by now. Neil Begley had suffered repeated bouts of malaria, and had problems with his eyes. Cruel to be kind, his parents were deliberately ungenerous with the goodies. 'My parents rationed us to a victory feast of two small cracker biscuits each with butter and cheese and a cup of instant coffee with powdered milk and sugar.' But even this was too much for Neil's mother who suffered a bilious attack.

The general happiness at the prospect of going home was marred by the untimely death of one of the older boys. On 3 September, the very day the Americans arrived in camp, Geoff Manley, a popular boy, succumbed to the physical and psychological pressures of prolonged privation. He was the second child to die in Yangchow, Sonny Rees having died in 1943 at the age of thirteen. In all there were only eight deaths in camp.

The cause of Geoff's death was not clear. Neil Begley believed that, hungry and weak, he lost the will to survive – a desperately sad situation for a young man on the threshold of life. He 'became despondent and lay on his bed saying he'd never get out of the camp alive ... Attempts to break his depression were to no avail and within a week he was dead. The doctors could find no explanation. These chaps were overcome by melancholy and dropped their bundle. No amount of jolly-up could break them from their lethargy.'[17] Colin Palmer, Keith Martin and another boy dug his grave. 'Not an experience we wanted,' Keith Martin observed, 'But he was one of us.'[18] Keith carried the processional cross at Geoff's funeral.[19]

The Allies were keen to empty the camp as quickly as possible as the political situation round Yangchow was highly volatile. The Communists were on the edge of the city, while the presence of warring groups of pro-Japanese Chinese, nationalist Chinese and non-aligned guerrillas and bandits made the surrounding countryside highly dangerous for Europeans. The internees left in groups of twenty-five or so, travelling down the Grand Canal to Chingkiang in barges, much as they had two and a half years earlier. On the journey Neil Begley observed how much life had changed in those two and a half years. A Chinese peasant woman sitting opposite the Begleys in the barge had been eating a pear. When she finished she produced a Chinese $500 note from her bag and, to Neil's horror, used it to wipe her hands. When they had gone into camp Chinese $100 possessed serious purchasing power. So did the 100 cents that made it up, and the four coppers that made up each cent. Now, thanks to the inflation caused by the distribution of Japanese occupation money, the Chinese currency was worthless and Chinese $500 was the lowest negotiable note.

The last leg of the journey from Chingkiang to Shanghai was made by train. In 1943 they had sailed up, but this time the authorities were worried that the Yangtze River might be mined. The Shanghai the returning prisoners encountered was a battered wreck, unrecognisable as the confident, glamorous Paris of the east they had left two and a half years earlier. Public services were hardly working, the collapsing Japanese occupation money meant people had to take large suitcases to carry the banknotes when they went shopping and exchange rates changed constantly. Neil Begley's mother bought him a modest pair of sandshoes for an eye-watering Chinese $250,000. Lack of fuel fostered ingenuity. Private cars carried gas producers on their running boards that converted coal into gas, which could be burnt by the engine. In the absence of public transport, Allied military vehicles took civilians where they needed to go. Homeless and destitute like most of the other ex-prisoners, the Begley family were rescued by the Red Cross. The organisation, which provided a lifeline for so many victims of war, gave them medical examinations, allocated them temporary housing and gave them money to buy necessities.

Soon after they arrived back in Shanghai the Begley family were separated once more. Neil's father was anxious to get back to his mission work in Hong Kong. He left the Bund on an RAF Catalina flying boat, waved off by his wife and children. Neil's mother, desperate to arrange for the family's repatriation to their native Australia, succeeded in getting places on a Navy troopship bound for Hong Kong. It was an exciting journey for Neil and his brother. Their ship was escorted by two corvettes whose job was to protect the travellers from mines. 'Whenever a mine was sighted our ship would be warned to proceed with caution while our escorts detonated the mine with gunfire. It was great sport to watch the huge water spouts as the mines exploded.' Sometimes the mines were too close by the time they were spotted: 'we'd reduce speed to a crawl and watch nervously as the mine with its menacing, protruding spikes bobbed slowly past us until it was far enough astern for one of the escorts to blow it up.'[20]

When they arrived in Hong Kong the family were allocated a flat in Kowloon, not far from Kai Tak airport. It was a carefree time for the brothers, who spent much of their time at the local YMCA hostel playing in the gym and swimming naked in the pool, as rules decreed. Even in such a trusting, seemingly innocent age, however, unsupervised youngsters could find they were courting danger. All over the colony Japanese prisoners were being put to work to restore the broken infrastructure and Neil's mother was allocated two to do her housework – the Japanese being 'required to bow respectfully to my mother', a tit-for-tat of which Neil thoroughly approved. As happened with the other children who passed through the colony on their way home, servicemen based in the area befriended them, taking them on trips, giving them goodies and war spoils. One RAF chap was particularly kind to Neil, taking him over to the island on a DUKW and showing him tricks, like how to burn his name in concrete using cordite from a bullet. The man had offered to show him the Spitfires he looked after and one afternoon Neil headed out to the airfield in search of him. Faced with an ocean of identical tents he had no idea how to locate his pal. He wandered over to one of the tents, which had about a dozen airmen in it and asked if they knew his friend. They said they didn't. Something in the atmosphere made Neil uneasy but as he edged towards the tent flap he found his exit blocked by two of the men.

'They took me by the arms and led me back to the middle of the tent ... They were laughing and the two who were holding me twisted my arms behind my back while some of the others pulled down my shorts.

'I was terrified. I struggled and tried to call out, but they forced me face down onto one of the camp stretchers and pushed a gag into my mouth. Then tying some ropes around my ankles they spread my legs apart. While a couple of them held me they each took it in turns to rape me.'

When, eventually, the ordeal was over, Neil ran home sobbing. He went up to his bedroom, rinsed the blood from his underpants and hid until his terror had subsided. His socks hid the welts the rope had cut into his ankles. Like many victims of sexual assault he felt he had done something wrong. 'I never breathed a word to anyone about my experience. If my father found out I was sure that I'd be in terrible trouble.'

17

Home Sweet Home

The mood of the youngsters returning to Britain on their various ships was one of eager anticipation. Unlike their parents, however, they had little idea how hard fitting into this new life would prove. It wasn't just the cold, though that would be bad enough for these children bred to the heat. The winter of 1945, and the following one, would turn out to be two of the coldest ever known. There were huge psychological problems facing these returning families. They were homeless and destitute. For the fathers, most well into middle age, finding new work would be a struggle. Many of the parents were psychologically scarred – as a result of the ordeals they had endured and because of anxiety about the uncertain future. Money was desperately tight – they had all lost all their material wealth in the war – and the status the men had enjoyed in the easy world of the colonies counted for nothing in hard-bitten austerity Britain, where everyone had troubles of their own. The majority of the homecomers threw themselves on the mercy of relatives. Grandparents up and down the country found their modest terraced houses and semis bulging at the seams. The missionaries were taken into mission hostels, thus postponing still further the resumption of normal family life. For the children there were problems of a different kind. Better than camp, it was nonetheless a sad and difficult time for many of them. Britain was not home to them. It was a cold, grey, unwelcoming place. A number were behind educationally due to the sketchy nature of schooling in camp. Many who had never been separated from their parents were packed off to cold unsympathetic boarding schools, where they felt excluded and misunderstood. Those who had spent the war apart from their parents struggled to fit back into the forgotten groove of family life. Trouble focused on the issue of authority for parents who couldn't accept the change wrought by the missing years. Those parents struggled to impose their authority on the stranger who in their eyes was still a child, but who, far from them in time and place, had turned into a young man or woman. Some youngsters returned to find new siblings had replaced them and felt shut out from the circle.

Joyce Kerry, fifteen now, whose mother had had two more children since Joyce had last seen her, was beside herself with excitement as her ship neared England. What thrilled her most was the prospect of sleeping in a proper bed.

On 15 November 1945 she wrote on paper headed SS *Arawa*: 'I know we shall be so terribly excited when we get near England. How lovely it's going to be! The last time I used one was Nov 3rd 1942 ... We weren't any of the lucky people to have a spring bed in camp. When we didn't sleep on the floor with a mattress we were on boxes. One thing about boxes was that they collected extra bed bugs. I hope we'll never see another!' Joyce had taken an affectionate interest in her new brother and sister, including them in her letters, remembering their birthdays and writing descriptions of life on board expressly destined for them. When fantasy became reality and she met them, however, she felt like a stranger in the warm family circle.

They went to stay in her grandfather's modest semi in Essex. 'The local church gave a Christmas party and I sat with my unfamiliar little brother on my lap, in the midst of all the happy chattering people, trying to hide the tears that were pouring down my face. I was surrounded by people I didn't know, and by my family whom I no longer knew. It was overwhelming. The family complained that I referred to my younger brother and sister as the children. But I didn't feel any connection to them.'

There were difficulties, too, to do with trying to adapt to a different culture. 'I had to learn, when calling the cat, to go "Puss, puss puss" and not to call "Mimi, mimi, mimi", the way the Chinese do. I called plimsolls "keds", which is perhaps American. My mother sent me to the shop to buy a reel of cotton and was cross when I came back with stiff button thread. I had asked for thread and in England, apparently, that meant button thread.'

Joyce's mother clearly struggled to understand just how deeply the privations of camp had affected her children. She was frequently critical of their behaviour. 'One day she was telling us about some trip or treat she had planned and we didn't react in an excited way. "Can't you two ever get excited about anything?" she would ask us. But in camp we had learned not to anticipate, as things that you desperately hoped for didn't happen. The Canadians and Americans were repatriated in 1943 and the British believed we would be too. We were told we might be going to India ... or South Africa. In the end we went nowhere. When other people are taking all your life decisions for you, you learn not to make plans. On one occasion when my behaviour failed to come up to my mother's expectations she burst out, "Well at least I didn't bring you up."'

Joyce found school was very difficult and had to be put down a year. Her poor sight caused endless misery. She had broken her glasses on the ship coming home and couldn't see. She had to stand on the platform right in front of the blackboard to see, which made her self-conscious. 'I made friends with another girl and we used to travel to school on the bus together. One morning she wasn't there and I got off at the wrong stop and couldn't see where I was. I felt completely lost. At home I used to cry myself to sleep. I tried to look on the bright side. At least I wasn't sitting on my bed for lessons, but I found school rules hard to understand. I landed up in the head's office – probably for talking – and then got told off for looking at the pictures in her room. But I hadn't been told this was wrong. To be set down in a place, where no one tells you the rules, and then get punished for breaking them seemed very hard.'

For some the contrast between longing expectation and cruel reality was made plain even before they reached home. Bill Macauley had left Stanley camp after three and a half years of internment and was sailing for his Belfast home when his ship, the *Empress of Australia*, put in at Gibraltar for mail.

A letter from his sister May was waiting for him. The letter broke the news that his father had died in September 1943 and his beloved brother Jim had gone missing in action in September 1944 – more than a year earlier.

Bill says: 'The four mates I had palled up with on board ship had all received good news. They did their best to comfort me. The shock took away my power of speech. I passed someone the letter and they handed it round. They didn't know what to say. I found out afterwards that they kept a round-the-clock watch on me. I felt I was surrounded by nothing. Everything that I had been looking forward to had dropped away. My brother Jim had been everything to me, my best mate. I loved him deeply and I looked up to him. He was such a fine man and I wanted to grow up like him. I'd been looking forward so much to telling him about everything that had happened since I said goodbye to him as a tearful fifteen-year-old at the docks in Kowloon in November 1941, a month before Pearl Harbor. I never for a moment thought then that that would be the last time I'd see him. If it hadn't been for those blokes I might well have topped myself.'

Bill docked at Liverpool on 28 October and took another ship to Belfast, missing his mother in the process as she had gone to Liverpool to meet him. He went to the family home and found it empty. A neighbour took him back to her house until his sister returned from work. As they arrived together at his mother's flat a telegram arrived. 'It was addressed to Mum but as she wasn't there our neighbour said I should open it. The words read "Confirmed. Sgt Jim Macauley killed in action." It meant that they had found the crew. He had been shot down over Hungary. That was it. It was true. Jim was dead. I felt as if I'd been kicked in the teeth.'

The first few months after his homecoming were a time of deep unhappiness. 'I wandered about in a daze. I used to get on the tram and ride round the city for hours on end. One of the drivers had been a good friend of my brother Jim's and he kept an eye on me. I had an attack of malaria while I was on the tram. The driver stopped the tram and took me home.'

He found family life particularly hard. 'My mother and my sister had two years and a year to get used to the death of my father and brother. I had had a week. My relationship with my mother wasn't easy. To her I was still the fifteen-year-old she'd seen off to boarding school before the war. She was just pleased that I had come through it and couldn't understand why I didn't feel more positive. She expected me to settle straight back into normal life, get a job, marry a good Belfast girl ...'

No one asked him what life had been like in camp. 'The family had got a Government leaflet on the mantelpiece about how to cope with returning prisoners. It warned about odd behaviour, disturbed sleep patterns ... I put it on the fire. We'd had lectures on board ship about what to expect when we got home. We were expressly told, "Don't tell your folks how bad it was. It will only upset them. England has had a rough time too. Concentrate on getting on with your life."'

The atmosphere at home became so strained that a family conference was arranged to decide what to do about Bill. 'Only my sister seemed to understand that I needed time. She said to my mother and my aunts, "Let him be. He'll find a way."'

Bill thinks that not talking about it was, on the whole, good advice. 'It's better not to dwell on the past.' He did, however, feel cut off from the world around him. The inflexible nature of post-war British bureaucracy didn't help. The Food Office refused to issue him with a ration book until he produced his birth certificate. 'It was only after my sister pointed out that I had just got off a troopship, having spent three and a half years in a prison camp, and that my birth certificate was probably on some rubbish heap in China, that the woman relented and issued me with clothing coupons.'

Another disappointment awaited him on the education front. In Stanley, unlike in other camps, educational records did not start being kept until 1943. Bill's classes had ended in 1942. 'I knew that I was behind educationally so I went to see the head of the local technical college about re-establishing my educational qualifications. He told me that it would take two years for me to retake School Certificate up to Matriculation standard. I had missed the boat educationally. Mum only had a widow's pension and she still had Joe, my younger brother, to raise. I had to get a job.' Three months after he returned from Stanley the doctor passed him as fit for work and he went to work in a factory.

Jose Chamberlain had also spent internment without parents, her mother having died in camp and her father having been a prisoner of the kempeitai. In a camp in Shanghai with her father after the end of the war she found herself facing the prospect of travelling to England alone. 'My father had been offered a job in Hong Kong, which was still a British colony. He asked if I would be prepared to go to England on my own, but I found the prospect of England rather daunting. I'd only been there once, when I was four. I said no. I regret that bitterly now as he could have got a proper job with a pension if he had stayed out east. Apparently, Dad had contacted a distant cousin who was wealthy and had no children. She lived in a big house in Weston-super-Mare with staff and she had agreed to bring me up and educate me. But when we docked there was a message for Dad. The cousin had died unexpectedly the previous week and her husband was not inclined to look after me.' Jose went to her maternal grandmother in Birmingham but they had been bombed out and were living with Jose's aunt and her daughter in cramped conditions over a shop. She then moved in with her father's sister while her father looked for work. She was struck by how much lower living standards were in Britain, which seemed to be a land of outside lavatories, gas lighting and outhouse kitchens. Eventually Jose's father put her into a convent boarding school. They lived on money from a handful of Chinese ornaments her father had managed to hang onto from their former life. Eventually he found work in Germany as a caretaker/security guard, far below his former status. Jose was the only non-Catholic at the school and was referred to by the nuns as the 'heathen'. At the convent all the pupils had to work. Jose was responsible for the younger children aged five and six. 'I had to get them up in the morning, get them ready for breakfast, put them to bed at night and then polish all their shoes.' The winter was so cold the children had to break the ice in the old-fashioned wash-basins in the mornings.

'When I went home for Christmas I told my aunt I was being picked on as a heathen and they baptised me. I don't know why I hadn't been christened before – maybe it was due to the war.' Jose, too, was behind educationally. She struggled with arithmetic because she didn't know her tables and later left the convent for a local state school to save her father money. Now she lived as a lodger with a widow with two daughters. 'After Dad went to Germany I never had any family life. The Christmas I was in digs I felt as if I were a complete outsider. The landlady had her own children and grand-children and she had bought them lots of presents. There was nothing for me. Dad had given me some money so I bought my own Christmas presents. I've always hated Christmas since then.' Jose left school, qualified as a shorthand typist and went to work as a kennel maid.

When Sylvia Williams sailed into Liverpool she found the welcome a total contrast to the warmth and compassion that had greeted her family in America. 'It was cold and grey. The British didn't seem particularly interested in people coming back from the Far East and what we had been through. Perhaps it wasn't surprising. Poor England had been through so much. The Salvation Army or Red Cross greeted us with cups of tea, but that was all. We were allowed double rations for a few weeks after we got back.' Sylvia's family moved in with her grandmother and she was put into boarding school in Northwood, Middlesex. 'Both parents accompanied me to the school by taxi. I had never been away from my parents before. I was received by Matron, who wore a big starched hat and a blue cloak. As my parents drove off she swirled her cloak round me and then I was shown to the room I was to share with other girls.'

Like so many other returning internees Sylvia was unhappy at school. 'I was left out and teased by the other girls. I was way behind the others educationally because of the years in camp. I'd never done algebra or geometry or Latin. By the second term I had turned in on myself and become a bookworm. I made one friend and although she was already part of a group she adopted me. That made it bearable.' The cold was almost as big a problem as the bullying. 'The winter of 1947 was bitterly cold. I counted thirty chilblains on my fingers. I was frozen in bed and was reduced to putting the bedside mat on my bed for extra warmth.'

Sylvia's father went back to Manila, but came back after a year and, in his mid-fifties, had to take early retirement. Sylvia believes internment was responsible. 'He had what we today would regard as post traumatic stress-type symptoms. I was allowed to go to Tilbury with my mother to meet him when he came back to England. I was always a bit afraid of him. He was very authoritarian and rather irritable. The war was very hard on men. That generation had been brought up to be the providers, the protectors, of their womenfolk and children. Internment prevented them from doing that and I think many felt unmanned by the experience. What he went through in the war, losing friends, enduring near-starvation changed his character.'

Getting over the ill-effects of camp took time. But there were up-sides. On occasion the shared experience of camp turned out to be a blessing. Cyril Mack and his family returned to England by troopship in April 1946, swapping exotic Shanghai for Briston, a small village in Norfolk, the home of his paternal grandparents. Cyril and his brother Roy put their names down for the local grammar school. First, however, they had to pass a pretty rigorous test set by the Norfolk Education Committee to establish if they would have passed the Eleven plus. They had missed, effectively, four of the most formative years of schooling. It was while they were facing this challenge that the old boy network of internment came to their aid. By remarkable coincidence, the Palmer family, who had also been interned in Yangchow, had also moved into Briston. Their son, Colin, who had helped in the hospital in camp, had taken his School Certificate in camp under P. C. Matthews, achieving very high marks. 'My father appreciating that', remembers Cyril, 'we would still be somewhat rusty, asked Colin if he would give us some tutoring and he was more than happy to do so. The three of us spent many hours in our grandfather's outhouse preparing for our test.'

Although Colin was four years older than the Mack boys there was an instant bond. They were all three strangers in a foreign land. Cyril recalls: 'There was much reminiscing and a kind of nostalgia because we missed our old friends – three ex-Shanghai boys sitting around a scrubbed outhouse table in a tiny village set in the heart of the wilds of Norfolk, it was a far cry from Yangchow ...'

It was the days when intellectual rigour was expected from the ablest pupils. The Mack brothers were subjected to a daunting raft of tests, administered by no less a figure than the Chief Education Officer; oral tests for English, Latin and French and a written test for maths. Both passed and started school in September 1946. Cyril went into Form IV. Roy should have been in the Lower VIth, but as he had not been able to sit for his School Certificate in 1945–46 due to the end of the war, he was put down a year.

Surprisingly, the major handicap Cyril suffered as a result of internment was not due to gaps in knowledge, but something far more basic – he had never written in pen. The teacher noticed that he used a pencil when writing an essay and handled the situation with sensitivity. At fourteen Cyril found himself having to master the challenge of writing neatly with a dip pen. 'It took me a little while to learn to write neatly in ink, certainly to get up to required speed, without corrections and blotches ... initially I kept digging the point of the nib into the paper ... and this would flick and spray the ink all over the place. If I had to nominate any one thing that I had missed in my education because of the war, it would have to be the use of pen and ink. '

Both Mack boys did well at school. Roy passed Higher School Cert. and became head boy. Cyril came third in his form order in the first term and from then on came top. He, too, passed School Cert. and Higher School Cert. He was offered the chance of going to university but decided he had had enough of schooling. Instead he went into the army and did National Service.

Margaret Blair and her family returned to her father's native Scotland aboard the ship appropriately named *Highland Chieftain*. Before they left Shanghai, they paid one last visit to the racecourse, focus of so much colourful Imperial-style pageantry in the pre-war world that already seemed like a dream. She recognised no landmarks. 'Everywhere we looked there were tangled grass and waist-high weeds, with discarded Japanese army tin plates and bottles lying in the undergrowth. The racecourse and tennis courts, cricket fields, baseball diamonds and bowling greens were all overgrown. It was hard to see where anything had been.' For a long time Margaret yearned for her old life in the east, hating the cold grey climate of Scotland and the 'bitter Calvinistic character of the Scots'. She and her brother Gordon were often ill in the years after they returned home. They caught cold frequently and suffered from a persistent lack of energy, which Margaret thinks may have been due to homesickness for China. Problems with her eyesight, which her family attributed to the years of neglect in camp, continued to worry Margaret's parents. Prolonged reading caused eyestrain, leading to the prescription of ever-stronger glasses. The children's health problems led their father to move the family away from the polluted air of Glasgow, where they were staying with relatives, to a small town where they gradually recovered their health. In the mercilessly cold winter of 1946–47 the deep pond of Margaret's teacher froze solid, killing her fish.

David Nicoll returned with his family to Edinburgh, where they too moved in with grandparents. David also was behind educationally. Though in many respects schooling in Chapei had been rigorous, there were gaps. There had been no professional teachers in camp, only businessmen and missionaries who did their best. Textbooks had been in very short supply. 'I knew nothing about science – physics and chemistry – and knew no Latin.' Because of this he was put in a class where he was a year and a half older than everyone else. However, he seemed to adapt to life in Britain with fewer difficulties than many and caught up educationally, reading Law at university.

Barbara Bruce's family decided to go back to England at the end of the war because Barbara's paternal grandmother was English and mother and son hadn't seen each other for twenty-five years. They embarked on SS *Antenor*. The Red Cross met them at Liverpool and directed them to their various trains, supplying sandwiches for the journey. The Bruces went to Deal in Kent where their grandmother's two-bedroom terraced house was stretched to the limit by the arrival of seven more people. Barbara's grandmother was overjoyed at being reunited with the son she had not seen for so long. Her 'welcome home' treat, however, failed to have the impact she hoped. 'We had a great family lunch together and then my Gran said, "I've a surprise for you Ernest", and promptly laid a large rice pudding on the table. After a few choice comments ... Gran explained that she had saved her precious food coupons from her ration book so that Dad could have his favourite pudding when he came home – not realising that we had seen and eaten enough of the stuff to last a lifetime!'"

18

Fighting Back

———

The shadow cast by internment has continued to make itself felt throughout the lives of many of the people in this story, long after they were reclaimed by freedom. Not all the effects have been negative, especially among those who remained with their families. Those effects may be superficial – being unable to discard paper used only on one side or hating certain foods. Many internees loathe rice to this day and Dick Germain, who grew a lot of tomatoes in his camp, still can't abide them. In some cases the effects are more profound. A lucky few found inspiration through close contact with dedicated professionals who led the way into satisfying careers. Some, forgetting the hunger and the illnesses, recall with nostalgia the wealth and variety of playmates. But others, parted from parents and loved ones, saw nearly four years of their childhood stolen. For them the shadow has been longest.

Few have had resort to counselling. Members of the war generation have little sense of self-entitlement. Moreover, they take the commendably unselfish view that others suffered more than they did and that it is better not to dwell on the past. But there have been breakdowns. Many believe the war is responsible in various ways for their underachieving professionally, while others feel life in an internment camp has left a legacy of emotional problems – anger, lack of confidence and feelings of isolation. Uniting both groups is a sadness caused by the premature deaths of so many of their parents.

Some ex-internees have largely happy memories. David Nicoll regards himself as having 'come through unscathed'. 'In a way the war was good for me. I did not have many friends prior to

World War II, but from Dec 24th 1941, three weeks after Pearl Harbor, and the day my family moved out of our flat and into the Church Hall, Shanghai, until September 17th 1945, the day we returned to the Custom House in Shanghai, I was never without pals.'

David spent fifteen years overseas and fully expected to remain single. He returned to Scotland in 1973 and married three years later at the age of forty-four. He has brought his own two children up very differently from the way he grew up. 'I was ultra-keen on stability. We have lived in the same house since a few months before my son's birth – nearly 33 years, which is quite a contrast with my own 46 places of abode and 60-odd moves.' David has also sought far greater involvement in the rearing of his children than was the case with his parents. 'When they were between four and twelve I increasingly had to attend meetings in London, for which purpose I could have flown down, had dinner and a night in a hotel, but I much preferred to take the night sleeper that enabled me to brush the children's shoes every evening. And I always read them a bedtime story.' His sister Ella, now eighty-five, is still active although she has had stomach problems and gets painful twinges when sitting or lying down, both the effects, she believes, of the blunt needle that broke off inside her in camp.

Keith Martin, the star of the Yangchow C sixth form, was predictably successful in his career, rising to become a top executive at Shell. For him, and for many other ex-internees, the legacy of camp was a horror of waste. This, he found, was a universal bond between men who had known prolonged hunger. He was once sent to a conference in the States consisting of thirty Americans and Britons. On his CV he put down that he had been a civilian prisoner of war. 'On the first day the leader said, "There are two former POWs here." I thought, I wonder who the other one is. That night we were dining at a long trestle table and the big burly American opposite me said, "So you're the other POW." I said, "How do you know?" And he said, "Look at your plate, look at mine and look at the others. They're the only clean plates on the table."'[1]

Colin Palmer was one of the lucky ones who found his way to a successful career as a direct result of what turned out to be the camps' old boy network. After he had sat his School Certificate he was expected to help with chores in camp, so he began helping one of the two doctors, cleaning the 'consulting room' and acting as a theatre assistant in operations. 'Dr Bolton was a very kind man. I was coming to the age when I would have to think about a career, if and when peace came. I had reached the required standard, having got three distinctions and two credits so he asked me if I would be interested in making medicine my career. If I was, he could open doors. I said I would and when we returned to Britain he took me under his wing. He was an old Barts man. When I applied it turned out that a contemporary of his was Dean of the Medical College so I was in.' Colin went on to specialise in ophthalmology and held the post of consultant in Sheffield for many years.

Ron Huckstep was another former internee who found his career – also in medicine – as a direct result of camp. He was in the middle of taking his School Certificate at the age of fifteen when the Japanese occupied Shanghai. He was lucky to be interned with a Cambridge-trained missionary surgeon of extraordinary dedication who taught him dissection and anatomy in the most unconventional, but thorough way. After the war the same surgeon was appointed as a lecturer in Pathology at Cambridge and became Ron's tutor. Ron went on to specialise in orthopaedics, achieving the rank of professor. What's more, Ron's unconventional training was so thorough that, far from holding him back, it ended up fast-tracking him.

'I went to Cambridge in March 1946 at the age of nineteen and would normally have spent a year with premedical studies before being accepted as a medical student there in October 1947. I would have then spent three years studying for the BA (Hons). I was allowed to take the exam in two years as a result of the work in the camp.'

The other truth he maintains camp revealed is that conventional education takes far more time than is necessary. 'I know now that about twelve years of schooling is twice the amount necessary for children willing to work.'

Richard Dobson, who was in a camp on Java, recovered from the ordeal of being tortured by sheer effort of will. 'I realised that if you think about these things all the time you have no energy left to do your job and create a life for yourself.' Richard fulfilled his dream, begun in camp, of becoming a naval architect and had a successful and enjoyable career. He believes internment has, however, left its mark.

'I learned in camp to keep a low profile; always to stand in the middle, never on the outside, never to put your head above the parapet – if you did you were more likely to get beaten. Unfortunately I have never been able to shed that habit and it affected my career. I did well, but, if I had not suffered from such a deep reluctance to draw attention to myself, I could have achieved even more.' Internment also had another, more unexpected effect.

'I only ever wear white shirts and I always wear a tie. After the war coloured shirts were fashionable and my mother used to buy me blue ones or yellow ones. But I would always tell her to take them back as I only wanted white. Today people dress in a more casual way, but I always feel the need to wear a tie. I get teased by my friends who say I make them feel under-dressed. I didn't really understand my motivation until one day, not long ago, the scene of the commandant in camp came back to me – me with my filthy shorts and bare feet and him with his white collar and highly shone black boots. I remembered the pledge I had made to myself – that when I was free I would have polished shoes and an immaculate white shirt.'

It was only when he retired that Richard allowed himself to think about what he had gone through during the war again. He remembered Wim, the fourteen-year-old who had also been tortured by the kempeitai. Uncannily, within a month of Wim coming into his thoughts he received a letter from him. 'He had found my address through a Dutch association of former internees. This was forty years after we were prisoners together.' The letter began: 'I hope you will reply to this letter!' Wim came to England for a reunion with Richard. 'He brought with him a postcard that had been sent by his mother to his father when the father was working as a prisoner on the Burma railway. She had just learned that her fourteen-year-old son had been arrested. She had written 'Wim has been picked up. Do not worry. He's with Richard.' To see that card, written in 1942 and sent to a place of such suffering, was very emotional. Internment has left its shadow on Wim, too. Richard's elder daughter Eleanor visited him in Canada and while they were chatting late one night, he became upset. 'He told her, "I betrayed your father." It is terrible to think he has been carrying that burden all these years.'

Bill Macauley had had a harrowing return to Britain, learning of the deaths of his father and brother on the way home. After a brief stint in a factory he joined the RAF and began training as a nursing orderly. He thought he had recovered, but seven years after the end of the war colleagues on night duty would find him sitting facing the wall, oblivious of his surroundings and chain smoking.

'Apparently I'd been doing this for some time. I wasn't sleeping properly. I don't remember much about it. I thought I was doing a good job. I was on the ophthalmic ward at the time in my second year of training. Several nights in a row the wing commander, who was a neuro psychiatrist, dropped in, ostensibly to see one of the patients, and would stay and chat to me over tea and biscuits. I thought it was a bit odd for a doctor of his seniority to make so many visits to one patient. He asked if I'd been in a prison camp, which struck me as odd. I didn't know about what they called FEPOW (Far East Prisoner of War) syndrome, which included disturbed sleep patterns and odd behaviour, but he did. I think one of the matrons must have had an unofficial word and asked him to have a look at me. Normally if there was anything wrong psychologically you were discharged, but in my case nothing was put on the record and I was simply sent to sickbay where I lay fallow for six months.'

This 'hiccup', as Bill calls it, cost him the promotion to sergeant that would otherwise have come his way. And there were other affects.

'I had a lot of nightmares, where I'd want to run away or be wanting to fight someone. For a long time I was very aggressive. I'd fight at the drop of a hat.'

Although Bill rose to the top of the nursing profession, retiring from the NHS as a charge nurse, he feels that, but for internment, he might have aimed higher on the career ladder.

'In Canton our GP, an Austrian refugee, thought I was bright enough for a career in medicine. I used to go to his consulting rooms every week in the summer of 1941 and do odd jobs there. He told me that if I was able to pass my Matric. I should stay on in Hong Kong and attend medical school there and then he would help get me into practice. I did my exams in camp, but unfortunately I did them in 1942 and they didn't keep them and send them in to the appropriate authorities after the war. They only did that from 1943 onwards.'

Bill has been back twice to Hong Kong. He wanted to make a private trip to the graveyard in what was once Stanley Civil Internment Camp to visit the graves of so many friends and acquaintances. There, among the graves of Hong Kong's earliest European pioneers, he remembered friends who had died so avoidably as a consequence of internment. The mass grave of the fourteen prisoners killed as a result of a misdirected US bomb which fell on the camp during the start of the fight-back on 15 January 1945 held a special poignancy. Among the dead was the wife of one of his schoolteachers in camp – 'she was young and gorgeous. They had only recently got married.' There was the father of someone he had known as a small and bubbly little girl in camp, who had died at fifty-four. Saddest of all for him was the grave of Muriel Hassard, the former matron of the Diocesan Boys' School. Bill had known her since the age of twelve and, in the absence of his mother, she had always kept an eye out for him in camp, remembering his birthdays and sending him notes and a small sum of money on that day. One note dated 1944, written, typically, on a tin label, and carefully kept for more than sixty years, reads:

Dear Bill,
Just to wish you many happy returns on your birthday tomorrow but not I hope in Stanley. I am sorry I cannot get out to buy you something so I am enclosing a small item that you can spend when the shops open ... I'll be seeing you. As ever,
Matron

It was on one of these trips that Bill finally learnt the identity of the young soldier he had helped to bury on Christmas Day 1941. Bill was told the soldier's name by the current headmaster when he visited his old school. He was Ronald Maxwell, who had joined the Hong Kong Volunteer Defence Corps and died at the age of twenty-two.

The soldier had been reinterred in the cathedral's main cemetery. In 2005 Bill spoke to the curator of the cemetery and asked to be directed to the grave. 'He told me, "That one has been reinterred", and I replied, "I know."' Bill went to the grave. 'I stood there and spoke to him. I told him, "I was one of the four who buried you the first time and since 1941 I have not known who the hell you were. Now I know. God Bless, Ronnie."'

As part of the campaign for compensation launched by the Association of British Civilian Internees Far East Region (ABCIFER), Jose Chamberlain put into words her thoughts about the effect being interned had had on her life.

'From the time I was interned and whilst growing to adulthood, I had no one to turn to for advice and comfort. I had to stand on my own feet. It was a very difficult and lonely time. My father would not discuss ... internment and I learned not to ask questions ... My own memories are still very few, and even things I would expect to have remembered remain blank. I put this down to the trauma suffered as a child during internment and the ensuing years.'

Jose was one of many ex-internees who spent her professional life working at a less demanding level than her intelligence should have directed, due to a disrupted education. She spent many years as a switchboard operator. Her father returned to England in 1958 and bought a house on the coast, but relations between them were not easy. 'I felt great affection for him, but he was still the same rather severe person he had always been.' Jose kept house for him until he remarried. He had two more children by his second wife, whom he met while working in Germany. Jose did not feel welcome in the new ménage and does not see her half sisters.

Jose has never married. 'I never really had boyfriends, though I get on well with men as friends. I've spent most of my life in single rooms. After being on your own a lot you get used to it. You get very selfish. I never wanted children.'

Iris Krass also did not marry and struggled with undiagnosed depression for many years after the war. Unlike Jose, however, she had her mother's support when she came to England. It was her mother who typed the legions of letters that eventually won Iris a place at medical school and led to the medical career she has found deeply fulfilling. Things didn't go so well for her brother and sister. Iris blames herself for not looking after her brother more in camp, although in Santo Tomas the sexes were segregated and she hardly saw him. 'Peter found it difficult to get work. He hadn't been trained for anything. No one had taken much notice of his needs while he was interned.' She found out after the war that her brother, whom she describes as a 'very meek sort of boy', was even put in prison in camp. It must have been a frightening ordeal for a young boy with no relations to comfort him – 'I think the prison was run by the internees, not the Japanese. He was sentenced to two weeks for having falsified his meal ticket. They were punched and he had pushed the punched bit back into place so that it looked new. He only did it because he was so hungry.' Peter never settled after the war. 'He took various office jobs. Then he had a breakdown. They said he was schizophrenic. He was in a mental hospital for quite a while.'

Iris's sister, who was four years younger, had what today would be termed learning difficulties. She was very distressed when she was parted from her mother in camp when she was only twelve. Iris feels she would have benefited from counselling when she came back, 'but of course people didn't in those days'. 'She managed to do simple jobs, like washing up. She married a kind man and he looked after her.' Life was a struggle for the family throughout the Fifties. Iris's father returned from Shanghai in 1950, having escaped internment due to his Russian nationality 'Things had been hard for him as he had had no idea what had happened to his wife and children from 1941 until the end of the war.' As was so often the way, he never spoke about the war, or asked his family what they had been through. A year later, Iris's mother died of a brain tumour at fifty-three. At the age of thirty, her brother Peter killed himself.

Iris feels the habit she developed in camp of withdrawing into herself has had an effect on her subsequent life. 'Children like me who were on their own had no means of developing as a person in camp. You withdrew into a kind of chrysalis where time stood still. You didn't emerge from that chrysalis until it was over, but for some of us it has seemed as if part of our personality has remained embedded in that camp experience. In my own case I have never married and I think perhaps this was linked to my lack of socialising, my "self-protecting" lack of engagement with people that seemed to continue after camp. Instead, I became totally absorbed in my medical studies. I think I was quite depressed over a period. However, all this passed over time and I loved my job and the contact it gave me with so many people.'

There have been physical effects too. A number of former internees have suffered all their lives from health problems that had their origins in camp. In a small number of cases the shadow of internment has returned to haunt them later in life. Dick Germain developed heart trouble in his late sixties. While he was in hospital, a blood test revealed that he had the potentially fatal liver condition hepatitis B.

'I had no idea how I contracted it. Apparently it had been dormant for many years and had now become active. The treatment was quite unpleasant. I had to inject myself with the drug interferon every day for nine months. I was very concerned as to how I got it and did some research. Eventually a friend located an American doctor who had contracted hepatitis B through the water. They took the drinking water from the ground where sewage had been disposed of.' The only silver lining is that Dick now receives a small war pension on account of having contracted 'chronic liver disease due to detention by the enemy'.

One of the saddest things many internees had to cope with after they returned to Britain, longing to enjoy normal family life again, was the early death of a parent. These deaths seem to have been more common among fathers. Their health, one suspects, was undermined, not just by the lack of food, or any ill-treatment they had undergone, but by the desperate, crushing burden of the future. These were educated, skilled men, trained in administering and running every aspect of a colonial society. That world had abandoned them. The question now was how to provide for wife and children in a ruined world where they had neither prospects, contacts or savings? Many fathers collapsed under the burden. Margaret and Gordon Blair lost their father at the age of fifty-four, David Nicoll's father died at fifty-two, Iris Krass's mother died at fifty-three. The father of Ron Bridge, the boy who had given his lead soldier to create a false palate for a baby girl born with a cleft palate in Weihsien camp, died of a heart attack at fifty. Sylvia Williams's father had to take early retirement due to stress. These deaths make very sad reading. Occasionally, however, in that harsh post-war world of despair and difficulty there appeared a spark of hope, a herald of better times to come. Paula Rose was one of these sparks. Barbara Bruce had found the physical side of life in England very hard to get used to after the tropical climate of Singapore. She shivered in that terrible winter of 1946–47, never thinking she'd be grateful for the scratchy woollen stockings the Red Cross had given her on the journey home. She pined for the warmth she had left behind, but in Paula Rose she had something that would be a permanent reminder of that other life. One day after the end of the war in Singapore, Barbara's mother noticed that one of the servants was missing. She was stunned when the woman's husband said that she was at the hospital having a baby, not having been aware that she was pregnant. When the woman returned to work the next day, Barbara's mother asked her where the baby was. 'I left it at the hospital for the orphanage to collect. I did not want a daughter,' the woman replied. Barbara's mother, who already had five children of her own, ordered her to go back and claim the baby, and told her she would bring her up.

'She adopted her at a week old. When we left Singapore to come to England we brought her with us.' Barbara and Paula Rose have remained on the fondest of terms. 'I loved her as a baby,' says Barbara. 'We grew up together. She's my little sister.' When Barbara recently moved to be nearer her daughter, Paula was worried that she might find the drive too arduous – so Barbara gave her a satellite navigation system for Christmas.

Settling into a 'normal' life seems to have been hardest for the children who had had to endure the ordeal of internment without their parents. These included the children of missionaries who had been left to board at Chefoo School in the far north of China and found themselves trapped by the war. These parents, deeply religious and inclined to be inflexible, clashed with their troubled children as they fought to resume the reins of parental authority in a changed world.

K Strange (later Foster), arrived back in England with her younger sister and her mother destitute and homeless. For five years they lived as guests in a mission house in a tough neighbourhood in London. The girls, who knew nothing about the facts of life and had never even been on a bus, attended a local girls' school where the pupils were as worldly as they were innocent. Tension grew as K's mother disapproved of everything her elder daughter did, especially opting to go to art school, which she regarded as 'wicked'.

'I began to question the kind of parenting I had received, even before I went into camp. Increasingly I felt my sister and I had been abandoned. This feeling increased when I married and had children of my own. I asked myself how my mother could have left me alone in a boarding school at the age of seven for years at a time. I saw then that my father had been a missionary first and a father second.'

K's mother refused to talk about her children's internment and was scandalised when, after an unhappy marriage, her daughter divorced. 'She couldn't cope with that. She was living in a mission home where everything had to be seen to be perfect.'

Having been unhappy for many years, in her fifties K began having counselling. 'It was the most liberating thing I've ever done. It helped me to evaluate what had happened to me. I realised that I didn't have to believe this and that and I stopped going to church. My mother told me she was ashamed of me.'

K says she is not angry with her parents. 'They thought what they were doing was for the best. But when you add being parted from them at seven onto two years of not having anyone put an arm round you, or hug and kiss you, the effects build up. My father died in 1941 while I was at school. A teacher sat me on her lap to break the news, but that sort of physical contact wasn't natural and it never happened again. The result of all this is that you are not at home in your own body and that makes things very difficult in marriage. One of the things I said in one of my counselling sessions was that I felt very unimportant.' K feels that with time, she has recovered. 'I don't know that I would say I'm happy, but I feel fine. I have three daughters and a son who are great. They are all married and they all work.'

As they launched themselves on the world of employment some internees sought to try to use their war experiences as a force for good in the world. Sylvia Williams was one of these. Sylvia not only had suffered hunger and a badly disrupted education in Santo Tomas, she had also seen the war destroy her father. She became passionately interested in peace when she started work, 'trying to think of ways I could help heal the dreadful thing that happened'. She became a Quaker, although she is not a pacifist. 'If it had not been for General MacArthur my family would not have survived. I am a moderate person but I believe you have to stand up to evil.' After a short career as a journalist, she found what she was looking for. 'I began working with the bereaved. I am interested in other people who have to live with unacceptable situations. Now I am a psychotherapist.'

Sylvia does not resent internment for what it took from her childhood. That does not mean, however, that she has entirely put it behind her. 'I feel sad at the way internment prevented my father from being able to work again. In my camp we saw fighting and death at close quarters and I still feel anguish over the deaths of so many of the internees and the young troops, some of whom I had got to know. They were happy, friendly young men who still had their life before them.'

In the mid-1990s a group of former internees, still angry at the lack of acknowledgement by the Japanese of the hardship endured by them and their families during the war, set up the Association of British Civilian Internees Far East Region. After years of dogged lobbying by ABCIFER, and despite failure to win either reparation or an apology from Japan, in 2000 the British Government decided it would settle what it termed a debt of honour, agreeing to a payment of £10,000 to every British citizen who had been interned by the Japanese. Although some claims, regrettably, have still not been settled, the gesture went some way to assuaging the bad memories for many former prisoners. For those who had been interned in Shanghai the new millennium brought more celebrations. In 2005 the crew of HMS *Belfast*, now moored on the Thames rather than Whangpoo River, threw a party to celebrate the sixtieth anniversary of the children's party held in Shanghai on 1 October 1945. Those who had attended the original party were guests of honour. As many of them had not seen each for half a century, name badges were the order of the day. The crew were determined the returning guests would feel at home, despite their advancing years. There was even a diver's suit, which they were invited to punch, just as they had in 1945. It was a poignant occasion. Dick Germain, who attended both parties, recalled, 'Not many of us would have been up to swings and slides this time around and we didn't eat so much that we were sick. We were quite happy nibbling canapés, sipping drinks and swapping memories.'

Father Thornton, an Irish Catholic priest who had become an inspirational teacher in internment, had loomed large in the life of the younger pupils in Yangchow. Most, embarked on a new life in

Britain, never expected to see him again. But in 1952 Cyril Mack unexpectedly found their paths crossing once more. Cyril had joined the army on leaving school and at that time was based in Hong Kong. After the war Father Thornton had been appointed pastor at Yangchow, but in July 1951 he had been imprisoned by the Communists who had starved, manacled and generally ill-treated him. By one of those coincidences which seem to link people who have shared extreme experiences, a year later Cyril was manning an observation post at the frontier between communist China and Kowloon, when he received word 'that he and three other ... very ill priests were going to cross the border'. Cyril watched through his binoculars and immediately identified the familiar tall figure of Father Thornton, now thin and wasted, supporting himself on one of the other priests, as he hobbled painfully to freedom. It was a moving moment. 'I remember wondering what he would say if he knew that one of his young pupils from Form Two in YC was up on the ridge watching him, making sure that he crossed over safely.' Much had happened in both their lives since they had last met as prisoners of the Japanese. But as Cyril watched him standing there on the station platform, 'the seven years that had passed since those days dropped away and the memories rushed in'. In spite of the tears that pricked, thinking of old times and the suffering the priest had endured at the hands of the Communists, Cyril was cheered when he saw the priest throw back his head in laughter: 'Although I could not hear him I knew that it would be the same guffaw that I used to hear in Yangchow.'

Father Thornton was taken to hospital in Hong Kong for several weeks but Cyril couldn't get leave to visit him. They never saw each other again. As for Father Thornton (who lived another forty years) a fragment of the past he had shared with those child prisoners remained etched affectionately on his memory, just as they treasured their memories of him. After the war the priest visited the old camp in Yangchow with the staff of the American Episcopal Mission who had reclaimed it. When they reached the old school room where he had introduced his hungry young charges to the spiritual nourishment of the cream of English literature, Father Thornton said: 'This was Form Two classroom where thirteen little heroes ... got down to their three Rs as they munched on their rusks and lard.

Should I teach till ninety they will ever remain my favourite pupils.'²

No other group of children in history has had the crucial years of their childhood stolen from them the way these children had. Their own offspring inhabit a different universe and take freedom, plenty and comfort for granted. To them eating foul food because one is hungry, or wearing peculiar clothes just to keep warm, belong to the long-vanished world of Hogarth's gin alley – not to the recent past. Their parents hoard leftovers and use and reuse every scrap of soap or paper. Old habits die hard. The young tease them for it and they put up with the teasing good-humouredly. The war changed their lives irrevocably and a sizeable chunk of their early lives was not happy, the way childhood is meant to be. But, in common with the rest of the war generation, they bear it lightly and rarely complain.

Father Thornton might have been speaking for all the children who endured internment when he called his charges little heroes. It is an epitaph that fits them well.

Notes

———

INTRODUCTION

1 Mrs T. Ellis, *Hear No Evil; Childhood Lessons Learned in Captivity*, unpublished manuscript, Imperial War Museum documents and sound section 95/14/1
2 Author interview with Richard Dobson

CHAPTER ONE: CAUGHT IN A NET

1 Mrs Olga Moss, Private papers, Imperial War Museum documents and sound section 93/21/1

CHAPTER TWO: PARADISE LOST

1 Mel Bruce, *Beneath the Rising Sun*, unpublished manuscript, Imperial War Museum documents and sound section 02/32/1
2 Greg Leck, *Captives of Empire: The Japanese Internment of Allied Civilians in China, 1941–1945* (Shandy Press, 2006)
3 Neil Begley, *An Australian's Childhood in China Under the Japanese* (Kangaroo Press, 1995)
4 David Nicoll, *Young Shanghailander*, unpublished memoir
5 Leck, *Captives of Empire*
6 Leck, ibid.
7 Leck, ibid.
8 Ron Huckstep, unpublished memoir
9 Hope Lee, unpublished manuscript and microfilm, Imperial War Museum documents and sound section PP/MCR/210

10 Cyril Mack, unpublished memoir
11 Huckstep, unpublished memoir
12 Huckstep, ibid.

CHAPTER THREE: MELTED LIKE BUTTER

1 Begley, *An Australian's Childhood*
2 Leck, *Captives of Empire*
3 Leck, ibid.
4 Leck, ibid.
5 Nicoll, *Young Shanghailander*
6 Leck, *Captives of Empire*
7 Leck, ibid.
8 Nicoll, *Young Shanghailander*
9 Nicoll, ibid.
10 Mack, unpublished memoir
11 Mel Bruce, private papers
12 Mack, unpublished memoir
13 Mack, ibid.
14 Mack, quoted in Leck, *Captives of Empire*
15 Mack, unpublished memoir
16 Mack, quoted in Leck, *Captives of Empire*
17 Nicoll, private papers

CHAPTER FOUR: GOODBYE TO ALL THAT

1 *Multicultural Japan* (Cambridge University Press, 1996)
2 Joyce Storey, interview with author
3 Irene Duguid, private papers, Imperial War Museum documents and sound section 85/29/1 and 1a
4 Leck, *Captives of Empire*
5 Leck, ibid.
6 Margaret Blair, *Gudao, Lone Islet: The War Years in Shanghai, A Childhood Memoir* (Trafford Publishing, 2007)
7 Leck, *Captives of Empire*
8 Nicoll, *Young Shanghailander*
9 Nicoll, ibid.
10 Leck, *Captives of Empire*
11 Nicoll, *Young Shanghailander*
12 Nicoll, ibid.
13 Nicoll, ibid.

14 Mack, unpublished memoir
15 Mack, quoted in Leck, *Captives of Empire*
16 Nicoll, *Young Shanghailander*
17 Fay Angus, *The White Pagoda* (Tyndale House, 1978)
18 Mack, unpublished memoir

CHAPTER FIVE: YOUR SAFEST REFUGE

1   Blair, *Gudao*
2   Leck, *Captives of Empire*
3   Article 1, Clause 1 of Regulations of the Civil Assembly Centre
4   Leck, *Captives of Empire*
5   *Shanghai Times*, 22 April 1943
6   Mary Dorothy Cornelius, *Changi* (Arthur H. Stockwell Ltd, Ilfracombe, 1953)
7   Bruce, *Beneath the Rising Sun*
8   Bruce, ibid.
9   Bruce, ibid.
10 Bruce, ibid.
11 Bruce, ibid.
12 Barbara Glanville (nee Bruce), interview with author
13 William Sewell, *Strange Harmony* (Edinburgh House Press, 1948)
14 Nicoll, *Young Shanghailander*
15 Ann Moxley, BBC WW2 People's War
16 Mary Wedekind, BBC WW2 People's War
17 Moxley, BBC WW2 People's War
18 Sewell, *Strange Harmony*
19 Nicoll, *Young Shanghailander*
20 Begley, *An Australian's Childhood*
21 Wedekind, BBC WW2 People's War
22 Grace Harvey, *Yangchow Years* (DreamStar Books, 2003)
23 Mack, quoted in Leck, *Captives of Empire*
24 Mack, ibid.

CHAPTER SIX: WRITING EXAMS ON SOUP TIN LABELS

1   Barbara Glanville, interview with author
2   Leck, *Captives of Empire*
3   Begley, *An Australian's Childhood*
4   Begley, ibid.
5   Lee, private papers, IWM

6 Sewell, *Strange Harmony*

7 Mr and Mrs E. L. Baker, unpublished manuscript, Imperial War Museum documents and sound section

8 Blair, *Gudao*

9 Blair, ibid.

10 Duguid, private papers, IWM

11 Duguid, ibid.

12 Nicoll, *Young Shanghailander*

13 Nicoll, ibid.

14 'Medical Students Behind Barbed Wire' by R. L. Huckstep, Professor of Traumatic and Orthopaedic Surgery, University of New South Wales, Sydney, Australia

15 David Michell, *A Boy's War* (Overseas Missionary Fellowship, 1988)

16 Harvey, *Yangchow Years*

17 Begley, *An Australian's Childhood*

18 Harvey, *Yangchow Years*

19 Mack, quoted in Leck, *Captives of Empire*

20 Harvey, *Yangchow Years*

21 Begley, *An Australian's Childhood*

22 Mrs J. Gittins, *I was at Stanley*, unpublished manuscript, Imperial War Museum documents and sound section P474

23 Harvey, *Yangchow Years*

24 Michell, *A Boy's War*

25 Mack, unpublished memoir

26 Begley, *An Australian's Childhood*

27 Begley, ibid.

28 Mack, quoted in Leck, *Captives of Empire*

CHAPTER SEVEN:
A HEALTHY MIND IN A HEALTHY BODY

1 Wedekind, BBC WW2 People's War

2 Blair, *Gudao*

3 Nicoll, *Young Shanghailander*

4 Nicoll, ibid.

5 Michell, *A Boy's War*

6 Lee, private papers, IWM

7 Begley, *An Australian's Childhood*

8 Begley, ibid.

9 Michell, *A Boy's War*

10 Duguid, private papers, IWM

11 Nicoll, *Young Shanghailander*
12 Nicoll, ibid.

CHAPTER EIGHT: FUN AND FATIGUES

1 Bruce, *Beneath the Rising Sun*
2 Harvey, *Yangchow Years*
3 Begley, *An Australian's Childhood*
4 Begley, ibid.
5 Begley, ibid.
6 Lee, private papers, IWM
7 Harvey, *Yangchow Years*
8 Nicoll ,*Young Shanghailander*
9 Sewell, *Strange Harmony*
10 Moxley, BBC WW2 People's War
11 Mack, quoted in Leck, *Captives of Empire*
12 Begley, *An Australian's Childhood*
13 Duguid, private papers, IWM
14 Duguid, interview with author
15 Albert Nissim, interview with author
16 Moxley, BBC WW2 People's War
17 Bruce, *Beneath the Rising Sun*

CHAPTER NINE: BOILS AND MALARIA

1 Lee, private papers IWM
2 Nicoll, *Young Shanghailander*
3 Mack, quoted in Leck, *Captives of Empire*
4 Mack, ibid.
5 C. E. Courtenay, *The Internment of Civilians in Singapore by the Nipponese Authorities February 1942 to August 1945*, unpublished report compiled from camp records circa 1946.
6 Bruce, *Beneath the Rising Sun*
7 Duguid, private papers, IWM
8 Blair, *Gudao*
9 Blair, ibid.
10 Begley, *An Australian's Childhood*
11 Nicoll, *Young Shanghailander*
12 Begley, *An Australian's Childhood*
13 Nicoll, *Young Shanghailander*
14 Begley, *An Australian's Childhood*

15 Blair, *Gudao*
16 Lee, private papers, IWM
17 Keith Gillison, *The Cross and the Dragon: A Medical Family in Central China* (Nottingham and Leeds, 1988)
18 Susan Dobson, interview with author
19 Nicoll, *Young Shanghailander*
20 Harvey, *Yangchow Years*
21 Harvey, ibid.
22 Harvey, ibid.
23 Mack, quoted in Leck, *Captives of Empire*

CHAPTER TEN: NOBODY'S CHILD

1 Harvey, *Yangchow Years*

CHAPTER ELEVEN: THE ENEMY

1 Sewell, *Strange Harmony*
2 Huckstep, unpublished memoir
3 Blair, *Gudao*
4 Ralph Armstrong, *A Short Cruise on the Vyner Brooke* (George Mann, 2003)
5 Armstrong, ibid.
6 Dick Germain, quoted in Leck, *Captives of Empire*
7 Bruce, *Beneath the Rising Sun*
8 Bruce, ibid.
9 J. G. Ballard, *Miracles of Life: Shanghai to Shepperton, An Autobiography* (Fourth Estate, 2008)
10 J. K. Stanton, unpublished manuscript, Imperial War Museum documents and sound section 05/5/1
11 National Archives and Records Administration Maryland USA section RG24 box 2154
12 Harvey, *Yangchow Years*
13 Moxley, BBC WW2 People's War
14 Bruce, unpublished memoir
15 M. Scovel, *The Chinese Ginger Jars* (Hodder and Stoughton, 1963)
16 Germain, quoted as personal correspondence in Leck, *Captives of Empire*
17 Begley, *An Australian's Childhood*
18 Sewell, *Strange Harmony*
19 Bill Ream, *Too Hot for Comfort: War Years in China 1938–50* (Epworth Press, 1988)

20 Stanton, private papers, IWM
21 Ream, *Too Hot for Comfort*

CHAPTER TWELVE: BAITING THE ENEMY

1 Bruce, *Beneath the Rising Sun*
2 Blair, *Gudao*
3 Blair, ibid.
4 Blair, ibid.
5 Blair, ibid.
6 Mack, quoted in Leck, *Captives of Empire*
7 Mack, ibid.
8 Leck, *Captives of Empire*
9 Patrick Scanlan, *Stars in the Sky* (Hong Kong Trappist Publications, 1984)
10 Stanton, private papers, IWM

CHAPTER THIRTEEN: 'THESE CHILDREN WILL BEAR THE BRAND OF CAMP LIFE AS LONG AS THEY LIVE'

1 Lee, private papers, IWM
2 Leck, *Captives of Empire*
3 Owen Gander, unpublished manuscript, Imperial War Museum documents and sound section 86/44/1
4 National Archives and Records Administration Maryland USA section RG24 box 2154
5 Mack, quoted in Leck, *Captives of Empire*
6 Begley, *An Australian's Childhood*
7 Mack, quoted in Leck, *Captives of Empire*
8 Estelle Cliff, interview with author
9 Frederic Stevens, *Santo Tomas* (Stratford House Inc., 1946)
10 Stevens, ibid.
11 Barbara Glanville, interview with author
12 Ream, *Too Hot for Comfort*
13 Sewell, *Strange Harmony*
14 Ream, *Too Hot for Comfort*
15 Sewell, *Strange Harmony*
16 John Barton, *Bamboo Wireless* (March 2002, Issue 25)
17 Sewell, *Strange Harmony*
18 Sewell, ibid.
19 Sewell, ibid.

20 Sewell, ibid.
21 Nicoll, *Young Shanghailander*
22 Duguid, private papers, IWM
23 The Red Cross 1945, unknown author, the Schmidt Collection, quoted in Leck, *Captives of Empire*
24 Leck, *Captives of Empire*
25 Nicoll, *Young Shanghailander*
26 Lee, private papers, IWM
27 Nicoll, *Young Shanghailander*
28 Mack, quoted in Leck, *Captives of Empire*
29 Stevens, *Santo Tomas*
30 Stevens, ibid.
31 Ballard, *Miracles of Life*
32 Sewell, *Strange Harmony*
33 Lee, private papers, IWM
34 Dr D. van Velden, *The Japanese Internment Camps for Civilians during the Second World War* (Groningen: J. B.Wolters, 1963)
35 Mack, interview with author

CHAPTER FOURTEEN: 'THEY HAVE TO GROW UP LIKE BEASTS, YOUR CHILDREN'

1 An Jacobs, *Ontwortleden* (*Uprooted*), unpublished manuscript translated from the Dutch by E. Macnamara, private papers of E. Macnamara, Imperial War Museum documents and sound section, 02/50/1
2 Moss, private papers, IWM
3 An Jacobs, private papers of E. Macnamara, IWM
4 Jacobs, ibid.
5 Ellis, private papers, IWM
6 An Jacobs, private papers of E. Macnamara, IWM
7 Ernest Hillen, *The Way of a Boy: A Memoir of Java* (Viking, 1994)
8 An Jacobs, private papers of E. Macnamara, IWM

CHAPTER FIFTEEN: WHAT, ALL DEAD?

1 An Jacobs, private papers of E. Macnamara, IWM
2 Armstrong, *A Short Cruise*
3 Armstrong, ibid.
4 Moss, private papers, IWM
5 Ernest Hillen, *The Way of a Boy*
6 An Jacobs, private papers of E. Macnamara, IWM

7 Jacobs, ibid.
8 Jacobs, ibid.
9 Jacobs, ibid.
10 Jacobs, ibid.

CHAPTER SIXTEEN: PRISONERS NO MORE

1 Leck, *Captives of Empire*
2 Duguid, private papers, IWM
3 Nicoll, *Young Shanghailander*
4 Huckstep, unpublished memoir
5 Nicoll, *Young Shanghailander*
6 Ballard, *Miracles of Life*
7 Nicoll, *Young Shanghailander*
8 Lee, private papers, IWM
9 Barbara Tilbury, interview with author
10 Sewell, *Strange Harmony*
11 Sewell, ibid.
12 Norman Cliff, *Prisoners of the Samurai: Japanese Civilian Camps in China 1941–1945* (Courtyard Publishers, 1998)
13 Far East Prisoners of War (FEPOW) website
14 Begley, *An Australian's Childhood*
15 Harvey, *Yangchow Years*
16 Begley, *An Australian's Childhood*
17 Begley, ibid.
18 FEPOW website
19 Harvey, *Yangchow Years*
20 Begley, *An Australian's Childhood*

CHAPTER SEVENTEEN: HOME SWEET HOME

1 Bruce, *Beneath the Rising Sun*

CHAPTER EIGHTEEN: FIGHTING BACK

1 FEPOW website
2 'Yangchow Revisited', Fr. J. Thornton, *North China Daily News*, April 1947

Index